Securitizing Youth

Securitizing Youth

*Young People's Roles in the Global Peace
and Security Agenda*

EDITED BY MARISA O. ENSOR

RUTGERS UNIVERSITY PRESS
NEW BRUNSWICK, CAMDEN, AND NEWARK,
NEW JERSEY, AND LONDON

Library of Congress Cataloging-in-Publication Data

Names: Ensor, Marisa O., editor.
Title: Securitizing youth : young people's roles in the global peace and security agenda / edited by Marisa O. Ensor.
Description: New Brunswick : Rutgers University Press, [2021] | Includes bibliographical references and index.
Identifiers: LCCN 2020050011 | ISBN 9781978822382 (hardcover) | ISBN 9781978822375 (paperback) | ISBN 9781978822399 (epub) | ISBN 9781978822405 (mobi) | ISBN 9781978822412 (pdf)
Subjects: LCSH: Youth and peace. | Youth in peace-building.
Classification: LCC JZ5579 .S44 2021 | DDC 327.1/720835--dc23
LC record available at https://lccn.loc.gov/2020050011

A British Cataloging-in-Publication record for this book is available from the British Library.

www.rutgersuniversitypress.org

Manufactured in the United States of America

To the young women and men whose stories of hope
and resilience inspired this book

Contents

Securitizing Youth

Introduction

Marisa O. Ensor

The recent proliferation of international activity on youth, peace, and security (YPS) has been motivated by demographic imperatives (there are more youth today than at any other time in human history) as well as geopolitical realities (more than six hundred million of those youngsters live in conflict-affected regions; Kujeke 2019). As the concept of national security has been expanded to the broader construct of "human security," security agendas have been globalized.[1] Security concerns in the Global North are linked to political unrest, environmentally induced displacement, and fragility in more peripheral regions of the global economy where most of this "youth bulge"—or "youth dividend," depending on one's standpoint—lives (United Nations 2005, 5). The global YPS agenda has been further driven by moral panics over the purportedly growing threat of radicalization of globally connected but marginalized youth by media-savvy extremist groups.

Adopted in December 2015, the United Nations Security Council Resolution (UNSCR) 2250 on youth, peace, and security formalized the global YPS agenda by establishing an international framework to address the critical role of youth in building and sustaining peace and preventing violent conflict. UNSCR 2250 represents the first time the U.N. Security Council (UNSC) had directly addressed the central role of youth in global security concerns (Williams 2016). This resolution is part of a set of recently developed international policies and conferences[2] on youth and security; together, they have formalized the global YPS agenda by establishing an international framework to address the critical role of youth in building and sustaining peace and preventing violent conflict. Additionally, a progress study on youth, peace, and security, as requested by UNSCR 2250, was recently made available (Simpson 2018). Titled *The Missing Peace: Independent Progress Study on Youth, Peace and Security*, it provides a blueprint for implementing UNSCR 2250 and the follow-up Resolution 2419.[3]

Supporters of UNSCR 2250 posit that this resolution is an important landmark for the recognition of the constructive role that young women and young men can play as agents for positive change. Recognizing youth's contributions as catalysts for peace and actors in preventing violence (Ortiz Quintana 2016) and acknowledging their civic engagement in the community and in formal institutions (Simpson 2018, xi), UNSCR 2250 urges member states to establish mechanisms to enable young people's meaningful participation in peace processes and conflict resolution (Simpson 2018, 1).

This "global youth as peacebuilders" discourse is, however, not without detractors. Indeed, critical views have emerged, observing that "such arguments do not hold up to scrutiny, as recent documents on global youth and security are saturated with concerns with youth as threat and liability" (Sukarieh and Tannock 2018, 855). The ideal of youth as peacebuilders is, some have argued, a pretext for instrumentalizing youth and a strategy for eliciting youth support for the current global social and economic order (854; see also chapters 4 and 5, this volume). Important issues of social justice, contested local understandings of peace and conflict (Sukarieh and Tannock 2018, 860), and the distinction between "productive and destructive forms of conflict" (Zembylas and Bekerman 2008, 197) have to date received scarce attention in YPS efforts. It has also been pointed out that "the inclusion and application of gender in the YPS agenda needs to be further developed and solidified as a key cross-cutting provision" (U.N. Women 2018, 5), correcting the lack of intersectional[4] approaches to peace and security policy and practice currently reflected in strategic documents (U.N. Women 2018).

Dominant gender discourses in the global peace and security agenda gained renewed impetus with the UNSC's adoption, on October 30, 2000, of Resolution 1325 on women, peace, and security (WPS; see chapter 8, this volume). UNSCR 1325 was the first resolution to link women's experiences of conflict to the maintenance of international peace and security. Seven related resolutions have been adopted since then. They focus on women's equal and meaningful participation in conflict prevention, peacemaking, and peacebuilding and the protection of women and girls from conflict-related violence. Together, these eight resolutions compose the global WPS agenda.[5] Despite the contribution that UNSCR 1325 and related resolutions have made in terms of highlighting the active and constructive role women play in advancing peace and security, the global WPS agenda has not fully incorporated the distinct realities, potential, and aspirations of young women and girls or documented how these differ from those of young men. Understandings of the role of gender dynamics in shaping the experiences of youth worldwide thus remain problematic and constitute a further point of contention (Pruitt 2013; Sebhatu 2017) that warrants far more attention than has been devoted to it in the available literature.

The interaction between youth and climate action critical for understanding, among other issues, the underlying mechanisms for how forced migration, conflict, and security challenges apply specifically to young people is being debated (see chapter 7, this volume). Forced migration—both internally and across borders—plays an important role in the debate around youth, climate change, peace, and security. Historically, most of the research on displaced populations had, however, been related to refugees fleeing armed conflicts and persecution, how they may contribute to conflict contagion (Salehyan and Gleditsch 2006; Stedman and Tanner 2003), and how diaspora populations influenced the opportunity for conflict (Smith and Stares 2007). Young women's and men's increasingly active role in environmental action and the ways in which climate change uniquely impacts the mobility, security, and development prospects of youth remain as of yet understudied. The limited availability of age- and gender-disaggregated data further hampers attempts to better understand how these dynamics differentially impact young women and men. *Securitizing Youth* seeks to advance these debates by sharing empirical findings on youth's engagement in the wide range of contexts relevant to the expanding peace and security field. Drawing on empirical evidence and policy analysis—and in some cases, the contributors' personal experiences—it offers new insights on the challenges and opportunities faced by young people in their efforts to build more peaceful, inclusive, and environmentally secure societies.

Janus-Faced Youth? Beyond Youth Bulges and Moral Panics

In April 2015, the UNSC[6] held a special session on the role of youth in countering violent extremism. "The role of youth lies at the heart of international peace and security," affirmed then U.N. secretary-general Ban Ki-Moon, voicing increasingly dominant standpoints linking youth as a social construct with global security concerns. The UNSC adopted Resolution 2250 in December of that same year. UNSCR 2250 was introduced by Jordan, a country with a large youth population, during its membership in the UNSC in 2015. The Global Forum on Youth, Peace and Security, which had promoted the resolution, was held in Amman under the patronage of Crown Prince Al Hussein bin Abdullah II. "Global patterns and growing incidence of violence, extremism and instability challenge the world community . . . to offer meaningful avenues to young people to shape the future of their countries," proclaimed the *Amman Declaration on Youth, Peace and Security* adopted at the forum (Global Forum on Youth, Peace and Security 2015, 1). Young people were thus linked to both grave security threats and the possibility of more peaceful prospects (see chapters 4, 6, and 10, this volume).

The duality evident in these documents has often been acknowledged in scholarly literature. As noted anthropologists Jean and John Comaroff remarked almost fifteen years ago, "Youth as a sign of contradiction, as the figuration of a mythic bipolarity, is enshrined in the foundations of the modern collective imaginary" (2005, 280). Simultaneously characterized as "makers and breakers" (Honwana and De Boeck 2005), "vanguard or vandals" (Abbink and Kessel 2005), spoilers and drivers of peace, contemporary youth remain uncomfortably situated in an ambiguous space where moral panics over threats of extremist violence and conflict are juxtaposed with idealized expectations of "youth as peacebuilders" and model citizens (Kennelly 2011).

This double-sided characterization is most common in countries with youthful age structures where youngsters are associated with possibility, opportunity, and panacea on the one hand and risk, threat, and social pathology on the other (Sukarieh and Tannock 2018, 855). Youth, particularly male youth, are often branded as the "main protagonists of criminal and political violence," and consequently, much of contemporary discussion carries unfavorable notions against them, demonstrated by negative connotations surrounding concepts such as the "youth bulge"[7] or "at-risk youth." These stereotypes are perpetuated by the media, where youth are simultaneously "infantilized" and "demonized," perceived to be vulnerable and in need of protection but also denounced as dangerous, violent, and apathetic (Ozerdem 2016).

Similarly problematic is the tendency to view the construct of "gender" as synonymous with women, while the category of "youth" is perceived as coterminous with young men. As a result, the role that prevalent and changing notions of masculinity play in conflict and peace tends to be disregarded, while the category of "female youth" has often been ignored. This has contributed to the victimization of young women and sexual and gender minorities, especially during conflict but also in times of peace.

Other approaches have engaged gender differences by juxtaposing the dichotomous narratives of "youth as threat" (referring almost exclusively to males) and "youth as resource" (applied mostly to young women and girls), which, as Izzi notes in chapter 5 (this volume), have contributed to the essentializing treatment of youth. Current policy and practice have not yet fully overcome these common shortcomings, thereby reducing the effectiveness of peacebuilding interventions.

Yet there is mounting evidence that gender-positive approaches to peace and security are more effective than traditional, militarized campaigns. The probability that a peace agreement will last at least two years is known to increase by 20 percent when women are included—a figure that increases to 35 percent over a time span of fifteen years (U.N. Women 2017). Groundbreaking research led by Valerie Hudson suggests that gender equality is the best predictor of a country's peacefulness and overall stability. Based on analysis of the largest global database on the status of women, she concludes that "in countries where males rule the home through violence, male-dominant hierarchies rule the state through violence" (Hudson et al. 2012).

UNSCR 2250 is largely silent on gender; subsequent related documents, such as *The Missing Peace*, are far more responsive to youth's gender-differentiated circumstances and experiences of violence, conflict, and peacebuilding, as are the chapters included in this volume. Young people themselves recognize the need to "engage with the gendered identities of both young men and young women, to support and promote positive, gender-equitable identities and roles, paying particular attention to cultivating non-violent masculinities" (Simpson 2018, viii).

UNSCR 2250, Global Youth, and the Peace and Security Agenda

While UNSCR 1325, adopted in 2000, established the global agenda on women, peace, and security (see chapter 8, this volume), and UNSCR 1612, adopted in 2005, addressed children and armed conflict, no similar framework was available for addressing youth's role in peace and security until 2015. That year, the UNSC adopted Resolution 2250 on YPS, which recognized both the rights of youth affected by conflict and their role in restoring long-term peace. In this document, youth are defined in chronological terms as persons between the ages of eighteen and twenty-nine (UNSCR 2015, 1).

There are no universally accepted definitions of adolescence and youth. The United Nations takes adolescents to include persons aged ten to nineteen years and youth as those between fifteen and twenty-four years for statistical purposes without prejudice to other definitions by member states (Patton et al. 2009). Article 1 of the U.N. Convention on the Rights of the Child (1989) defines a child as a person below the age of eighteen, and the Committee on the Rights of the Child, the monitoring body for the convention, has encouraged states to review the age of majority if it is set below eighteen and to increase the level of protection for all children under eighteen. Other international entities, like the Africa Union Commission, consider the youth cutoff age as thirty-five years old. The U.N. itself sometimes defines youth from ages eighteen to twenty-four for statistical purposes (Simpson 2018).

UNSCR 2250 identifies five "pillars for action"—participation, protection, prevention, partnerships, and disengagement and reintegration—and calls for a case study to be implemented on youth's contributions to peace and conflict-resolution processes (UNSC 2016). The first pillar urges member states to increase the participation of young people in decision-making at all levels in local, national, regional, and international institutions and in mechanisms for the prevention and resolution of conflict. It also stresses the critical importance of considering young people's needs—for example, rehabilitation and reintegration—during the missions of the Security Council (UNSCR 2015, 3).

The protection pillar calls on states to comply with obligations concerning youth as dictated by international law under the Geneva Conventions of 1949 and the Additional Protocols of 1977. Further, the protection pillar calls on states to adopt necessary measures to protect youth from sexual and gender-based violence. It also exhorts countries to end impunity by bringing to justice those who commit genocide, crimes against humanity, and war crimes against youth civilians (UNSCR 2015, 3).

The prevention pillar urges the facilitation of youth-inclusive environments to be provided with adequate support to implement violence-prevention activities. It also stresses the importance of policies for youth designed to grow local economies and support youth employment opportunities and entrepreneurship (UNSCR 2015, 3). Member states are exhorted to support education initiatives that equip youth with the ability to constructively engage in inclusive political processes. This pillar also stresses the need to create policies for youth that positively contribute to peacebuilding efforts, including for their social and economic development (3).

The fourth pillar, partnerships, encourages states to increase political, financial, technical, and logistical support to U.N. bodies engaged in promoting peace, development, and equality that address the needs and participation of youth, particularly in peace efforts in conflict and postconflict environments (UNSCR 2015, 3). The Peacebuilding Commission, the Office of the United Nations High Commissioner for Human Rights, and the United Nations Entity for Gender Equality and the Empowerment of Women (U.N. Women) are proposed as illustrative examples of the kind of organizations with which member states could establish fruitful partnerships. Any other collaborative endeavor that advances youth's role in the global YPS agenda would also satisfy the requirements of the partnerships pillar. Member states are further encouraged to engage local communities and nongovernmental actors in the development of strategies to prevent violent extremism and promote social cohesion and inclusion (3).

The fifth and final pillar, disengagement and reintegration, urges those involved in planning for disarmament, demobilization, and reintegration (DDR) to incorporate evidence-based and gender-sensitive opportunities for youth. National youth employment action plans are among the initiatives that could contribute to the reintegration of youth in postconflict areas. Aspects to be considered include establishing opportunities and policies in the field of education, facilitating training and employment to prevent the marginalization of youth, and promoting a culture of peace. The need for investing in building young persons' capabilities and skills designed to promote a culture of peace is also emphasized (UNSCR 2015, 4).

The UNSC called for a comprehensive case study to be conducted on young people's experiences and contributions to peace and conflict resolution processes, articulated in their own words (Conciliation Resources 2018). Titled *The Missing Peace: Independent Progress Study on Youth, Peace and Security*, this case study advances our understanding of the global youth and security agenda and informs the substantive chapters of this volume. Conducted independently from any U.N. agency, *The Missing Peace* study identifies a significant deficit in trust among youth and their governments, multilateral bodies, and civil society organizations (Simpson 2018). This ubiquitous lack of trust is believed to stem, at least partly, from young people's opposition to the simplistic, binary, and gendered stereotypes of youth either as perpetrators of violence or as passive victims (Simpson 2019, 42), noted earlier. These limiting perceptions constrain youth's ability to contribute to peacebuilding processes, let alone advocate for their rights as youth.

Discussed in further detail throughout this volume, a critical finding of *The Missing Peace* is the urgent need to "address the perceptions of injustice and what young people describe as 'the violence of their exclusion'" (Simpson 2019, 42). The data collected for this study show that young people around the globe often experience insurmountable exclusion in the form of structural, psychological, or even kinetic (or physical) violence. Youth demand to be included in political arenas and policy-making processes. Yet a considerable lack of confidence often colors the interactions between youth and their adult counterparts in their communities and, at the national and international level, negatively impacts peace and security efforts. This finding should prompt advocates of the YPS agenda to carefully consider what constitutes positive agency and meaningful political inclusion.

Accompanying *The Missing Peace* is a study produced by the Sustainable Development Solutions Network—Youth (SDSN Youth) discussing the impact of climate change and ecological crises on the peace and security of young people. United Nations Secretary-General António Guterres submitted both documents to the Security Council and General Assembly in December 2017. Titled *Impacts of Climate Change on Youth, Peace and Security*, this SDSN Youth report outlines a series of policy and program recommendations for the U.N. Security Council in its mandate to address the impacts of climate change on youth populations with a focus on Africa and the Middle East as primary case studies (Payne, Warembourg, and Awan 2017). These issues are discussed at greater length in chapter 7.

Youth, Security, and the Agenda for Sustainable Development

Global approaches to peace and security, development, and humanitarian action are becoming increasingly interrelated and youth inclusive, at least at the discourse level. A case in point was the first-ever World Humanitarian Summit, which took place in Istanbul, May 23–24, 2016. Responding to a global call to action by the then United Nations Secretary-General Ban Ki-Moon, this event brought together governments, humanitarian organizations, people affected by humanitarian crises, and new partners, including in the private sector, to propose solutions to our most pressing challenges and set an agenda to keep humanitarian action fit for the future.

Young people were recognized as a critical part of that response, as evidenced by the summit's special session, "Transforming Humanitarian Action with and for Young People," held on May 24, 2016. "Youth participation and leadership should be the rule, rather than the exception—institutionalized in humanitarian processes and policies, and explicitly stipulated in operational plans and budgets," said UNFPA Executive Director Dr. Babatunde Osotimehin during the opening of the session. UNSCR 2250 is a compelling—if not unproblematic—call to action defining a new vision for the role of young people in this global YPS agenda. Supporting this vision will require the mobilization of global and local stakeholders and a better understanding of the interplay between peace, security, and youth empowerment. "We can no longer afford to leave young people behind," he added.

While it is still far from being the norm, the international community has progressively embraced a recognition of the importance of working collaboratively on shared commitments, moving toward abandoning the "silo approach" that still characterizes the field. A case in point, *Pathways for Peace: Inclusive Approaches to Preventing Violent Conflict* is a joint United Nations and World Bank study that considers how development processes can better interact with diplomacy and mediation, security, and other tools to prevent conflict from becoming violent (United Nations and World Bank 2018). A further indication of the increasing attention in international frameworks to youth's role in the interconnected arenas of peace, security, and development is the *World Bank Group Strategy for Fragility, Conflict, and Violence 2020–2025.* Drawing on the premise that "preventing and mitigating FCV [fragility, conflict, and violence] challenges is key to making progress toward the Sustainable Development Goals (SDGs) and to the international community's broader efforts to promote peace and prosperity" (World Bank Group 2020, viii), the proposed strategy seeks to "promote women's empowerment and youth inclusion" (95). The World Bank Group (WBG) further underscores that "it is essential to give youth hope by signaling to them that they have an important role to play in society, and that their country is on a positive trajectory" (87). Newly released at the time of writing, it remains to be seen whether the new WBG strategy succeeds in accomplishing the stated outcomes.

Significantly, the 2030 Sustainable Development Agenda (UNGA 2015) was adopted in 2015, the same year as UNSCR 2250. One key feature of the 2030 Agenda is the recognition that the Sustainable Development Goals are global in nature and universally applicable, taking into account national realities, capacities and levels of development, and specific challenges. In addition, the 2030 Agenda integrates the three dimensions of sustainable development—economic, social, and environmental. Three years later, in 2018, the *World Youth Report on Youth and the 2030 Agenda for Sustainable Development* provided insight into the role of young people in sustainable development (U.N. DESA 2018). Discussing youth in the context of the implementation of the 2030 Agenda for Sustainable Development and related frameworks, this report noted that "the active engagement of youth in sustainable development efforts is central to achieving sustainable, inclusive and stable societies by the target date, and to averting the worst threats and challenges to sustainable development, including the impacts of climate change, unemployment, poverty, gender inequality, conflict, and migration" (U.N. DESA 2018, 1). World Bank analyses conclude that one basic measure of a country's success in turning "youth bulges" into "demographic dividends" is the youth (un)employment rate. As young adults enter the working age, the country's dependency ratio—that is, the ratio of the nonworking age population to the working age population—will decline. If the increase in the number of working-age individuals can be fully employed in productive activities, other things being equal, the level of average income per capita should increase as a result. "Youth bulges" will thus become "demographic dividends" with the potential to positively impact economic growth, political stability, and sustainable human development (see chapter 5, by Valeria Izzi, for a critical assessment of this approach). Despite their significant present and projected numbers, young people are nevertheless often confronted with age-related challenges and barriers to participation in economic, political, and social life, greatly hindering their own development and, by extension, the sustainable development of their communities and nations. "Youth bulges" thus risk becoming "demographic bombs," as large numbers of frustrated youth unable to attain social adulthood are likely to become a potential source of social and political instability (World Bank 2011).

The particular circumstances of potentially vulnerable or disenfranchised youth—for example, young women and girls; indigenous youth; youth in conflict and postconflict situations; migrants, refugees, and stateless youngsters; members of sexual and religious minorities; youth with disabilities; and rural youth and those living in poverty—point to the recognition that the 2030 Agenda will not succeed unless it is grounded on a recognition of diversity and inclusiveness (U.N. DESA 2018, 12). Recent efforts to promote positive youth development (PYD; see chapter 1, this volume) are among the initiatives being attempted to prevent this from happening. Yet as MacNeil acknowledges, PYD- and youth-focused programming more generally have only recently begun to acknowledge that insights derived from high-income countries (HICs)—or WEIRD (Western, educated, industrialized, rich, and developed) societies—tend not to be directly applicable to youth in lower- and middle-income countries (LMICs). Emerging research from LMICs does nonetheless seem promising, she reports.

It is worth noting that both development and youth have long been linked to security agendas (Hettne 2010), although the emphasis has moved from local to global contexts. Sukarieh and Tannock (2018) argue that current perspectives on youth, especially those in developing countries, have shifted from perceptions of young people as a matter of local and national interest to constructions of youngsters as a global security concern: "Underdevelopment in peripheral regions of the global economy is thus reconstrued not just as a development problem for those living in these regions, but a security concern for those living in metropolitan centres of global wealth accumulation" (Sukarieh and Tannock 2018, 856). The chapters included in *Securitizing Youth* represent an effort to broaden our current understanding of the diversity of roles that young people play in a variety of contexts of peace, development, conflict, and fragility across the globe. Lessons learned interrogate, inform, expand, and at times also critique and challenge the international YPS agenda, contributing to make it more reflective of the lived realities encountered by the young women and men whose lives the agenda purports to positively impact.

Rationale and Organization of This Book

Conflicts, particularly civil wars, have increased markedly since 2008, after declining in the late 1990s and early 2000s. Global interest in the complexity of young people's roles in conflict and engagement for peace has consequently burgeoned in the last decade. Their experiences often differ significantly from those of their adult counterparts and must be examined accordingly; at the same time, youth's realities cannot be properly understood on the basis of the larger and more established body of scholarly literature on children and childhood (Cuthbert and Cregan 2014; Ensor 2012; James and James 2012; James and Prout 1997; Lancy 2015; MacBlain, Dunn, and Luke 2017). As they engage in peace and security agendas, young women and men must navigate complex, intersectional realities where gender and age are but two of many intersecting considerations.

There has also been an increased recognition that gender roles and gendered relationships in conflict and postconflict settings are often subject to modifications that may force young women and young men into "nontraditional" activities (U.N. Women 2018, 5) that defy cultural norms. Youth in conflict-affected settings and those engaged in peacebuilding efforts may at times find themselves "modifying or transforming the adult and gender roles they have assumed" (U.N. 2005, 151). Drawing on his fieldwork on conflict, development, and youth in Africa, anthropologist Marc Sommers suggests that the social category of youth is increasingly being identified as an "outcast majority" and defined as "a young person with a tenuous social status and a hoped-for social transformation into adulthood . . . which may not happen" (2015, 14). The experiences of conflict-affected youth, he adds, are markedly gender differentiated; they respond to patterns and pressures not fully acknowledged in policy-oriented literature and technocratic interventions, which are often guided by uncritical assumptions of youth resilience.

Another anthropologist and childhood scholar, David F. Lancy, reminds us that the relatively recent Western emphasis on privileging children's voices—which he terms "neontocracy"—does not easily fit in with the traditional power structures prevalent in gerontocratic societies (2015)—that is, those ruled by (typically male) elders despite youth constituting the demographic majority. Those benefitting from gerontocratic social configurations are thus likely to perceive the global YPS agenda as a threat to the status quo. Similarly, the WPS agenda's emphasis on gender equality and female agency may be resisted by those seeking to uphold the patriarchal order. The combination of patriarchal and gerontocratic attitudes often results in young females' exclusion and marginalization. As I discuss in my own chapter on youth and environmental action in South Sudan (chapter 7, this volume), engaging in counterhegemonic initiatives and opposing what youth scholars Christiansen, Utas, and Vigh term "gerontophallic post-colonial Africa" (2006, 21) often come at a high price that many of these young women are nonetheless willing to pay (Ensor 2013).

Rationale and Significance

The body of scholarly work on youth, peace, and security, while still rather limited, has nevertheless experienced a recent upsurge. The growing number of opinion pieces and articles on specific aspects of the global YPS agenda recently published in a variety of journals (see Del Felice and Ruud 2016 for an annotated bibliography) attests to this expanding interest. Until recently, however, most of the available information on youth's involvement in the peace and security field was to be found in policy-oriented materials and agency reports[8] that have often sought to advance a particular agenda and are either very narrowly focused or not based on rigorous empirical research or robust policy analysis.

Securitizing Youth presents a coherent compilation of the latest research on youth's wide-ranging experiences in peace and security contexts across the globe in one edited volume. Our work serves as a comparative lens highlighting the points of convergence and divergence among various world settings. Contributions acknowledge that "youth as a demographic category includes and conceals a diversity of beliefs, values, worldviews, and expectations about the future, as well as differing senses of agency and responsibility" (O'Brien, Selboe, and Hayward 2018, 2). This collection deepens our understanding of the normative frameworks that regulate the global and local links connecting youth, peace, and security. It is aimed at multidisciplinary academic audiences as well as policy makers, sociolegal and development practitioners, and youth rights advocates. Additionally, the case studies included in the volume shine light on the violence of exclusion, identify barriers to youth's meaningful participation, and suggest strategies for overcoming such barriers. A focus on field-based evidence and the voices of young women and men themselves allows intergenerational differences regarding the impact of and attitudes toward YPS-inspired approaches to come to the fore.

We present findings on the experiences of young women and young men engaged in peace work in different countries—Afghanistan, Brazil, Colombia, Kenya, Romania, Rwanda, South Sudan, Uganda, United Kingdom, and several other locations across the globe—and in different types and phases of war and violence, including both conflict-affected and relatively peaceful societies. The chapters included in *Securitizing Youth* offer a clear, broad, and multidisciplinary view of who these young people are and what peace and security mean for them. Efforts were made to avoid reproducing the very problem we seek to address—the exclusion of youth. Several chapters were either authored (chapters 2, 3, 4, 9, and 10) or coauthored (chapter 8) by young people actively engaged in the peacebuilding field. Chapter contributors, young peacebuilders and seasoned scholars and practitioners alike, propose ways to support youth's agency and facilitate their meaningful participation in decision-making. Overall lessons learned contribute to our understanding of the diversity and complexity of young people's engagement for peace and security and are synthesized and discussed in more detail in the concluding chapter. The following section provides a brief outline of the organization of this volume.

The Following Chapters

Securitizing Youth is organized into five broad thematic issues that correspond to UNSCR 2250's five pillars for action. In part I, "Participation," which follows this introductory chapter, contributors address issues related to UNSCR 2250's first pillar. Authors Carole MacNeil and Grace Atuhaire discuss, in their respective chapters, the ways in which young people have been involved in conflict prevention and resolution and in the promotion of social cohesion. Drawing from her experience working with young people, youth associations, and communities in various fragile and postconflict contexts throughout Africa and the Middle East, MacNeil explores the concept of "participation" by examining it through a PYD lens. Her chapter, "Peace *by, for,* or *with* Youth? How a PYD Lens Enhances Our View of Young People's Role in Peacebuilding" (chapter 1), considers how emerging trends in PYD research might inform program design for youth engagement in general and participation in the global YPS agenda in particular. MacNeil proposes that a PYD perspective allows for a shift toward an asset-based, social-ecological approach with proven potential for positive outcomes for youth, adults, and the larger community. In chapter 2, "And Then They Came for Me: Youth's Role in Mediating for Peace in Kibera, Kenya," Atuhaire examines the dynamics of youth participation using peace activism in Nairobi, Kenya, as a primary case study. More specifically, the chapter explores young people's role in the events that took place in Nairobi's Kibera slum, where a government-sponsored urban development plan resulted in the eviction of a large number of resident families. Atuhaire examines the intersecting structural, age, and gender dimensions of exclusion facing Kibera residents. Led by a young female activist using online and offline tactics, the young people of Kibera served as a "bridge of mediation" between community members and local institutions. She concludes that despite the enormous challenges they face, these young activists belied the unfavorable views of marginal youth prevalent in gerontocratic Kenya and succeeded in deescalating the conflict created by the unlawful evictions.

Part II of the volume, "Protection," opens with Diana Budur's chapter, "Protecting Marginalized Youths: Romani Children and Formal Education" (chapter 3). Budur discusses the concept of protection in the context of one of Europe's largest underprivileged, impoverished, and predominantly illiterate minority—Romani youths, particularly those born in Eastern Europe and now residing in Western Europe, where they often experience high levels of ethnic discrimination. Budur also addresses gender dynamics examining the plight of Romani girls, often married off as young as thirteen and deliberately prevented from acquiring much of a formal education so they will not acculturate into mainstream society, as well as boys, largely viewed by society as at heightened risk of becoming petty criminals. She proposes several best practices to empower young Romani through educational pursuits. Ali Altiok's chapter, "Squeezed Agency: Youth Resistance to the Securitization of Peacebuilding" (chapter 4), critically considers what protection means in an increasingly securitized context. He examines the often fraught involvement of youth in the prevention of violent extremism (PVE) efforts and the YPS framework—two important normative policy developments that recognize youth's role in peace and security matters. Altiok argues that despite the conflicting perceptions of youth agency presented by these two normative frameworks, many youth-led peacebuilding organizations continue to engage with both of these agendas simultaneously. He suggests that effective protection measures require a more nuanced understanding of the complex relationships between policies, institutions, and actors—youth and their adult/older counterparts—working in the PVE and YPS fields.

The third pillar for action, discussed in part III of the volume, "Prevention," is represented by the chapters by Valeria Izzi and Nasrat Khalid. In chapter 5, Izzi offers a critical assessment of the way employment fits within the overall discourse and practice around youth policy and programming and, more specifically, the role it plays in relation to the securitization of youth. Titled "Lost in Translation? Youth Employment and Peacebuilding—from Policy to Programs," Izzi's chapter investigates how youth unemployment is constructed at the policy level within the peace and security agenda, noting the transition "from early accounts of youth unemployment as a security threat to the inclusion of youth employment as part of the prevention pillar of the United Nations Security Council Resolution 2250." Izzi notes the limited empirical evidence that employment programs targeting youth in postconflict countries and other fragile settings are indeed effective peacebuilding strategies—or that they actually benefit young participants. She argues for closer attention to the way in which the problem is conceptualized at the policy level and how this framing translates into programmatic responses. Chapter 6, "Community Ties, Training, and Technology: A More Effective Framework for Peace, Security, and Development for Afghan Youth" by Nasrat Khalid, wraps up part III. Khalid discusses current understandings of security and the potentially vital role of quality education and economic development as contributing elements in conflict prevention strategies. He presents his three Ts framework, which centers on community ties, technical training, and access to today's technology and is intended to supplement traditional approaches to peacebuilding, postconflict reconstruction, and development. The case of Afghan youth, Khalid argues, illustrates the reasons most peacebuilding efforts have to date met with limited success. Lessons learned from the application of the three Ts framework in Afghanistan could, by qualified extension, guide YPS initiatives in other conflict-affected regions.

My chapter, "Climate Change, Environmental Action, and the Youth, Peace, and Security Agenda: Global Policies, Local Efforts" (chapter 7), together with the chapter on "Putting Youth on the Agenda: Intersections with the Women, Peace, and Security Framework" (chapter 8), coauthored by Jeni Klugman and Matthew Moore, make up part IV, "Partnerships." Starting with the premise that conflicts over natural resources and the environment are among the greatest challenges in twenty-first-century geopolitics, I explore young women's and men's increasingly active role in environmental action. I draw on my ongoing longitudinal fieldwork in South Sudan—a war-torn country whose very young population must confront the interrelated challenges of conflict and climate change—and in the refugee camps in neighboring Uganda, where many young South Sudanese refugees live. My chapter also examines the interaction between youth and climate change, acknowledged as critical for understanding the underlying mechanisms for how forced migration, conflict, and security challenges apply specifically to young people. Partnerships between youth-led organizations and broader institutions, I argue, are critical if these endeavors are to succeed. Klugman and Moore continue the partnership theme by identifying the links and synergies between the WPS and the YPS agendas. Their discussion is informed by the Women, Peace and Security Index, an innovative analytical tool elaborated by the Georgetown Institute for Women, Peace and Security in partnership with the Peace Research Institute of Oslo, designed to measure and track progress on women's inclusion, justice, and security. Their chapter reflects upon the extent to which the YPS agenda has addressed evident shortcomings in the WPS agenda in light of the almost twenty years of WPS implementation experience. A better understanding of these linkages aims at informing policy and practice, resulting in a more gender-sensitive global YPS agenda.

Part V, "Disengagement and Reintegration," the final section of this volume, opens with Victoria R. Bishop's discussion of "Securitized Youth, Transitional Justice, and the Politics of Disengagement in Rwanda" (chapter 9). An analysis of the transitional justice process in this country offers valuable lessons on young people's experiences as both objects of and actors in a range of postgenocide rehabilitation and reintegration mechanisms whose implementation has been complicated by increasingly securitized constructions of youth. Bishop's discussion underscores that although Rwanda's youth involvement in their country's transitional justice and DDR initiatives is not without contradictions and inconsistencies, their engagement in their country's sociopolitical life is essential in advancing Rwanda's progress postgenocide. In chapter 10, "Digital Media as the Next Frontier for Fighting Violent Extremism among Youth?," Willice Onyango examines the path toward the meaningful reintegration of young women and men involved in violence and/ or violent extremism through the use of digital media platforms. The author examines the effectiveness of public diplomacy programs on social media and the building of virtual networks as strategies to reduce young people's susceptibility to radicalization online. The Youth Café, a platform established to facilitate young people's sharing of experiences on constructive strategies to prevent radicalization and extremist violence, is presented as the primary case study. Onyango examines internet browsing patterns of at-risk/potential extremists and discusses communication strategies among the under-thirty-fives. Building on analyses of online and offline consultations on countering violent extremism, the lessons learned through this case study provide insights into the real and assumed beliefs of extremist groups that can guide more effective disengagement efforts.

The final chapter, "Conclusions: Securitizing Youth—Lessons Learned," is authored by myself, the editor of this volume. I draw on the main lessons stemming from the various case studies of *Securitizing Youth* to discuss the prospects facing the largest generation of youth as they prepare for the way ahead and confront the forces of change shaping the world in which they live. As the individual contributions to this volume reveal, young women and young men across the world are actively seeking opportunities to participate socially, politically, and economically—advocating for the needs of their communities in Kenya, engaging in environmental peacebuilding in South Sudan and Uganda, fighting ethnic marginalization in Europe and Latin America, becoming educated against violence and conflict in Afghanistan, struggling to reach social adulthood in Rwanda, or seeking meaningful employment and using media to fight violent extremism across the globe. Some of these experiences have been successful; others have been met with as yet unresolved challenges. By contributing to a better understanding of the changing nature of conflict and fragility, assessing the impact of emerging approaches to peacebuilding undertaken by young women and young men, and identifying potential strategies to reverse the negative manifestations of youth exclusion, this volume takes an important step forward in our path toward sustaining peace.

NOTES

1. In *Human Security in Theory and Practice* (2009, 5), the U.N. defines "human security" as a concern with political, social, environmental, economic, military, and cultural "threats and situations" that block "human freedoms and human fulfilment," including "chronic and persistent poverty . . . climate change, health pandemics . . . and sudden economic and financial downturns."

2. These include the White House Summit on Countering Violent Extremism in February 2015; the European Youth against Violent Extremism conference in June 2015; the Global Forum on Youth, Peace and Security in August 2015; the Global Youth Summit against Violent Extremism in September 2015; and the *Arab Human Development Report 2016*, which focuses on the role of youth in the Arab region.

3. Unanimously adopted in June 2018, UNSCR 2419 calls on all relevant actors to consider ways for increasing the representation of young people when negotiating and implementing peace agreements. Particularly attention is paid to the purported link to youth's marginalization, seen as "detrimental to building sustainable peace and countering violent extremism, as and when conducive to terrorism" (United Nations 2018, para. 2).

4. Intersectionality, as introduced by critical race and gender theorist Kimberlé Williams Crenshaw (2005), refers to the ways in which overlapping or intersecting social identities, particularly among minorities, relate to systems and structures of oppression, domination, or discrimination.

5. The eight Security Council resolutions composing the global women, peace, and security agenda are Resolution 1325 on Women, Peace and Security (2000); Resolution 1828 (2008) on sexual violence during wars; Resolution 1888 (2009), which calls for the appointment of the special representative on sexual violence in conflict and establishes women protection advisors (WPAs) within peacekeeping missions as well as a team of experts meant to rapidly deploy to situations of sexual violence; Resolution 1889 (2009), which calls for the development of indicators to measure the implementation of UNSCR 1325 both within the U.N. system and by member states; Resolution 1960 (2010), which calls for an expanded mandate to comprehensively address sexual violence when used as a tactic of conflict or emerging as a consequence of conflict; Resolution 2106 (2013), which emphasizes the investigation and prosecution of sexual violence crimes; Resolution 2122 (2013) on the creation of stronger measures to include women in peace processes; and Resolution 2242 (2015), which calls for the WPS agenda to be placed as a central component of efforts to address the challenges of the current global context, including rising violent extremism, climate change, and unprecedented numbers of displaced people.

6. The U.N. Security Council, one of the six arms of the U.N., is charged with the maintenance of international peace and security. Under the United Nations Charter (1945), the UNSC has the power to (1) investigate any dispute or situation that might lead to international friction, (2) recommend terms for settling such disputes, and (3) determine the existence of threats to peace and decide which actions should be taken (United Nations 1945). The UNSC publishes resolutions as formal documents representing the opinion and will of the U.N. (United Nations 1945).

7. In demographic terms, a population bulge refers to an age group that is larger than the groups both younger and older than it, thus forming a bulge. Youth bulges are most prevalent in Africa, with pockets in the Middle East, Central America, and parts of Asia (Lin 2012).

8. Examples include ILO's *Global Employment Trends for Youth, 2017*; United Nations Department of Economic and Social Affairs' *World Youth Report 2015: Youth Civic Engagement*; United Nations Inter-agency Network on Youth Development's *Guiding Principles on Young People's Participation in Peacebuilding*; World Bank's *Preventing Youth Violence: An Overview of the Evidence*, 2015; and USAID's *Promising Practices in Engaging Youth in Peace and Security and PVE/CVE*, 2017.

REFERENCES

Abbink, Jon, and Ineke Kessel, eds. 2005. *Vanguard or Vandals: Youth, Politics and Conflict in Africa*. Boston: Brill.

Christiansen, Catrine, Mats Utas, and Henrik E. Vigh. 2006. Introduction to *Navigating Youth, Generating Adulthood: Social Becoming in an African Context*, edited by Catrine Christiansen, Mats Utas, and Henrik Vigh, 9–28. Uppsala: Nordiska Afrikainstitutet.

Comaroff, Jean, and John Comaroff. 2005. "Reflections on Youth, from the Past to the Post-colony." In *Makers and Breakers*, edited by A. Honwana and F. De Boeck, 267–281. Oxford: James Currey.

Conciliation Resources. 2018. "Youth Aspirations for Peace and Security." *Conciliation Resources Report*. www.c-r.org/downloads/Youth%20aspirations%20for%20peace%20and%20security.pdf. (URL inactive.)

Crenshaw, Kimberlé. 2005. "Mapping the Margins: Intersectionality, Identity Politics, and Violence against Women of Color." In *Violence against Women: Classic Papers*, edited by R. K. Bergen, J. L. Edleson, and C. M. Renzetti, 282–313. Auckland: Pearson Education New Zealand.

Cuthbert, Denise, and Kate Cregan. 2014. *Global Childhoods: Issues and Debates*. London: Sage.

Del Felice, Celina, and Helene Ruud. 2016. *Annotated Bibliography: The Role of Youth in Peacebuilding*. United Network of Young Peacebuilders and Humble Bees. https://unoy.org/wp-content/uploads/Annotated-Bibliography-Youth-and-Peacebuilding-November-2016.docx-2.pdf.

Ensor, Marisa O., ed. 2012. *African Childhoods: Education, Development, Peacebuilding and the Youngest Continent*. New York: Palgrave Macmillan.

———. 2013. "Youth Culture, Refugee (Re)integration, and Diasporic Identities in South Sudan." *Postcolonial Text* 8, no. 3, 1–19.

Global Forum on Youth, Peace and Security. 2015. *Amman Declaration on Youth, Peace and Security*. United Nations, August 22, 2015. https://unoy.org/en/amman-youth-declaration.

Hettne, Björn. 2010. "Development and Security: Origins and Future." *Security Dialogue* 41, no. 1, 31–52.

Honwana, Alcinda, and Filip De Boeck, eds. 2005. *Makers and Breakers: Children and Youth in Postcolonial Africa*. Oxford: James Currey.

Hudson, Valerie M. 2012. "What Sex Means for World Peace." Foreign Policy, April 24, 2012. https://foreignpolicy.com/2012/04/24/what-sex-means-for-world-peace/.

Hudson, Valerie M., Bonnie Ballif-Spanvill, Mary Caprioli, and Chad F. Emmett. 2012. *Sex & World Peace*. New York: Columbia University Press.

James, Allison, and Adrian James. 2012. *Key Concepts in Childhood Studies*. London: Sage.

James, Allison, and Alan Prout, eds. 1997. *Constructing and Reconstructing Childhood: Contemporary Issues in the Sociological Study of Childhood*. Oxon, U.K.: Routledge.

Kennelly, Jacqueline. 2011. *Citizen Youth*. New York: Palgrave Macmillan.

Kujeke, Muneinazvo. 2019. "Young Refugees Can Help 'Silence the Guns by 2020.'" Reliefweb, OCHA Services, May 9, 2019. https://reliefweb.int/report/world/young-refugees-can-help-silence-guns-2020.

Lancy, David F. 2015. *The Anthropology of Childhood: Cherubs, Chattel, Changelings*. Cambridge: Cambridge University Press.

Lin, Justin Yifu. 2012. "Youth Bulge: A Demographic Dividend or a Demographic Bomb in Developing Countries?" World Bank Blogs, January 5, 2012. http://blogs.worldbank.org/developmenttalk/youth-bulge-a-demographic-dividend-or-a-demographic-bomb-in-developing-countries.

MacBlain, Sean, Jill Dunn, and Ian Luke. 2017. *Contemporary Childhood*. London: Sage.

O'Brien, Karen, Elin Selboe, and Bronwyn M. Hayward. 2018. "Exploring Youth Activism on Climate Change: Dutiful, Disruptive, and Dangerous Dissent." *Ecology and Society* 23, no. 3, 42.

Ortiz Quintana, Romeral. 2016. "United Nations Security Council Resolution 2250: Youth, Peace and Security." Policy Paper no. 14 (September 2016). Barcelona: Institu Catala Internacional per la Pau.

Ozerdem, Alpaslan. 2016. "The Role of Youth in Peacebuilding: Challenges and Opportunities." Oxford Research Group, October 26, 2016. www.oxfordresearchgroup.org.uk/blog/the-role-of-youth-in-peacebuilding-challenges-and-opportunities.

Patton, George C., Carolyn Coffey, Susan M. Sawyer, Russell M. Viner, Dagmar M. Haller, Krishna Bose, Theo Vos, Jane Ferguson, and Colin D. Mathers. 2009. "Global Patterns of Mortality in Young People: A Systematic Analysis of Population Health Data." *Lancet* 374, no. 9693, 881–892.

Payne, Julian, Antoine Warembourg, and Jalal Awan. 2017. *Impacts of Climate Change on Youth, Peace and Security*. Sustainable Development Solutions Network Youth. Paris: SDSN Youth. www.unsdsn.org/resources/publications/impacts-of-climate-change-on-youth-peace-and-security/. (URL inactive.)

Pruitt, Lesley. 2013. *Youth in Peace and Conflict, Youth Peacebuilding: Music, Gender and Change*. Albany, N.Y.: SUNY Press.

Salehyan, Idean, and Kristian Skrede Gleditsch. 2006. "Refugees and the Spread of Civil War." *International Organization* 60:335–366.

Search for Common Ground. 2017. Youth, Peace and Security: Insights from Engaged and Disengaged Young Women and Men in Nepal, Niger, Nigeria and Tunisia. October 30, 2017. www.youth4peace.info/system/files/2018-04/UNSCR%202250%20Hard%20to%20Reach%20Consultations%20-%20Comparative%20Report%20SFCG%20final.pdf.

Sebhatu, Rahel Weldeab. 2017. "(En)gendering Youth for Gender-Just Peace with UN Security Council Resolution 2250." *Gender-Just Peace and Transitional Justice*. No. 3. Lund, Sweden: Lund University.

Simpson, Graeme. 2018. *The Missing Peace: Independent Progress Study on Youth, Peace and Security*. UNFPA. www.unfpa.org/sites/default/files/youth/youth-web-english.pdf.

———. 2019. "Youth, Peace and Security: Addressing the Violence of Exclusion." *Accord* 28. www.c-r.org/downloads/Youth,%20Peace%20and%20Security.pdf. (URL inactive.)

Smith, Hazel, and Paul Stares, eds. 2007. *Diasporas in Conflict: Peace Makers or Peace Wreckers?* Tokyo: United Nations University Press.

Sommers, Marc. 2015. *The Outcast Majority*. Athens: University of Georgia Press.

Stedman, Stephen J., and Fred Tanner. 2003. *Refugee Manipulation: War, Politics, and the Abuse of Human Suffering*. Washington, D.C.: Brookings Institution.

Sukarieh, Mayssoun, and Stuart Tannock. 2018. "The Global Securitisation of Youth." *Third World Quarterly* 39, no. 5 (September): 854–870.

U.N. DESA (United Nations Department of Economic and Social Affairs). 2018. *World Youth Report on Youth and the 2030 Agenda for Sustainable Development*. New York: U.N. DESA.

UNGA (United Nations General Assembly). 2015. *Transforming Our World: The 2030 Agenda for Sustainable Development*. A/RES/70/1. October 21, 2015. Accessed October 5, 2019. www.refworld.org/docid/57b6e3e44.html.

United Nations. 1945. *The Charter of the United Nations*. www.un.org/en/charter-united-nations/.

———. 2005. *World Youth Report, 2005: Young People Today, and in 2015*. United Nations Publications. October 2005. www.un.org/esa/socdev/unyin/documents/wyr05book.pdf.

———. 2009. *Human Security in Theory and Practice: Application of the Human Security Concept and the United Nations Trust Fund for Human Security*. New York: Human Security Unit, U.N. Office for the Coordination of Humanitarian Affairs (OCHA).

———. 2015. "Security Council, Unanimously Adopting Resolution 2250 (2015), Urges Member States to Increase Representation of Youth in Decision-Making at All Levels." U.N. Meetings Coverage, December 9, 2015. www.un.org/press/en/2015/sc12149.doc.htm.

———. 2018. "Adopting Resolution 2419 (2018), Security Council Calls for Increasing Role of Youth in Negotiating, Implementing Peace Agreements." July 6, 2018. www.un.org/press/en/2018/sc13368.doc.htm.

United Nations and World Bank. 2018. *Pathways for Peace: Inclusive Approaches to Preventing Violent Conflict*. Washington, D.C.: World Bank.

United Nations Security Council (UNSC). 2016. "UNSCR 2250 Introduction." www.youth4peace.info/UNSCR2250/Introduction.

United Nations Women. 2017. "Media Advisory: U.N. Women Highlights the Voices of Women Building Sustainable Peace and Mobilizing for Justice and Equality." October 23, 2017. www.unwomen.org/en/news/stories/2017/10/media-advisory-un-women-at-open-debate-on-security-council-resolution-1325.

———. 2018. *Young Women in Peace and Security: At the Intersection of the YPS and WPS Agendas*. April 2018. www.unwomen.org/-/media/headquarters/attachments/sections/library/publications/2018/research-paper-young-women-in-peace-and-security-en.pdf?la=en&vs=2849.

Williams, Margaret. 2016. "Youth, Peace and Security." *Journal of International Affairs* 69, no. 2. https://jia.sipa.columbia.edu/youth-peace-security-new-agenda-middle-east-north-africa.

World Bank. 2011. *World Development Report 2011: Conflict, Security, and Development*. Washington, D.C.: World Bank.

———. 2018. *Pathways for Peace: Inclusive Approaches to Preventing Violent Conflict*. Washington, D.C.: World Bank. https://openknowledge.worldbank.org/handle/10986/28337.

World Bank Group. 2020. "World Bank Group Strategy for Fragility, Conflict, and Violence 2020–2025." Washington, D.C.: WBG. http://documents.worldbank.org/curated/en/844591582815510521/pdf/World-Bank-Group-Strategy-for-Fragility-Conflict-and-Violence-2020-2025.pdf.

Zembylas, Michalinos, and Zvi Bekerman. 2008. "Education and the Dangerous Memories of Historical Trauma: Narratives of Pain, Narratives of Hope." *Curriculum Inquiry* 38, no. 2, 125–132.

PART I

Participation

CHAPTER 1

Peace *by*, *for*, or *with* Youth?

HOW A PYD LENS ENHANCES OUR VIEW OF YOUNG PEOPLE'S ROLE IN PEACEBUILDING

Carole MacNeil

If "true peace is not merely the absence of tension, it is the presence of justice," as Martin Luther King Jr. (1958) once suggested, then working on behalf of peace means working on behalf of justice more broadly defined, including issues of voice, inclusion, and power. Peacebuilding efforts that exclude entire groups within a community fail to create a foundation of justice, diluting the effectiveness of such efforts—or worse, dooming them to failure.

Much needed—and much deserved—attention is finally being given to the roles that youth can and should play in peacebuilding and security, most notably with the passing of U.N. Security Council Resolution (UNSCR) 2250, which encourages member states to work toward greater inclusion of youth and recognizes young peoples' real and potential contributions to peacebuilding. Even with growing recognition of the important contributions that young people have made toward peace and social justice (e.g., Simpson 2018; UNOY Peacebuilders and SFCG 2017), challenges remain regarding how to fully support youths' peace and justice work and how to integrate that work more broadly throughout the community rather than marginalizing it in silos, disconnected from systems and structures of power.

Over more than two decades of working with young people, I have facilitated countless youth-focused community change processes in places such as Kenya, the Democratic Republic of the Congo (DRC), Tanzania, Lebanon, Turkey, the West Bank, numerous U.S. urban settings, and others. These involved diverse groups of youth and adults, including those in refugee camps and host communities, those living in informal settlements ("slums"), those isolated by geography, those marginalized by existing power structures, and those living in conflict-affected settings. In these processes, community members come together to envision the short- and long-term changes they would like to help make happen in their community(ies), with an intentional bias toward hearing and acting on the perspectives, needs, and goals of diverse young people. Many of these processes have focused on building peaceful communities. This chapter draws from these personal experiences, from other youth peacebuilding research, and from the broader base of research in positive youth development (PYD), as summarized later.

This chapter suggests that PYD's particular lens for seeing youth and their relationship to society supports—even obligates—a shift in young people's roles and power within the community, helping undergird the justice side of peace and justice work. Further, by building on young peoples' assets and supporting their *meaningful* and *authentic* engagement, PYD shifts the focus from programs and policies "for" youth to those "by" and "with" youth, creating a foundation for a peaceful and just future for all of a community's young (and not-so-young) people. The chapter begins with an overview of the evidence-based principles of PYD and then explores how those principles might guide social and political policies away from the securitization of youth toward an integrative approach that invests in youth and community resilience.

Understanding the PYD "Lens"

While the growing global youth population is frequently referenced in youth-related policies and issues, even more important may be how those numbers are used (or misused) to shape programs, policies, and practices. Is the so-called youth bulge a threat to society, requiring security-based policy responses? Are large numbers of youth a vulnerable target for those who would seek them out as actors in violence, suggesting another set of responses within a securitization framework? Or are youth "an undervalued asset" who could help solve some of the world's most pressing economic, social, and political issues, both now and in the future? Perhaps it depends on which lens we use to view youth as we work with and on behalf of them.

Like a photographer who switches lenses to view the same scene with a new perspective, changing "lenses" to examine a social phenomenon may help us see it in a new way. PYD's extensive body of research, amassed over several decades, may provide that new lens for understanding how best to support the efforts of youth in peace and security (YPS). Using a PYD lens is like "zooming out" from a focus on the circumstances of a unique young person (or a group of young people) to focus on the entire social ecology in which that young person is situated.

PYD and the Social Ecology of Youth: An Overview

PYD is at once a philosophy, an approach, and a concrete integration of principles and practices for working directly with or on behalf of young people. PYD is a holistic approach to working with youth that intentionally sees beyond youths' needs, instead regarding young people as individuals with existing assets to be recognized and nurtured. More than "future" citizens, PYD suggests that youth are capable and important citizens in their own right, who have the right to participate in the decisions that affect their lives and the capability to make significant contributions to their organizations and communities (Lansdown 2001; MacNeil 2012; USAID 2012). Since neither youth issues nor the solutions to address them are isolated, PYD focuses both on youth programs (microlevel) and on the larger social-ecological context (macrolevel) in which youth are situated.

PYD is described in different ways, according to somewhat different paradigms, but most of these descriptions share the following characteristics (Catalano et al. 2004; Lerner 2005; National Research Council and Institute of Medicine 2002; Pittman et al. 2002; Scales and Leffert 1999):

- PYD is assets-based. A PYD approach starts with the talents, skills, and interests of the individual—or the group or community—not with the deficits, needs, or risks. PYD doesn't ignore needs and risks; it just doesn't start there.
- PYD nurtures supports and opportunities. PYD supports learning and skills building and then creates authentic and meaningful opportunities to apply and expand those skills. This reinforces youth agency, supporting youth as leaders and citizens of today, not only tomorrow.
- PYD places a high priority on supportive, nurturing relationships, both youth-adult and peer-to-peer relationships.
- PYD is inclusive at both the micro- and macrolevels. At the microlevel, it's attentive to issues of inclusion and diversity, including gender, age, ethnicity, and other aspects of identity. At a macrolevel, it casts a wide net through the community or society, with opportunities that are appropriate, accessible, and effective for all youth.
- PYD starts with the tenet of "safe spaces." This includes ensuring that youth involved in PYD programs will feel and be safe both physically and emotionally.
- PYD works "outside the program box," focusing on the larger social-ecological context. PYD can happen within any program or organization concerned with youth but is also attentive to the relationships among the various programs and sectors and with the larger economic, social, and political systems.

PYD has evolved into this holistic, ecological model over the course of many decades of learning from both researchers and practitioners who found that simply focusing on intervention (fixing a problem) or prevention (stopping a problem before it happens) doesn't do enough to build on the inherent potential of young people.[1] Earlier models of PYD tended to focus on future leadership or citizenship roles, while contemporary models of PYD seek to support young peoples' full engagement both now and in the future.

Recent research in PYD has begun to include an increasing number of studies focused on contexts in lower- and middle-income countries (LMICs) and other lesser-researched settings (e.g., Alvarado et al. 2017; Catalano et al. 2019; Lerner et al. 2018; Naudeau et al. 2008; YouthPower Learning 2017). While the research base in these settings is growing, it is still far from robust, particularly in terms of experimental, quasi-experimental, or longitudinal research on specific PYD outcomes in LMICs (Alvarado et al. 2017; Catalano et al. 2019). Still, there are many years of case studies and anecdotal evidence documenting success in PYD programs (Naudeau et al. 2008). There is also evidence to suggest that programs for and with youth may be integrating PYD principles without a consistent PYD language or PYD outcome measures, which hinder our ability to truly understand outcomes across programs, contexts, and sectors (Alvarado et al. 2017; Lerner et al. 2018). The evidence that does exist across LMICs suggests that PYD is happening in diverse contexts and that, while the need for cultural adaptation cannot be minimized, PYD principles hold true—and has great potential—across these contexts (Catalano et al. 2019).

As research in PYD continues to expand in both high-income countries (HICs) and LMICs, several important trends have emerged that are particularly relevant for thinking about YPS. These include the centrality of relationships, the importance of youth agency for both youth and communities, and the positive role of intergenerational partnerships.

The Centrality of Relationships

Emerging research on PYD highlights that for all youth, sustained relationships with caring adults are critical. In fact, of all the things we do with young people, our focus on building and supporting a caring connection with a caregiver or other significant adult may be the most important thing we do. These important "developmental relationships" have been shown to increase social-emotional learning, academic motivation, and the sense of personal responsibility and to reduce future high-risk behaviors (National Scientific Council on the Developing Child 2018; Pekel et al. 2018; Roehlkepartain et al. 2017).

Importantly, the research also shows that, while these caring connections are important for all youth, they may have a particular power for those impacted by trauma, hardship, and other circumstances of risk, providing critical "social buffering" (Act for Youth Center of Excellence 2014; National Scientific Council on the Developing Child 2015). Even for those who experience what is referred to as "toxic stress," developing from war, violence, poverty, or a combination of these or other factors, the caring, sustained relationship with a caregiver or other adult can serve as a buffer against the effects of that stress (Harper Browne 2014; Masten 2014; National Scientific Council on the Developing Child 2015).

Because of their power to buffer against the negative effects of stresses such as violence, war, and related hardships, these relationships take on particular significance in the context of YPS. We know that children and youth are among those most adversely affected by peace and security issues. Some recent estimates suggest that more than six hundred million youth are living in conflict-affected and fragile regions (UNDP 2014); this makes them more likely to be out of school and undernourished (UNICEF 2016) in addition to the direct effects of the conflict itself. And as UNSCR 2250 states, "Among civilians, youth account for many of those adversely affected by armed conflict, including as refugees and internally displaced persons, and . . . the disruption of youth's access to education and economic opportunities has a dramatic impact on durable peace and reconciliation" (1).

Relationships are critical to help young people develop a sense of belonging and to buffer conflict- and trauma-affected youth from the negative effects of conflict while supporting them in proactively participating in their communities rather than becoming alienated from those communities. In LMICs, some evidence suggests that PYD programs in schools may have particular potential to build this sense of connectedness (Naudeau et al. 2008), but other case study evidence suggests that relationship building isn't limited to schools (MacNeil, Krauss, and Zeldin 2016). More evidence is needed to see how and where these important relationships can be strengthened.

Developmental relationships play a vital role in supporting youth in meaningful and authentic engagement in peacebuilding processes. Relationships build a foundation that expands the power and possibility of youth agency (discussed in the following section) while addressing issues of marginalization through the strengthening of intergenerational partnerships (also discussed in the next section).

The Importance of Youth Agency

One of the characteristics that distinguish PYD from other approaches to youth work, such as prevention or intervention programs, is its focus on engaging youth not only as future citizens and leaders but also as citizens and leaders of today.[2] A PYD approach actively builds the skills youth need to engage in constructive ways, then it identifies or creates opportunities for youth to apply those skills in ways that make a positive difference in their own lives and in their communities and world.[3]

> Like, you're in a group and the decision matters, and it's your decision. . . . I get to be involved in all these great opportunities, like these conference calls from people all over the world. . . . And I get to go to all these places, and it's kind of invigorating . . . like my existence makes a difference.
>
> U.S. female teen participant in a study of youth-adult collaborative leadership, as cited in MacNeil 2000, 299

I use two key concepts to distinguish engagement from other forms of youth participation: (1) meaningful and (2) authentic. *Meaningful* refers to opportunities for action that matter to the individual. *Authentic* refers to actions that involve real decisions or, at minimum, influence real decisions (rather than tokenistic groups operating on the sidelines while real decisions are made elsewhere). Defined thusly, youth engagement leading to agency involves real power and the renegotiation—or disruption—of power structures that have typically excluded youth from participating in the processes and decisions that affect them.

Agency has particular significance in discussions of YPS, as it can inform the first pillars for action of UNSCR 2250. This pillar—"participation"—calls for the "inclusive representation of youth in decision-making at all levels in local, national, regional and international institutions and mechanisms for the prevention and resolution of conflict" (3). But working out how to accomplish this within social, political, and economic structures that typically exclude youth is no small task. Those who hold power do not easily relinquish it, as is particularly the case in some deeply gerontocratic societies. PYD offers evidence-based approaches for fostering youth agency and creating opportunities for contribution that build on the needs and assets of diverse young people.

Research has consistently revealed the importance of PYD's emphasis on fostering agency through meaningful and authentic engagement experiences. Important benefits of civic engagement and activism for overall youth development have been documented, perhaps especially for youth who may experience discrimination or marginalization (Ginwright and James 2002; Gambone et al. 2004). Recent large-scale, longitudinal research has highlighted the positive correlation between certain forms of civic engagement and better health outcomes, positive emotions, fewer risky health behaviors, increased school performance, and higher levels of income and education later in life (Ballard, Hoyt, and Pachucki 2018).

Research in LMICs shows that developing agency through civic engagement benefits both youth and community, enhancing social cohesion and building social trust (MacNeil 2013). Programs that incorporated youth agency were associated with individual outcomes such as increased self-esteem and sense of empowerment, decreased school dropout rates, and decreased rates of substance abuse (Naudeau et al. 2008). Integrating agency into youth programming can promote youths' participation in prosocial civic engagement and decrease their participation in and support for violence (Slachmuijlder 2017; Tesfaye 2016).

> The youth can bring a different perspective and a fresh approach. Involving youth into the decision making process is a fundamental way of gaining legitimacy. Opening up space to the civil society in this manner is bound to bring in fresh perspectives, technical expertise and ground support.
> —Nepalese youth, as cited in MacNeil, Ragan, and Solberg 2012, 10

Further, a study by the United Nations Human Settlements Programme on seventy youth-led community development projects in forty-four countries showed a range of positive outcomes not only for those projects' youth leaders and participants but also for their communities. These positive outcomes included community information and communications technology (ICT) and vocational training, social entrepreneurship ventures, or improvements to basic urban services (MacNeil, Ragan, and Solberg 2012).

In an example from the West Bank, youth participated in leadership development, service learning, peacebuilding, and other educational programs through hubs known as Youth Development Resource Centers (YDRCs). The project utilized a PYD approach, tailored for the Palestinian context. Through the combination of learning and authentic engagement, the project showed results that benefited both youth and, by extension, the larger communities. For example, intentionally developing leadership skills and attitudes, accompanied by opportunities to practice those skills, led to significant positive attitude changes regarding the participant's personal capacity: to make a difference in the community (an increase from 46 percent to 83 percent pre/post, compared with 44 percent of comparison group respondents), to solve personal conflicts (an increase from 62 percent to 92 percent pre/post, compared with 77 percent of comparison group respondents), and to get along with people who are different (an increase from 53 percent to 93 percent pre/post, compared with 69 percent of comparison group respondents). While reported changes were not equally strong among female and male youth, potentially due to rates of participation connected to the cultural context and differing expectations for females, the project was successful in reaching certain groups of marginalized youth (IREX 2015).

By now we know that marginalization of youth in the civic arena can fuel discontent (USAID 2012; Simpson 2018) and that youth agency can sometimes be channeled into less constructive directions. Research shows some connection between the alienation of youth—including their sidelining by governments who may view youth agency as a security threat rather than a force for positive change—and the vulnerability of youth to recruitment by violent extremist organizations (Sommers 2018). The connections between youth and engagement in violence are complex, but "there is a growing body of research that demonstrates the link between significant levels of social, economic and political exclusion and lack of opportunities faced by young people, with the result that their transition to adulthood is blocked or prolonged" (U.N. IANYD Working Group on Youth and Peacebuilding 2016, 12).

In the midst of unraveling the possible connections among youth, alienation, agency, and conflict, it is important to keep in mind that the vast majority of young people do not get involved in violence (Simpson 2018; U.N. IANYD Working Group on Youth and Peacebuilding 2016). Still, in contexts where youth policies and approaches are highly securitized, youth agency—as important for the positive development of the community as it is for the positive development of the young person—gets squelched because of fears that youth agency may be destructive (Simpson 2018, 26).

But seen through the PYD lens, youth agency can have as great or greater capacity for impact in a positive direction. Engagement is critical for both present peace and security and for future justice. Later, this chapter explores how PYD and its support of youth agency might directly address some of the complex factors associated with youth involvement in violent extremism.

The Positive Role of Intergenerational Partnerships

Relationships and agency come together in an important way in youth work—including YPS work. In some community contexts, the roles of youth are highly structured and constrained by cultural norms that delineate what roles youth may play compared to adults or elders. Supporting youth agency, then, requires sensitivity to those norms. By developing intergenerational partnerships, young people have found ways to negotiate those norms and create opportunities to take on new leadership roles while at the same time building new and often meaningful relationships with the elders in their communities (MacNeil, Krauss, and Zeldin 2016). In essence, they are creating agency and finding a caring connection simultaneously.

Relationships are strengthened by agency: for relationships to have the greatest developmental impact, power needs to be shared between adults and youth. This builds trust, develops skills, and reinforces confidence in the young person's ability to take on leadership roles (Pekel et al. 2018). Conversely, agency is strengthened by relationships: for youth agency to serve youth optimally, particularly those youth affected by hardship or trauma, it must be coupled with appropriate supports, including opportunities to build relationships and safe spaces in which youth can act without fear (Williams and Drury 2011).

It's great, it's like we're equals . . . like [my adult partner in the project] asks me for advice. . . . I mean, it's not like I'm [the youth], it's like we're partners . . . and he asks for my input and stuff. . . . So, it's pretty cool, I feel like I'm giving a lot more.

—U.S. male teen participant in a study of youth-adult collaborative leadership, as cited in MacNeil 2000, 265

For example, in Dadaab, groups of Somali refugee youth activists doing "social cohesion" projects[4] built intergenerational partnerships as a way to increase their own agency within the community and cultural context. They needed elders to build broader support for their work or to access resources to which youth alone had no access. Those relationships helped them accomplish their goals while also building visibility and relationships throughout the community (MacNeil, Krauss, and Zeldin 2016).

Beyond supporting the positive development of youth, intergenerational partnerships also support the positive development of the adults/elders part-nering with the youth by reshaping perceptions and forming relationships that are meaningful to adults and youth alike (Zeldin et al. 2000). Intergenerational partnerships have the power to dismantle negative stereotypes of youth held by adults and strengthen social ties at multiple levels within a community. One of the major barriers to youth engagement in peacebuilding or security (or other types of social justice work) is the negative perceptions held by adults, leading to stereotypes, fear, or "policy panic" (Simpson 2018; UNOY Peacebuilders 2018). As these stereotypes further stigmatize youth, they make it increasingly difficult for youth to engage in meaningful and authentic ways to the peace- and justice-building work of their communities. By dismantling negative stereotypes, inter-generational relationships have the power to overcome the distrust that creates such barriers to youth inclusion in civic and political processes, resulting in ben-efits to youth, adults/elders, and the larger community. Research has shown that intergenerational partnerships contribute to positive outcomes in policy making and organizing (Tolman et al. 2001), organizational decision-making (MacNeil and McClean 2006; Zeldin et al. 2000), and urban planning and community develop-ment efforts (Chawla 2002). In short, the benefits of youth engagement are only expanded through these intergenerational partnerships (O'Donoghue, Kirshner, and McLaughlin 2002). In conflict-affected contexts, in particular, some evidence suggests that intergenerational partnerships successfully diminish the lure of armed groups and strengthen community resilience (United Nations 2016).

YPS FROM A POSITIVE YOUTH DEVELOPMENT PERSPECTIVE

The evidence base for PYD provides a new lens for viewing youths' role in YPS and a foundation for strengthening and supporting that role. First, PYD's focus on inclusion and diversity and its emphasis on tailoring program approaches to meet developmental needs according to age and gender increase its adaptability to diverse contexts and make it useful for informing peace- and justice-focused pro-grams happening with or by youth in communities. In this way, PYD can inform YPS at a micro- or programmatic level.

Second, the evidence base for PYD informs our thinking about the larger con-text in which youth live, learn, work, and play, including the systems, sectors, and structures that impact young people and their communities. It can thus help shape how we conceptualize and develop YPS approaches more broadly at the macro- or community/social level. Given that UNSCR 2250 calls for youth participation locally, nationally, regionally, and internationally, the fact that PYD evidence informs both the micro- and macrolevels may prove useful for YPS initiatives.

The Microlevel (or Programs Matter)

The microlevel focuses at the level of the individual, where programs operate, and where activities seek to meet the needs of specific individuals or specific groups of young people. A PYD approach compels programs to be culturally responsive and to adapt programs, policies, and practices to a young person's unique developmental needs as they evolve at different ages and as they vary according to gender, ethnicity, and other facets of identity.

In the PYD literature, the healthy development of a young person is influenced by the combination of individual, family, and community-level "risk" factors that she or he faces as well as the positive strengths ("protective" factors) that exist or are fostered intentionally. Risk factors make a young person more vulnerable to problems and are associated with negative outcomes, while protective factors "buffer" a young person and reduce the negative impact of risk factors.

In contexts where peace and security are especially problematic, particularly those contexts where attention is focused on preventing or countering violent extremism (PVE/CVE), PYD can be a powerful alternative lens to the framework and language associated with PVE/CVE. The research on PVE/CVE identifies "push" and "pull" factors as a way to understand the drivers related to the recruitment of young people into violent extremism. Push and pull factors describe what attracts a young person to violent extremism (VE), including the environmental characteristics (push factors) making the young person's environment more conducive to VE and the psychosocial conditions (pull factors) incentivizing the young person toward VE (Elsayed, Faris, and Zeiger 2017; UNESCO 2017; YouthPower Learning 2017). By sorting these factors into spheres of influence (individual/peer/family/community) and then superimposing PVE/CVE's push/pull factors over PYD's framework of risk/protective factors, a significant pattern of overlap emerges. Table 1.1 illustrates this overlap.

This suggests that framing the push and pull of a young person into violent extremism as a human developmental issue may hold some merit as an alternative "lens."[5] That is, youth are meeting their heretofore unmet developmental needs through the exploration of, and possible participation in, VE groups. Or said another way, *youth will find ways to meet their developmental needs*. It is the community's and larger society's responsibility to ensure that constructive opportunities for meeting those developmental needs are available and accessible for all youth.

Since PYD is supported by a robust body of literature from HICs and a growing body of evidence in LMICs that substantiate the importance of building protective factors and that can guide program developers to do so (Lerner et al. 2005; National Research Council and Institute of Medicine 2002; National Scientific Council on the Developing Child 2015; USAID 2012), could it not also help guide YPS programs to do the same? In particular, in conflict-affected contexts, PYD research might help shift the thinking about push/pull factors not as a process that needs to be stopped but as part of the natural human developmental process that has some internal logic to it. With that shift in perspective, communities might provide alternative supports and opportunities to respond constructively to those factors. This has implications for the development of programs for, by, and with youth.

TABLE 1.1

COMPARISON OF SELECTED PYD RISK/PROTECTIVE FACTORS VS.
C/PVE PUSH/PULL FACTORS[6]

Factor	PVE/CVE[7]		PYD[8]	
	CONSIDERED A "PUSH" FACTOR	CONSIDERED A "PULL" FACTOR	CONSIDERED A "RISK" FACTOR	CONSIDERED A "PROTECTIVE" FACTOR
Individual/peer				
To develop a sense of belonging	X			
To have a sense of belonging				X
Negative peer influences within communities	X			
Interaction with friends involved in problem behaviors		X		
Expression of religion (as an alternative for religious institutions)		X		
Belief in the moral order; religious and club affiliations				X
To develop a sense of purpose			X	X
Family				
Decreased role of parents in education and social support	X			I=X
A low level of positive parental involvement			X	
Role models or charismatic leaders (esp. replacing father figures)		X		
The presence of a positive adult in the family to mentor and be supportive				X
Social/community/ education				
Lack of socioeconomic opportunities; lack of jobs	X			

Factor	PVE/CVE[7]		PYD[8]	
	CONSIDERED A "PUSH" FACTOR	CONSIDERED A "PULL" FACTOR	CONSIDERED A "RISK" FACTOR	CONSIDERED A "PROTECTIVE" FACTOR
Economic disadvantage			X	
Lack of education	X			
Poor academic performance			X	
Unresolved conflict (social)	X			
Social disorganization in the community			X	
Discrimination; disenfranchisement	X			I=X
Low community attachment			X	

Note: I=X indicates that the inverse of a push or risk factor is supported in the research as a protective factor. For example, if "discrimination" is a push factor toward involvement in VE, I=X indicates that the inverse (a lack of discrimination) would serve as a protective factor.

PYD may also inform PVE/CVE efforts through its focus on agency (and intergenerational partnerships). Emerging research has shown the importance of agency in PVE/CVE efforts: "Although improving access to secondary education through this program reduced youth participation in political violence by 16%, it increased support for political violence by 11%. However, when combining secondary education with civic engagement opportunities that allow youth to carry out community action campaigns, both participation in and support for violence drop significantly, by 14% and 20% respectively" (Tesfaye 2016, 2). This important research showed that it was the combination of education and civic engagement opportunities—or, said another way, learning plus agency—that led to a reduction in both participation in and support for political violence rather than education alone.

PYD research and practice tell us that intentionally promoting young peoples' positive development at a micro- or program level—including youths' need for agency, relationships, and inclusion—will create positive outcomes for youth and also align with a vision for peaceful, just, engaged communities.

The Macrolevel (or Context Matters)

Young people don't live in isolation. They live in families and communities and interact in a wide variety of ways with school, work, and other social networks, all situated within a larger community. A second, important way that PYD may be able to inform YPS efforts is through its focus on the larger context in which youth are situated. PYD's focus on the macrolevel includes the community, youth-serving and community-based organizations, social groups, schools, health systems, religious organizations, and any group or institution that touches or impacts the lives of young people. Importantly, PYD focuses not only on individuals or individual programs but also on the intersection between and among the groups in which youth are situated and their larger economic, social, and political systems, described as the "social ecology" of young people.

We have some understanding of how the social ecology affects the well-being of the young person and vice versa. Recent estimates are that 263 million children and youth are out of school worldwide (UNESCO Institute for Statistics 2017), which has long-term effects on the young person, her/his family, and the larger community. Youth make up between 50 and 70 percent of the population in areas affected by civil war (U.N.-Habitat 2013), which hinders access to education, economic participation, medical care, and other social needs. In many contexts, the economic participation of female youth is unequal to that of males, which negatively impacts the life of the young woman, the well-being of her family and community, and the community's overall economic growth (Gonzales et al. 2015).

In other words, we know that context matters, for or against the positive development of a young person, for or against her/his resistance to recruitment into violence or VE, for or against her/his engagement in peacebuilding and social justice. We know that communities and the institutions within them can be important participants in buffering individual youth from the effects of the drivers toward violence but may also be instrumental in building community resilience against extremism (Fink et al. 2013; Hedayah, n.d.; UNESCO 2017). Thus communities and their institutions are essential in the work of promoting peace and justice (Simpson 2018; UNESCO 2016; United Nations and World Bank 2017).

UNSCR 2250 takes a macroview of YPS in that it encourages the participation of youth at multiple levels of society. It also encourages member states to work cross-sectorally, including governmental and nongovernmental actors; civil society organizations; educational, cultural, and religious leaders; and the private sector. However, PYD can provide the specificity that UNSCR 2250 lacks by laying out an expanded view of youth participation and offering detailed guidance on implementation in various contexts. Evidence shows that this social-ecological approach benefits both youth and communities—in the short and long term—particularly when youth themselves develop agency to act on their own and others' behalf within that community (i.e., through various forms of civic engagement, activism, or volunteerism; Ballard, Hoyt, and Pachucki 2018; Conner 2011; Ginwright and James 2002; MacNeil, Ragan, and Solberg 2012; Mauto 2012).

As discussed earlier, the factors "pushing" or "pulling" a young person toward VE are influenced by his or her relationships with family, peers, and others (the microcontext). However, those push and pull factors are operating not in isolation but within a context of group, community, and social dynamics. UNSCR 2250 calls on member states to address the underlying social, economic, and political conditions that lead to violence, VE, and lack of peace. However, it is beyond the scope of UNSCR 2250 to provide detailed explanations of how to address some of these macrolevel issues and concerns. PYD's evidence base regarding the social-ecological context can provide promising practices on integrating a macrolevel focus—where programs reach both vertically and horizontally and cut across multiple sectors—into any PVE/CVE work happening within the larger community.

Working Further "Upstream":
Implications for Programs and Policy

With an ever-expanding research base in PYD and increased understanding of developmental processes, youth work has slowly migrated "upstream." With the realization that approaches need to be more inclusive and holistic, programs have focused more on engagement and potential, not simply on reaching so-called at-risk youth or on solely avoiding negative outcomes (Pittman et al. 2002).

Each time youth work moves upstream, the lens changes from trying to solve problems associated with youth to instead searching for ways to meet the developmental needs of all youth and to support them in reaching their fullest potential. Moving upstream in PYD includes more youth. But what does "moving upstream" mean in the context of YPS? The target population upstream is certainly bigger; the focus upstream is not simply on working *against* violence or insecurity but on working *for* peace, justice, and human rights. Or said another way, the focus is on building spaces where justice and hope and possibility are so expansive that they crowd out the opportunities for violence and insecurity!

Just as moving upstream in youth programming has significant implications for the ways we fund, design, deliver, recruit for, and evaluate youth programs, so too does moving upstream in YPS to a more community-based and holistic approach that incorporates the tenets of PYD. Moving upstream is linked to greater inclusiveness and to increased support for authentic and meaningful engagement of youth in peacebuilding and other forms of engagement and away from seeing youth in dichotomous terms of perpetrators or victims of violence.

Moving upstream in YPS and looking through a developmental lens would mean that the target of intervention would no longer be simply youth "at risk" nor even youth writ large. Rather the target would shift to the larger social ecology where youth live, work, learn, and play. Rather than "fixing" youth, we can buffer youth. But that is not the whole of our work. We can also buffer communities, build resilience at the community level, and support communities in fostering resilience in all of their youth (not just a small subset of youth deemed to be at high risk). This involves connecting youth to their communities and vice versa; building supportive, sustained relationships; creating intergenerational partnerships; and developing meaningful and authentic opportunities to express agency toward community development, peacebuilding, and social justice.

For this to happen, the work must not be left to "youth workers" to accomplish. Rather, the work must be seen as the responsibility of multiple sectors, multiple agencies within sectors, and multiple levels within agencies. It must be seen as the work of multiple generations. Looking through a PYD lens to support the role of youth in peacebuilding, we would see institutions that work directly with youth (e.g., youth-serving organizations, schools) collaborating with those who work with youth in the context of a broader focus on families or communities (e.g., health or social service agencies, religious organizations, civic organizations). In addition, those groups who work with youth would partner with those who do not but whose policies and practices impact young peoples' lives (e.g., government and business). The more extensive the partnerships, the broader and stronger the web of support would be created for a community's youth. As youths' assets are recognized and are integrated into these partnerships in meaningful ways, negative perceptions will start to shift. More positive perceptions and decreased stereotypes can help address the "policy panic" that occurs when policy makers develop solutions in a vacuum and without input from the youth who are often the target of those very policies. While these things are not easy to do, they can help young people feel less marginalized within their communities as their needs and concerns are heard and more valued as they see their skills and talents recognized and engaged.

CONCLUSION

Using lessons learned from the research in PYD and related fields as well as from the author's own PYD work with marginalized, fragile, and conflict-affected communities, this chapter has examined the possible conceptual and practical benefits of framing YPS through a PYD lens. The methods, strategies, and possible applications of PYD are too numerous and rich to discuss them all at length in one chapter. Certainly, this work will be supported by increasing the evidence base for PYD in LMICs, with particular attention to diverse cultural contexts and the inclusion of marginalized groups (Alvarado et al. 2017). PYD must be investigated more systematically, rigorously, and longitudinally in LMICs, and measures must be developed that are culturally and contextually appropriate so they can adequately capture the broader developmental outcomes for youth (Catalano et al. 2019). Far from a strictly defined road map, this chapter is intended to be a conceptual contribution toward applying PYD to YPS efforts and perhaps to inspire further investigation that will support youth—and adults—to take on new roles and develop new kinds of relationships in their communities and beyond.

A PYD lens helps shift the framing of youth away from that of perpetrator or victim and toward a new perception as agent of change (including in partnership with other agents of change, such as adults/elders who currently hold social, economic, or political power). In addition, a PYD lens reminds us of the larger perspective demanded when reframing the role of youth in society. Of course, there is the issue of a young person's right to be involved and her/his potential and actual contributions once involved. However, PYD pushes us further, toward a larger socioecological paradigm in which we consider both the short- and long-term outcomes from the authentic and meaningful engagement of youth, from their partnerships with older individuals, and from their engagement with systems and processes that do and will impact their lives in an ongoing way (and on which they also can and will have an impact). It is not simply about what adults can do for youth, such as increasing the chances of education, livelihood, or good health, nor is it simply about what youth can do for adults, such as improving the chances of creating peaceful and just communities and countries and improving the efficiency and effectiveness of peacebuilding efforts. From a purely practical standpoint, those are all true. But a PYD perspective pushes us to a much larger and longer view. It is what all of us, working together, do with and for each other and for the generations to come. What kind of community do we build together? What kinds of foundations do we lay for the generations that will come after us?

These conceptual ideals are aligned with the calls to action regarding representation and participation of youth affirmed in UNSCR 2250. PYD pushes these ideals further by drawing on decades of research and practical knowledge that can inform programs, policies, and practice and can be applied to YPS efforts at the micro- and macrolevels. A PYD approach applied to YPS means going beyond the obvious application of PYD to youth-serving organizations or social services and integrating the principles to multiple sectors of the community. It means horizontally and vertically weaving a web of support that will include all youth (and others) in developing protective factors and building resilience, actively fostering youth agency, and intentionally creating supportive relationships and intergenerational partnerships. It means supporting youth to become active leaders of peacebuilding and social justice, connected in positive ways to their families, organizations, and communities. In this way, it has the potential to address the "violence of exclusion" reported by youth as so disempowering and detrimental to their efforts as peace builders and community leaders (Simpson 2018, 63).

While youth programs or policies may often be framed in terms of what can or should be done "for" youth, a PYD perspective encourages youth agency—thus programs or policies "by" youth. The centrality of relationships and power of intergenerational partnerships encourages collaboration—thus programs or policies "with" youth. In YPS, then, a PYD perspective leads us to shift toward this asset-based, social-ecological approach not only because of its proven potential for positive outcomes for youth but also for the adults and communities working with them.

PYD at its best offers a more inclusive view, one that includes individuals and systems; youth and elders; and public, private, and nongovernmental sectors. Being asset-based, it moves away from dependency models and toward a focus on identifying and harnessing the strengths found in every community and in every individual. It sees communities differently and youth differently: not as perpetrators, not as victims, and not "at risk" but rather "at promise." Improving the human condition for everyone means improving the odds for one of the largest segments of that human population, the youth. This is a human rights imperative. It is also a pragmatic demand to fully understand that the challenges of our shared humanity will only be solved in partnership with those young people by supporting their development toward their fullest potential and promoting their inclusion in the issues that matter most, regardless of age, gender, cultures, or borders.

NOTES

1. This evolution in thinking does not mean, however, that there is no longer a place for intervention and prevention programs. Indeed, those programs may serve important purposes in certain situations.

2. Because of this focus, I use the language of "engagement," rather than "participation," to describe the type of involvement that most benefits both youth and the context in which they are involved (organization, community, etc.). Further, it is the fully engaged form of involvement (compared to just "showing up") that develops one's sense of agency, which

is important as both a means (knowledge and skills building) and an end (outcomes at the community level and beyond) when thinking about YPS.

3. "Agency" as seen through a PYD lens is inherently constructive, based on principles of contribution and inclusion. Seen through a security lens, however, youth agency may not always be perceived as positive, as is the case when marginalized or alienated youth turn to violent or extremist groups or activities to meet very real developmental needs (see discussion following). Some have referred to this as "negative resilience" (e.g., Simpson 2018, 33).

4. During this project, "social cohesion" programming included conflict mediation, peace-building, community development, social action, and leadership development.

5. This is not to suggest that there is a singular pathway into VE or that a developmental lens would be equally useful in all scenarios. A full exploration of the many possible pathways toward extremism, violence, and violent extremism (all different outcomes) is beyond the scope of this chapter. However, evidence suggests that meeting developmental needs (the PYD "lens") might have explanatory merit in some cases.

6. This comparison table highlights only a few factors for illustration; additional overlaps exist in each sphere. Some research suggests that the push/pull factors may vary between Organisation for Economic Co-operation and Development (OECD) countries and non-OECD countries (YouthPower Learning 2017); these distinctions are not delineated here.

7. These push/pull factors are based on the work of Elsayed, Faris, and Zeiger (2017) and UNESCO (2017).

8. These risk/protective factors are based on the work of Youth.gov (2009) and USAID (2012).

REFERENCES

Act for Youth Center of Excellence. 2014. "Positive Youth Development Outcomes." New York: Cornell University, Bronfenbrenner Center for Translational Research. www.actforyouth .net/youth_development/development/outcomes.cfm.

Alvarado, G., M. Skinner, D. Plaut, C. Moss, C. Kapungu, and N. Reavley. 2017. *A Systematic Review of Positive Youth Development Programs in Low- and Middle-Income Countries.* Washington, D.C.: YouthPower Learning, Making Cents International.

Ballard, P., L. Hoyt, and M. Pachucki. 2018. "Impacts of Adolescent and Young Adult Civic Engagement on Health and Socioeconomic Status in Adulthood." *Child Development* 23 (January): 1138–1154. https://doi.org/10.1111/cdev.12998.

Catalano, R., M. L. Berglund, J. A. M. Ryan, H. S. Lonczak, and J. D. Hawkins. 2004. "Positive Youth Development in the United States: Research Findings on Evaluations of Positive Youth." *The ANNALS of the American Academy of Political and Social Science* 591, no. 1, 98–124. Accessed February 12, 2019. https://doi.org/10.1177/0002716203260102.

Catalano, R., M. Skinner, G. Alvarado, C. Kapungu, N. Reavley, G. Patton, C. Jessee, D. Plaut, C. Moss, K. Bennett, S. Sawyer, M. Sebany, M. Sexton, C. Olenik, and S. Petroni. 2019. "Positive Youth Development Programs in Low- and Middle-Income Countries: A Conceptual Framework and Systematic Review of Efficacy." *Journal of Adolescent Health* 65, no. 1 (July): 15–31. Accessed August 18, 2019. https://doi.org/10.1016/j.jadohealth.2019.01.024.

Chawla, L. 2002. "Insight, Creativity, and Thoughts on the Environment: Integrating Children and Youth into Human Settlement Development." *Environment and Urbanization* 14:11–21.

Conner, J. O. 2011. "Youth Organizers as Young Adults: Their Commitments and Contributions." *Journal of Research on Adolescence* 21:923–942. Accessed May 30, 2018. https://doi.org/ 10.1111/j.1532-7795.2011.00766.x.

Elsayed, L., T. Faris, and S. Zeiger. 2017. *Undermining Violent Extremist Narratives in the Middle East and North Africa: A How-To Guide.* Abu Dhabi: Hedayah.

Fink, N. C., I. VeenKamp, W. Alhassen, R. Barakat, and S. Zeiger. 2013. "The Role of Education in Countering Violent Extremism: Meeting Note." Center on Global Counterterrorism Cooperation and Hedayah. Accessed February 12, 2019. https://globalcenter.org/wp-content/uploads/2013/12/Dec13_Education_Expert_Meeting_Note.pdf.

Gambone, M., H. Yu, H. Lewis-Charp, C. Sipe, and J. Lacoe. 2004. "A Comparative Analysis of Community Youth Development Strategies." CIRCLE Working Paper. College Park: University of Maryland School of Public Policy.

Ginwright, S., and T. James. 2002. "From Assets to Agents of Change: Social Justice, Organizing, and Youth Development." *New Directions for Youth Development* 96:27–46.

Gonzales, C., S. Jain-Chandra, K. Kochhar, M. Newiak, and T. Zeinullayev. 2015. *Catalyst for Change: Empowering Women and Talking Income Inequality.* Washington, D.C.: International Monetary Fund.

Harper Browne, C. 2014. *Youth Thrive: Advancing Healthy Adolescent Development and Well-Being.* Washington, D.C.: Center for the Study of Social Policy.

Hedayah. n.d. *Education for Preventing Violent Extremism (EPVE): Working Group Paper.* Abu Dhabi: Hedayah.

IREX. 2015. "21st Century Youth Competencies Assessment: Midline Assessment Report." IREX. Accessed February 12, 2019. www.irex.org/sites/default/files/node/resource/midline-youth-competencies-assessment-full-report.pdf.

King, M. L., Jr. 1958. *Stride toward Freedom: The Montgomery Story.* New York: Harper.

Lansdown, G. 2001. *Promoting Children's Participation in Democratic Decision-Making.* Florence: UNICEF Innocenti Research Center.

Lerner, R. 2005. "Promoting Positive Youth Development: Theoretical and Empirical Bases." Workshop on the Science of Adolescent Health and Development white paper, National Research Council, Washington, D.C., September 9, 2005. Washington, D.C.: National Academy of Sciences.

Lerner, R., J. B. Almerigi, C. Theokas, and J. V. Lerner. 2005. "Positive Youth Development." *Journal of Early Adolescence* 25:10–16.

Lerner, R., J. V. Lerner, G. J. Geldhof, S. Gestsdottir, P. E. King, A. T. R. Sim, M. Batinova, J. M. Tirrell, and E. Dowling. 2018. "Studying Positive Youth Development in Different Nations: Theoretical and Methodological Issues." In *Handbook of Adolescent Research and Its Impact on Global Policy,* edited by J. E. Lansford and P. Banati, 68–83. Oxford: Oxford University Press.

MacNeil, C. 2000. "Youth-Adult Collaborative Leadership: Strategies for Fostering Ability and Authority." PhD diss., University of Colorado Boulder.

———. 2012. *The Challenge and Promise of Youth-Led Development.* Nairobi: United Nations Human Settlements Programme.

———. 2013. "Supporting Asset-Based Youth and Community Development in Conflict Zones: A Training Example from the Democratic Republic of the Congo." *Children, Youth and Environments* 23, no. 1, 211–220.

MacNeil, C., S. Krauss, and S. Zeldin. 2016. "Voluntary Association, Youth Voice, and Collective Action: Youth Work in Places Where There Are No [Professional] Youth Workers." In *The Changing Landscape of Youth Work: Theory and Practice for an Evolving Field,* edited by B. Kirshner and K. Pozzoboni, 11–30. Charlotte, N.C.: Information Age.

MacNeil, C., and J. McClean. 2006. "Moving from 'Youth Leadership Development' to 'Youth in Governance': Learning Leadership by Doing Leadership." *New Directions for Youth Development* 109 (March): 99–106.

MacNeil, C., D. Ragan, and J. A. Solberg. 2012. *State of the Field in Youth-Led Development: Through the Lens of the UN-Habitat's Urban Youth Fund.* Nairobi: United Nations Human Settlements Programme.

Masten, A. S. 2014. "Global Perspectives on Resilience in Children and Youth." *Child Development* 85, no. 1, 6–20.

Mauto, T. 2012. *Experiences and Lessons from the Urban Youth Fund Grantees in Africa and Asia.* Nairobi: United Nations Human Settlements Programme.

National Research Council and Institute of Medicine. 2002. *Community Programs to Promote Youth Development.* Washington, D.C.: National Academies.

National Scientific Council on the Developing Child. 2015. "Supportive Relationships and Active Skill-Building Strengthen the Foundations of Resilience: Working Paper 13." Accessed January 4, 2018. www.developingchild.harvard.edu.

———. 2018. "Understanding Motivation: Building the Brain Architecture that Supports Learning, Health, and Community Participation: Working Paper No. 14." Accessed June 4, 2018. www.developingchild.harvard.edu.

Naudeau, S., W. Cunningham, M. K. A. Lundberg, and L. McGinnis. 2008. "Programs and Policies that Promote Positive Youth Development and Prevent Risky Behaviors: An International Perspective." In "Core Competencies to Prevent Problem Behaviors and Promote Positive Youth Development," edited by N. G. Guerra and C. P. Bradshaw. Special issue, *New Directions for Child and Adolescent Development* 122:75–87.

O'Donoghue, J., B. Kirshner, and M. McLaughlin. 2002. "Introduction: Moving Youth Participation Forward." *New Directions for Youth Development* 96 (Winter): 15–26.

Pekel, K., E. C. Roehlkepartain, A. K. Syvertsen, P. C. Scales, T. K. Sullivan, and J. Sethi. 2018. "Finding the Fluoride: Examining How and Why Developmental Relationships Are the Active Ingredient in Interventions that Work." *American Journal of Orthopsychiatry*, June 21, 2018. Advance online publication. https://doi.org/10.1037/ort0000333.

Pittman, K., M. Irby, J. Tolman, N. Yohalem, and T. Ferber. 2002. *Preventing Problems, Promoting Development, Encouraging Engagement: Competing Priorities or Inseparable Goals?* Washington, D.C.: Forum for Youth Investment.

Roehlkepartain, E. C., K. Pekel, A. K. Syvertsen, J. Sethi, T. K. Sullivan, and P. C. Scales. 2017. *Relationships First: Creating Connections that Help Young People Thrive.* Minneapolis: Search Institute.

Scales, P. C., and N. Leffert. 1999. *Developmental Assets: A Synthesis of the Scientific Research on Adolescent Development.* Minneapolis: Search Institute.

Simpson, Graeme. 2018. *The Missing Peace: Independent Progress Study on Youth, Peace and Security.* UNFPA. www.unfpa.org/sites/default/files/youth/youth-web-english.pdf.

Slachmuijlder, L. 2017. *Transforming Violent Extremism: A Peacebuilder's Guide.* Washington, D.C.: Search for Common Ground.

Sommers, M. 2018. *Youth and the Field of Countering Violent Extremism.* Washington, D.C.: Promundo-US.

Tesfaye, B. 2016. *Critical Choices: Assessing the Effects of Education and Civic Engagement on Somali Youths' Propensity towards Violence.* Portland, Ore.: Mercy Corps.

Tolman, J., and K. Pittman, with B. Cervone, K. Cushman, L. Rowley, S. Kinkade, J. Phillips, and S. Duque. 2001. *Youth Acts, Community Impacts: Stories of Youth Engagement with Real Results.* Community and Youth Development Series, 7. Takoma Park, Md.: Forum for Youth Investment and International Youth Foundation.

UIS (UNESCO Institute for Statistics). 2017. *More Than One-Half of Children and Adolescents Are Not Learning Worldwide.* UIS Fact Sheet no. 46. Montreal: UIS. http://uis.unesco.org/sites/default/files/documents/fs46-more-than-half-children-not-learning-en2017.pdf. (URL inactive.)

UNDP (United Nations Development Programme). 2014. "UNDP Youth Strategy 2014–2017: Empowered Youth, Sustainable Future." www.undp.org/content/undp/en/home/librarypage/democratic-governance/youthstrategy.html.

UNESCO (United Nations Educational, Scientific, and Cultural Organization). 2016. *A Teacher's Guide on the Prevention of Violent Extremism*. Paris: United Nations Educational, Scientific, and Cultural Organization.

———. 2017. *Preventing Violent Extremism through Education: A Guide for Policy-Makers*. Paris: United Nations Educational, Scientific, and Cultural Organization.

U.N.-Habitat. 2013. *Cities of Youth: Cities of Prosperity*. Nairobi: United Nations Human Settlements Programme.

U.N. IANYD Working Group on Youth and Peacebuilding. 2016. *Young People's Participation in Peacebuilding: A Practice Note*. New York: U.N. Inter-agency Network on Youth Development.

UNICEF (United Nations Children's Fund). 2016. *The State of the World's Children 2016: A Fair Chance for Every Child*. New York: United Nations Children's Fund.

United Nations. 2016. *World Youth Report: Youth Civic Engagement*. New York: United Nations.

United Nations and World Bank. 2017. *Pathways for Peace: Inclusive Approaches to Preventing Violent Conflict—Main Messages and Emerging Policy Directions*. Washington, D.C.: World Bank. https://doi.org/10.1596/978-1-4648-1162-3.

United Nations Security Council. 2015. Resolution 2250, S/RES/2250, December 9, 2015. www.un.org/en/ga/search/view_doc.asp?symbol=S/RES/2250(2015)&referer=/english/&Lang=E.UNOY Peacebuilders. 2018. *Beyond Dividing Lines: The Reality of Youth-Led Peacebuilding in Afghanistan, Colombia, Libya and Sierra Leone*. The Hague: UNOY.

UNOY Peacebuilders and Search for Common Ground. 2017. *Mapping a Sector: Bridging the Evidence Gap on Youth-Driven Peacebuilding*. The Hague: UNOY.

USAID (U.S. Agency for International Development). 2012. *Youth in Development: Realizing the Demographic Opportunity*. Washington, D.C.: USAID.

Williams, R., and J. Drury. 2011. "Personal and Collective Psychosocial Resilience: Implications for Children, Young People and their Families Involved in War and Disasters." In *Children and Armed Conflict: Cross-disciplinary Investigations*, edited by D. T. Cook and J. Wall, 57–75. New York: Palgrave Macmillan.

Youth.gov. 2009. "Risk and Protective Factors." Accessed January 4, 2018. https://youth.gov/youth-topics/youth-mental-health/risk-and-protective-factors-youth.

YouthPower Learning. 2017. *Promising Practices in Engaging Youth in Peace and Security and PVE/CVE: Summary of Key Interventions and Examples*. Washington, D.C.: USAID and Making Cents International. www.youthpower.org/sites/default/files/YouthPower/resources/Peace%20and%20Security%20Brief%209-21-17%20PRINT%20FINAL-OK.pdf.

Zeldin, S., A. McDaniel, D. Topitzes, and M. Calvert. 2000. *Youth in Decision-Making: A Study on the Impact of Youth on Adults and Organizations*. Chevy Chase, Md.: University of Wisconsin-Madison and Innovation Center for Community and Youth Development.

CHAPTER 2

And Then They Came for Me

YOUTH'S ROLE IN MEDIATING FOR PEACE IN KIBERA, KENYA

Grace Atuhaire

This chapter explores the concept of participation—one of the "pillars for action" promoted in the United Nations Security Council Resolution (UNSCR) 2250—as it applies to youth action in Kibera, an underprivileged urban settlement in Nairobi, Kenya; young people in Kibera actively participated in a successful campaign to de-escalate the conflict that ensued in the aftermath of an illegal eviction that took place in 2014. The study on which the chapter is based documents the efforts of youth activists who, under the leadership of a young woman I will call Miriam,[1] succeeded in mobilizing fellow youth to work together with the people uprooted by the illegal evictions in Kibera to reclaim their rights. This young woman and her followers used social media to effectively mitigate the top-down approach used in the implementation of the Nairobi Integrated Urban Development Master Plan (NIUPLAN) in Kibera, described later. The use of digital technology is discussed as evidence of the creativity and innovation demonstrated by the young people of Kibera who, acting as agents of peace, are leveraging social media as a mediation tool. The gender dynamics evident in the leadership of the social media campaign are discussed to examine the participation of females—both the young activists and the uprooted women in the case study (Lamoreux 2018).

This chapter explores the relationship between the young people living in the urban settlement of Kibera and the development programs implemented by the government of Kenya aimed at achieving Kenya Vision 2030 (2008).[2] The analysis of the events referenced here is grounded in a critical view of the securitization theory that questions the primacy of militaristic approaches and that of the state in the conceptualization of security. Buzar and Wæver use the concept of securitization to describe the presentation of an issue as posing "an existential threat, requiring emergency measures and justifying actions outside the normal bounds of political procedure" (Buzar, Wæver, and de Wilde 1998). Study findings help widen traditionally narrow understandings of (national) security in strategic studies that privilege militaristic approaches to include issues in the economic, environmental, and societal sectors (Buzar, Wæver, and de Wilde 1998). Additionally, the chapter contributes to a better understanding of the conditions facing young people in poor urban settlements in Kenya specifically—and Africa more broadly—whose fluid relationship to the physical and emotional space its inhabitants call "home" is often questioned and unsettled.

Despite the pervasive state of anomie that often affects African youth, young people in the continent have been leading impactful peacebuilding initiatives on the ground (Olaiya 2020). As I have discussed elsewhere, from Burundi to Rwanda, the Democratic Republic of the Congo, and Kenya, youth have often sought to pursue sustainable and lasting peace by advocating, creating, and providing spaces for inclusivity (Atuhaire 2019). Nevertheless, the dominant discourse has largely depicted youth—especially male youth—as perpetrators of conflict and prone to violence (Adhiambo 2008; Ismail 2017; Burcar 2013; Simpson 2018). Traditional constructions of the agency of youth in the peace and security arena view youth as an issue to be addressed or even a threat to be neutralized lest they become what Barry Buzan, Ole Wæver, and Jaap de Wilde (1998) refer to as a "security problem." This chapter does not claim that negative stereotypes of youth as violence-inclined may not at times be based on reality; rather, it contends that prevalent views seem to speak to the consequences of youth's participation in conflicts and violence rather than attending to the root causes and motivations of their actions. The events examined in this chapter offer a counterpoint to the prevalent securitized narrative on youth and conflict by discussing a case study that evidences youth's efforts as active agents of mediation in their families and communities, the urban settlements where many live, and beyond.

In line with UNSCR 2250, the African Union (AU) youth frameworks, and *The Missing Peace: Independent Progress Study on Youth, Peace and Security* (Simpson 2018), this chapter examines some of the ways in which youth have been contributing to the overall peace and security of the country by engaging in conflict mediation in Kibera. Through the use of youth-inclusive approaches, the oft neglected important contributions of young people to peace and security can be uncovered, documented, and supported. More specifically, the research undertaken to investigate this case study draws on qualitative exploratory methods that include the use of both primary[3] and secondary research. While the verification of events discussed in the study has been challenged by a lack of consistent documentation, young people's engagement has been verified through their footprint on social media platforms traced under the hashtag #Kiberademolitions.[4]

FRAMEWORKS AND STEREOTYPES:
THE SECURITIZATION OF YOUTH IN KENYA

International and regional agendas reframing perceptions of youth's roles in the global peace and security agenda are important tools for countries like Kenya where constructions of youth have long reflected negative stereotypes. UNSCR 2250 and the Peace and Security Council (PSC) of the African Union in meeting 807 recognize the existence of knowledge gaps on the contribution of the youth to global peace and security. The respective resolutions mandated the creation of the youth study to understand the youth agency in peace and security. UNSCR

2250 mandated the appointment of the U.N. Office of the Secretary-General's Envoy on Youth; the creation of the Global Coalition on Youth, Peace and Security (YPS); and the implementation of a youth study entitled *The Missing Peace*, which affirmed that young people are "the connective tissue that bridges the silos of development, human rights, humanitarian affairs and peace and security, from the local to the global level" (Simpson 2018). In addition, the study, which involved a number of consultations with youth from several countries, including Kenya, revealed the existing mistrust of youth toward their governments, multilateral institutions, and international organizations.

The process of regionalizing UNSCR 2250 in Africa has followed the global agenda proposed by the United Nations. In 2018, the PSC of the African Union 807 meeting committed to prioritizing youth agency in peace and security. The meeting set into motion the subsequent adoption of the resolution that mandated the creation of the Envoy on Youth, regional youth ambassadors, and the Youth for Peace Program to conduct a study focusing on bridging the knowledge gap of African youth's contribution to peace and security. In 2019, the Youth for Peace Program conducted a validation workshop of the study that included the participation of selected African youth to affirm the findings and recommendations to the PSC. Although the contents of the study are not yet available to the public, the press release includes an overview of the existing frameworks at a regional level. However, it leaves room for speculation regarding the current status of the existing national youth policies as well as how these policies incorporate issues of peace and security.

Indeed, the African Union's initiatives to acknowledge the positive agency of youth can be traced in other foundational frameworks—for example, article 3(f) of the AU Constitutive Act; article 17 of the 2006 African Youth Charter, "which recognizes the importance of youth in promoting peace and nonviolence, and working to end physical and psychological scars that result from involvement in violent armed conflict and war"; article 20 of the protocol relating to the establishment of the PSC; aspiration 4 and 6 of Agenda 2063, which aims for an integrated, prosperous, and peaceful Africa, driven by its own citizens and representing a dynamic force in the international arena; and the existence of a number of national youth policies in member states (African Union 2015). However, youth agency in peace and security is based not on the existence of frameworks but on the implementation of these instruments that contest the extent of youth securitization, particularly on whether youth have been securitized at the national level.

UNSCR 2250 and the PSC meeting 807 are both important steps forward on paper, but their implementation remains a challenge at both the international and regional levels. For the former, there is still an unfulfilled need to provide adequate financing for various programs—for example, the action plans of the Envoy on Youth offices—within the overall institutional budget system to ensure their efficiency. Additionally, there is a need for institutionalizing a reporting mechanism to underscore member states' progress in the domestication of UNSCR 2250 at the national level.

Member states like Kenya have taken a leadership role in nationalizing youth peace and security frameworks through the 2019 approval of the Kenya Youth Development Policy (KYDP), which seeks to mainstream issues affecting the youth. The implementation of these policies is critical to the advancement of the agency of youth and sustainable peace. Interpeace's annual report on "Youth at the Center for Peacebuilding" (2017) documents youth's active involvement in transforming conflict and building peace. Young people's digital mediation efforts and advocacy campaigns in Kibera are other examples.

THE SETTING OF THE STUDY:
KIBERA, THE PLACE WE CALL HOME

The city of Nairobi, of which Kibera is a part, has operated for the past forty-seven years under the guidance and recommendations of the 1973 Nairobi Metropolitan Growth Strategy. This strategy incorporated a package of new guidelines, followed by the 1984–1988 Nairobi City Commission Development Plan and the 1993 Nairobi City Convention; it expired in the year 2000. However, "many recommendations of the 1973 Master Plan were not realized due to shortages in capacity by the old City Council, as well as lack of commitment and political will" (Smart Cities Dive 2017).

Nairobi has seen continuous urbanization, increased industrialization, and increased densification. The pace of its urban sprawl has accelerated over the years, especially along highway corridors. The once rich agricultural suburbs are increasingly becoming residential, while slums expand along rivers, railways, and roads. The failure to realize much of the old plan, combined with the pressing need to program a livable city for its projected 5.2 million inhabitants by 2030, led to the development of the NIUPLAN. This seeks to integrate all existing sectoral plans in the city and align them to the Kenya Vision 2030 (2008), providing a framework for coordinating urban development (Smart Cities Dive 2017). The Kenyan Vision 2030 aims to transform Kenya into a newly industrialized, middle-income country that provides a high quality of life to all its citizens. The Nairobi Metro 2030 strategy is part of the overall national development agenda for Kenya and is aimed at transforming Nairobi into an African metropolis by 2030 (GOKenya 2008). The Kenya Railway Upgrading Project is part of the overall NIUPLAN (2014–2030). It was implemented as a pilot program in Kibera jointly by the Nairobi Railway Relocation Action Plan (the Railway Project) and the National Youth Service (NYS), led by the Kenya Slum Upgrading Programme. Pamoja Trust, a nongovernmental organization (NGO) in Kibera, was also an implementing partner (Urban Africa Risk Knowledge 2017).

National and county stakeholders began work on the NIUPLAN in November 2012 with assistance from the Government of Japan through its Japan International Cooperation Agency (JICA). Consulting members of the private and public sectors—national government ministries, universities, and civil society organizations, which included institutions like the World Bank, the Kenya Railways Corporation, U.N.-Habitat, and the GoDown Arts Center—provided input and critically analyzed the existing sector plans and the city's situation (Solés 2014). The plan's formulation covers six thematic areas: (1) land use and human settlements, (2) population and urban economy, (3) governance and institutional arrangements, (4) environment, (5) urban infrastructure, and (6) urban transport. Key among the challenges identified are insufficient infrastructure, transport problems, high demand for mid- and low-income housing, and, directly relevant to the situation in Kibera, uncontrolled urban development (Smart Cities Dive 2017).

Kibera, where the main events that form the basis of this chapter took place, is a neighborhood in the city of Nairobi, 6.6 kilometers (4.1 miles) from the city center. Kibera, whose name means "forest" or "jungle" in the local Kinubi language, is the largest slum in Nairobi and the largest urban slum in Africa (McKinney 2006). The majority of Kibera residents are poor and live in tinned or mud-walled shelters with corrugated roofs. The houses are usually overcrowded, often with small rooms and accommodating as many as six to eight people.[5]

A World Bank study of the slums in Nairobi concluded that 63 percent of residents in these settlements reported feeling unsafe within their neighborhoods. It is worth noting that 80 percent of Kibera residents are tenants of illegal makeshift housing, which places them in vulnerable positions (U.N.-Habitat 2011). Demolitions in Kibera are not a new phenomenon (Otiso 2003; U.N.-Habitat 2008). As Otiso notes (2003), these forced evictions are embedded in the country's political economy, which features high levels of inequitable property laws, making it difficult for the poor to access land and shelter. Kibera residents have often pursued legal redress against the government as evidenced by the numerous court cases seeking to halt development projects, often citing a notoriously corrupt system of land allocation and profit extraction. What is unprecedented is youth's effective leveraging of social media platforms to advocate for their communities and act as mediators of peace in Kibera.

While official demographic figures are not available, it is estimated that a large portion of Kibera's inhabitants are youth. Kenya's National Youth Policy defines a young person as being fifteen to thirty years old. This definition reflects the socioeconomic particularities of Kenya, especially the nature and length of transition into social adulthood. This explains its divergence from internationally adopted definitions by the U.N. (fifteen to twenty-four years), the East African Community (EAC, fifteen to thirty-five years), the African Union (fifteen to thirty-five years), and the World Bank (twelve to twenty-four years; Ismail 2017). According to the 2009 Kenya Population and Housing Census (KNBS 2010), Kenyan youth constitute two-thirds of the country's population. Although Kenya is generally considered to be a country in transformation, this is yet to be manifested due to a range of factors. These include the existing structural barriers limiting the ability of youth to participate in decision-making, violations of their human rights, and the history of lack of effective implementation of mechanisms for youth inclusion in the country's sociopolitical life.

YOUTH'S PLACE IN PEACE AND SECURITY IN KENYA

For the last ten years, the peace and security situation in Kenya has been punctuated with incidences of political violence, radicalization, and violent extremism; interethnic and intercommunal clashes; pastoralist violence; and state-led violence (Ismail 2017). Many of those involved in these various forms of violence are youngsters. Violence is, however, not an inherent attribute of young people and should not be constructed as analogous to youth (Ismail 2017). In spite of the markedly gerontocratic power relations that characterize the patchwork of societies that compose the country, Kenya is making headway regarding the implementation of UNSCR 2250. Over the years, the country has taken significant steps in placing youth at the center of a number of policy frameworks, even if the effective implementation of these youth-inclusive instruments has been uneven at best.

The 2007 Kenya National Youth Policy did not explicitly prioritize youth in peace and security programming. In 2015, Safer World—an international NGO—reported that the Kenyan National Council had established and adopted a series of policies and structures, including those from the National Peace Council, the National and County Peace Secretariats, the National and County Peace Fora, the Local Peace Committees and Mediation Support Units (Safer World 2015). These structures were expanded in 2019 with the approval of the Kenya Youth Development Policy (KYDP), which seeks to mainstream issues affecting the youth, including the coordination of youth programs, to address unemployment, youth exclusion, cybercrime, and human trafficking, among other challenges.

Accounts on youth participation and engagement in peace and security issues in Kenya have nevertheless long been reflective of negative constructions of violent youngsters. A case in point is Adhiambo's detailed account of the 2007/2008 Kenyan postelection violent conflicts (2008). The Office of the United Nations High Commissioner for Human Rights (OHCHR), reporting on the violence after the 2007 elections, acknowledges that violent events were triggered by the anger of opposition supporters at what they perceived as the rigging of the presidential election. OHCHR further reports that the first occurrences of violence—most notably the burning and looting of shops, houses, and commercial outlets in the slums of Nairobi and Kisumu[6]—were carried out by youth groups. Several additional incidents of violence, for which youth have shouldered the greatest blame and registered the highest number of casualties, have been reported in Kenya in recent years (U.N. OHCHR 2008). Popular narratives of youth that depict them as perpetrators of violent acts from 1992 to 2008 are well documented (Adhiambo 2008; Ismail 2017). Some of the actions reported are driven by not only frustration toward government projects being implemented in Kibera but also some other contentious issues that could perhaps be considered signs of national pride. For example, in 2009, the youth of Kibera tore apart the railway line that runs to Uganda in protest of the alleged invasion of Lake Victoria Island of Migingo, which resulted in tensions between Kenya and Uganda (Observer 2009).

According to the OHCHR's accounts, these violent episodes stem from accumulated frustrations generated by poor living conditions and historical disenfranchisement. In 2016, an event in which a local leader, Maurice Akuk, introduced a project that sought to distribute water tanks to the community turned violent when youths protested against the leader's purported corruption and ineptitude (Wekesa 2016). Social factors such as poor living conditions; exclusion and inequality; ethnic stereotypes; economic factors such as poverty, unemployment, and underemployment in the informal sector; and political factors ranging from inciting statements from politicians to the overreach of security forces in the slums have all drawn youth into violence (Adhiambo 2008).

In 2016, young people expressed their frustration with the political leadership in Kibera because of youth's continued exclusion and marginalization from different government programs and the mismanagement of resources. "We want Akuk to go! Akuk must go because he has let us down! Even in today's event, no local leader was consulted and that's an insult to us" (Wekesa 2016). These incidents illustrate the underlying root causes of youth protests. Adhiambo observes that the youth in Kibera are impoverished and are often compelled to resort to violence as their only available means to express their frustration over their social, political, and economic marginalization (Adhiambo 2008). These accounts of youth involvement in violence have all emphasized their role as perpetrators, ignoring the root causes of the conflict and disregarding the role youth have often played in bringing about peace.

Conversely, the positive agency of Kibera youth has been evidenced in the active role they have played in peace and development projects that have embraced the use of technology and social media through youth organizations such as Map Kibera, Carolina for Kibera, and Amani Kibera (Peace Insight 2015). Founded in 2009, Map Kibera has been particularly influential in producing the first complete free and open map of the Kibera neighborhoods (Hagen 2011). Carolina for Kibera, a group that advocates for peacebuilding processes, has been among the organizations that have led campaigns against forced evictions in various informal settlements in Nairobi since 2004 (Habitant 2008). Amani Kibera has operated since 2007 on issues of peacebuilding, conflict management and health, and cultural and educational awareness (Peace Insight 2015). These youth-led, community-based organizations' efforts were also engaged during the implementation of the contentious NIUPLAN in Kibera.

CONTEXTUALIZING THE CASE STUDY:
AND THEN THEY CAME FOR ME

The case study of young people in Kibera is grounded on the often tense and contested relationship between the government and its citizens. These youth sought to address the perceived inefficiency and heavy-handed implementation of government projects that negatively impacted their livelihood, family, and community. My analysis captures the events in 2014 surrounding the implementation of the NIUPLAN.

On July 30, 2014, a construction company—H-Young—contracted by Kenya Railways, demolished the houses that had been built along the railway line in Kibera (Hurley 2014). Prior to the events in 2014, a local resident named Kepha Omondi Onjuro and 234 other petitioners from Kibera filed a case against the Kenyan government before Kenya's high court in Nairobi (Kepha Omondi Onjuro and Others v. Attorney General et al. 2014). They protested what they considered to be unfair remuneration schemes within the project. The petitioners' case denounced the railway development's infringement of rights of the businesses, churches, schools, and clinics operating along the railway reserve in the Kibera and Mukuru slums in Nairobi. The court advised all parties to maintain the status quo for the time being and indicated that further guidelines and orders were to be issued on October 14, 2014. Despite having won the case and having obtained a court injunction halting the demolitions, Miriam and her family, together with other residents, were awoken at dawn on September 8, 2014, to the sound of the H-Young bulldozers demolishing their homes. Residents had not been given an eviction notice prior to the illegal demolitions (Hurley 2014).

The Railway Project was essentially an attempt by Kenya Railways to recover the land reserve and establish extended safety corridors along the railway line. It was estimated to cost about US$30 million, which would be funded by the World Bank. The project sought to secure a sixty-meter land reserve along the railway line in the Kibera and Mukuru slums, purportedly to improve the safety of the Kenya-Uganda railway line (also known as the Rift Valley Railways), boost train speeds, and increase trade volumes between Kenya and Uganda. The significance of the Kenya Railways upgrade project in Kibera is not contested (Hurley 2014). Kibera residents sued the government over the project's implementation, not its overall objective. Reclaiming the land in question involved uprooting and relocating ten thousand residents who lived along the railway (KNCHR 2015). A total of 3,022 families and 2,775 business occupants were directly affected (UPFI 2015).

Some commentators have argued that "the land around the railway lines does not formally belong to Kenya Railways Corporation (KRC); it is public land reserved for railway operation and maintenance" (Charbonneau 2016). A number of Kibera residents, schools, and businesses had long occupied and claimed the land along the railway line (Urban Africa Risk Knowledge 2017). All these various parties contested Kenya Railways' claim to the ownership of the land. Specifically, they cited irregularities in the implementation of NIUPLAN and in the guidelines for compensation of victims of the demolitions. As mentioned, they were successful in their claim. It is also worth noting that the railway track itself doubles as an informal market and pathway for pedestrians in many areas around Kibera. To recover the land, the government adopted the Relocation Action Plan (RAP) for slum dwellers living along railway lines in Nairobi. RAP included the provision of two-story conventional model units that would be given to the residents as permanent, livable housing as an incentive to be relocated away from the land in contention (UPFI 2015).

On September 8, 2014, several young activists from all over Kenya met for a week in Nairobi to be trained in advocacy and campaign strategies at the Global Platform,[7] a center for youth activists. Miriam was one of the participants and had been selected to participate in the training because of the outstanding role in her community and the country at large, including raising awareness on health, education, and cultural issues in Kibera as a member of the Activista Movement.[8] On the first day of the training, she was given the opportunity to introduce herself, and she narrated the experiences of her family and neighbors in Kibera. She told of how H-Young, contracted by Kenya Railways, had demolished houses along the railway line in Kibera, including their house. These documented events supported claims of the continued illegal evictions taking place in the Kibera neighborhoods (Otiso 2003; Habitant 2008).

At another advocacy and campaign training, participating youth activists supported their colleagues by designing a campaign to draw attention to the various actors that were implicated in the implementation of the project. The campaign was aimed at raising awareness of the previous and ongoing illegal demonstrations in Kibera. The campaign targeted the late Hon. Keneth Okoth using the hashtag #Kiberademolitions on Twitter and Facebook. Okoth was a Kenyan politician who served as a member of Parliament for the Kibra Constituency from March 2013 until his death on July 26, 2019 (Mureu 2019). Young people addressed their messages to Okoth and appealed to him to lobby for and support the affected families by providing them with immediate shelter and to facilitate a meeting where all aggrieved parties would dialogue with the implementing actors and discuss the sustainability of the project.

In response to the social media movement that was generated, Okoth agreed to meet with young people to identify a way forward and support the affected families. Subsequently, different stakeholder meetings to resolve the conflict and humanitarian crisis were first held at the premises of the Global Platform in Nairobi and later at a venue called Forty-Two (42) in Kibera. Stakeholders involved included Okoth himself, representatives of the affected families, and several young Kenyan activists, particularly those who had participated in the advocacy training discussed earlier. At the meetings, the government representatives were hard-pressed to explain why the implementation of the project had violated the World Bank guidelines for resettling project-affected persons (PAPs) and the 2010 Relocation Action Plan. Okoth committed to further consultations on the issue to ensure that the families were duly compensated. The youth who participated in the meetings resolved to establish a network to work with Okoth to safeguard the interests of the victims, engage with humanitarian aid organizations like ActionAid Kenya, and ensure that victims were indeed duly compensated.

Subsequently, ten displaced families had an opportunity to hold a meeting with Okoth, together with their representatives. What could have been a direct and possibly violent confrontation between the residents and the government was thus successfully forestalled (Jaffar 2014). Miriam noted that the Kenyan police had intervened on behalf of the victims and apprehended the workers of the H-Young company who had carried out the demolitions. National organizations such as ActionAid Kenya and Amnesty Kenya offered immediate support of food and basic necessities to the affected families. The families whose houses had been demolished were temporarily sheltered in a school within Kibera, and their names were added to the compensation list, which was critical to ensure that relocation took place as per the agreed-upon guidelines.

Miriam's account of the events is illustrative of the conditions they endured in the temporary shelter: "We live in an eight-by-eight room with more than ten families, no privacy, sleeping in turns. Men sleep in the day, and women sleep at night so as to protect the women against anything that might happen, including rape. Food has become a luxury, and sleeping for the hours you want is no longer an option." Such an account is not unique for Kenyan slum dwellers (Otiso 2003; Habitant 2008). Evictions in urban settlements continue to be a very asymmetrical process of negotiation between the slums dwellers and the state—the state, on the one hand, works toward upgrading road, power, railway, and other utility reserves; for those earmarked for eviction, on the other hand, the realities they must endure are often characterized by violence and the threat of aggression (Pamoja Trust 2008).

Responding to these circumstances, the young people in Kibera have organized themselves in pursuit of social justice, peace, and security. As they bridge the gaps between the policies and implementation of government projects, they at times put their lives on the line in their efforts to mediate between their communities and the government actors. Youth-led, community-based organizations like Map Kibera, Carolina for Kibera, and Amani that promote the participation of young people like Miriam in peacebuilding and advocate for their inclusion in all government processes have been an integral aspect of the implementation of structural, cultural, and social peace and security processes since 2004.

DISCUSSION AND LESSONS LEARNED

The U.N.'s *Missing Peace* progress study advances the argument for recognizing the remarkable ingenuity of young people in their efforts to prevent violence and consolidate peace across the globe in both devastated and conflict-affected societies as well as those enjoying relative peace (Simpson 2018). The continued participation of young people in actions to promote democracy, inclusiveness, and human rights, as the case of Kibera illustrates, is an indication that they need to be taken seriously as meaningful stakeholders. Young activism in Kenya further evidences the use of online platforms as a strategy to raise awareness and inspire mobilization that can also promote and support offline actions.

Youth as Digital Mediators

The internet and social media have brought with them a new form of empowerment that is fundamentally altering the relations between citizens and states at both global and local levels. The discussion on digital mediation in Kibera is situated in the context of the historical changes in the activities and social languages that mediate the lives of young people (Kibere 2016). For the purposes of this study, digital mediation was traced and analyzed as illustrative of the transformative potential of young people's engagement with digital technologies and media within and across securitized settings.

Technology is rapidly becoming an integral element of everyday life for many young people across sociocultural and geographic borders. Mobile networks and the internet have enabled people to communicate globally in real time.

As Farrah, de Boer, and Muggah (2017) report in their discussion of "Digitally-Enabled Peace and Security" for Youth4Peace, "The dramatic spread of digital technologies and the Internet in fragile and conflict affected contexts has opened new possibilities for political, economic and social transformation. Access to social media and other forms of cyber-enabled communications facilitates new avenues for civic participation and engagement. Millions of youth have taken to the Internet to promote peace and help construct a new future for themselves and their countries" (1–2). Internet penetration and its adoption have grown at an exceedingly fast pace in Africa, and particularly in Kenya (Mukhongo 2014; see also chapter 10, this volume). This has resulted in social media platforms becoming a primary sociotechnical system that shapes and is shaped by different ways of life—and activism. Apart from finding information online, the internet is used as a platform for collectively creating new information. Digitally enabled youth are on the frontlines of the peace and security agenda. Internet use is, however, not without serious risks, as young users can also be exposed to and influenced by predatory agents (see the conclusions chapter, this volume). Potential challenges notwithstanding, social media sites, such as Facebook, Twitter, and blogs, have given people of all ages the enhanced opportunity to network, share, discuss, and create information together.

Young people have traditionally been excluded from political debates in Kenya (Larsson 2017). Yet in today's new media landscape, there are greater chances for young women and young men to participate in social and political life and have their voices heard. In the Kenyan context, bloggers and activists are successfully using social media to reach out and create social mobilization and awareness. On the other hand, if young people are not heard or if their voices are heard but their requests, proposals, and solutions are not acted upon, can they really effect change (Larsson 2017)? The case of Kibera illustrates the importance of distinguishing between frameworks and agreements written on paper but ignored in practice and effective action on the ground.

In Kibera, young people used Twitter and Facebook to share targeted messages to and about the late Hon. Kenneth Okoth. Acquiescing to young people's persistent requests, Okoth met with a delegation of youngsters to listen to what they had to say. He then facilitated the subsequent steps, which included meetings with the aggrieved families, after which a way forward was jointly agreed upon by the parties involved (Hurley 2014). Hurley concluded that these actions by young people from Kibera and beyond led to the intervention of the Kenyan police on behalf of the evicted families, ultimately resulting in the apprehension of the workers of the H-Young company, which carried out the demolitions (Hurley 2014). Miriam reiterated that thanks to young people's digital activism, the families whose houses had been demolished were temporarily sheltered in a school within Kibera and their names included in the compensation list, which ensured their safe relocation by the government, as already noted. Digitally enabled youth in Kenya are on the frontlines of efforts to bring peace and security to their communities. As Farrah, de Boer, and Muggah caution, however, these youth "can be powerful agents for peace, but can also be exposed to and influenced by predatory agents" (2017, 3). The upside and downside of digital engagement, as tends to be the case with other aspects of social life, are framed by the prevalent gender dynamics.

The Role of Young Women in Mediating Peace at the Community Level

Young women have largely been portrayed as passive victims and devoid of agency. Their participation in peace and security processes is often either unacknowledged or mischaracterized and relegated to the category of "supporting role" (Lamoreux 2018). Young men, on the other hand, tend to be perceived as risk factors, prone to turning to violence and vulnerable to being recruited by armed groups, criminal gangs, and violent extremists (Lamoreux 2018). The exclusionary narrative traditionally associated with "being young" and being a "woman" can, conversely, be analyzed from a standpoint of visibility, inclusion, and participation, ensuring that young women themselves have opportunities to meaningfully contribute to building and sustaining peace.

The examples of women's participation as high-level mediators in Africa are sources of inspiration that illuminate the realities of the institutionalized platforms for women, how these spaces have been defined for women in general, and what these spaces would be like for young women more specifically. Young African women like Miriam have an increasing number of role models to look up to for encouragement and inspiration. Betty Bigombe, a former state minister of Northern Uganda who spearheaded the dialogues with warlord Joseph Kony;[9] Hamsatu

Allamin, a teacher who dared to speak to the Boko Haram;[10] the late Wangari Mathai, who sought to end the devastation of Kenya's forests and lands;[11] and the late Winnie Mandela, who contributed tremendously to the antiapartheid regime in South Africa (Chalumbira 2018) are some oft mentioned examples.

Preventing Conflict, Transforming Justice, Securing the Peace, a 2015 global study on the implementation of UNSCR 1325, reported a substantial increase in the frequency of gender-responsive language in peace agreements and the number of women, women's groups, and gender experts who serve as official negotiators, mediators, or signatories. Nevertheless, as Klugman and Moore discuss in chapter 8 of this volume, the inclusion of women in peace and security processes demanded by UNSCR 1325 has at times been met with resistance as well as numerous obstacles. It is, for instance, still the case that high-level AU mediation efforts have in the past included very few women and that almost all AU special envoys to conflict zones are men—mostly former heads of state and other former senior officials (Ani 2018). Furthermore, women's official participation in mediation processes in Africa and elsewhere is often temporary, and their delegated roles may be seen as more symbolic than substantive, while their capacity to influence directly resisted local cultural norms (U.N. Women 2015).

Women's participation in high-level peace mediation processes continues to be challenged by stereotypical political and sociocultural narratives questioning women's skills, knowledge, or social status and thus their ability to bring about change in postconflict environments (O'Reilly, Súilleabháin, and Paffenholz 2015).

Countering prevalent stereotypes, the actions that took place in Kibera as discussed in this chapter were initiated by a young female, Miriam, who, alongside her fellow young women and young men, strategized on how best to raise awareness on the illegal house demolitions in Kibera and pushed the advocacy process forward. Miriam's initiative and participation in the Twitter advocacy campaign illustrate young women's agency as peacebuilders and active digital mediators. Her team faced challenges persuading the men from the affected families to participate, as they were initially unconvinced that young people could help their current situation. Miriam, whose family had also been affected and had a personal relationship with each family, reached out to the affected women, who then persuaded their husbands to attend the meeting. This in turn led to each house being represented in full at the first meeting. Thanks to Miriam's initiative, conflict was prevented in Kibera.

CONCLUDING THOUGHTS

This chapter contributes to the modern understanding of youth's roles in peace and security that reject uncritical one-sided characterizations of youth people as violence- and conflict-prone (Adhiambo 2008; Ismail 2017; Burcar 2013; Simpson 2018). While Kenyan youth have, at times, resorted to violence as a means to have their voices heard, such violence has been largely contextual and is not an inherent attribute of youth (Ismail 2017). To counter prevailing negative stereotypes, the positive contributions of youth to peace and security need to be uncovered, supported, and documented (Simpson 2018). Kenya, a demographically youthful country where young people may be described as members of an "outcast majority"

(Sommers 2015), is nonetheless making headway regarding the implementation of UNSCR 2250. Over the years, the country has taken significant steps in centering on the youth, although the effective implementation of its youth instruments is yet to be seen in peace and security.

Profiling the circumstances of young people living in the poor urban settlement of Kibera, this chapter examines youth's positive agency exerted in their efforts to mitigate a conflict escalation after an illegal eviction in 2014. Prominent in this study are the experiences of Miriam, whose initiative, leadership, and savvy of online and offline advocacy and mediation succeeded in preventing the escalation of conflict in the context of the implementation of the NIUPLAN in Kibera.

As a young female peace activist, Miriam personifies the oft uneasy intersection of gendered and generational dynamics highlighted in the parallel women, peace, and security (WPS) and youth, peace, and security (YPS) global agendas. Examples of women's participation in high-level mediation processes, coupled with a realization that the number of women involved in this type of processes remains very small, provided inspiration to showcase the experiences of a young female who, defying cultural expectations, became the lead facilitator and mediator in a series of events that captured the imagination of the Kenyan public in 2014. Miriam's involvement in the events discussed in this chapter may have been the outcome of thoughtful decision-making, or it could have been her spontaneous response to compelling circumstances. Either way, what transpired in Kibera and the country at large contributes to the growing number of case studies of young women's positive involvement in peace and security at the community and national levels.

The internet and social media are powerful tools and spaces for peace promotion. The rapid spread of the internet and social media have made them vehicles for peace promotion, particularly by youth (Larrauri and Kahl 2013). Digital tools may serve to amplify the voices of young people through communication technologies to support global peace and security, as this case study has illustrated. They are, however, not a panacea. Apart from the potential risk of manipulation and "cyberbullying," social media engagement is unlikely to effect impactful results if it is not followed up with meaningful offline action: "For the Youth, Peace and Security agenda to be successful, engaging youth and supporting their contribution to peace both offline and online is essential" (Farrah, de Boer, and Muggah 2017, 3). Fortunately, it does not seem to have been the case in 2014 Kibera, but it is widely recognized that young girls and women often constitute prime targets of predatory behavior online (3). There is much promise in leveraging youth and technology for peace in Kibera, Kenya, Africa, and beyond. To fully realize that objective, young women and young men must not be securitized—that is, construed as risks to peace and security—but acknowledged as full of potential as enthusiastic peacebuilders.

NOTES

1. The young woman I call Miriam in this chapter was born and has lived all her life in Kibera and can trace four of her family generations as residents of the same urban settlement. Her name has been changed to preserve her anonymity and protect her privacy and that of her family.

2. In 2008, Kenyan president Mwai Kibaki launched Kenya Vision 2030 as a vehicle for accelerating the transformation of the country into a rapidly industrializing middle-income nation by the year 2030. The Kenya Vision 2030 (2008) aims to transform Kenya into a newly industrializing, middle-income country providing a high quality of life to all its citizens by 2030 in a clean and secure environment.

3. This case study could not have been possible without the documentation of the participants of the training at the Global Platform in Nairobi through blogs and Twitter in 2014. I would further like to note that in 2014, I was a social media trainer at the Global Platform in Nairobi. I would like to thank Miriam for agreeing to relive with me the events of 2014.

4. The messages of youth that raised the awareness of the 2014 illegal evictions in Kibera were shared mainly through Twitter, using the hashtag #Kiberademolitions. The hashtag continues to be used to this day by different activists to decry the demolitions in Kibera, which have continued to take place at the time of this writing, May 2020.

5. Kibera is made up of the following villages: Soweto East, Kianda, Gatwekera, Kisumu Ndogo, Lindi, Laini Saba, Silanga, Undugu, Makina and Mashimoni, Kichinjio, Raila, Soweto West, Kambi Muru, and Saragombe (KNCHR 2015).

6. Kisumu is the third-largest city in Kenya after Nairobi and Mombasa and the second-largest city after Kampala, Uganda, in the Lake Victoria Basin.

7. Global Platform Nairobi is one of the youth-led activism networks supported by an NGO called ActionAid International.

8. The Activista Movement is a youth network involving young members from all over the world fighting for social, political, and cultural justice. The Activista Movement is facilitated by ActionAid International.

9. Joseph Rao Kony is the leader of the Lord's Resistance Army, a guerrilla group that formerly operated in Uganda and is currently operating in the Central African Republic.

10. Boko Haram is a jihadist terrorist organization also known as the Islamic State in West Africa.

11. Wangari Mathai is the first African woman to win the Nobel Prize.

REFERENCES

Adhiambo, Christabel A. 2008. "Youth and Violent Conflicts in Nairobi's Kibera Slum 1992–2008." Master's thesis, University of Nairobi Research Archive. Accessed January 10, 2021. http://erepository.uonbi.ac.ke:8080/xmlui/handle/123456789/9701. (URL inactive.)

African Union (AU). 2002. Protocol Relating to the Establishment of the Peace and Security Council of the African Union. July 9, 2002. Accessed January 11, 2021. www.refworld.org/docid/3f4b1d374.html.

———. 2006. African Youth Charter. July 2, 2006. Accessed January 11, 2021. www.refworld.org/docid/493fe0b72.html.

———. 2015. "Agenda 2063: The Africa We Want." January 31, 2015. Accessed January 11, 2021. https://web.archive.org/web/20191213181702/https://au.int/en/agenda2063/overview.

———. 2018. "Peace and Security Council 807th Meeting." November 8, 2018. Accessed January 11, 2021. www.peaceau.org/uploads/psc.807.comm.psc.youth.peace.and.security.8.11.2018.pdf.

———. 2019. "AU Youth for Peace Africa (Y4P) Program Validates the Continental Framework on Youth, Peace and Security and Study on the Roles and Contributions of Youth to Peace and Security in Africa." Accessed May 3, 2020. www.peaceau.org/en/article/press-release-au-youth-for-peace-africa-y4p-program-validates-the-continental-framework-on-youth-peace-and-security-and-study-on-the-roles-and-contributions-of-youth-to-peace-and-security-in-africa.

Ani, Ndubuisi Christian. 2018. "FemWise-Africa Set to Boost Women's Role in Peace Pro-
    cesses." Institute for Security Studies. Accessed January 11, 2021. https://issafrica.org/iss
    -today/femwise-africa-set-to-boost-womens-role-in-peace-processes.
Atuhaire, Grace. 2019. "African Union's Securitization of Youth: A Milestone for Regional
    Coordination of Youth Programmes in Peace and Security." Institute for Peace and Secu-
    rity Studies. Accessed March 6, 2019. www.ipss-addis.org/publications.
Burcar, Veronika. 2013. "Doing Masculinity in Narratives about Reporting Violent Crime:
    Young Male Victims Talk about Contacting and Encountering the Police." *Journal of
    Youth Studies* 16, no. 2, 172–190.
Buzan, Barry, Ole Wæver, and Jaap de Wilde. 1998. *Security: A New Framework for Analysis.*
    London: Lynne Rienner.
Chalumbira, Nomvelo. 2018. "South Africa's Anti-apartheid Heroine Winnie Mandela
    Laid to Rest." Reuters. Accessed January 11, 2021. www.reuters.com/article/us-safrica
    -winninemandela/south-africas-anti-apartheid-heroine-winnie-mandela-laid-to-rest
    -idUSKBN1HL0LF.
Charbonneau, Adèle. 2016. "Managing Conflicts in Slums within a Relocation Project: Case
    Study of Soweto East, Kibera, Nairobi." *Mambo!* 14, no. 2, 1–4.
Farrah, Raouf, John de Boer, and Robert Muggah. 2017. "Digitally-Enabled Peace and
    Security: Reflections for the Youth, Peace and Security Agenda." SecDev Group. www
    .youth4peace.info/system/files/2018-04/2.%20TP_Social%20Media_SecDev.pdf.
Fernandez, Rosa Flores, and Bernard Calas. 2011. "The Kibera Soweto East Project in Nairobi,
    Kenya." *Les cahiers d'Afrique de l'Est* 44:129–146.
GOKenya. 2008. "Nairobi Metro 2030." Government of the Republic of Kenya—Ministry
    of Nairobi Metropolitan Department.
Hagen, Erica. 2011. Mapping Change: Community Information Empowerment in Kib-
    era. *Innovations: Technology, Governance, Globalization.* Volume 6. Issue 1, Winter 2011.
    p.69–94. Accessed January 11, 2021. https://www.mitpressjournals.org/doi/pdfplus/10
    .1162/INOV_a_00059.
Hurley, Kat. 2014. "They Came for Us." The Year of Magical Dreaming. Accessed January 7,
    2019. https://theyearofmagicaldreaming.wordpress.com/2014/10/06/they-came-for-us
    -guest-post.
Interpeace. 2017. *Youth at the Center of Peacebuilding.* Annual report. Accessed January 11,
    2021. https://reliefweb.int/sites/reliefweb.int/files/resources/2017-Annual-Report-WEB
    -draft-spreads.pdf.
Ismail, Olawale. 2017. "Youth, Peace and Security in Kenya." Accessed January 11, 2021. www
    .youth4peace.info/system/files/2018-04/7.%20CFR_Kenya_Wale_0.pdf.
Jaffar, Asha. 2014. "And Then They Came for Me." Brainstorm. Accessed January 15, 2019.
    http://brainstorm.co.ke/2014/09/16/and-then-they-came-for-me.
Kepha Omondi Onjuro and Others v. Attorney General et al. 2014. Before the Hon. Mr.
    Justice Odunga. Petition no. 239 of 2014. High Court of Kenya at Nairobi. Accessed Jan-
    uary 15, 2019. http://kenyalaw.org/caselaw/cases/view/105457.
Kibere, Faith Njeri. 2016. "The Capability of Mobility in Kibera 'Slum,' Kenya: An Ethno-
    graphic Study of How Young People Use and Appropriate New Media and ICTs." Thesis,
    Department of Media and Communication, University of Leicester.
KNBS (Kenya National Bureau of Statistics). 2010. *The 2009 Kenya Population and Housing Cen-
    sus: Counting Our People for the Implementation of Vision 2030.* Volume IC, Population Distri-
    bution by Age, Sex and Administrative Units. August 2010. Accessed January 11, 2021. https://
    s3-eu-west-1.amazonaws.com/s3.sourceafrica.net/documents/21195/Census-2009.pdf.
KNCHR (Kenya National Commission on Human Rights). 2015. "The Implementation of
    Petition No. 304 of 2015." Accessed January 11, 2021. http://kenyalaw.org/caselaw/cases/
    view/117266.

Lamoreux, Natasha. 2018. *Young Women in Peace and Security: At the Intersection of the YPS and WPS Agendas*. United Nations Entity for Gender Equality and the Empowerment of Women. Accessed January 11, 2021. www.unwomen.org/-/media/headquarters/attachments/sections/library/publications/2018/research-paper-young-women-in-peace-and-security-en.pdf?la=en&vs=2849.

Larrauri, P.-H., and A. Kahl. 2013. "Technology for Peacebuilding." *Stability: International Journal of Security and Development* 2, no. 3, 61.

Larsson, Carl. 2017. "Online Activism in Kenya." *Act Blog*, October 3, 2017. http://wpmu.mah.se/nmict172group4/2017/10/03/online-activism-kenya.

McKinney, Taja. 2006. "A Trip through Kenya's Kibera Slum." International Medical Corps. https://web.archive.org/web/20141006104222/https://internationalmedicalcorps.org/sslpage.aspx?pid=1561#.VDJyFJ77TBI.

Mukhongo, Lynete. 2014. "Negotiating the New Media Platforms: Youth and Political Images in Kenya." *TripleC* 12, no. 1, 328–341.

Mureu, Lynester. 2019. "Tribute—Hon. Ken Okoth (1978–2019)." Kenya National Commission on Human Rights. Accessed May 13, 2020. www.knchr.org/Articles/ArtMID/2432/ArticleID/1082/Tribute-Hon-Ken-Okoth-1978-2019.

Observer. 2009. "Kibera Youth Always Primed for Violence." Accessed January 5, 2019. www.observer.ug/viewpoint/83-staff-writers/3357-kibera-youth-always-primed-for-violence.

O'Reilly, Marie, Andrea Ó. Súilleabháin, and Thania Paffenholz. 2015. *Reimagining Peacemaking: Women's Roles in Peace Processes*. International Peace Institute. Accessed January 11, 2021. www.ipinst.org/wp-content/uploads/2015/06/IPI-E-pub-Reimagining-Peacemaking.pdf.

Organization of African Unity (OAU). 2000. *Constitutive Act of the African Union*. July 1, 2000. Accessed January 11, 2021. www.refworld.org/docid/4937e0142.html.

Otiso, Kefa M. 2003. "Forced Evictions in Kenyan Cities." *Singapore Journal of Tropical Geography* 23, no. 3, 252–267.

Pamoja Trust. 2008. "An Inventory of the Slums in Nairobi." Know Your City. Accessed May 13, 2020. https://knowyourcity.info/wp-content/uploads/2015/04/Nairobi_slum_inventory_jan_09.pdf.

Peace Insight. 2015. "Amani Kibera." Accessed February 20, 2019. www.peaceinsight.org/conflicts/kenya/peacebuilding-organisations/amani-kibera.

Safer World. 2015. "Finally! A Peace Policy for Kenya." November 4, 2015. www.saferworld.org.uk/resources/news-and-analysis/post/174-finally-a-peace-policy-for-kenya.

Simpson, Graeme. 2018. *The Missing Peace: Independent Progress Study on Youth, Peace and Security*. UNFPA. www.unfpa.org/sites/default/files/youth/youth-web-english.pdf.

Smart Cities Dive. 2017. "Nairobi, Kenya's 1973 Master Plan Receives an Update." www.smartcitiesdive.com/ex/sustainablecitiescollective/nairobi-kenya-s-1973-master-plan-receives-update/308991.

Solés, Gemma. 2014. "New Master Plan for Nairobi." UrbanAfrica.Net, August 12, 2014. www.urbanafrica.net/urban-voices/new-master-plan-nairobi.

Sommers, Marc. 2015. *The Outcast Majority*. Athens: University of Georgia Press.

U.N.-Habitat (United Nations Human Settlements Programme). 2008. *UN-Habitat and the Kenya Slum Upgrading Programme*. Strategy document. Nairobi, Kenya. https://unhabitat.org/sites/default/files/2020/09/un-habitat_and_the_kenya_slum_upgrading_programme_-_strategy_document.pdf.

United Nations Habitat. 2011. "Building Urban Safety through Slum Upgrading." Accessed January 11, 2021. https://unhabitat.org/sites/default/files/download-manager-files/Building%20Urban%20Safety%20through%20Slum%20Upgrading.pdf.

United Nations Women. 2015. "Preventing Conflict, Transforming Justice, Securing Peace: A Global Study on the Implementation of United Nations Security Council Resolution 1325."

Accessed January 11, 2021. www.peacewomen.org/sites/default/files/UNW-GLOBAL
-STUDY-1325-2015%20(1).pdf.

U.N. OHCHR (United Nations Office of the High Commissioner for Human Rights). 2008.
"Fact-Finding Mission to Kenya." Accessed January 11, 2021. www.ohchr.org/documents/
press/oHCHRKenyareport.pdf.

UNSC (United Nations Security Council). 2015. *Security Council Resolution 2250 (2015)
[on Youth, Peace and Security]*, S/RES/2250. March 18, 2016. www.refworld.org/docid/
56ebfd654.html.

U.N. Women. 2015. *Preventing Conflict, Transforming Justice, Securing the Peace: A Global
Study on the Implementation of United Nations Security Council Resolution 1325.* Accessed
January 11, 2021. https://wps.unwomen.org/pdf/en/GlobalStudy_EN_Web.pdf.

UPFI (Urban Poor Fund International). 2015. "Nairobi Railway Relocation Action Plan
Design: Kibera." Accessed February 1, 2019. http://upfi.info/projects/nairobi-railway
-relocation-action-plan-design-kibera.

Urban Africa Risk Knowledge. 2017. "Developing Risk or Resilience? Effects of Slum
Upgrading on the Social Contract and on Social Cohesion in Kibera, Nairobi." Accessed
January 11, 2021. https://pubs.iied.org/pdfs/G04118.pdf.

Vision 2030. 2008. "Kenya Vision 2030." Accessed February 27, 2019. https://vision2030.go.ke.

Wekesa, Chrispinus. 2016. "Kibera Youths Turn Violent as Kidero Donates 23 Water Tanks."
Star-Kenya, November 13, 2016. www.the-star.co.ke/news/2016/11/13/kibera-youths-turn
-violent-as-kidero-donates-23-water-tanks_c1454775.

PART II

Protection

CHAPTER 3

Protecting Marginalized Youths

ROMANI CHILDREN AND FORMAL EDUCATION

Diana Budur

This chapter argues for furthering the educational opportunities available to marginalized Romani youngsters, construed as active agents participating in their own protection and doing so on their own terms. Efforts toward this goal would be in line with the implementation of the guidelines put forth by the United Nations Security Council Resolution (UNSCR) 2250 and its global agenda for youth, peace, and security (YPS), as discussed in the introduction of this volume. Education is an integral component of the UNSCR 2250 protection pillars for action, which establishes the obligation to protect young people during armed conflict as well as in postconflict and peace times; this includes protection from all forms of sexual and gender-based violence. Education as a form of protection also figures prominently in the UNSCR 2250–mandated *The Missing Peace: Independent Progress Study on Youth, Peace and Security* (Simpson 2018).

Romani children and teens constitute a significant proportion of their ethnic diaspora present worldwide. These youths' challenges, the educational opportunities available to them, and their contributions to the global YPS agenda are explored in a comparative study primarily centered on Romania and Brazil. These two countries are, by qualified extension, also illustrative of the broader situation in the European and Latin American Romani diasporas. Romani youths in these two contexts share some similarities but also face comparatively different obstacles regarding their education, security risks, and overall well-being. The analysis of these cases reveals a range of best practices that can help empower young Romani people through educational pursuits.

For the purposes of this study, Romani youths are defined as members of any Romani subgroup between the ages of fifteen and twenty-four. According to *The Missing Peace*, "Resolution 2250 defines youth as 18 to 29 years, but it notes the variations that exist on the national and international levels. The United Nations defines 'youth' as between the ages of 15 and 24" (Simpson 2018, 9). However, individual United Nations entities use different age parameters, adding to the overall lack of consistency in chronological definitions of youth. It is, furthermore, worth noting that most Romani communities recognize only two age categories: childhood and adulthood—that is, there is no "youth" category. The transition between these two sharply differentiated statuses is accomplished through marriage, which represents the socially prescribed rite of passage into adulthood.

As a twelve-year-old boy in my study remarked, "I can't wait to get my driver's license, get married, and become a man!" noting the importance of acquiring a driver's license to be ready to work as an apprentice alongside the older men and thus become more credible as an eligible bachelor. "*Chej* [girl] marries *chavo* [boy], then she moves in with him and his parents," he further elaborated. Marriage in Romani culture is an arranged union, often between minors who are afterward allowed to live together as a married couple. Marriage ceremonies, which are not legally documented, are generally considered unlawful by non-Romani standards. Nevertheless, married Romani youths, whose ages typically range between twelve and twenty-five years, would be considered "adults" in their own culture regardless of chronological age.

The discussion of the role of education in the protection of Romani youth that constitutes the basis of this chapter is a partial adaptation of my cultural anthropology doctoral dissertation, "Gypsy Myths and Romani Cosmologies in the New World: Roma and Calons in Brazil"; I defended my dissertation at Princeton University in 2015 (Budur 2015).

METHODS AND FRAMEWORKS

My analysis was initiated with an in-depth literature review of the subject. Romanian and Brazilian Romani youths made up the primary interlocutors contributing to the analysis presented in this chapter: these included twenty-four youths in Brazil and forty Romanian-born Romani, including migrants across Europe, both pools with a slightly higher representation of females than males. As noted, portions of this chapter are an adaptation of the dissertation I completed as part of my doctoral work (Budur 2015). My dissertation was based on fieldwork I undertook in Brazil, Rio de Janeiro, and Sao Paulo and prolonged visits to several EU countries; these include Romania, my native country, as well as France and Italy. I speak fluent Romanian, Portuguese, French, some Italian, and Romani, which greatly facilitated my ethnographic fieldwork. In Brazil, my fieldwork focused on the Roma and Calon subgroups.[1]

My fieldwork in Brazil revealed that local Roma, unlike Calons, often choose not to reveal their ethnicity to avoid discrimination similar to what they had experienced in Europe. Romani population estimates thus remain misleadingly smaller than the actual numbers. According to the 2012 Basic Municipal Information Research census conducted by the Brazilian Geography and Statistics Institute, only half a million *Ciganos* (*Gypsies* in Portuguese) live in Brazil (Vasconcelos 2013). Argentinean Romani activist Jorge Bernal argues that agencies and associations with access to these communities can provide more accurate figures; their estimates indicate that there are between eight hundred thousand and a million Romani people living in Brazil. However, Bernal suggests that even this number is a conservative estimate: "According to UNESCO data in 1991, the Romani population of Latin America was approximately 1,500,000 individuals, taking into account that many Roma deny their origin" (2003, 14). My study relies on qualitative fieldwork rather than quantitative data—a more suitable approach to research with people who do not wish to be known.

My literature review includes an analysis of EU member states' initiatives. I was particularly concerned with identifying potential shortcomings in the implementation of EU guidelines for promoting Romani social inclusion and equal education and for reducing ethnic discrimination. A key agency in this regard is the Alliance against Antigypsyism (AAA). Its published reference paper, "Antigypsyism," defines this very term as reflective of the multifaceted discrimination that Romani people have been subjected to and clarifies that the term *Gypsy* is a misnomer associated with exoticizing stereotypes (Alliance against Antigypsyism 2016). I commend the Organization for Security and Cooperation in Europe (OSCE), the European Agency for Fundamental Rights (FRA), and the Council of Europe (COE) in particular as pioneers in exploring political agendas to fight anti-Romani discrimination. I further argue that the associations with the term *Gypsy* that non-Romani dislike or resist reflect an antagonism toward a fictitious creation of their own collective imaginary rather than factual knowledge about Romani and their diverse cultures.

In line with the previous argument, this chapter is written on the premise, shared with the aforementioned research paper, that there is no such thing as *gypsyism*; what exists is *Rromanipen*, a Romani term indicating a register of values shared among all Romani worldwide and also coexistent with the diversity found among subgroups (Weyrauch 2001). Using examples from different countries, I highlight the diversity of this widespread diaspora characterized by its intercontinental albeit marginalized presence. My analysis engages diverse materials, including other ethnographies, news articles, official policies, documentary films, and various organizations' research reports. My sources reveal ongoing U.N. and EU commitment to the development of national education policies for Romani children. The COE pioneered such involvement with Romani youth by adopting the first official text on *The Situation of Gypsies and Other Travelers in Europe* (Wiklund 1969). Additionally, in 1983, COE organized the first training for teachers working with Romani youth; in 2009, COE adopted the Committee of Ministers' recommendation, which is drawn specifically on the topic of Romani youth education, as the main strategy for positive change: "Overall, the legal framework and initiatives undertaken at international and national levels reflect the presence of political commitment to ameliorate the situation of Roma, specifically through education" (COE 2019). It follows that education-oriented initiatives for the Romani constitute a fundamental strategy for addressing the security deficits of this ethnic minority.

Background

Western Europeans often confuse Romanian Romani migrants with majoritarian citizens of Romania. Meanwhile, some Romanian Roma do not recognize their new "politically correct denomination." A cinnamon-skinned, slender Rom in a village in Eastern Romania joked wittily, "Today they call us Rom. Tomorrow they'll call us Euro. All I know is that I'm Tsigan." *Tsigan* is Romanian for "Gypsy"—it is also a misnomer. The term comes from the Greek *athinganoi*, meaning *pagan*. The denomination *Gypsy*, on the other hand, erroneously indicates Egyptian origins. Europeans have misidentified and misunderstood Romani since their arrival in the 1300s to the present day. Romani represent quintessential *others* in most societies, particularly where they constitute an ethnically visible minority. In the Americas, however, Romani have often chosen to integrate—pass for or blend in—with the local population, and in public, they may hide or even deny belonging to their ethnic minority.

In Brazil, for instance, the Roma subgroup insists on maintaining its ethnicity undisclosed to avoid being associated with the Calons. Members of the Calon subgroup started arriving in Brazil with the Portuguese in the 1500s and choose to display their ethnicity by wearing traditionally colorful clothes and living in tents. The discrimination that Calons encounter on rare occasions in Brazil, such as being called disparaging names when reading palms in the street, is milder compared to what Romani people often experience in Europe. *Ciganos* fare much better in Brazil than in Europe, possibly due to the fact that women's traditional occupation—fortune-telling—is enjoying renewed popularity and prosperity. As a new bride of the Calon tribe explained, "Here in Brazil, we are living the good life." Women from both Brazilian Roma and Calon tribes make a living as fortune-tellers; they express pride in their ethnicity and contend that it would be far below their dignity to ever beg like European Romani, as they see them do on the news or on the internet.

The negative stereotypes associated with Gypsies, such as begging, swindling, or thieving, are still circulated by European laymen, politicians, and journalists, despite resistance from activists and members of academia. This stigma pervades European imaginaries due to sensationalistic depictions of the Romani minority. The police and society at large continue to portray Romani youths as perpetrators of crimes rather than as potential victims of highly challenging circumstances. The media do occasionally report on the vulnerability of Romani youth and highlight the need to support them. More often, however, they focus on their poverty, illiteracy, and criminality—and even their alleged link to human trafficking. A popular narrative involves the belief that hundreds of Romani migrant children are being used by other adult ethnic-group members as pickpockets, burglars, or even sex slaves (Pieters 2018).

Members of the Romani ethnicity have, in effect, been involved in trafficking—this does not, however, mean that Romani are culturally predisposed toward inflicting such harms on themselves or others. Moreover, although human trafficking does occur, it does not account for the majority of Eastern European Romani migrations westward, in spite of what officials from France, Italy, Finland, and Canada have claimed. "French NGOs working with Romani migrants report that the vast majority are not trafficked and that they come to France voluntarily," according to the report *Breaking the Silence: Trafficking in Romani Communities* issued by the European Roma Rights Center and the People in Need (ERRC 2011). These migrations seem to be largely driven by structural poverty, social marginalization, and ethnic discrimination, all of which can be prevented or alleviated by providing meaningful educational opportunities for young Romani students.

My fieldwork has led to similar conclusions. For example, my study revealed that when Romanian Romani migrants traveled to Brazil, they often did so primarily in search of a way to make a living; some even tried begging. However, since begging is considered illegal in Brazil, most of these families ended up being deported back to Romania within a few weeks, with a free one-way ticket for everyone in their extended families. In the context of such frequent international mobility, educational measures are a valuable strategy for young people to learn the local language and understand the culture of the new lands they encounter. On the other hand, schools may not be the most suitable places for Romani youth to learn: "We do not like to sit in and be told what to do. We learn fast, but we learn in the streets. If we like something, we will learn it. We are very smart. Smarter than *gadjos*," noted a persnickety boy of Calon background. As this remark illustrates, Brazilian Romani fear cultural assimilation resulting from schooling.

Intermarriages between Romani and locals, on the other hand, tend to happen rather frequently because "Brazilians are so friendly," as offered by a Sao Paulo–residing Calon youth. He was referring to mixed marriages between young men like himself and non-Romani women. This practice is allowed, unlike the marriages between female members of the Romani ethnic group and male nonmembers, which remain taboo. Brazilian non-Romani sometimes pretend to be of Romani origins: "*Gadjos* want to be like us and be psychics," I was told by a young Romani fortune-teller in Rio de Janeiro. Both Roma and Calons reported being aware of the existence of *Ciganos* impersonators working as musicians, psychic readers, and belly dancers. Others admitted that they themselves were progressively losing old-fashioned *Rromanipen*, including their mother tongue, *chib*.

Addressing the security deficits of these youths would require multipronged efforts. These should include helping them (re)learn their ancestral language by providing them with instruction in Romani language and history similar to that now available in Romani public schools. On the other hand, as a young Romanian Roma woman in Florence, Italy, noted, "We don't need to go to museums or learn about history. Why should we be told what we are supposed to be? We know what we are." Perhaps in the same way, it is not really feasible to teach the Romani language, given that each group speaks its own dialects. The existence of an "official" or standard Romani is being debated, and some representatives have even argued against "wasting time with it."

In Brazil, Romani report a preference for studying materials on Romani culture privately and argue against making them public knowledge disseminated in regular schools. Some fear that non-Romani impersonators might thereby be able to acquire their main identifier—their Romani language. Standardized Romani-language textbooks, written primarily by Romanian linguist Gheorghe Sarău, are part of the minority-specific education initiatives implemented by the Romanian Ministry of Education (Sarău 2014). This standardized version of the language remains controversial as a wide variety of spoken dialects compete for authenticity status and serve as key ethnic subgroup identifiers. Nonetheless, these Romani language, history, and traditions textbooks and pioneering courses have created an innovative infrastructure of minority education in the Romanian public schools. These courses could eventually be translated and made available to Romani youths in other countries.

Youth would benefit from access to ethnic-specific language and history coursework, offering them the option to transfer their cultures and dialects from orality to the written form. Giving written expression to important elements of Romani culture—from policies to literature—in their own *chib* is a realistic present-day possibility. Educated Romani youths worldwide can now read, write/type, and communicate globally with each other, making it easier for them to unite in their efforts toward equality, protection, and representation. Ethnic-specific education for Romani youth would likely increase their sense of belonging in school, reduce their fear of assimilation, and encourage them to continue their formal education. Furthermore, a shared curriculum of Romani language and history textbooks could unite youths belonging to various subgroups through a sense of shared *Rromanipen* and mutual understanding. Schools would then no longer be perceived as places of cultural loss and assimilation.

All Romani youths across continents share a common interest in breaking the intergenerational cycle of social marginalization and stigmatization; formal education enhanced by ethnic-specific coursework can provide significant tools. The voices of Romani youth from different ethnic subgroups at the local, national, and international levels should be heard on this issue.

PROTECTION DEFICITS AND THE CONTEXT OF MARGINALIZATION

The Gypsy race does not exist; nonetheless, Romani themselves often make remarks pointing out perceived ethnic differences like "We are not like the others" or "Calons are not real Ciganos." Romani have been stereotyped as a group needing "special treatment," including "special schools" segregated from those for the rest of society. While Romani remain a quintessential minority in the popular imaginary in both Latin America and Europe, pronounced differences can be noted in the living situation and status of the Romani youth in those two regions.

In Brazil, most of the youth living in impoverished communities receive a very different quality of education than their wealthier peers; this applies to both Romani and non-Romani (Muggah 2017). Some Roma in Brazil, on the other hand, are in fact quite wealthy and live in upscale neighborhoods. Yet investments in Romani-specific youth education (e.g., language, history) that would help young people rise as community leaders while maintaining their ethnic identity are rather restricted.

Limited education attainment, unemployment, and poverty remain the main protection risks Romani face in Europe, on a wider scale and more visibly so than in the United States or in Latin America. For historical reasons, they remain Europe's largest underprivileged, impoverished, and predominantly illiterate ethnic minority, numbering ten to twelve million people, six million of whom live in the EU member states, according to the ERRC. Those born in Eastern Europe may choose to migrate with their extended families to Western Europe on short-term visas, where they strive to meet their financial needs. As poorly integrated migrants, some live as squatters in illicit housing and remain vulnerable to forced evictions and deportations—a pattern particularly common in Italy and France.

Due to their lack of a stable address, Romani children in France are denied access to schools, or they get wait-listed for a year (ERRC 2011). A ten-year-old Romanian Roma girl in France complained, "They don't let us get into schools. We have to wait until the next school year, and by that time, we have to move." Due to poverty and constantly forced displacements, schooling often gets altogether interrupted. A UNESCO document titled *Evolution in Approaches to Educating Children from Mobile and Nomadic Communities* (Dyer 2015) commissioned by the Education for All Global Monitoring Report has identified a number of strategies that would also be applicable to Romani students.

Additional reasons for Romani youngsters to drop out of school are fear of losing their culture, gender bias, and negative stereotyping—most girls drop out several years prior to being married to prepare for marriage by learning to take care of younger siblings and doing household chores. *Rromanipen* shared values include ethnic-specific moral purity taboos, such expectations of virginity for young girls at marriage, and the practice of arranged marriages. Both younger and older people often contend that any extended period of schooling entails the potential for cultural assimilation into the rest of society. As a young Romani from Brazil explained, "If a girl goes to school, she starts having a crush on a *Gagjo* [non-Romani boy], sending love notes, and soon enough, she elopes with him, then she is *perdida* [lost]."

My research indicates that this is indeed an increasing trend; schooling, as a powerful vehicle for socialization, may have led certain girls to lose some of the traditional cultural values upheld by Romani elders. An eleven-year-old French Sinti girl traveling in Southern France with her family emphatically stated, "When I grow up, I'm going to be my own driver. I'm not going to get married," expressing her critical views on the patriarchal customs of her elders, who insist that the man drives the van, representing the leadership in the family, whereas the woman is the one to cook, clean, and take care of the children.[2] Other girls proclaimed that when they got older, they wanted to become judges, lawyers, or doctors—all occupations that would require access to higher education and are thus out of reach for most Romani youth—and more so for girls.

Many other young women reported a preference for undeclared, informal work either in Romania or abroad. More often, they opted for availing themselves of the benefits of the social security system. Owing to the combination of these factors, the incidence of early school dropouts among Roma youth is up to 19 percent (Meirosu 2018, 3). This high dropout rate, compounded by discrimination, subsequently results in poor integration into the labor market. All of these issues are related to the high incidences of poverty. In effect, poverty is "almost three times higher among Roma people than the rest of the population in Romania, which makes their social inclusion even more difficult" (Meirosu 2018).

Romani have often been singled out as an ethnic minority and have even been segregated into "special schools." In the Czech Republic, almost a third of Roma youth were placed in "practical schools" or "institutions that use a simplified curriculum for children who have mild mental disabilities or who need remedial training," while "others are segregated into Roma-only schools that keep them isolated from the mainstream education system" (Flanagin 2014). It is unusual that such practices continue in a present-day EU member state, since all it does is retain the stigma of dysfunction and backwardness attached to Romani youth, who without proper education may well enough lean into petty theft to survive their circumstances.

In other contexts, such segregated schools have, however, been turned to the benefit of Romani youth. Leila de Morais, a Brazilian *romolog* (Romani studies expert), has written extensively on the topic of Calon space appropriation. Her 2018 article published in *Áltera*, a Latin American anthropology journal, discusses how the Calon Gypsies who are "stopped" in Carneiros, a city in the backcountry of Alagoas, manage to appropriate the space through the relationship built inside and outside the city (Morais 2018). The concept of appropriation has close relationships with the conception of "being a Calon" and with the constant mobility of the community. Calons establish a range of effective and economic relationships they engage in externally (with neighboring municipalities) and internally (those established within Carneiros); they differentiate themselves from the local population through cultural practices that include nomadism, mourning rituals, quarrels, business practices, the specific vocabularies used for different occupations, and so forth, all of which have important implications for the type of education that would be more suitable to Calon students.

As already alluded to, an additional protection challenge for these youngsters stems from negative perceptions of Romani youth as untrustworthy, violence-prone, dangerous, and likely thieves. This attitude thwarts Romani people's efforts at local integration and may result in a self-fulfilling prophecy that perpetuates social relations of mutual distrust. As the chief of a particular tribe remarked, "One bad apple gives all of us bad fame. But there's a bad apple in every batch. So why stereotype?" Dispelling unhelpful negative stereotypes and promoting youth education represent key strategies to overcome protection risk and facilitate Romani youngsters' integration into the larger society.

EDUCATION AS PROTECTION IN THE GLOBAL YPS AGENDA

Romani youths have had limited access to equal education in many countries, particularly in Romania. This is related to the fact that many still live in rural areas or other similarly marginalized, impoverished, ghettoized, and "disadvantaged communities, which make youth integration and access to education more difficult" (Meirosu 2018, 3). When these youths travel abroad with their extended families, who are often seeking financial well-being, they find themselves having to drop out of school and struggling to make ends meet. In such foreign countries, these youths' opportunities for education are even more scarce or difficult to access. As outlined in the following discussion, many formidable challenges remain. The situation is, nevertheless, slowly changing due to social activism at a higher political scale. Recent developments include the establishment of special programs offered by the EU and the provision of targeted materials for the education of nomadic students. Furthermore, teachers and social workers have acted as intermediaries between young people who wish to study and parents who have limited experience with schooling and do not see education as a valuable asset.

If provided with the right opportunities, Romani youths can make a positive contribution to the global YPS agenda by addressing their security deficits in their own terms—for example, mitigating the risks created by poverty, unemployment, segregation, discrimination, stigmatization, criminalization, violence, human trafficking, and sexual abuse. Formal education, I argue, is the best strategy toward empowering Romani youths of any gender and lowering their potential risks. Education is part of the global YPS agendas outlined in UNSCR 2250's pillars for action in *The Missing Peace* (Simpson 2018). Education policies specifically designed with at-risk young men and women in mind can support them as they participate in efforts to ensure their own protection.

A recent Harvard FXB[3] project titled "Reclaiming Adolescence: Roma Transitions to Adulthood, 2012–2014" (Harvard FXB 2019) concluded that Romani youth are eager to be included in policy making and research projects on their education. This project involved training and supporting Romani youth in Eastern Europe to conduct fieldwork about their own schooling. These youths conducted interviews with Roma and non-Roma peers on topics like discrimination, racism, affirmative action measures, transitioning into the workforce, experiences and fears of bullying at school, and parental support or the resistance toward continued education. "Reclaiming Adolescence" showcases how Romani youth can actively help design research-based educational policies to meet their needs while working together with authorities and organizations on both local and broader scales.

Romani-specific educational programs are necessary due to Romani students' lack of a stable residence. Many schools in European counties—for example, French and Italian—have refused access to Romani migrant youths, which is both illegal and against human rights principles (Bryant 2017). Several Romanian Roma children in France agreed with a twelve-year-old girl who proclaimed, "We want to go to school, but they won't let us. We don't have an address." In some states, even native-born Romani find it hard to access schools because of their lack of documents, including birth certificates. This poses additional and particularly serious protection risks for Romani—that of statelessness. As a case in point, Roma are the largest undocumented group in Ukraine, and without legal documents, they cannot defend their rights to citizenship (EERC 2018). As a result, Roma youth in this country have been excluded from schools or detained by the police and have resorted to begging for survival. Their situation is a case of administrative failure resulting in poor educational attainment. This, in turn, leads to unemployment or underemployment as unskilled day laborers with unstable salaries.

Even Romani migrant youths who manage to enroll in foreign schools often struggle to meet their requirements. A study conducted by the British Office for Standards in Education, Children's Services and Skills (OFSTED) on *Overcoming Barriers: Ensuring That Roma Children Are Fully Engaged and Achieving in Education* (2014) analyzed the situation of Romanian Roma migrant youth integrated into eleven schools in Derby, Manchester, and Sheffield. The study concluded that when newly arrived pupils had little prior experience with formal education, they faced obvious difficulties adhering to their school routine and meeting expectations for good behavior. Being able to communicate in the official language of the host country is a strong predictor of migrant youths' education level and subsequent quality of employment. Romani children whose reading skills in the official language are at least "good" are up to twice as likely to work later on with a formal contract compared to those who have lesser knowledge of the official language. My research further shows that Romani youth who did not experience ethnicity-based violence, harassment, or discrimination are more likely to work with a formal contract. Antigypsyism thus constitutes one of the key obstacles to obtaining stable employment.

The European Union Agency for Fundamental Rights suggests that poverty also interferes with the process of a continuing education. Poverty motivates the bulk of

Romani migrations from Eastern Europe westward and continues to plague many of those who remain as well as those who go. In 2016, nine European countries found that as many as 80 percent of Romani live below the poverty line, while one in three has no access to tap water or even sanitation (FRA 2016). Survey results further concluded that "every third Roma child lives in a household where someone went to bed hungry at least once in the previous month; and 50% of Roma between the ages of six and 24 do not attend school." These findings indicate that the majority of this Romani diaspora continues to face infrastructural discrimination and unequal access to vital services. Youth access to schooling is hindered by factors like poverty, the lack of proper clothing and shoes, no means of transportation to school, and the necessity to provide for a struggling family.

To alleviate students' poverty and encourage their attendance in schools, some organizations are offering free textbooks and food incentives. In Romania, children who live in poverty, frequently belonging to the Romani minority, have received help from the Alex Fund Agency for Early Education. This nonprofit organization is based in Tarrytown, New York. It funds programs such as OvidiuRo, active in Romania, where it works closely with public officials and educational staff to provide teacher training and educational resources. In the past, the Alex Fund provided a free lunch consisting of a croissant and milk box. Romani parents who were initially resistant to sending their children to school now encourage them to attend daily and take advantage of the free meal. My field visits revealed that for some youths, this constituted the only meal they had for the entire day.

Since the fall of 2017, the agency has distributed over sixty thousand books. It also has involved over five thousand parents, barely literate themselves, in reading activities so they learn to value literacy. This project has resulted in significantly improved school registration rates and attendance rates among disadvantaged children: "In the 2016–2017 school year, 70,000 children were registered and 40,000 were benefiting from daily attendance and food coupons" (Alex Fund Agency 2018).

Similar incentive programs could be developed in other EU states to reduce the educational gap for Romani as well as other impoverished, at-risk youngsters. Food incentives and parent remuneration for youths' school attendance would empower these students to strive for a brighter, more secure future. As the previous examples have illustrated, in order to thrive and fulfill the promise of the global YPS agenda, Romani youths need to be provided with the right opportunities and adequate resources, including legal documentation, if this is lacking, as well as access to suitable, culture-appropriate educational opportunities.

Conclusions and Recommendations

UNSCR 2250 calls for action to ensure that youth voices are heard and that young people, even—or perhaps especially—at-risk youths, are provided with adequate culturally appropriate opportunities. Striving for higher educational attainment requires the engagement of these at-risk youth in efforts to counter negative stereotypes. Youth can best fight negative misperceptions by proving them all wrong. To counteract the characterization of Romani youths as "troublemakers" or as disinterested in formal education, these youths must replace the racist fatalism that underestimates their potential contributions with optimism about their involvement in academics and participation in gainful employment. Gifted, dedicated students become leaders in the fight for peaceful social inclusion and equality. As such, they must be recognized as allies in civil rights actions and rewarded with scholarships. Policies and interventions must also facilitate young people's transition from education to employment, leading to meaningful participation in the workforce with stable contracts and salaries.

Their culture is of utmost importance to Romani parents, and their wishes must be respected as valid concerns. Romani parents are more likely to support Romani-specific education than mainstream education, which they mistrust, as it carries the risk of turning their children into members of the majority group, an outcome they fear. Parental interest in youngsters' education can be more effectively encouraged by also stressing its importance for success in any area of life. The research on best practices for Romani social integration shows that migrant youths whose level of knowledge of the official local language is "excellent" or "native-like" are much more likely to be working with a formal contract than those whose language proficiency in the official language is deemed only "good" (OFSTED 2014, 29). This makes education especially important for migrant youths who do not speak the official host language proficiently. The risk of unemployment that limited education entails for Romani youth also carries the additional threat of leading others to perceive them as dangerous or criminals and leaving Romani youth as mistrusted and stigmatized.

With poverty-motivated mass migrations among Eastern Europe–born Romani, the EU faces additional challenges for Romani education as protection from unemployment. Affirmative action measures are currently encouraging university-level students. However, these students represent a negligible percentage of Romani to this day, with the majority of youths dropping out before reaching high school. The European Platform for Roma Inclusion (EPRI 2017) outlines in *Transition from Education to Employment* the call for governments, social partners, and employers to promote work-based learning for Roma youth, including quality apprenticeships, traineeships, and entrepreneurial education, such as training for start-ups and support for self-employment.

This report also calls on governments to introduce Romani history and the concept of antigypsyism in regular school curricula to foster diversity training in classrooms. The transition from education to employment must involve multifaceted youth support. The report shows that schooling among sixteen- to twenty-four-year-olds has remained low: "Currently not attending education: 81%; Currently attending vocational training: 13%; Currently attending upper secondary education: 3%; Currently attending lower secondary education: 3%" (EPRI 2017). According to this report, only 3 percent of Roma youth aged twenty to twenty-four are still in education, meaning few are enrolled in universities.

Adequate development of Romani youth must start when they are young and ensure their continued education. Proper preschool enrollment can prepare children and parents to value formal education, which would help prevent early dropouts, particularly for girls. The World Bank report insists this can only be achieved through the consistent involvement of institutions in implementing and monitoring local educational policies and programs; specifying clearly institutional budgets, responsibilities, and expected results; and requesting progress reports.

Affirmative action measures can help combat the low expectations some Romani students have by promoting those who excel with scholarships toward university admissions. In 2018, thirty-five Romanian Romani students received medical scholarships—an unprecedented and promising outcome in Central and Eastern Europe, according to the Open Society Foundation (OSF 2018). These medical scholarships were part of the Decade of Roma Inclusion Program. "Discrimination and limited resources have created barriers for Roma access to quality health care. The education of Roma in the medical field will help tear down these barriers," said Alina Covaci, program officer of the Roma Health Project (OSF 2018). Romani youth who study medicine contribute to the betterment of their communities by providing them with nondiscriminatory health care and by becoming positive role models for new generations. Romani graduates have also been excelling in other fields such as history, law, and political science. They secure a more prosperous future for themselves and other members of their ethnic diaspora by becoming professors, activists, and politicians able to defend their cultural and human rights.

Romani youth have, in effect, been excelling in many fields. The Snétberger Music Talent School in Felsőörs village in Western Hungary is a training center created for disadvantaged Roma youths. The school is led by world-famous Romani guitarist Ferenc Snétberger. Every year, sixty gifted young musicians receive scholarships for achieving world-class training at this center. They bring positive recognition to their diaspora, along with those excelling in many other fields. European Romani activist organizations emphasize the support for youth educational excellence. For example, the Roma Education Fund (REF) based in Hungary and Switzerland has been promoting Romani children's rights to inclusive, high-quality education since 2005.

According to its mission statement, the REF has been reaching out to over "150,000 beneficiaries through its projects and programs that target all aspects of formal education, from early childhood development to parenting, from after-school tutoring to university scholarships" (REF 2019). Each year, REF awards university students and graduates with scholarships as well as additional support for higher academic results and employability. The Roma Versitas Agency in Albania likewise disburses forty-five scholarships per year to university students and graduates based on merit as well as additional support. European Romani affirmative action measures do help high school graduates and college-enrolled students and can be expanded upon to support the high achievers.

In addition, just like Romani males, Romani females must address the risks that jeopardize their future employment and financial stability by overcoming the conservative, patriarchal values with which they are frequently raised and that prevent them from attending school after their usually early marriage—as early as after having their first menstruation. As a result of traditional gender roles, a significantly lower number of Romani women have jobs compared to men. According to the *Transition from Education to Employment* report, "Across all nine Member States, on average, more than twice as many Roma men are in employment than Roma women, 26 % and 11 % respectively" (EPRI 2017, 15). Since child rearing is typically delegated to women, it is hardly surprising that "if they lived in a household with a small child, Roma women were less likely to be in employment and Roma men were more likely to be in employment" (20). Of the employed Romani youth, only

29 percent are women, while the remaining 71 percent are men aged sixteen to twenty-four. The gender gap in Romani employment clearly persists.

Romani youths can empower themselves by successfully continuing their formal education. This would also require challenging them to reinterpret some of their cultural and gender norms, possibly contravening the assumptions and expectations of their parents, who are often barely literate and do not value schooling. As more young Romani women and men become educated and start being engaged in well-respected professional occupations, scapegoating Romani as petty criminals is likely to decline over time. This is indeed a trend I saw increasing during my field research. The field of criminal justice is reported as particularly appealing to young boys and girls because of the historical association of Romani people with crime. Rising to the upper echelons of society, including its justice system, is seen as the best strategy to facilitate social life as a minority living harmoniously within a larger majority group.

The education of marginalized youth represents a key component of the Security Council's global YPS agenda since it calls for youth of all genders as equal, active agents and cocreators of their peaceful social integration. Much remains to be done toward Romani youth participation in formal education and employment opportunities. Furthering the YPS agenda means empowering collaborative action where Romani youths are considered equal and are essential partners in improving their lives and choosing the content of their course curricula as relevant to their own lifestyles. Addressing structural inequalities and facilitating marginalized youths' access to culture-appropriate education are necessary steps in supporting them as they strive to make a better future for themselves while ensuring the protection of their communities against long-standing risks.

NOTES

1. The Roma do not constitute a homogeneous ethnic entity; rather, they are subdivided into linguistically, economically, culturally, or socially distinct subgroups.

2. The Sinti are a Romani subgroup believed to be originally from Central Europe. They were traditionally itinerant, and in earlier times, they frequently lived on the outskirts of communities. Today only a small percentage of Sinti remain unsettled.

3. Harvard University's François-Xavier Bagnoud Center for Health and Human Rights is popularly known as the Harvard FXB.

REFERENCES

Alex Fund Agency. 2018. "Agency for Early Education: Programs." Accessed August 5, 2020. www.alexfund.org/agency-for-early-education/. (URL inactive.)

Alliance against Antigypsyism. 2016. "Antigypsyism: A Reference Paper." Accessed August 1, 2020. www.antigypsyism.eu.

Bernal, Jorge. 2003. "The Rom in the Americas." Sub-commission on Promotion and Protection of Human Rights Working Group on Minorities. Ninth session. Geneva: Office of the United Nations High Commissioner for Human Rights.

Bryant, Alice. 2017. "Europe's Roma Do Not Have Equal Access to Education." VOA Learning English. https://learningenglish.voanews.com/a/europes-roma-still-struggle-to-get-good-education/4108678.html.

Budur, Diana. 2015. "Gypsy Myths and Romani Cosmologies in the New World: Roma and Calons in Brazil." PhD diss., Princeton University.

COE (Council of Europe). 2019. "Roma and Travelers: Education of Roma Children." Accessed August 3, 2020. www.coe.int/en/web/roma-and-travelers/education-of-roma-children. (URL inactive.)

Dyer, Caroline. 2015. *Evolution in Approaches to Educating Children from Mobile and Nomadic Communities*. UNESCO and Education for All Global Monitoring Report. ED/EFAT/MRT/2015/PI/15. https://unesdoc.unesco.org/ark:/48223/pf0000232422.

EPRI (European Platform for Roma Inclusion). 2017. *Transition from Education to Employment*. Accessed August 1, 2020. https://ec.europa.eu/info/sites/info/files/report_roma_platform_2017_final.pdf.

ERRC (European Roma Rights Center). 2011. *Breaking the Silence: Trafficking in Romani Communities*. European Roma Rights Center and the People in Need, March 11, 2011. www.errc.org/uploads/upload_en/file/breaking-the-silence-19-march-2011.pdf.

———. 2018. "Roma Belong—Statelessness, Discrimination and Marginalisation of Roma in Ukraine." European Roma Rights Center. Accessed August 1, 2020. www.errc.org/reports-and-submissions/roma-belong--statelessness-discrimination-and-marginalisation-of-roma-in-ukraine.

Flanagin, J. 2014. "The Roma May Be Just What Europe Needs to Recover." *Quartz Daily*. Accessed August 3, 2020. https://qz.com/280695/the-roma-may-be-just-what-europe-needs-to-recover/.

FRA—European Union Agency for Fundamental Rights. 2016. "Second European Union Minorities and Discrimination Survey (EU-MIDIS II) Roma." Accessed August 5, 2020. https://fra.europa.eu/en/publication/2016/eumidis-ii-roma-selected-findings.

Harvard FXB. 2019. "Reclaiming Adolescence: Roma Transitions to Adulthood, 2012–2014." Accessed August 5, 2020. https://fxb.harvard.edu/research/adolescent-empowerment/roma-program/rights-and-participation/.

Meirosu, Catalina. 2018. "Tackling Roma Youth Unemployment in Romania: The Role of Youth Guarantee Programme." Trans European Policy Studies Association TEPSA Briefs—August 2018. Accessed August 3, 2020. www.tepsa.eu/wp-content/uploads/2018/08/Catalina-Meirosu_in-template-3.pdf.

Morais, Leila Samira Portela de. 2018. "Space Appropriation, Identity and Displacements: Calon Experiences in the Backcountry of Alagoas." *Áltera—Revista de Antropologia, João Pessoa* 2, no. 7 (July/December): 153–177. Algoas Federal University (PPGS/UFAL).

Muggah, R. 2017. "Youth, Security and Peace: Brazil Revisited." U.N. Country Focused Research. Accessed January 9, 2020. www.youth4peace.info/system/files/2018-04/2.%20CFR_Brazil_Robert%20Muggah_0.pdf.

OFSTED (Office for Standards in Education, Children's Services and Skills). 2014. *Overcoming Barriers: Ensuring That Roma Children Are Fully Engaged and Achieving in Education*. Accessed August 10, 2020. https://assets.publishing.service.gov.uk/government/uploads/system/uploads/attachment_data/file/430866/Overcoming_barriers_-_ensuring_that_Roma_children_are_fully_engaged_and_achieving_in_education.pdf.

OSF (Open Society Foundations). 2018. "Romanian Students Receive First-Ever Roma Medical Scholarships." December 14, 2018. www.opensocietyfoundations.org/newsroom/romanian-students-receive-first-ever-roma-medical-scholarships.

Pieters, Janene. 2018. "Hundreds of Roma Children Trafficked in Netherlands as Sex Slaves, Pickpockets." *NL Times*, January 22, 2018. https://nltimes.nl/2018/01/22/hundreds-roma-children-trafficked-netherlans-sex-slaves-pickpockets.

REF (Roma Education Fund). 2019. "Six University Students and Graduates in Bosnia and Herzegovina Will Be Awarded Scholarships and Offered Support towards Improved

Academic Results and Employability." Roma Education Fund. Accessed August 10, 2020. www.romaeducationfund.org.

Sarău, Gheorghe. 2014. "Începuturile învățământului pentru rromi (1990–1994)." *Revista Inovația Sociala* 6, no. 1, 1–9.

Simpson, Graeme. 2018. *The Missing Peace: Independent Progress Study on Youth, Peace and Security*. UNFPA. www.unfpa.org/sites/default/files/youth/youth-web-english.pdf.

Vasconcelos, Maria. 2013. "Dados Estatísticos Sobre os Povos Romani no Brasil: Avanços e Retrocessos." AMSK—Associação Internacional Maylê Sara Kalí, August 27, 2013. http://amskblog.blogspot.com/2013/08/dados-estatisticos-sobre-os-povos.html.

Weyrauch, Walter O. 2001. *Gypsy Law*. Berkeley: University of California Press.

Wiklund, Daniel. 1969. *The Situation of Gypsies and Other Travelers in Europe*. (Former) Social, Health and Family Affairs Committee. Strasbourg: Council of Europe.

CHAPTER 4

Squeezed Agency

YOUTH RESISTANCE TO THE SECURITIZATION
OF PEACEBUILDING

Ali Altiok

Youth, peace, and security (YPS) and the prevention of violent extremism (PVE) are the two new normative policy agendas that globally acknowledge the positive agency of young people in the international peace and security field. The global agenda on YPS was officially recognized by the adoption of the United Nations Security Council Resolution (UNSCR) 2250 in December 2015. In the same month, the then current secretary-general, Ban Ki-Moon, proposed his Plan of Action to Prevent Violent Extremism to the United Nations General Assembly (2015), which was welcomed by the member states. Both of these major policy developments and the short time within which they were successfully brought forward highlight increased attention to youth on the part of the global political elite. This turning point marks the category of youth becoming a major international peace and security policy priority. However, as some critics highlight, it also signals the global securitization of youth as a social group (Sukarieh and Tannock 2017).

The global political elite play an important role in the securitization of policies, resources, institutions, and even spaces. However, the elite are not the only actors who shape securitization policies and practices. There are multiple peacebuilding institutions and actors, including young people and youth organizations, who rather than embrace often demonstrate resistance to securitization locally and globally. As such, analyzing and critically evaluating the relationships young people build with these two policy agendas are critical to ascertain whether, when, and how young people are being securitized. There is a need to understand the dynamics of the securitization process of youth and the roles not just the elite but others play in that process. Do youth blindly embrace these policies, or do they show resistance to the global securitization of youth? I argue that there is a complex relationship between the global peace and security structures and the agency of young people, which is being shaped by the structure but also shapes the structure itself.

This analysis draws in part on my own experiences as a member of the United Network of Young Peacebuilders (UNOY Peacebuilders) and my active involvement in multiple global, regional, and community research and advocacy projects associated directly with the YPS agenda. First, I served as a researcher at the joint United Nations Peacebuilding Support Office (U.N. PBSO)–United Nations Population Fund (UNFPA) Secretariat for the Progress Study on Youth, Peace and Security at the U.N. headquarters in New York. Over that two-year period, I took personal notes in regional youth consultations, expert groups, and multistakeholder and intergovernmental gatherings that exclusively focused on the development of the YPS agenda. As a rapporteur, I listened to the peace and security priorities of hundreds of young people from all regions of the world and participated personally in youth gatherings in the Arab states, Asia and the Pacific, Eastern European and Central Asia, and Western Europe. Second, working as a researcher for the Office of the Secretary-General's Envoy on Youth (OSGEY) for six months, I conducted over twenty in-depth interviews with youth leaders involved in political dialogue and mediation activities to shape peace processes in their own contexts. Third, I conducted an analysis of the internal advocacy strategies between 2012 and 2015 of youth-led peacebuilding organizations that demanded a U.N. Security Council resolution on youth and peacebuilding. Last, through interviews with young peacebuilders in Sri Lanka and Turkey for master's-level research together with an independent audiovisual research project, I also gathered data on how young people interact with state security institutions. I analyzed these diverse data sources to examine the role that young people play in their resistance to securitization at multiple levels. The names of some of the individuals, organizations, and institutions discussed in this chapter are kept confidential for privacy and security reasons.

This chapter is structured into four parts. The first part briefly explains the global securitization of young people and the resistance young people demonstrate against it. While global securitization legitimizes the violence of the state against young people, youth-led peacebuilding organizations and movements employ diverse sets of political tactics and strategies to resist securitization processes. Youth resistance against securitization builds the connection between their personal experience of injustices and the broad political structures responsible for the securitization of young people. Their resistance not only protects their own personal safety but defends their rights and freedoms. However, resistance to securitization puts young people at risk of arbitrary arrest, mass incarceration, aggression, repression, and various other forms of state violence, particularly under the guise of counterterrorism.

The second part reviews how the category of "youth" became a major policy priority in the counterterrorism field through the adoption of the PVE policy agenda. Although adoption of the PVE policy agenda brings some positive developments for the recognition of rights and freedoms of young people, all counterterrorism frameworks continue to legitimize state violence against young people, especially state security forces' violation of young people's rights in the name of counterterrorism. Nonetheless, many youth-led peacebuilding organizations continue engaging with counterterrorism actors and building links between the counterterrorism frameworks (particularly with the PVE agenda) and the YPS agenda.

The third section sheds light on the ties and differences between the PVE and the YPS agendas and discusses the extent to which YPS is another securitization agenda. This section argues that the YPS agenda did not emerge merely as a result of the political elite sitting at the Security Council or by civil society organizations who advocated for a shift on the dominant narrative on youth; it is a combination of the opposing interests of multiple actors that led to the adoption of a new youth agenda at the Security Council. This discussion provides reasons for seeing UNSCR 2250 as a tool for resistance against the securitization of youth in global policy-making platforms. The YPS agenda offers an opportunity for youth-led peacebuilding organizations to contest the top-down international counterterrorism policies, which securitizes young people but also the field of peacebuilding at large.

The last part of this chapter argues for a broader understanding of protection, which can support young people and youth-led peacebuilding organizations in their resistance to securitization. While the protection pillar of UNSCR 2250 almost exclusively focuses on the physical safety of youth, the virtue of young people's resistance to securitization lies in their ability to protect civic spaces, rights, and freedoms. In order to reverse the securitization of youth and that of the peacebuilding field through counterterrorism, efforts need to be directed to highlighting the role and agency of young people in protecting human rights and fundamental freedoms conducive to peace and peacebuilding.

THE GLOBAL SECURITIZATION OF YOUTH

The securitization of youth is not a new phenomenon that emerged in the post-9/11 period (Maira 2016). Young people have long been (mis)perceived as a security threat or as violent criminals to be feared in the state-society relationship throughout the world. For example, in Britain, the fear of young people traces back to the early nineteenth century, when the concept of "juvenile delinquent" was invented to build direct causal relationships between delinquency and adolescence (Muncie 2004). Similarly, during the Ottoman rule in sixteenth-century Anatolia, young people, particularly young men, were labeled as *delikanli* (those with wild blood) and as a potential threat to organized society (Neyzi 2001).

Yet the globalization of youth securitization can be considered relatively new. In international relations, youth-bulge theorists were the first to introduce the notion that young people pose a security threat to social order (Moller 1968; Choucri 1974; Huntington 1997; Urdal 2006; see also the introduction in this volume). Youth-bulge theorists conducted various quantitative studies to find a correlation between youthful populations and violence. Although there are significant variations among youth-bulge theories regarding the assumptions tested in these studies, there is one common thing among all of them. All youth-bulge studies ignore the violence of the state against youthful populations (Nordås and Davenport 2013), which is the most crucial consequence of the securitization of youth.

State violence against youth through securitization practices intensified with the beginning of the war on terror in 2001. The war on terror has been directed at young people across the world with zero-tolerance approaches, as critical scholars Brad Evans and Henry Giroux (2015) summarize: "The 'war on terror' is in reality a war on youth who are both its target and the vehicle for targeting others." The global political elite have been waging this war against youth for nineteen years through a securitization logic that is legitimized in the name of counterterrorism policies.

Although the concepts and issues that are being used to reinforce the (mis)perception that young people pose a threat to social order change over time and locations (Muncie 2004), the process of securitization brings similar consequences. In a broad sense, the process of securitization stereotypes young people as a threat to be contained or as passive vulnerable actors who are at risk of violence (Simpson 2018). These stereotypes are also often highly gendered. While young women are perceived as victims of crime, violence, and terrorism, young men are portrayed as potential criminals, violent perpetrators, or terrorists (Hendrixson 2004).

Youth-Led Resistance to Securitization

Young people's resistance to securitization is manifested in their activities seeking peace and justice in a broad sense. Many of the organizations and movements in which young people are involved are driven by the urgent necessity of dealing with injustice felt by them in their everyday lives. Yet these engaged youth are also able to associate their own lived experiences of injustice with the structural problems that are their underlying causes. Youth-led peacebuilding and protests for peace and justice offer a salutary counterpoint to the most fundamental sources and problems of securitization.

Youth-led peacebuilding organizations resist global securitization trends, for instance, by mobilizing for the eradication of illicit arms trades and light weapons. As a case in point, the Coalition on Rights and Responsibilities of Youth (CRY) is a youth-led peacebuilding organization from Pakistan involved in such action. The CRY's community-level work uses peer-to-peer education as a tool to empower young people for the protection of their rights. The CRY's peace education training aims to access the most vulnerable and marginalized social groups in order to build community-level resilience against forced recruitment by militant groups. This youth-empowerment strategy at the community level also aims to build a bottom-up approach to target the policies of securitization at the national and international levels. Through establishing advocacy groups and raising public awareness of the control of small arms, the CRY contests armament and militarization. The vision of CRY in building resistance against securitization is summarized in their press release to condemn the 2014 Peshawar school massacre, which caused the loss of 149 people, including 132 children: "We are aware that this massacre didn't happen in vacuum [sic], it is result of the weak state policies towards the militancy and terrorism in Pakistan despite of huge national budget [sic] spending on military and defense" (Aware Girls and CRY 2014).

Youth-led peacebuilding organizations reduce the securitized approaches of the state by engaging in criminal justice and prison reform processes. As a case in point, the Local Youth Corner (LOYOC) in Cameroon is an organization that works closely with criminal justice and law enforcement institutions to transform the securitization policies of the state. The LOYOC as a youth-led peacebuilding organization employs sociopolitical, cultural, and economic empowerment methods to counter the exclusion and marginalization of young people. The work of this organization particularly targets the rehabilitation and reintegration of criminal and violent extremist offenders. The LOYOC uses peer-to-peer approaches to transform prisoners into entrepreneurs and calls them "prisonpreneurs." Achaleke Christian Leke, national coordinator of the LOYOC, shared the story behind how his organization started from practice to policy: "Since we [the LOYOC] have conducted over 300 hundred projects, we could build trust-based relationships with the Government and its security-focused departments. . . . We even provide training for various Government departments, including Police forces, on Criminal Justice Reform, Human Rights and CVE related issues." As a result of this proactive engagement, the LOYOC gained legitimacy to penetrate the policy sphere for initiating structural change. As Leke explains, "We created a national YPS coalition between Government, Civil Society and youth-led organizations for the implementation of the UNSCR 2250" (Facebook direct message to author, March 26, 2019). The Global YPS policy agenda and UNSCR 2250 in this context provide a powerful political tool for youth-led peacebuilding to challenge rigid power structures and top-down securitization practices in the policy sphere.

There are also many examples of how youth-led peacebuilding organizations resist the securitization of the state through peaceful protest and dissent across the world. The Okay Africa Foundation, a South Sudanese youth-led peacebuilding organization, resists securitization through their campaign titled #NadafaLeBeledna (Let us clean our country). #NadafaLeBeledna is a monthly youth gathering to clean the street of Juba, the capital city of South Sudan. Since the securitized streets of Juba provide limited civic space to protest against corruption, this organization transmits messages of young peacebuilders through cleaning the dirty streets of the city. Wani Michael, the leader of this collective youth-led action, shared, "Cleaning is a protest, because we are tired of wars. If we clean the streets, we can also clean the bushes. We can clean this country out of corruption, nepotism and tribalism" (Altiok and Grizelj 2019, 33). The success of this initiative can be observed in its ability to bring young people who are working in state security institutions and youth peace activists in a collective action to raise public concerns on corruption. A South Sudanese national newspaper, *Juba Monitor*, reported that "the army and the civilians used the same brooms and sacks to dump rubbish and use the same language as people from the same organization" (Balla and Emmanuel 2018). This type of youth-led protests build a societal trust to protect freedoms and resists the shrinking civic space (see also chapter 7 in this volume for a broader discussion of youth activism in South Sudan).

It is worth noting that the securitization of youth is also being contested in the Global North. One of the most remarkable examples of this is the youth-led #NeverAgain movement in the United States. Student survivors of the 2018 school shooting in Parkland, Florida, initiated this movement to protest for gun-control laws to protect their schools from mass shootings. The #NeverAgain movement demands the protection of schools through legal reforms but also openly targets the financial relationships between gun lobbyists and lawmakers. David Hogg, an eighteen-year-old student survivor of the Parkland massacre, speaking at a public demonstration in Washington, D.C., remarked that "ninety-six people die every day from guns in our country, yet most representatives have no public stance on guns. . . . We are going to make this the voting issue. We are going to take this to every election, to every state, in every city. . . . We will get rid of these public servants that only serve the gun lobby." Later in his speech, Hogg openly expressed how the #NeverAgain movement will deliberately work to save the democratic decision-making process that is being hijacked by the corporate interests of gun manufacturers and the powerful progun lobby: "When politicians say that your [youth] voice doesn't matter because the NRA [National Rifle Association, the largest gun lobby in the United States] owns them . . . and to those politicians supported by the NRA, that allow the continued slaughter of our children and our future, I say: Get your résumés ready" (2018). The #NeverAgain movement illustrates how youth-led peace activism is able to build the relationships between their very personal experiences and the political-economic dimension of securitization.

All these examples show that youth-led peacebuilding organizations and movements resist securitization processes through various political tactics. Their strategic resistance addresses injustices both incrementally and structurally. Youth-led peacebuilding organizations are often inclined to engage and negotiate with law-enforcement actors in the implementation of security policies at community and city levels. This is a form of peacebuilding action that sees young people incrementally addressing their everyday experiences of injustice. In order to address injustice structurally, youth-led peacebuilding organizations and movements also occupy the streets in peaceful protest and through mass mobilization online.

Due to their engagement in diverse modes of political action in resisting securitization, youth-led peacebuilding organizations and movements often put themselves at risk of arbitrary arrest, mass incarceration, aggression, repression, and various other forms of state violence. As Graeme Simpson (2018), the lead author of *The Missing Peace: Independent Progress Study on Youth, Peace and Security*, noted, young peacebuilders across the world express their frustration about how "peaceful political organizations and legitimate organized political protest were frequently shut down in the name of counter-terrorism or the prevention of violent extremism" (102). Thus these state counterterrorism approaches push youth-led peacebuilding organizations into a cycle of repression. While youth-led peacebuilding organizations resist the securitized approaches of the state, they experience the violence of the state security apparatus under the pretext of countering terrorism. In order to get out of this cycle, many youth-led peacebuilding organizations develop specific tactical and strategic peacebuilding practices.

Youth-led peacebuilding organizations engage with the state security apparatus and even often associate themselves with the counterterrorism policies, frameworks, agencies, and programs to pursue their strategic peacebuilding goals. Collaborating and cooperating with security actors entail the risk of tokenistic youth participation to whitewash repressive behaviors of the security sector. Yet this also allows youth-led peacebuilding organizations to penetrate national and international policy-making spaces and build political alliances for transforming securitization policies.

Youth-led peacebuilding organizations are in fact often proud of working with the state security apparatus and being active in the field of counterterrorism. This can be observed especially in their active involvement in the PVE programs. Youth-led peacebuilding organizations perceive their role in the PVE field as one of the top achievements (Thapa 2017). There is also an observable interest among the counterterrorism actors to engage, consult, and even partner with youth-led peacebuilding organizations to counter terrorism and prevent violent extremism. This mutual interest reveals the delicate relationship between youth organizations and counterterrorism actors, which needs to be unpacked. In order to this, we need to understand why and how youth organizations and young people became important actors in the eyes of counterterrorism agents.

Growing Interest in Youth in the Counterterrorism Field

The emphasis on the positive role of young women and men in countering and preventing violent extremism grew gradually within the counterterrorism field. This growing emphasis on youth as key actors closely followed the trend of developing more comprehensive and inclusive counterterrorism policies. Since 9/11, the international community at the U.N. adopted three main approaches that were built upon each other: counterterrorism, countering violent extremism, and the prevention of violent extremism (Abu-Nimer 2018).

Counterterrorism was the first strategy adopted by the international community in this vein. This approach construed increasing numbers of young people of Middle Eastern, South Asian, and Arab descent; Muslims; and people of color in the Global South and in the West as international security threats (Hendrixson 2004). It heavily relied on military operations, surveillance, and intelligence gathering (Abu-Nimer 2018). Its hard-security orientation claimed to tackle the root causes of terrorism through punishing and preventing recruitment processes of extremist armed groups. However, the militaristic nature of this approach generated counterproductive security practices and fueled grievances that were then exploited by terrorist organizations (Keen and Attree 2015). Its military interventions also visibly targeted racially profiled communities (Patel 2013) and created conditions for the securitization of youth spaces, such as schools and youth clubs in both the Global South and North (Novelli 2017).

With the introduction of the term *violent extremism*, the international community started to highlight the positive role young people can play within the counterterrorism field. Countering violent extremism (CVE) was the second major approach adopted by the international community and emphasized the necessity of engaging civil society actors, including young people, for building social cohesion and community resilience (Abu-Nimer 2018). Yet the central concern of CVE frameworks in engaging youth is not to build socially cohesive and resilient societies per se but rather "to keep young people from expanding the ranks of violent extremist groups" (Sommers 2019, 37). Thus although the CVE approach claimed to engage young people from a positive angle, it continued stereotyping them as "at risk" of recruitment into extremist armed groups (Simpson 2018).

PVE, the third and most comprehensive counterterrorism policy, was adopted by the U.N. and its member states in 2016. This newest approach underscores the necessity of engaging, consulting, and partnering with a wide range of actors, including young people, to identify the root causes of extremism and encourages community-level solutions. As referenced in the U.N. Plan of Action to Prevent Violent Extremism (A/70/674), this approach recognizes youth agency in promoting peace and security and suggests that youth empowerment is an essential part of prevention efforts.

The emphasis on youth inclusion and empowerment highlighted in the U.N. Plan of Action to Prevent Violent Extremism was touted as an important step for youth empowerment. This recognition of young people as positive actors to oppose terrorism allows youth-led peacebuilding organizations to take part in formal policy-development processes at international and national levels, build strategic relationships with multiple actors at the international peace and security platforms, and receive financial support to implement youth inclusion and empowerment programs. However, this begs the question, What is youth empowerment for?

A Paradoxical Relationship: Youth Empowerment and Counterterrorism

Despite all the steps taken toward the recognition of young people's agency from a positive perspective, all counterterrorism approaches, including the PVE approach, securitize youth. On the one hand, the field of counterterrorism embraces the new narrative of "youth as peacebuilders" that is promoted by the youth, peace, and security agenda and invests in youth empowerment and inclusion programs. On the other hand, counterterrorism approaches continue portraying young people as "at risk" of violence and perceive them as susceptible to joining violent extremist groups. This dualistic notion demonizes, victimizes, and instrumentalizes young people and harms and limits the peacebuilding agency and leadership of youth under empowerment and inclusion programs serving for the field of counterterrorism.

Implementing youth empowerment and inclusion programs under counterterrorism frameworks represses young people instead of empowering them. As Mayssoun Sukarieh and Stuart Tannock (2015) point out, such formalized youth programs are used to establish "spaces of social control and containment, seeking to inculcate in their young participants a narrowly prescribed set of legitimate practices and viewpoints, and offer little to no real opportunity to effect radical or significant social or political change" (29). Thus developing youth empowerment programs and facilitating youth inclusion under the framework of PVE are risky and counterproductive paths, as these formalized youth engagement methods provide new tools and mechanisms for state security institutions to expand, strengthen, support, and supplement hardfisted law enforcement approaches that actually harm youth spaces and control young people.

Counterterrorism approaches also criminalize dissenting youth voices in civic spaces. In the name of counterterrorism frameworks, governments denigrate, potentially undermine, and often repress the legitimate processes of youth-based political organizations, social movements, peaceful protests, and expressions of dissent (Simpson 2018). This means that governments use the counterterrorism label to excuse their policies and practices disrespecting and stifling their citizens' rights to freedom of assembly, expression, association, and movement. Governments' use of such repressive practices crushes youth's dissent on issues like corruption and limit civic spaces and their access to the internet.

Although all counterterrorism approaches pose serious security risks for youth-led peacebuilding organizations, many of them continue to associate the PVE agenda with youth-led peacebuilding and also with the global YPS policy agenda. Considering all the dangerous policies and practices that come with the PVE agenda, it is an important question to consider why many youth-led organizations continue to build links between the YPS and the PVE agendas.

Is YPS Another Securitization Agenda?

Although multiple country-level resolutions with positive references to youth were in place (UNOY Peacebuilders 2013) prior to the adoption of UNSCR 2250 in 2015, no document officially recognized young people's peacebuilding agency at the U.N. Security Council. Since UNSCR 2250 is the first thematic resolution acknowledging the positive agency of young people, institutions supported it and introduced it as a "historic landmark" and a "groundbreaking step" toward building trust among young people, their governments, and multilateral institutions.

UNSCR 2250 was unanimously adopted in December 2015, just a month before the then U.N. secretary-general Ban Ki-Moon introduced his Plan of Action to Prevent Violent Extremism to the members of the U.N. General Assembly. The temporal proximity between the two events suggests that UNSCR 2250 was influenced by the interests of the member states in developing policies and new solutions to violent extremism. In fact, the text of UNSCR 2250 contains a strong focus on PVE, indicative of the obvious overlap between member states' support for the YPS and the PVE agendas. As such, former U.S. president Barack Obama hosted a summit on countering violent extremism in February 2015 to push the international community further in the development of a counterterrorism agenda with an emphasis on youth (U.S. Department of State 2015). That event and President Obama's (2015) remarks both had a particular focus on the need to address young people's vulnerability to violent extremist groups and suggested that empowering young people is key to the prevention of future violent extremist threats. In April 2015, just a couple of months after the White House summit, the Hashemite Kingdom of Jordan organized a ministerial debate on the role of youth in countering violent extremism at the Security Council (OSGEY 2015). Jordan then also shepherded the YPS resolution at the Security Council while the OSGEY was still occupied by Ahmad Alhendawi, who is also Jordanian.

Member states' interest in the overlap of the two policy agendas continued in the following years. The majority of the member states who joined the Group of Champions of SCR 2250, officially launched in September 2018, were also members of the Group of Friends of Preventing Violent Extremism (Norway in the U.N. 2017). Most of the member states organizing or participating in YPS events at the U.N. headquarters in New York exclusively speak about the instrumental value of the YPS agenda in supporting international and national efforts to counter and prevent violent extremism. For example, in March 2018, at the first open debate on YPS at the Security Council, the overwhelming majority of member states focused on the usefulness of the YPS agenda for combating, countering, or preventing violent extremism. Yet the meeting was organized for the presentation of *The Missing Peace*. Ironically, *The Missing Peace* highlighted that governments' insistence on implementing counterterrorism frameworks tends to yield counterproductive results by exacerbating youth marginalization and exclusion instead of harnessing the positive agency of young people to build peace (Simpson 2018). In September 2018, when the long version of *The Missing Peace* was launched, the title of the event was *The Youth, Peace and Security Agenda, towards Sustaining Peace and Preventing Violent Extremism* (United Nations 2018). The title and main objective of this meeting once again evidenced that most member states' main interest in the

YPS agenda was related to their investment in the counterterrorism frameworks to a great extent.

The majority of member states are interested in the YPS agenda due to its tie to the PVE agenda; nevertheless, there are also other member states who are not interested in seeing YPS just as a useful element or extension of the PVE agenda (Nwaozuzu 2018). Since the language of extremism does not necessarily resonate with their national security concerns, a handful of these countries have drawn a clear line between the YPS and the PVE agendas. Some of the other Member States are also interested in the YPS agenda due to its emphasis on inclusion. Therefore, it must be noted that member states' standpoint is not monolithic and that they approach the relationship between YPS and PVE from various perspectives.

The Role of Civil Society Organizations and U.N. Entities

The Hashemite Kingdom of Jordan, as a temporary member of the Security Council, obviously played a critical role in the adoption of UNSCR 2250. Jordan first hosted the Global Forum on Youth, Peace and Security in Amman in August 2015 and then led the political processes at the Security Council through December 2015. Jordan's role as a Security Council member state could not have been performed by a nonstate actor. Yet Jordan would not have been able to initiate this particular political process at the Security Council without the contributions of civil society organizations and other U.N. entities (UNOY Peacebuilders 2015a).

The Global Forum and its outcome, the *Amman Youth Declaration*, were prepared as a result of a multistakeholder collaboration among civil society organizations, U.N. entities, and Jordan. Search for Common Ground (SFCG, a youth-inclusive international nongovernmental peacebuilding organization) and the UNOY Peacebuilders (a network of youth-led peacebuilding organizations) were the two civil organizations actively involved in shaping the agenda of these two developments. These two organizations had advocated with U.N. entities and member states for a Security Council resolution on youth and peacebuilding long before this event took place in August 2015. For this event, these two organizations played an instrumental role to consult around ten thousand young people to draft the *Amman Youth Declaration*.

On the U.N. side, OSGEY, UNFPA, PBSO, and the United Nations Development Programme (UNDP) were the other co-organizers of the Global Forum to represent the U.N. system in this process. The involvement of these U.N. institutions was critical to transmitting the demands of youth and peacebuilding organizations to Jordan and other member states, shaping global peace and security policies at the U.N. Security Council.

Most member states were interested in adopting a resolution on youth due to their interest and investment in counterterrorism frameworks. Nevertheless, the YPS agenda emerged, to a great extent, as a result of the advocacy efforts of youth-led peacebuilding organizations and their alliance-building activities with U.N. entities and international nongovernmental peacebuilding organizations. This is evident in the *Amman Youth Declaration*, which shaped the actual language of UNSCR 2250. Thus the YPS agenda was not born solely as a result of the political elite sitting at the Security Council nor through civil society organizations who advocated for a shift on the dominant narrative on youth; it was born as a result of political processes initiated and then partially shaped by youth-led peacebuilding organizations, which sought to tackle the injustices they faced.

For many, the groundbreaking aspect of UNSCR 2250 is that it provides and formalizes a new narrative on youth agency at the Security Council. Yet for most youth-led peacebuilding organizations, the significance of UNSCR 2250 lies in its usefulness as a political tool to negotiate with state institutions for the transformation of the state-society relationships and advocate for incremental and structural change to address injustices. The adoption of UNSCR 2250 in this sense evidences that youth agency can be radical enough to challenge the hegemony of counterterrorism discourse and smart enough to build alliances that influence individuals and institutions shaping the policies and practices of the global securitization of youth.

Youth Agency in Global Policy Development Processes

Youth-led peacebuilding organizations demanded a Security Council resolution on youth and peacebuilding many years before the adoption of the UNSCR 2250. This request became increasingly loud and visible between 2012 and 2015. During these years, the UNOY Peacebuilders conducted yearly advocacy missions to the U.N. headquarters in New York to initiate a process for the recognition of youth as peacebuilders (UNOY Peacebuilders 2012, 2015b). Through these advocacy missions, UNOY Peacebuilders built relationships and informal alliances with multiple U.N. entities, agencies, and personnel. These relationship- and alliance-building activities played an important role in preparing the groundwork for the adoption of UNSCR 2250 and mobilizing political support among the members of the Security Council. The advocacy efforts taken by the members of youth-led peacebuilding organizations were supported by their civil society partners and allies within the U.N. system, which enabled them to bring their demands to the member states of the U.N.

The alliance-building activities of the UNOY Peacebuilders' Youth Advocacy Team also pushed for the creation of an informal Working Group on Youth and Peacebuilding. This informal working group was established in 2012 as part of the U.N. Inter-agency Network on Youth Development. The Working Group on Youth and Peacebuilding started providing space for youth-led peacebuilding organizations to build trust with U.N. entities and youth-focused civil society organizations. The Working Group on Youth and Peacebuilding is currently called the Global Coalition on Youth, Peace and Security and is co-led by UNOY Peacebuilders, SFCG, and U.N. PBSO.

Prior to the adoption of UNSCR 2250, youth-led peacebuilding organizations also took multiple important steps toward the recognition of "youth as peacebuilders." First, by involving the Working Group on Youth and Peacebuilding, youth-led peacebuilding organizations shaped the document *Guiding Principles on Young People's Participation in Peacebuilding* (Working Group Youth and Peacebuilding 2012). This document offered a response to the secretary-general's report on *Peacebuilding in the Aftermath of Conflict* (United Nations 2012). The document proposed a normative set of principles for organizations when working with young people as partners in their peacebuilding initiatives and in the development of youth-sensitive peacebuilding policies and programs. Second, the UNOY Peacebuilders published another key document, *Agreed Language on Youth, Peace and Security*, in 2013. This document analyzed the reference to young women and men in the U.N. General Assembly and the Security Council resolutions from the perspective of youth-led peacebuilding organizations and has publicly asked for a Security Council resolution on YPS. Third, the *Amman Youth Declaration* was the outcome of the Global Youth Forum hosted by Jordan in 2015. Youth-led peacebuilding organizations drafted this document after consulting over eleven thousand young women and men around the world. Lastly, just a month after the Global Youth Forum, youth-led peacebuilding organizations were involved in shaping The Global Youth Summit against Violent Extremism with the support of the White House and the U.S. Department of State (UNOY Peacebuilders 2015c). This event was critical for getting the support of a permanent member of the Security Council for a resolution on youth.

Youth-led peacebuilding organizations took small but strategically important steps for mobilizing political support for the YPS agenda. Youth-led peacebuilding organizations alone were neither powerful nor connected enough to shift or influence the policy orientation of the Security Council on youth-related issues. Yet through building strategic partnerships with civil society organizations and informal alliances with relatively young U.N. staff, youth-led peacebuilding organizations initiated a political process. The outcome of this political process challenged the global securitization of youth, which has been the dominant approach of counterterrorism policies for almost two decades.

To push for the adoption of UNSCR 2250, youth-led peacebuilding drew on the urgency of the international community to respond to the challenge posed by violent extremist groups. While the number of attacks committed by the Islamic State (ISIS) in Iraq and Levant increased between 2012 and 2015 (Miller 2016), member states with veto powers were unable to reach a consensus to respond to these attacks at that time (von Einsiedel, Malone, and Ugarte 2015). These divisions among member states of the Security Council provided a justification for youth-led peacebuilding organizations to push for an inclusion-oriented youth agenda. This opportunity was intentionally and cautiously employed by youth-led peacebuilding organizations to be recognized as new actors in the international peace and security platforms. During this process, youth-led peacebuilding organizations capitalized upon member states' interest in developing more comprehensive approaches to countering and preventing violent extremism to insert a new narrative—that is, "youth as peacebuilders."

Youth-led peacebuilding organizations did not detach themselves from global counterterrorism policies but rather sought to compromise with, engage, and build communications to challenge member states and U.N. agencies to transform securitized approaches to youth agency. Since global counterterrorism policy frameworks are being used by national governments to justify their arbitrary actions to target young people and youth-led peacebuilding organizations, they are unsurprisingly interested in transforming these policies and frameworks (Thapa 2017). Their interest is not necessarily driven by a grand political strategy to challenge the securitization of the entire peacebuilding, development, or humanitarian fields but rather shaped by their lived experiences of injustice in their communities due to already existing securitization practices of states and counterterrorism policies. This motivated youth organizations to walk a fine line between advocating for the recognition of youth peacebuilding agency and being instrumentalized by the political elite for the revitalization of failed, costly, and damaging counterterrorism projects. Consequently, young people in general, and youth-led organizations more specifically, entered into a complex relationship with global peace and security policies as new actors.

Youth-led peacebuilding organizations strategized to maneuver between policy orientations (peacebuilding and counterterrorism) with conflicting visions on youth agency. This goal evolved through the years in the advocacy strategies of the UNOY Peacebuilders (2012, 2015b). Through maneuvering between the complex relationships among actors with diverse interests in youth as a social category, youth-led peacebuilding organizations reached their goal to shift the dominant narrative on youth from "victim" or "perpetrator" of violence to "youth as peacebuilders."

This new characterization of "youth as peacebuilders" is being considered as a counternarrative tool against violent extremism by a number of member states and counterterrorism institutions and even some youth-led peacebuilding organizations themselves. However, the essential value of UNSCR 2250 lies in its ability to legitimize young people's demands to challenge and contest top-down international counterterrorism policies and transform state-society relations.

Considering UNSCR 2250 from this perspective demonstrates the agency of youth-led peacebuilding organizations to challenge the global securitization of youth rather than passively accept the stereotypes promoted through securitized approaches of counterterrorism policies. The emergence of the new narrative of "youth as peacebuilder" and the YPS agenda in this respect thus represent a sort of resistance that is promoted by youth-led peacebuilding organizations themselves.

The success of youth-led peacebuilding organizations' resistance against global securitization is noticeable when the text of UNSCR 2419 is compared to the text of UNSCR 2250. The second resolution on the YPS agenda—UNSCR 2419, adopted in 2018—mentions the term *violent extremism* only once and predominantly focuses on the inclusion of young people in formal peace processes. While this change was welcomed by some member states, some members of the council pushed back against it. The division among member states was observable at the Security Council meeting on the adoption of UNSCR 2419: "The United States regrets, however, that the resolution did not contain language on preventing violent extremism. This concept is not new, and it should not be controversial" (United Nations Security Council 2018). Despite such pushbacks from member states bent on linking the YPS and PVE agendas, the YPS agenda is currently being directed by the U.N. Security Council toward the participation and inclusion of young people in formal peace processes.

Youth inclusion in formal peace processes remains a limited but increasingly recognized vital aspect of youth's engagement in peacebuilding. UNSCR 2419 opens a significant space for youth-led peacebuilding organizations to influence criminal justice and security sector processes in the context of peace processes. Thus such normative arguments may significantly help youth-led peacebuilding organizations to resist securitization practices in conflict-affected countries. Inclusion in formalized political settings may help youth-led peacebuilding organizations to shape the state security apparatus and reform criminal justice processes as well (Altiok and Grizelj 2019).

It is, nevertheless, important to recognize that this shift in focus from PVE to formal peace processes may engender new problems. The issues attached to formal peace processes are almost exclusively focused on the conflict-affected countries of the Global South, which limits the YPS agenda's scope. Maintaining this narrower role as a field centered on formal peace processes may decrease the universality of this agenda. This could result in the creation of roadblocks for youth-led peace-building organizations seeking to invoke UNSCR 2250 as a policy tool for challenging securitization in the Global North. These potential hurdles notwithstanding, the adoption of UNSCR 2419, with its focus on formal peace processes, constitutes another important political win for youth-led peacebuilding organizations looking to distance the YPS agenda from the securitized nature of the PVE agenda at global peace and security platforms.

It is also worth noting that reforming the behavior of law enforcement institutions or making criminal justice systems more transparent is not always sufficient to resist securitization when state institutions operate as the repressive apparatuses used by the financial elite to maintain their privilege (Giroux 2016). As such, a fundamental component of efforts to contest securitization is the exposure and subsequent reversal of corrupt relationships between the security apparatus of the state and the financial elite. Such challenges are echoed in youth protests and dissent that seek to challenge corruption, nepotism, elitism, favoritism, and tribalism across the world. Although these activities of youth-led peacebuilding organizations and movements may be brutally pushed back by the violence of the state, demands for justice continue to be expressed as efforts to contest the global securitization of youth at all levels.

From Right Holder to Rights Defender

A squeezed youth-led peacebuilding agency emerged in between the opposing stereotypical narratives on youth that were promoted by the peacebuilding and counterterrorism agendas. This tension offered a political opportunity for youth-led peacebuilding organizations to shift the dominant narrative on "youth as victims" and "youth as perpetrators" of violence to a positive narrative: "youth as peacebuilders." This is a political win for those seeking to resist and counter the global securitization of youth. Young people have had a say and will continue to have a say on whether they are securitized or empowered in the international peace and security policy developments on youth. Youth-led peacebuilding organizations do not have a seat at the U.N. Security Council, but they have insights and strategies to resist global securitization.

Young people have raised their voice against arms trafficking to Pakistan; they have worked to rebuild the trust between state and society through penetrating criminal justice reform processes in Cameroon; they have opened the civic space to question corruption in South Sudan; and they have protected democratic values from the hegemony of corporate interest in the United States. Youth-led peace-building agency motivated by personal experience of injustice aims to tackle the most systemic problems of global securitization by speaking truth to power. All these activities demonstrate the agency of youth-led peacebuilding organizations and youth movements' struggles to exercise their rights and freedoms.

Youth-led peacebuilding resists securitization mainly at the community level, but it is also able to resist the influence of securitized approaches at national and international levels through strategic political actions. This multilevel dimension of youth agency manifests itself through its ability to relate very personal experiences of injustice to the global securitization of young people. This expertise and strength of youth also resist the violence of the state security apparatus.

Understanding, valuing, and protecting this multilevel resistance to securitization also offers an important critique of the protection pillars for action of the UNSCR 2250. This pillar of the resolution focuses almost exclusively on the protection of young people from violence. The peacebuilding agency of youth-led organizations and movements, on the other hand, indicates that it is the protection of civic spaces, rights, and freedoms that matters most to advance the YPS agenda. As Simpson (2018) rightly noted, the conversation on protection needs to move .from youth as "right-holder to human rights defender" (103–104). In practice, this requires mainstreaming "the rights and participation of young people into the work of the human rights treaty bodies, special procedures and other human rights mechanisms" (122) to tackle and reverse the global securitization of young people.

When it comes to scholarship, there is a need to (re)insert the agency of young people into the debate on the global securitization of youth. The expression of youth agency incorporates linkages between global securitization policies and young people's lived experiences of injustices resulting from these global processes. Across the world, young people are contesting the expansion of securitized approaches that are uncritically imposed under the umbrella of counterterrorism measures. Yet their ability to resist through maneuvering between these competing priorities of global policy agendas—namely, between peacebuilding and counterterrorism—remains extremely limited. Many of these youth are in fact not immune to the risk of co-optation and may even face brutal state repression of their political actions in the civil society arena. Additional scholarly efforts need to be directed toward investigating the role and agency of young people in protecting the human rights and fundamental freedoms that are conducive to peace and peacebuilding.

Denying or overlooking young people's agency in resisting securitization—or worse, stereotyping young people as passive or helpless to oppose global securitization trends—just adds additional obstacles to building broad-based peace and justice movements. As a global youth-led peacebuilding movement, #Youth4Peace should be regarded as an opportunity to challenge the problematic securitization of peace and peacebuilding.

REFERENCES

Abu-Nimer, Mohammed. 2018. "Alternative Approaches to Transforming Violent Extremism: The Case of Islamic Peace and Interreligious Peacebuilding." In *Transformative Approaches to Violent Extremism*. Berghof Handbook Dialogue Series no. 13, edited by Beatrix Austin and Hans J. Giessmann, 1–23. Berlin: Berghof Foundation.

Altiok, Ali, and Irena Grizelj. 2019. *We Are Here: An Integrated Approach to Youth Inclusive Peace Processes*. New York: Office of the Secretary-General's Envoy on Youth, 2020.

www.un.org/youthenvoy/wp-content/uploads/2019/07/Global-Policy-Paper-Youth
-Participation-in-Peace-Processes.pdf.

Aware Girls and CRY. 2014. "Young Peacebuilders Condemn Taliban Attack on Peshawar School." Accessed April 29, 2020. https://unoyadvocacy.wordpress.com/2014/12/17/young -peacebuilders-condemn-taliban-attack-on-peshawar-school/.

Balla, Loruba, and Woja Emmanuel. 2018. "Cleaning Takes Center Stage towards Peace Celebration." *Juba Monitor*, October 29, 2018. www.jubamonitor.com/cleaning-takes-center -stage-towards-peace-celebrations/.

Choucri, Nazli. 1974. *Population Dynamics and International Violence: Propositions, Insights, and Evidence*. Lexington, Mass.: Lexington Books.

Evans, Brad, and Henry Armand Giroux. 2015. "The War on Terror Is a War on Youth: Paris and the Impoverishment of the Future." *Truthout*, November 24, 2015. https://truthout .org/articles/the-war-on-terror-is-a-war-on-youth-paris-and-the-impoverishment-of -the-future/.

Giroux, Henry Armand. 2016. *America's Addiction to Terrorism*. New York: Monthly Review Press.

Hendrixson, Anne. 2004. "Angry Young Men, Veiled Young Women: Constructing a New Population Threat." *Corner House Briefing* 34 (December): 1–16. www.thecornerhouse.org .uk/sites/thecornerhouse.org.uk/files/34veiled.pdf.

Hogg, David. 2018. "The Transcript of David Hogg's March for Our Lives Speech Will Bring Tears to Your Eyes." Bustle, March 24, 2018. www.bustle.com/p/the-transcript-of-david -hoggs-march-for-our-lives-speech-will-bring-tears-to-your-eyes-8596305.

Huntington, Samuel Philipps. 1997. *The Clash of Civilizations and the Remaking of World Order*. New Delhi: Penguin.

Keen, David, and Larry Attree. 2015. "Dilemmas of Counter-terror, Stabilisation and Statebuilding: A Discussion Paper." Saferworld. Accessed June 19, 2019. www.saferworld.org .uk/downloads/pubdocs/dilemmas-of-counter-terror-stabilisation-and-statebuilding .pdf.

Maira, Sunaina. 2016. *The 9/11 Generation: Youth, Rights, and Solidarity in the War on Terror*. New York: New York University Press.

Miller, Erin. 2016. *Patterns of Islamic State-Related Terrorism, 2002–2015*. START. www.start .umd.edu/pubs/START_IslamicStateTerrorismPatterns_BackgroundReport_Aug2016.pdf.

Moller, Herbert. 1968. "Youth as a Force in the Modern World." *Comparative Studies and History* 10, no. 3 (April): 237–260. www.jstor.org/stable/177801.

Muncie, John. 2004. *Youth and Crime*, 2nd ed. London: Sage.

Neyzi, Leyla. 2001. "Object or Subject? The Paradox of 'Youth' in Turkey." *International Journal of Middle Eastern Studies* 33, no. 3, 411–432.

Nordås, Ragnhild, and Christian Davenport. 2013. "Fight the Youth: Youth Bulges and State Repression." *American Journal of Political Science* 57, no. 4 (April): 926–940. https://doi.org/ 10.1111/ajps.12025.

Norway in the United Nations. 2017. "Group of Friends of Preventing Violent Extremism." Accessed March 31, 2019. www.norway.no/en/missions/un/news/news-from-norwayun/ PVE/.

Novelli, Mario. 2017. "Education and Countering Violent Extremism: Western Logics from South to North?" *Compare: A Journal of Comparative and International Education* 47, no. 6 (July), 835–851. https://doi.org/10.1080/03057925.2017.1341301.

Nwaozuzu, Ijechi. 2018. "Security Council Open Debate on Youth, Peace and Security." Accessed June 19, 2019. www.peacewomen.org/security-council/security-council-open -debate-youth-peace-and-security-april-2018.

Obama, Barack. 2015. "Remarks by the President at the Summit on Countering Violent Extremism." The White House Summit on Countering Violent Extremism in Washington,

D.C. Accessed March 31, 2019. https://obamawhitehouse.archives.gov/the-press-office/2015/02/19/remarks-president-summit-countering-violent-extremism-february-19-2015.

OSGEY (Office of the Secretary-General's Envoy on Youth). 2015. "Jordan to Convene a Security Council Ministerial Debate on the Role of Youth in Countering Violent Extremism and Promoting Peace." Office of the Secretary-General's Envoy on Youth. Accessed June 19, 2019. www.un.org/youthenvoy/2015/04/jordan-convene-security-council-ministerial-debate-role-youth-countering-violent-extremism-promoting-peace/.

Patel, Tina. 2013. "Ethnic Deviant Labels within a Terror-Panic Context: Excusing White Deviance." *Ethnicity and Race in a Changing World* 4, no. 1 (Autumn): 34–49. https://doi.org/10.7227/ERCW.4.1.3.

Simpson, Graeme. 2018. *The Missing Peace: Independent Progress Study on Youth, Peace and Security.* UNFPA. www.youth4peace.info/ProgressStudysecurity. (URL inactive.)

Sommers, Marc. 2019. *Youth and the Field of Countering Violent Extremism.* Washington, D.C.: Promundo-US. https://promundoglobal.org/wp-content/uploads/2019/01/Youth_Violent_Extemism.pdf.

Sukarieh, Mayssoun, and Stuart Tannock. 2015. *Youth Rising? The Politics of Youth in the Global Economy.* New York: Routledge.

———. 2017. "The Global Securitisation of Youth." *Third World Quarterly* 39, no. 5 (September): 854–870. https://doi.org/10.1080/01436597.2017.1369038.

Thapa, R. 2017. *Mapping a Sector: Bridging the Evidence Gap on Youth-Driven Peacebuilding.* The Hague: UNOY Peacebuilders and SFCG. http://unoy.org/wp-content/uploads/Mapping-a-Sector-Bridging-the-Evidence-Gap-on-Youth-Driven-Peacebuilding.pdf.

United Nations. 2012. *Peacebuilding in the Aftermath of Conflict,* A/67/499 and S/2012/746. www.un.org/ga/search/view_doc.asp?symbol=A/67/499.

———. 2018. *The Youth, Peace and Security Agenda, toward Sustaining Peace and Preventing Violent Extremism.* United Nations Secretary-General. New York. Accessed March 31, 2019. www.un.org/sg/en/content/sg/remarks-sg-team/2018-09-28/remarks-youth-peace-and-security-agenda-towards-sustaining.

United Nations General Assembly. 2015. *Plan of Action to Prevent Violent Extremism,* A/70/674. New York. Accessed January 5, 2021. www.undocs.org/pdf?symbol=en/A/70/674.

United Nations Security Council. 2018. *8277th Security Council Meeting: Maintenance of International Peace and Security.* New York. Accessed March 31, 2019. www.unmultimedia.org/avlibrary/asset/2170/2170458/.

UNOY Peacebuilders. 2012. "Strategy of Global Youth Advocacy Team." Unpublished manuscript, The Hague.

———. 2013. *Agreed Language on Youth, Peace and Security.* The Hague: UNOY Peacebuilders. http://unoy.org/wp-content/uploads/2015/03/Agreed-UN-Language-on-Youth-Participation-in-Peacebuilding-2-FLAT.pdf.

———. 2015a. *Amman Youth Declaration.* March 31, 2019. http://unoy.org/en/amman-youth-declaration/.

———. 2015b. "Strategy of the Global Youth Advocacy Team." Unpublished manuscript, The Hague.

———. 2015c. *Youth Advocacy Team at the Global Youth Summit against Violent Extremism.* March 31, 2019. http://unoy.org/en/youth-advocacy-team-at-the-global-youth-summit-against-violent-extremism/.

Urdal, Henrik. 2006. "A Clash of Generations? Youth Bulges and Political Violence." *International Studies Quarterly* 50, no. 3 (September): 607–629. https://doi.org/10.1111/j.1468-2478.2006.00416.x.

U.S. Department of State. 2015. "Countering Violent Extremism." Accessed March 31, 2019. www.state.gov/j/cve/.

von Einsiedel, Sebastian, David M. Malone, and Bruno Stagno Ugarte. 2015. "The UN Security Council in an Age of Great Power Rivalry." United Nations University Working Paper, no. 4. February 2015. Tokyo. https://collections.unu.edu/eserv/UNU:6112/UNSCAgeofPowerRivalry.pdf.

Working Group Youth and Peacebuilding. 2012. "Guiding Principles on Young People's Participation in Peacebuilding." Accessed June 19, 2019. http://unoy.org/wp-content/uploads/Guiding-Principles.pdf.

PART III

Prevention

CHAPTER 5

Lost in Translation?

YOUTH EMPLOYMENT AND PEACEBUILDING— FROM POLICY TO PROGRAMS

Valeria Izzi

In the prevalent peacebuilding discourse, job creation for youth is seen as both a short-term stabilization tool to generate "quick wins" and a long-term peace-building strategy to create more stable, cohesive, and resilient societies. While youth-employment programs and projects[1] vary greatly in terms of scope, target, and ambition, they share a common rationale: young people should be provided with jobs and opportunities in order to harness their energy toward peace instead of violence.

The extent to which these programs have made a difference is a matter of spec-ulation: evaluations—when they are carried out at all—usually focus on outputs (e.g., number of young people trained or number of short-term jobs created) and stand clear of the tricky topic of the impact of long-term peacebuilding. Even so, there is little ground for optimism. Examples of success stories are hard to come by, and there are emerging accounts of interventions unintentionally "doing harm" by reinforcing frustration, disillusionment, and existing dynamics of marginal-ization and exclusion (NSRP 2014; Sikenyi 2017; Sommers 2015).

Yet the mantra of "youth employment for peacebuilding" remains unquestioned among donors and international agencies alike. This unwavering belief (seemingly at odds with the emphasis on evidence-based programming and aid effectiveness) can only be understood in light of the evocative power conveyed by images of large cohorts of unemployed young people. The perceived threat of idle youth has long been represented through metaphors such as "deadly time bomb" or "social dyna-mite." More recently, this scaremongering narrative has been outshined by a much more celebratory image of youth as an "opportunity" or "untapped resource" with the potential to drastically reshape the future of the Global South.

Whether young people are feared as "breakers" or celebrated as "makers" (Hon-wana and De Boeck 2005), the transmission mechanisms from unemployment to violence remain scarcely understood. The dominant intervention paradigm assumes a simple causal relation between labor market status and the propensity for violent mobilization—in spite of compelling evidence of this correlation being far more complex.

U.N. Security Council Resolution (UNSCR) 2250 (2015) lists the provision of employment and vocational training opportunities for youth among the policies that are needed to "positively contribute to peacebuilding efforts" (par. 11). *The Missing Peace: Independent Progress Study on Youth, Peace and Security* debunks many of the myths frequently associated with the "youth unemployment and violence" discourse, effectively catching up with over a decade of evolving reflection by scholars and practitioners (Simpson 2018). This acknowledgment of complexity is an important first step toward more evidence-based and effective programming. Still, for policy to translate into meaningful impact, a reflection is needed on what has hampered success so far—starting with the essential (but still largely unaddressed) question of what the "success" of a youth-employment program looks like from a peacebuilding perspective.

This chapter explores how employment fits within the overall discourse and practice around youth, peace, and security and the role that labor-related factors play in relation to the securitization of youth. It investigates how youth unemployment—and its identified solution, employment creation for youth—is discursively constructed at the policy level within the peace and security agenda, from early accounts of youth unemployment as a security threat to the inclusion of youth employment as part of the prevention pillar of UNSCR 2250 (2015). The chapter further analyzes the extent to which the elements of this discursive construction are retained in the translation from policy to programmatic interventions,[2] focusing, in particular, on exploring the related questions of program rationale (why youth?) and targeting (which youth?) and how these play out in the measurement of impact.

THE SECURITIZATION OF YOUTH (UN)EMPLOYMENT: A BRIEF POLICY OVERVIEW

Given the hype that surrounds the discourse on youth employment in peacebuilding today, one may be excused for forgetting that this focus is relatively recent. Seminal documents like the U.N. secretary-general's *An Agenda for Peace* (U.N. 1992) or its supplement (U.N. 1995) all but failed to mention youth or make any reference to unemployment even in passing.[3]

Things drastically changed in the intervening decade. In 2001, the *UN Secretary-General's Report on the Prevention of Armed Conflict* dedicated a full paragraph to the risk of "young people with limited education and few employment opportunities" and little hope for the future, providing "fertile recruiting ground for parties to a conflict"—particularly in countries with "a 'youth bulge', a population comprised of [a] large number of youth compared to other age groups" (U.N. 2001, 29). Three years later, *A More Secure World: Our Shared Responsibility*, a report by the High-Level Panel on Threats, Challenges and Change, pointed to youth unemployment as both a cause of violence and a consequence of failed postconflict peacebuilding, potentially leading to further violence. The report compellingly quoted a woman who, during the panel's consultation with civil society organizations in Africa, wondered, "How have we let what should be our greatest asset, youth, become a threat to our security?" (U.N. 2004, 26).

This high profiling of youth unemployment has different roots. Much of the initial momentum came from West Africa, where conflicts in the 1990s have been famously dubbed "crises of youth" (Richards 1995, 1996; Peters 2011). A much-quoted 2005 report by the United Nations Office for West Africa, titled *Youth Unemployment and Regional Insecurity in West Africa*, characterizes youth unemployment as a "ticking bomb" for the region and job creation as "a key tool for conflict prevention" (2005, 8).

The terrorist attacks of September 9, 2001, and their aftermath reinforced the focus on youth unemployment as a possible explanation for violent radicalization (Bagchi and Paul 2018; Ismail and Amjad 2014), strengthening the policy case for youth employment as a way to "win hearts and minds" in countries targeted by the war on terror (Fishstein and Wilder 2012) and as a preventive strategy in regions considered at risk of violent extremism (Aldrich 2014). In a 2014 address to the United Nations, then U.S. president Barack Obama cited the jobless young as vulnerable to extremist ideology, identifying investments to support entrepreneurship as "the best antidote to violence" (Mercy Corps 2015, 16).

Finally, the Arab Spring brought to the world's attention the plight of young people in North Africa and the Middle East (Murphy 2012). Contrary to the assumption that a "lack of education" went hand-in-hand with a "lack of employment opportunities," rates of youth unemployment in the region are exceptionally high even among those with higher education, trapping Arab youth "in a liminal phase of pre-adulthood" (Muldering 2013, 4). The Arab uprising showed the potential for youth activism to be a nonviolent force for democratic change—but also contributed to igniting fears of the disruptive potential of youth anger and frustration as well as the risk of youth protests to be hijacked by radical agendas (LaGraffe 2012; Bradley 2012; Chamkhi 2014).

These diverse roots converged into shaping the dominant policy narratives of youth unemployment as a security risk. While it is undeniable that an overwhelming number of young people around the globe are struggling to access decent work, the price to pay for making youth employment a policy priority has been a "blanket securitization of economically marginal youth" (Enria, n.d., 2). This has a number of important consequences—including the prevalent gender bias in the policy and practice of youth employment (reflecting the notion of young men as dangerous troublemakers) and the frequent conflation of the overall category of (male) youth with that of combatants or former combatants (in spite of the fact that, in any conflict, combatants only account for a small portion of the youth population).

Not surprisingly, these biases trickle down from policy to programs, resulting in a tendency for programs to prioritize young men (Simpson 2018, 15) and, among them, those who have been previously involved with violence. A review of youth employment projects carried out by the Youth Employment Network in West Africa found that a significant percentage of interventions generically labeled as "youth employment" in postconflict countries targeted primarily (or exclusively) former combatants; in Liberia, it was over half of all the projects surveyed (Lopes and Pasipanodya 2008, 8).

UNSCR 2250 and the Missing Peace Report

In recent years, policy narratives on youth have gained both nuance and optimism. UNSCR 2250, adopted in December 2015, embodies the shift from the image of youth as perpetrators of violence to that of youth as peacebuilders and agents of positive social change. Under its prevention pillars for action, the resolution stresses the importance of "youth employment opportunities and vocational training" as well as "youth entrepreneurship" among the policy measures that would enable youth to "positively contribute to peacebuilding efforts" (par. 11). However, most of the substantive focus on employment is in relation to the disengagement and reintegration of former combatants, where the need for "evidence-based and gender-sensitive youth employment opportunities" is stressed (par. 17). The way in which this is positioned in the resolution perpetuates the misleading conflation between youth and former combatants and misses the opportunity to encourage a more in-depth reflection on the needs and priorities of noncombatant (male and female) youth.

The Missing Peace study, released in March 2018, provides an overdue debunking of common myths and assumptions about youth, offering a cautionary tale about the counterproductive impact of policy panic around youth bulges and reframing youth as a diverse and sometimes divided "microcosm of wider society" rather than a homogenous category (Simpson 2018, 4). The report addresses the long-standing gender bias in depictions of youth, recognizing the fundamentally gendered nature of youth as a transition phase and warning against the reliance on stereotypes of "young men as violent predators or potential spoilers of peace" and "young women . . . as passive victims at best, or invisible at worst" (5).

In relation to employment, the report deplores the fact that "in large part, peace and security programming and policies continue to be driven by a widely presumed causal relationship between youth unemployment and violence," while, in fact, "there is little reliable evidence for a correlation, let alone causation" between the two (13). Other important factors need to enter the equation—including the way in which violent conflict may be explained by "experiences of horizontal inequality and identity-based factors" (13). While postconflict job creation is undoubtedly important, it should not be viewed as a silver bullet: a key message of the report is the need to go beyond jobs, seeing employment as only one piece of the puzzle in solving young people's exclusion.

From "Youth as Threat" to "Youth as Opportunity"—Plus Ça Change?

The emerging focus on youth as peacebuilders can be situated in the context of a more general turn toward optimism in the development discourse of governments and international agencies. Young people are presented as a resource, a country's most important asset and hope for the future (Sukarieh and Tannock 2008). Investing in young people is seen not just as "the right thing to do" but also as a good value for the money; they can generate significant social and economic returns, thus maximizing aid effectiveness (Pereznieto and Harding 2013, 1). Urban youth, long "condemned as a lost generation of deprived, restless agents of lawlessness," are now celebrated as resilient, creative, flexible catalysts of development (Dolan and Rajak 2016, 514).

This cheerful attitude is not without its critics. It has been argued that the call to look at youth through rose-colored glasses (Meagher 2016, 484) is ultimately not about youth at all but rather about incorporating youth as willing and enthusiast participants of the neoliberal project and instrumentally using them as a political construction and rhetorical frame to deflect attention from structural inequalities (Sukarieh and Tannock 2008, 2014, 2018).

At a closer look, there is significant continuity between the apparently antithetic labels of "youth as threat" and "youth as opportunity." In both cases, youth remains a "black box"; it is not contextually understood in its plurality or acknowledged in its agency. Young people are to be either "mobilized" (by violence entrepreneurs) or "capitalized upon" (by the private sector, governments, donors, or nongovernment organizations [NGOs]): in both cases, the key agency resides outside the realm of youth. Gender-wise, the "youth as threat" narrative refers almost exclusively to young men, seen as the most at risk for violent recruitment, while the "youth as resource" narrative calls for significantly scaled-up investments in girls and young women because they offer the greatest returns and value for money—an argument that has become popularly known as the "girl effect" (Chaaban and Cunningham 2011; Hickel 2014; Sumberg and Hunt 2019).

Discourses on youth share many of the characteristics of what in gender studies is called "essentialism"—that is, the belief that certain categories have an underlying "true nature" or "essence" that gives them their identity and is responsible for intragroup similarities that transcend differences (Cornwall, Harrison, and Whitehead 2007). Examples of essentialism can be found in peace studies, where women are depicted as naturally peaceful by virtue of their role as mothers, spouses, and caretakers (El-Bouchra 2007); environmental studies, where women are seen as "mothers of the earth" and intrinsically closer to nature (Leach 2007); and governance studies, where women are often seen as inherently less corrupted than men (Goetz 2007).

Feminist scholars have vocally criticized the stereotype of women as "vulnerable" and "virtuous" and more generally the "unreflective use of the term 'women' as if it describes a pre-determined interest group with shared concerns" (Cornwall, Harrison, and Whitehead 2007, 14). Similar considerations can be made for youth narratives, including the discursive rescue of youth from the realm of "threat" and its glorification as an "opportunity" (Sumberg and Hunt 2019). Just like the "gender discourse," the "youth discourse" shows an evident pressure to "simplify, sloganize and create narratives with the 'power to move'" (Cornwall, Harrison, and Whitehead 2007, 13), resorting to "sound bites," "short, punchy messages preferably accompanied by seductive statistics" that have the power to mobilize attention and funding but end up creating "a fictional object of study or a category of analysis based on uncritical monolithic and ahistorical assumptions and cultural clichés" (Della Faille 2011, 226).

In the case of youth, these "seductive statistics" have often to do with unemployment data. While often unreliable, these figures have an undeniable mobilizing power. Undoubtedly, data and statistics about youth unemployment have proved their worth in generating compelling narratives with the "power to move." There are, however, major problems about these data-powered narratives, starting with the fact that they are not really about "youth" or "unemployment"—at least not in the sense in which these terms are conventionally understood.

"Youth"? "Unemployment"? A Quest for Analytical Clarity

Essentialist thinking about youth—be it in its original form of "youth as threat" or in its more recent incarnation of "youth as opportunity"—represents an essential component of the securitization of youth (un)employment. Policies and programs about job creation for youth in fragile settings are predicated on the two concepts of "youth" (as a demographic group that can be separated, for both analytical and practical purposes, from the population at large) and "unemployment" (as a defined status related to participation in the labor market). As I briefly discuss in this section, both notions are inherently problematic.

Much has been written about "youth" as a transition phase that is socially constructed, has less to do with age than with status and behavior, and is intrinsically linked with rites of passage of some kind (UNDP 2006). It is also widely recognized that in many parts of the world, young people are finding it increasingly difficult to negotiate their transition to adulthood and are instead "stuck" in an enduring youth limbo (Sommers 2012). Employment plays an important role both as a milestone in its own right and as an enabler of other forms of transition to adulthood, such as moving out of the parental home and starting one's own family (UNDP 2006; Batmanglich and Enria 2014).

Age-based definitions are a necessarily imperfect proxy to capture the complexity of this transition—yet from the perspective of policy making and related interventions, they are hard to do without. The phenomenon of youth as a stalled transition has been reflected in a "stretching" of the age brackets conventionally associated with the term. For statistical consistency among member states, the U.N. defines youth as the section of the population between the ages of fifteen and twenty-four; however, many governments around the world have adopted far more extensive classifications. This trend is particularly evident in Africa: at the regional level, the 2006 African Youth Charter defines youth as any individual between the age of fifteen and thirty-five; most African governments have followed suit. But if the attainment of full adulthood is dependent on external socioeconomic and political conditions, there is of course no guarantee that these conditions will fall into place on one's thirty-fifth birthday. Louisa Enria notes that during her fieldwork in Sierra Leone, it was not uncommon to encounter individuals well above the official threshold of thirty-five years of age who would still define themselves as "youth" while also feeling a sense of shame for the absence of status and resources that prevented them from meeting social expectations of adulthood (Enria 2018, 116).

Gender norms, values, and practices often "stretch" the youth category for males while "shrinking" it for females. Cultural practices of early marriage and/ or early motherhood inevitably shorten girls' period of transition (Gebremariam 2017). Maurice Sikenyi describes teenage mothers' frustrations of not being able to qualify for participation in Kenya's Youth Enterprise Development Fund (YEDF)[4] by virtue of not being socially regarded as "young" (Sikenyi 2017, 133).

What follows is that the so-called unemployed youth are not necessarily "young" in a conventional (age-based) sense. Neither, in fact, are they "unemployed"—at least if we apply the official definition of unemployment as "the share of the workforce without work but available for and seeking employment" (ILO 2011).[5] The notion of "employed" and "unemployed" as neatly distinct and mutually exclusive categories does not reflect the experience of a large part of the population in the Global South. Rather than being inactive, young (and less young) individuals are eking out a living in a variety of precarious economic activities in the informal sector (Mallet, Atim, and Opio 2017, 3). These creative attempts—variedly termed "hustling" (Munive 2010; Thieme 2013) or "straining" (Finn and Oldfield 2015)—are as far as they can be from the mobilizing narratives on youth idleness.

Beyond semantics, reconsidering the meanings of "youth" and "unemployment" has crucial implications for policy making and programming. It is one thing to design interventions aimed at keeping teenagers busy and out of trouble; it is a completely different thing to design a comprehensive agenda to lift people in their thirties from the hopelessness of low-quality jobs and the social shame of a stalled transition.

Beyond Unemployment: Unpacking the Relation between Labor Market Status and Violence

While the idea of a causal link between youth unemployment and violence has proved a powerful mobilizer of policy attention and funding, there is no evidence of straightforward correlation—let alone causality (Cramer 2010; Holmes, McCord, and Hagen-Zanker 2013). The notion that poor, unemployed youth are more likely to be violent is "intuitive but analytically reductive" (Enria 2018, 216), representing "the triumph of theory and intuition over evidence" (Blattman 2010, 3).

It follows from the discussion in the previous section that a focus on "unemployment" is likely to miss the point; rather, it is labor market status that matters *in some way*. Two main lines of analysis have emerged in an attempt to broaden and deepen this reflection—focusing, respectively, on the quality of jobs as a more relevant variable compared to the simple employment/unemployment dichotomy and on the dynamics of job access and distribution.

"Bad Jobs" as a Possible Cause of Violence

Writing about the prevalence of informal and precarious work for youth in Egypt, Ghada Barsoum notes that youth unemployment rates continue to be seen as the main yardstick to measure youth well-being and economic integration—while in fact bad jobs, as "traps of poverty and precariousness," could be a more useful lens to understand the emergence of the Arab Spring (2016, 430–431).

The experience of most young people in the Global South is not one of idleness but rather one of chronic job insecurity, an absence of workers' rights, long (and often unpaid) hours, and little or no prospects of upward mobility (Mallet and Atim 2014).[6] If one accepts the hypothesis of "bad work"—that is, work that is "precarious, underpaid and exploitative" (Mallet, Atim, and Opio 2017)—as a possible explanation for violence, the policy and practice implications for the peacebuilding agenda are enormous. The real "elephant in the room," in this regard, is the role of the informal economy in postconflict and other fragile settings.

In development circles, informal economies used to have a bad name, and high levels of informality in the Global South have traditionally been considered a burden to economic growth. More recently, though, informality has been reevaluated as a hidden engine for innovation (World Bank 2013; Kraemer-Mbula and

Wunsch-Vincent 2016). This comeback of informality has proceeded in parallel with the discursive reframing of the youth workforce as an untapped resource and as entrepreneurial "job creators" rather than hapless "job seekers." There are concerns that this double shift may lead governments and donors to put less focus on the need to understand how the labor market actually works (Mallet, Atim, and Opio 2017, 5), in turn increasing the vulnerability of youth and their "adverse incorporation" into the economic system (Meagher 2016).

The role of informality in development is a highly complex topic, and there are compelling arguments on both sides of the debate to which this chapter cannot do justice. What should be noted, however, is that in postconflict settings, the majority of activities in the informal economy tend to be small scale and only profitable enough to ensure subsistence, and moreover, the borders between the "legal" and "illegal" sectors are blurred, with the conflict economy casting its shadow well past the signing of peace agreements.

Contrary to the widespread assumptions that young people "prefer" to be self-employed entrepreneurs, studies have shown that self-employment is often a constrained choice, "grounded less in any sort of inherent aspiration to become an entrepreneur, and more in the young people's negative experiences of employment" and the dearth of available opportunities for decent salaried work (Mallet and Atim 2014, 32–33).

From a programming perspective, there is a very concrete trade-off between quality and quantity: if emphasis is put on "decent" jobs, it is likely that the scale of job creation would remain relatively small (Jütersonke and Kobayashi 2015, 22). Yet if we accept the argument that bad jobs are potentially conflict inducing, inadequate attention to the quality of job creation, at the expense of quantity, can at best be ineffective for stabilization and peacebuilding and at worst backfire.

Inequality in Access to Jobs as a Possible Cause of Violence

It has been argued that the determinant factor in the individual's choice to fight may not be one's own employment situation in isolation but instead may be how this is perceived in relation to the wider societal context (Mercy Corps 2015). Thus horizontal inequalities in access to the labor market can hold more explanatory power in relation to violence than unemployment statistics (Stewart 2012).[7]

One implication of this is the need for a better understanding of the role played by networks, connections, and power dynamics in accessing jobs in the context of labor markets as social institutions (Solow 1990; Zweig 2015).[8] Louisa Enria writes at length about the relation between "connectocracy" and employment in Sierra Leone and the way in which "exclusion from redistributive networks with powerful big people (sababu) determined young people's perceptions of themselves in relation to social hierarchies defined by socio-economic status" (2018, 113). To further complicate things, in postconflict settings, networks of redistribution tend to be strongly intertwined with the legacy of the war economy (Cramer 2006).

What derives from this—who gets which jobs and how—is just as important, from a peacebuilding perspective, as the overall quantity of jobs created. Whether programs are successful or not will depend, to a large extent, on the way in which they interact with the political economy of jobs. This leads us to the next part of our analysis: how international actors select, out of the large population of unemployed youth, the "lucky few" who will participate in employment programs.

Jobs for Some, Peace for All:
The Paradox of Targeting in Youth-Employment Programs

When it comes to youth employment for peacebuilding, the translation from policy to practice embodies a fundamental paradox. The reason young people are a policy priority is their sheer number, along with their socioeconomic marginalization: they are "a demographic majority that sees itself as an outcast minority" (Sommers 2003, 1). Most program documents state in unequivocal terms that youth unemployment is a fundamental problem in the countries under consideration and provide some data to support this statement.

Yet by their very nature, these donor-funded interventions only target a limited number of the youth population, often with little potential to be scaled up. The key (but implicit) assumption is that by reaching out to *some* of these young people, the programs will benefit the *overall* youth population and society as a whole.

Increasingly extensive definitions of youth, as discussed earlier, compound this paradox by raising the percentage of the general population *potentially* eligible to be targeted—and thus (all other things being equal) reducing the portion of the youth population that will *actually* be reached by the intervention.

The all-encompassing use of the term *youth* also makes it more challenging to provide forms of support that address the needs of different age cohorts. The operational definitions adopted during program implementation are often even broader than the official one: a review of programs in Sierra Leone and Liberia found that that in one case, the age group was extended "to include 'youths' of 56 years of age alongside 15-year olds" (Batmanglich and Enria 2014, 18).

Youth-employment programs tend to have vague criteria to determine who—among this large youth population—should be targeted by the program (Sikenyi 2017). Most program documents use generic terms such as *at-risk youth*, *youth in need*, or *vulnerable youth*—yet in situations where the majority of young people face great hardship, these broad indications are unhelpful in determining who should be included (and, crucially, who will be excluded).

Moreover, optimal targeting may look very different from an employability perspective (according to which young people with the greatest motivation and ability would have the best chances of success), from a poverty alleviation perspective (which would prioritize the poorest and most in need among the youth), and from a short-term stabilization perspective (which would target young people most at risk of violent recruitment). Without an a priori recognition of these potential tensions, it is unlikely that the intervention will manage to match its stated purpose with its beneficiary selection.

ASSESSING IMPACT

Evaluations of youth-employment programs tend to focus on how the activities were delivered during the project cycle, with little or no follow-up assessment of what happens to participants after the end of the funding (Batmanglich and Enria 2014, 24).

Besides, the question of participants' long-term employability is only one dimension (and, arguably, not even the most important one) of peacebuilding impact. As the stated raison d'être for the interventions is their potential to reduce violence and promote peace, this is the yardstick against which its impact should be measured. Most of the evaluations reviewed from this analysis either ignore the peacebuilding question altogether, explicitly state that such a positive effect on peace could not be demonstrated (e.g., Koekebakker 2007 for Timor Leste), or else admit that a peacebuilding impact is unlikely given the limited size of the intervention (e.g., Larrabure and Ouledi 2011 on Comoros). While this conclusion is not surprising, it does stand in stark contrast with the bold claims of the expected impacts that are made *ex ante* in program documents.

The U.N. program Empowerment of Youth at Risk through Job Creation Programs in Areas of Tensions in Lebanon, which specifically targeted Palestinian job seekers, exemplifies some of the points made earlier.[9] The midterm evaluation found that the intervention only involved a relatively small number of youth—and, in all likelihood, not those who were most at risk of violent recruitment (Moran 2013, 56–57). Moreover, the final evaluation found that the program was solely focused on providing employment with not enough emphasis on decent working conditions, thus leaving participants in a condition of vulnerability (Zakkar 2013, 8, 22).

Any discussion of impact cannot shy away from the acknowledgment of the possibility that programs may "do harm" and unintentionally increase, rather than reduce, the risk of violence. This risk plays out at different levels. To start with, the program may have a negative effect on participants by frustrating their expectations and making them—even if not materially worse off—more disillusioned than they were before. For example, skill training that is inadequately matched to market demands and thus does not translate into improved prospects for graduates may lead to frustration and despondency (Batmanglich and Enria 2014, 40; Mercy Corps 2015, 36). To avoid this risk, policy makers and practitioners need to acquire a better understanding of the cost-opportunity considerations that inform individuals' choices: participants of a vocational training course, for example, are not just filling in empty time but rather foregoing the income and network potential that they would come from participation in the informal economy—and thus expect to have something in return.

Beyond participants, the program can create resentment in those who are not included in the program—particularly when this exclusion overlaps with preexisting dynamics of marginalization and exclusion. If an employment program makes some young people better off but at the same time increases a sense of powerlessness and injustice in many others, its peacebuilding impact may be offset, and indeed surpassed, by its conflict-inducing potential.

Given the role that patrimonialism plays in job allocation (Irwin, Mader, and Flynn 2018) and the fact that donor-funded jobs are such a coveted resource, there is a very concrete risk that programs—particularly with loose criteria for targeting—can be "captured" by powerful interests and feed into preexisting dynamics of favoritism and clientelism. Indeed, there is no reason to believe that "connectocracy" will disappear just because jobs are provided through donor-funded programs.

An evaluation commissioned by the Nigeria Stability and Reconciliation Program (NSRP)[10] found that youth-employment programs were used by local politicians as "a source of funds to mobilize political support" and "as political point-scoring between and within parties over job creation" (2014, 29, 33). Flawed outreach and beneficiary selection processes left ample room for "manipulation by officials according to political, ethnic or religious affiliation" (9). Many interviewed youth claimed that only those close to powerful men could get access to the program (28). Ultimately, for many young people, these programs "have served to exacerbate a sense of exclusion and frustration, with opportunities perceived to be unjustly distributed, largely ineffective or otherwise beyond reach. . . . This state of affairs risks exacerbating, rather than reducing, conflict tensions where perceptions of exclusion are a factor" (8, 29).

Analyses of youth-employment programs elsewhere reach similar conclusions. In Kenya, it was found that young people widely see the YEDF as part of the dominant logic of using employment to build political loyalty, particularly at election times (Sikenyi 2017, 135). Marc Sommers recalls conversations with members of the poor and marginalized youth in Sierra Leone, who saw participation in donor-funded employment programs as an unattainable wish, not just because there were "few slots and high demand for them," but also because "nepotism drove access to the treasured program." As local chiefs could not afford to pay supporters, "becoming program participants was a compensation in another form." In so doing, the program "ran the risk of negatively affecting large numbers of young people that were not in the program. In unsteady Sierra Leone, a country with enduring legacies of inequality, corruption, and violent resistance, such a result promises to exacerbate youth anger and fatalism in the face of still more elite favoritism" (Sommers 2015, 2).

A recognition of the weakness in monitoring and evaluation systems for employment-creation programs has led to calls for more robust qualitative and quantitative methodologies for impact assessment (Holmes, McCord, and Hagen-Zanker 2013; Rosas and Sabarwal 2016; Brück et al. 2016), and attempts have been made to use experimental and quasi-experimental methods that compare the treatment group with a control group (Blattman and Annan 2016). But even as we rightly strive for better and more rigorous evaluation, it is important to consider that nonparticipants are not a neutral control group that is unaffected by the program: they are closely looking, and their sense of marginalization and exclusion may be worsened by what they see. In principle, one could imagine a situation in which the control group is indeed more violent than the intervention group—but this is due to not a "violence-reducing" effect on the latter but rather a "violence-inducing" effect on the youth that were excluded from participation.

Conclusions

Employment programs are the international community's tool of choice to capitalize on the development and peacebuilding potential of youth. Yet after more than a decade of intensive investments in job creation for youth in postconflict and other fragile settings, evidence of impact is scant. Disappointing results are often blamed on contextual factors and implementation challenges and even written off as unavoidable, given the sheer size of the challenge they confront. This chapter has argued that closer attention should be given to the way in which the problem is conceptualized at the policy level and how this framing translates into programmatic responses.

The policy discourse on youth unemployment and violence has morphed significantly over the years. One-dimensional images of angry mobs of idle (male) youth have been overshadowed by optimistic portraits of youth as agents of positive change, peace activists, and enablers of social cohesion. In many ways, this can be seen as a manifestation of a larger trend of positive thinking in relation to youth, now seen as agents of innovation and entrepreneurship (Sumberg and Hunt 2019).

Yet the key elements of the securitization of youth employment linger in these celebratory accounts. Youth are still represented as a group that can be neatly set apart from the rest of the population and has essential characteristics by virtue of its youthfulness. Employment is presented as the factor that can tip youth one way or the other: not having a job makes youth a threat to be feared, while work and entrepreneurship opportunities turn young people into a resource to be celebrated and empowered.

The 2018 *Missing Peace* report represents a welcome attempt to overcome this threat/opportunity dichotomy and to recognize youth as a diverse microcosm rather than a homogenous category (Simpson 2018). The report also goes beyond the simple equation between unemployment and violence and challenges the idea of "giving jobs" as a panacea to peacebuilding—embracing instead a more nuanced understanding of how work-related issues affect individuals' sense of self and their relationship with others and how employment relates to other political, social, and economic dynamics.

More of this nuanced thinking is needed. Having recognized the importance of job quality, the international community needs to engage in an in-depth reflection on the interface between the youth, peace, and security agenda and the "decent work" agenda embodied in the Sustainable Development Goals (ILO 2018a; 2018b). It needs, in particular, to take a clearer, evidence-informed policy position on the role of informality in postconflict employment creation and peacebuilding.

Yet there is no guarantee that even an enriched reflection at the policy level will trickle down to programs. While the problem is framed at the macrolevel (with regard to the overall youth population), it is addressed programmatically at the microlevel (through individual targeting). For (microlevel) interventions to translate into (macrolevel) impact, one or both of the following need to happen: programs need to reach precisely those individuals who would otherwise be violent and/or they need to generate virtuous catalytic effects that benefit society at large. There is little evidence that these considerations guide program design: criteria for identification of beneficiaries are, on the whole, extremely loose and at times inherently contradictory, and no indication is given on how positive spillover effects for society are supposed to be generated. This logical gap between "work for some" and "peace for all" is probably the greatest weaknesses of the "youth employment for peacebuilding" agenda.

Analytical clarity does not guarantee good programming, but certainly an incorrect identification of the problem at the design stage increases the chance of programs being ineffective—or, worse, harmful. The perception of young people that are equally eligible to participate but are not selected is an area that deserves exploration if we want to fully understand the impact that employment programs can have on society at large.

NOTES

1. Programs have normally a longer timescale and larger budget and are more complex than projects. For simplicity, for the remainder of this chapter, we use "programs" to indicate any donor-funded intervention.

2. The evidence base for this reflection is given by a meta-analysis of 432 employment interventions, implemented by U.N. agencies and the World Bank in 47 postconflict and fragile countries (Brück et al. 2016). Of these, 147 interventions specifically identified youth as a target group.

3. Technically, *An Agenda for Peace* does mention youth once, in the context of "cultural exchanges and mutually beneficial youth and educational projects" as a confidence-building measure among states after international conflict (U.N. 1992, par. 56).

4. The YEDF was started in 2006 and focuses on microfinance and enterprise development, with the aim of ensuring that young people (aged eighteen to thirty-five) have access to affordable loans to develop their small and medium businesses (Muthee 2010; Sikenyi 2017). See www.youthfund.go.ke/ (accessed June 29, 2019).

5. The ILO recognizes that the third condition (actively looking for work) can "make the scope of the measurement somewhat restrictive and ill-suited to capture the prevailing employment situation in developing countries," and thus at times uses a "relaxed" definition, including people that satisfy the first two conditions but not the third ("available non-seekers"; Luebker 2008).

6. This is particularly the case in conflict and postconflict countries. The *World Development Report 2013: Jobs* notes that people work even during wars; however, those jobs offer little pay and no security and may involve illegal and dangerous activities (World Bank 2013, 193).

7. In their study of the role of aid in "winning hearts and minds" in Afghanistan, Paul Fishstein and Andrew Wilder discuss the meaning of the Dari word *mahroum*, which translates as "deprived" or "left out" but also conveys a more profound sense of alienation, being discriminated against, or being deliberately deprived at the hands of others (Fishstein and Wilder 2012, 58).

8. On the importance of social connections to get jobs, see, for example, Mallet and Atim (2014) on Uganda; Banks (2016) on Tanzania; Gukurume (2018) and Oosterom (2019) on Zimbabwe; and Gough, Chigunta, and Langevang (2016) on Zambia.

9. The program was funded by the Peacebuilding Fund for a total of US$2,002,719 and implemented jointly by ILO, UNICEF, and the United Nations Relief and Works Agency for Palestine Refugees in the Near East (UNRWA) from 2011 to 2013.

10. The NSRP was a five-year program (2013–2017) funded by the U.K. Department for International Development (DFID) that has the overall goal of reducing violent conflict in Nigeria.

REFERENCES

Aldrich, Daniel. 2014. "First Steps towards Hearts and Minds? USAID's Countering Violent Extremism Policies in Africa." *Terrorism and Political Violence* 26, no. 3, 523–546.

Bagchi, Aniruddha, and Jomon A. Paul. 2018. "Youth Unemployment and Terrorism in the MENAP (Middle East, North Africa, Afghanistan and Pakistan)." *Socio-economic Planning Sciences* 64:9–20.

Banks, Nicola. 2016. "Youth Poverty, Employment and Livelihoods: Social and Economic Implications of Living with Insecurity in Arusha, Tanzania." *Environment and Urbanization* 28, no. 2, 437–454.

Barsoum, Ghada. 2016. "'Job Opportunities for the Youth': Competing and Overlapping Discourses on Youth Unemployment and Work Informality in Egypt." *Current Sociology* 64, no. 3, 430–446.

Batmanglich, Sara, and Luisa Enria. 2014. *Real Jobs in Fragile Contexts: Reframing Youth Employment Programs in Liberia and Sierra Leone.* London: International Alert.

Blattman, Christopher. 2010. "Can Youth Employment Programs Foster Social Stability in Africa?" Speech to the World Bank Africa Management Retreat, April 2010. https://chrisblattman.com/files/2010/09/Blattman-Can-youth-employment-reduce-social-instability-April-2010.pdf.

Blattman, Christopher, and Jeannie Annan. 2016. "Can Employment Reduce Lawlessness and Rebellion? A Field Experiment with High-Risk Men in a Fragile State." *American Political Science Review* 110, no. 1, 1–17.

Bradley, John. 2012. *After the Arab Spring: How Islamists Hijacked the Middle East Revolts.* London: Palgrave Macmillan.

Brück, Tilman, Neil Ferguson, Valeria Izzi, and Wolfgang Stojetz. 2016. *Jobs Aid Peace: A Review of the Theory and Practice of the Impact of Employment Programs on Peace in Fragile and Conflict-Affected Countries.* Berlin: International Security and Development Center.

Chaaban, Jad, and Wendy Cunningham. 2011. *Measuring the Economic Gain of Investing in Girls—the Girl Effect Dividend.* Washington, D.C.: World Bank.

Chamkhi, Tarek. 2014. "Neo-Islamism in the Post-Arab Spring." *Contemporary Politics* 20, no. 4, 453–468.

Cornwall, Andrea, Elizabeth Harrison, and Ann Whitehead. 2007. "Gender Myths and Feminist Fables: The Struggle for Interpretive Power in Gender and Development." *Development and Change* 38, no. 1, 1–20.

Cramer, Chris. 2006. "Labour Markets, Employment, and the Transformation of War Economies." *Conflict, Security & Development* 6, no. 3, 389–410.

———. 2010. "Unemployment and Participation in Violence." Background Paper for the World Development Report 2011, London, School of Oriental and African Studies.

Della Faille, Dimitri. 2011. "Discourse Analysis in International Development Studies: Mapping Some Contemporary Contributions." *Journal of Multicultural Discourses* 6, no. 3, 215–235.

Dolan, Catherine, and Dinah Rajak. 2016. "Remaking Africa's Informal Economies: Youth, Entrepreneurship, and the Promise of Inclusion at the Bottom of the Pyramid." *Journal of Development Studies* 52, no. 4, 514–529.

El-Bouchra, Judy. 2007. "Feminism, Gender, and Women's Peace Activism." *Development and Change* 38, no. 1, 131–147.

Enria, Luisa. 2018. *The Politics of Work in a Post-conflict State: Youth, Labour and Violence in Sierra Leone.* Woodbridge, Suffolk: Boydell & Brewer.

———. n.d. "An Idle Mind Is the Devil's Workshop? The Politics of Work amongst Freetown's Youth." Summary of DPhil thesis, Oxford Department of International Development.

Finn, Brandon, and Sophie Oldfield. 2015. "Straining: Young Men Working through Waithood in Freetown, Sierra Leone." *Afrika Spectrum: Deutsche Zeitschrift für Gegenwartsbezogene Afrikaforschung* 50, no. 3, 29–48.

Fishstein, Paul, and Andrew Wilder. 2012. *Winning Hearts and Minds? Examining the Relation between Aid and Security in Afghanistan.* Medford, Mass.: Feinstein International Center, Tuft University.

Gebremariam, Eyob Balcha. 2017. "The Politics of Youth Employment and Policy Processes in Ethiopia." *IDS Bulletin* 48, no. 3, 33–49.

Goetz, Anne Marie. 2007. "Political Cleaners: Women as the New Anti-corruption Force?" *Development and Change* 38, no. 1, 87–105.

Gough, Katherine, Francis Chigunta, and Thilde Langevang. 2016. "Expanding the Scales and Domains of (In)security: Youth Employment in Urban Zambia." *Environment and Planning* 48, no. 2, 348–366.

Gukurume, Simbarashe. 2018. "Navigating Precarious Livelihoods: Youth in the SME Sector in Zimbabwe." *IDS Bulletin* 49, no. 5, 89–104.

Hickel, Jason. 2014. "The 'Girl Effect': Liberalism, Empowerment and the Contradictions of Development." *Third World Quarterly* 35, no. 8, 1355–1373.

Holmes, Rebecca, Anna McCord, and Jessica Hagen-Zanker. 2013. *What Is the Evidence on the Impact of Employment Creation on Stability and Poverty Reduction in Fragile States: A Systematic Review.* London: Overseas Development Institute.

Honwana, Alcinda, and Filip De Boeck, eds. 2005. *Makers and Breakers: Children and Youth in Postcolonial Africa.* Oxford: James Currey.

ILO (International Labour Organization). 2011. *Policy Options to Support Young Workers during Economic Recovery.* Geneva: International Labour Organization.

———. 2018a. *Decent Work for Sustainable Development—Transformation towards Sustainable and Resilient Societies.* Geneva: International Labour Organization.

———. 2018b. *Decent Work and the Sustainable Development Goals: A Guidebook on SDG Labour Market Indicators.* Geneva: International Labour Organization.

Irwin, Stacie, Philip Mader, and Justin Flynn. 2018. *How Youth Specific Is Africa's Youth Employment Challenge?* K4D Emerging Issues Report. Brighton, U.K.: Institute of Development Studies.

Ismail, Aisha, and Shehla Amjad. 2014. "Determinants of Terrorism in Pakistan: An Empirical Investigation." *Economic Modelling* 37:320–331.

Jütersonke, Oliver, and Kazushige Kobayashi. 2015. *Employment and Decent Work in Fragile Settings: A Compass to Orient the World of Work.* Geneva: International Labour Organization.

Koekebakker, Welmoed. 2007. *Timor Leste—Work for Peace Project—UNDP Final Evaluation.* https://erc.undp.org/evaluation/documents/download/2355.

Kraemer-Mbula, Erika, and Sacha Wunsch-Vincent. 2016. *The Informal Economy in Developing Nations Hidden Engine of Innovation?* Cambridge: Cambridge University Press.

LaGraffe, Daniel. 2012. "The Youth Bulge in Egypt: An Intersection of Demographics, Security, and the Arab Spring." *Journal of Strategic Security* 5, no. 2, 65–80.

Larrabure, Juan Luis, and Ahmed Oueledi. 2011. "Final Evaluation—Peace Building Fund Program in the Comoros 2008–2011." Unpublished manuscript. New York, NY: UNDP.

Leach, Melissa. 2007. "Earth Mother Myths and Other Ecofeminist Fables: How a Strategic Notion Rose and Fell." *Development and Change* 38, no. 1, 67–85.

Lopes, Thais, and Tendai Pasipanodya. 2008. *Youth Employment Initiatives in West Africa: An Overview of Survey Results.* Dakar: YEN-WA.

Luebker, Malte. 2008. *Employment, Unemployment and Informality in Zimbabwe: Concepts and Data for Coherent Policy-Making.* Harare: International Labour Organization.

Mallet, Richard, and Teddy Atim. 2014. *Gender, Youth and Urban Labour Market Participation: Evidence from the Catering Sector in Lira, Northern Uganda.* London: Overseas Development Institute.

Mallet, Richard, Teddy Atim, and Jimmy Opio. 2017. *"Bad Work" and the Challenges of Creating Decent Work for Youth in Northern Uganda.* London: Overseas Development Institute.

Meagher, Kate. 2016. "The Scramble for Africans: Demography, Globalisation and Africa's Informal Labour Markets." *Journal of Development Studies* 52, no. 4, 483–497.

Mercy Corps. 2015. *Youth and Consequences: Unemployment, Injustice and Violence.* Portland, Ore.: Mercy Corps.

Moran, Gerard. 2013. *Empowerment of Youth at Risk through Job Creation Programs in Areas of Tensions in Lebanon—Mid-Term Evaluation.* http://mptf.undp.org/document/download/10690.

Muldering, M. Chloe. 2013. "An Uncertain Future: Youth Frustration and the Arab Spring." The Pardee Papers 16. Boston, Mass.: Frederick S. Pardee Center for the Study of the Longer-Range Future, Boston University.

Munive, Jairo. 2010. "The Army of 'Unemployed' Young People." *Young* 18:321–336.

Murphy, Emma C. 2012. "Problematizing Arab Youth: Generational Narratives of Systemic Failure." *Mediterranean Politics* 17, no. 1, 5–22.

Muthee, Margaret Wamugu. 2010. *Hitting the Target, Missing the Point: Youth Policies and Programmes in Kenya.* Washington, D.C.: Woodrow Wilson International Center for Scholars.

NSRP (Nigeria Stability and Reconciliation Program). 2014. *Winners or Losers? Assessing the Contribution of Youth Employment and Empowerment Programs to Reducing Conflict Risk in Nigeria.* Nigeria Stability and Reconciliation Program. www.nsrp-nigeria.org/wp-content/uploads/2014/06/WINNER-OR-LOSER-final-6.2.2014.pdf.

Oosterom, Marjoke. 2019. "Youth and Social Navigation in Zimbabwe's Informal Economy: 'Don't End Up on the Wrong Side.'" *African Affairs* 118, no. 472, 485–508.

Pereznieto, Paula, and James Hamilton Harding. 2013. *Investing in Youth in International Development Policy—Making the Case.* London: Overseas Development Institute.

Peters, Krijn. 2011. *War and the Crisis of Youth in Sierra Leone.* Cambridge: Cambridge University Press.

Richards, Paul. 1995. "Rebellion in Liberia and Sierra Leone: A Crisis of Youth?" In *Conflict in Africa,* edited by Oliver Furley, 134–170. London: I. B. Tauris.

———. 1996. *Fighting for the Rainforest: War, Youth and Resources in Sierra Leone.* Oxford: James Currey.

Rosas, Nina, and Shwetlena Sabarwal. 2016. *Public Works as a Productive Safety Net in a Post-conflict Setting—Evidence from a Randomised Evaluation in Sierra Leone.* Washington, D.C.: World Bank.

Sikenyi, Maurice. 2017. "Does Kenya's Youth Enterprise Development Fund Serve Young People?" *IDS Bulletin* 48, no. 3, 127–140.

Simpson, Graeme. 2018. *The Missing Peace: Independent Progress Study on Youth, Peace and Security.* UNFPA. www.unfpa.org/sites/default/files/youth/youth-web-english.pdf.

Solow, Robert M. 1990. *The Labor Market as a Social Institution.* Cambridge, Mass.: Blackwell.

Sommers, Marc. 2003. *Urbanization, War, and Africa's Youth at Risk towards Understanding and Addressing Future Challenges.* Washington, D.C.: United States Agency for International Development (USAID).

———. 2012. *Stuck: Rwandan Youth and the Struggle for Adulthood.* Athens: University of Georgia Press.

———. 2015. *The Outcast Majority: War, Development, and Youth in Africa.* Athens: University of Georgia Press.

Stewart, Frances. 2012. "Employment Policies and Horizontal Inequalities in Post-conflict Situations." In *Horizontal Inequalities and Post-conflict Development,* edited by Arnim Langer, Frances Stewart, and Rajesh Venugopal, 61–83. London: Palgrave Macmillan.

Sukarieh, Mayssoun, and Stuart Tannock. 2008. "In the Best Interests of Youth or Neoliberalism? The World Bank and the New Global Youth Empowerment Project." *Journal of Youth Studies* 11, no. 3, 301–312.

———. 2014. *Youth Rising? The Politics of Youth in the Global Economy.* Abingdon, Va.: Routledge.

———. 2018. "The Global Securitisation of Youth." *Third World Quarterly* 39, no. 5 (September): 854–870.

Sumberg, James, and Stephen Hunt. 2019. "Are African Rural Youth Innovative? Claims, Evidence and Implications." *Journal of Rural Studies* 69:130–136.

Thieme, Tatiana. 2013. "The 'Hustle' amongst Youth Entrepreneurs in Mathare's Informal Waste Economy." *Journal of Eastern African Studies* 7, no. 3, 389–412.

UNDP (United Nations Development Programme). 2006. *Youth and Violent Conflict: Society and Development in Crisis?* New York: UNDP.

United Nations. 1992. *An Agenda for Peace: Preventive Diplomacy, Peacemaking and Peace-Keeping, A/47/277.* www.un.org/ruleoflaw/files/A_47_277.pdf.

———. 1995. *Supplement to an Agenda for Peace: Position Paper of the Secretary-General on the Occasion of the Fiftieth Anniversary of the United Nations, A/50/60-S/1995/1.* https://digitallibrary.un.org/record/168325?ln=en#record-files-collapse-header.

———. 2001. *UN Secretary-General's Report on the Prevention of Armed Conflict, A/55/985-S/2001/574.*

———. 2004. *A More Secure World: Our Shared Responsibility: Report by the High-Level Panel on Threats, Challenges and Change, A/59/565.* www.un.org/ruleoflaw/files/gaA.59 .565_En.pdf.

UNOWA (United Nations Office for West Africa). 2005. *Youth Unemployment and Regional Insecurity in West Africa.* Dakar: United Nations Office for West Africa.

World Bank. 2013. *World Development Report 2013: Jobs.* Washington, D.C.: World Bank.

Zakkar, Wael. 2013. "Final Independent Evaluation—Project of Empowerment of Youth at Risk through Job Creation Program in Areas of Tension in Lebanon." Unpublished manuscript. New York, NY: UNDP.

Zweig, Michael. 2015. "Complicating Labour Markets as Social Institutions." *Review of Radical Political Economics* 47, no. 4, 572–578.

CHAPTER 6

Community Ties, Training, and Technology

A MORE EFFECTIVE FRAMEWORK FOR PEACE, SECURITY, AND DEVELOPMENT FOR AFGHAN YOUTH

Nasrat Khalid

Poor economic conditions and a history of civil war combined with youth bulges and high rates of unemployment create the perfect storm for radicalization and sustained conflict (Collier and Hoeffler 2004; Goldstone 2010; Urdal 2004, 2006; Urdal and Hoelscher 2012). Historically, insurgent groups like the Taliban have recruited youth from their native Pakistan or from neighboring countries like Afghanistan to fuel their wars. When U.N. Security Council Resolution (UNSCR) 2250 on youth, peace, and security (YPS) was adopted in 2015, this complex relationship between youth and conflict was a primary consideration. In some cases, recruitment is systematic, and families have been fighting for so many generations that the very war itself is part of a community identity. Recruiters of warring groups may have invoked a glorious past where youth could find a worthy, God-chosen path to follow. Solutions to prevent this violent radicalization of youth often involve the provision of (usually limited) access to education, job training, hiring opportunities, and related interventions. International organizations have often also sought to expose youth from isolated parts of the world to "modern" or Western culture as a way of promoting alternative narratives. The impact of these approaches is often fleeting at best. The root causes of extremist violence and radicalization are too deeply ingrained for superficial solutions to be effective.

This chapter centers on Afghanistan, one of the countries most deeply impacted by protracted conflict and radicalization, as a primary case study. It draws on the premise that it will take more than basic socioeconomic development or education programs to promote a lasting culture of peace and tolerance in Afghanistan that involves all ages and genders. It argues that youth have the potential to play a larger role in conflict prevention, but to do so, they will need what we will call the three Ts framework: stronger community ties, technical training, and access to today's technology. These three Ts will complement current international development efforts in Afghanistan centered on socioeconomic- and education-driven programs. Implementing both strategies in concert is more likely to move Afghanistan away from war and toward peace and inclusive development. The three Ts framework is applied in the context of ongoing efforts to engage Afghan youths in peace, security, and development initiatives. A combination of personal experience and fieldwork in Afghanistan, together with an examination of previous programs[1] centered on preventing the radicalization of young women and men, constitutes the basis of the discussion. By examining the radicalization of youth at the ground level and at the level of national programs, the three Ts framework proposes middle-ground solutions—that is, it connects local systems with national and international ones to create lasting solutions for development in Afghanistan.

This framework directly aligns with UNSCR 2250's pillars for action on prevention, which "urges member States to facilitate an inclusive and enabling environment in which youth actors . . . from different backgrounds, are recognized and provided with adequate support to implement violence prevention activities and support social cohesion." Creating, fostering, and institutionalizing better community ties to connect local and state levels of government and community members to each other will allow youth in Afghanistan to have a more impactful political voice in their country's peace process. Second, the resolution "stresses the importance of creating policies for youth that would positively contribute to peacebuilding efforts, including social and economic development, supporting projects designed to grow local economies, and provide youth employment opportunities and vocational training, fostering their education, and promoting youth entrepreneurship and constructive political engagement." The three Ts framework focuses on training to bolster young people's ability to handle their local political circumstances and to prepare them to help Afghanistan better integrate with the political and economic landscape of the rest of the world. Another component of the prevention pillar "urges the Member States to support, as appropriate, quality education for peace that equips youth with the ability to engage constructively in civic structures and inclusive political processes" (UNSC 2015). This chapter argues that the most effective way to accomplish this in Afghanistan is by providing youth with quality technical training and access to technologies to prepare them for the fast-paced, technology-based, and globalized economy that exists today and allow them to sustain the peace they promote.

With programs centered on this framework, Afghan youth will receive the tools necessary to improve their communities and integrate Afghan society with the rest of the world. Increased access to the necessary ties, training, and technology will foster a more modernized, freer environment for education and economic opportunity, ultimately addressing the final subcomponent of UNSCR 2250's prevention pillar, which "calls on all relevant factors to consider instituting mechanisms to promote a culture of peace, tolerance, intercultural and interreligious dialogue that involve youth and discourage their participation in acts of violence, terrorism, xenophobia, and all forms of discrimination" (UNSC 2015). If the goal for Afghanistan is peace, then engaging youth (and women) to be not only beneficiaries of that process but also an active part of it is crucial to the implementation and sustainment of UNSCR 2250 and, more broadly, efforts toward sustaining peace and security.

The rest of the chapter is structured as follows. Following a vignette about how insurgent groups and inadequate educational opportunities radicalize vulnerable Afghan youth and marginalize women, I present a brief discussion of larger socioeconomic and political challenges that prevent a peaceful conflict resolution and economic development. I then analyze previous international programs in Afghanistan that missed the mark or barely hit the target for sustained results. This analysis involves a series of interviews with youth in Afghanistan who are enrolled in educational programs or otherwise receiving training so as to become more involved in the current peace processes. While not a primary source of data for this chapter, these interviews nonetheless offer some helpful context on how the youth in Afghanistan assess the current international aid programs. Following the discussion of those assessments, this chapter will conclude by framing the three Ts framework as the key to creating programs to engage youth and women in Afghanistan's peace process, arguing that the implementation and sustainment of these programs will contribute to Afghanistan's progress as a more peaceful, economically stable nation.

SHAMSHATO REFUGEE CAMP:
A VIGNETTE ON CONFLICT AND RADICALIZATION IN AFGHANISTAN

In the early 1990s, 6.3 million Afghan refugees fled the Afghan civil war to refugee camps at the Afghanistan-Pakistan border. The civil war, an aftermath of the war with the Soviets, involved Afghan ethnic leaders fighting against the Soviet-backed, communist regime (Coleville 1997). Countless Afghans fled their homes seeking safety in neighboring countries such as Pakistan and Iran. In many cases, these refugees headed toward these countries found that they had not moved as far away from the conflict as they had hoped. As a case in point, the largest Afghan refugee camps in Pakistan were created and run by warlords who controlled political factions, not international organizations or the government.

Homes in these refugee camps typically consisted of tents or rudimentary structures with mud walls and dirt floors, housing multiple families in each.[2] Few opportunities were available to their occupants. The land did not belong to the refugees, restricting the possibility of engaging in agriculture-based livelihoods. International organizations gave limited support to the hospitals and at times also to schools. Job opportunities were limited to the kinds of work needed to maintain the camps. Taking advantage of this situation, extremist leaders urging groups in Afghanistan to take a stand against the Soviets and the Afghan government managed to maintain high levels of control over the population.

Shamshato was one of the largest of these refugee camps in Pakistan (Redden 2002). It housed thousands of refugees and was built around a religious context that shaped community rules and mindsets. The Islamic Party of Afghanistan under the leadership of Gulbuddin Hekmatyar established their bureaucratic units to administer to the health, education, and policing of Shamshato. In Shamshato, every part of a refugee's life was beholden to the camp structure: for food, medical treatment, law and order, and education. Social order was defined by *sharia* (Arabic for "Islamic rules"), and the *amniyat* (meaning "security" in Pashto) maintained order with a heavy hand. Children playing marbles could be slapped for engaging in a game considered too close to gambling. Television was not permitted because the programs were too Western and not religious enough. Marriage was strictly controlled; music was practically forbidden. In the camps, religion by the ruling *mujahideen*—meaning "freedom fighter" in Pashto—defined politics, education, and the refugees' entire way of life.

Afghan women and girls, already accustomed to considerable strictures, saw the restrictions imposed on them greatly intensified in the camp. The constraints on their freedom significantly expanded, and they were allowed no say in their own lives. Schools for young girls did exist, yet schooling ended once a girl married, and the only jobs available to women involved the provision of limited education to other young girls. Women could not own shops or run their family's businesses from the camp's markets. If they were not at school, either studying or teaching, they were at home, maintaining their household or maybe sowing or embroidering clothes.

Religion also constituted the basis of the school systems. Along with writing, arithmetic, geography, history, and languages, young kids would learn *faqih* (Arabic for "Islamic jurisprudence"), *aqayad* (meaning "Islamic beliefs"), and *tajweed* (roughly translated as "the proper way of reading the Quran in Arabic"). There were no libraries or laboratories to explore outside ideas or acquire scientific knowledge, nor was there any way to learn modern technologies or even study other cultures. High school education was the only accreditation that a refugee received in the camps, since no higher education was available.

As another strategy employed to control the lives of the refugees and sometimes indoctrinate them into a particular ideology was the expectations that boys and girls would attend *madrasas* ("religious education center" in Pashto), which taught whatever interpretation of religion mixed with politics the faction running the camps happened to support. The political parties in conflict with the Afghan government until the end of 2016 saw these refugees as a population ripe for the picking and were able to take from the camps the troops they needed for their wars. Although Shamshato was more ideologically moderate than other tribal areas of Pakistan, children in the *madrasas*, both girls and boys, learned to normalize even extreme violence as an expected aspect of their experience (Human Rights Watch 2016). Everyday life in their bleak mud-and-straw houses and bare market streets offered no personal fulfillment or better opportunities. The refugee camps in Pakistan originally represented the promise of an escape from the violence in Afghanistan. Sadly, refugees' dependence on the wishes of the camp administrators left them vulnerable to manipulation. Camp administrators' laws and schools encouraged an extremely violent form of religion. Young boys were taught to revere religious martyrs as role models; their tales of violence were spun into romantic legends for children. Once boys finished primary school, a few could be called away from their houses in Shamshato and taken back to Afghanistan, back into the *jihad* (Arabic for "holy war"). Some might make it back; most would not. The ones who did not return were revered as heroes for younger children to admire.

Multiple generations of Afghan youth have been indoctrinated into these extremist beliefs; recruited as soldiers, young men saw themselves deeply connected to the religious drives of the insurgents in the war in Afghanistan. Young girls, raised to marry freedom fighters and raise another generation to fight in the war, ended up internalizing the dictum that it was their duty to do so. It is not possible to extricate young people from these circumstances without first understanding how conditioned they have become to fight in this war (Radio Free Radio Europe Radio Liberty 2009). Offering them economic incentives or making Western education programs available to them are only partial—and ultimately inadequate—solutions to a larger systemic problem. Afghanistan is politically and technologically decades behind much of the rest of the world. The widening gap between Afghanistan and more developed countries is more than the traditional socioeconomic and educational aid programs that have been implemented in the past—or are currently in place—can possibly address. The outcomes of these interventions will be short term at best and largely ineffectual in the long term as they fail to tackle the root causes of the problem. To break free of these extreme and ingrained mindsets, this chapter argues, Afghan youth must receive training and access to technology alongside social ties and the proper context to expand their worldviews and avail themselves of opportunities to shape their community.

MISSED OPPORTUNITIES FOR PEACE: STATE FRAGILITY AND POLITICAL STALEMATE

Afghanistan's current generation of youth is one of the largest in the world and accounts for a large proportion of the global caseload of refugees and displaced persons affected by conflict. Around 63.7 percent of Afghans are under the age of twenty-five. According to the United Nations Population Fund (UNFPA), this reflects a "steep pyramid age structure whereby a large cohort of young people is slowly emerging." Afghani society nevertheless remains deeply gerontocratic, a cultural reality that poses considerable challenges to international efforts to advance the position of youth, especially those unresponsive to local circumstances, as discussed later in the chapter.

In theory, "with education and access to jobs, good health care, and empowerment, young people could emerge and develop into a large working-age population with few dependents, collectively bringing prosperity to their society" (UNFPA 2015). As of 2015, Afghan unemployment had reached over 40 percent (Tolo News 2015). As per an Afghanistan Living Conditions Survey, Afghanistan's poverty levels rose from 38 percent in 2011–2012 to 55 percent in 2016–2017 (Jain 2018).

Afghanistan faces significant challenges in the areas of health, education, employment, and gender equality. There are additional serious challenges that youth face in political and security contexts, as will be discussed in subsequent sections. Ironically one of the biggest factors preventing youth and women from engaging in the peace process is the discouraging lack of tangible progress toward achieving peace outcomes in the past few years. On the contrary, the last forty years in Afghanistan have been marked by persistent upheaval and war. After a communist government ended the monarchy in 1973, what followed included the invasion of the Soviet Union in 1979, decades of civil war, and the rise of the Taliban regime in the mid-1990s; Afghanistan has long been plagued by unabated political instability.

Efforts toward reaching a peace agreement between the Afghan government and the Taliban have remained at a stalemate over the past fifteen years. This prolonged, violent stalemate is frustrating to Afghan citizens, particularly young people who have grown up with nothing but conflict. Nasrin, a twenty-five-year-old from Herat, remarks that there is no "spiritual commitment to ending the conflict," which leads to a "lack of effective and practical strategies" that could lead to lasting policies.[3] The peace efforts most often publicized are traditional *jirgas* (Pashto for "gatherings") between male elders in Afghanistan and Pakistan. The Afghan High Peace Council was established in 2010, but it has made little progress despite high initial expectations. Peace negotiation efforts by the Afghan government have relied almost exclusively on the efforts of the older generation of male tribal elders.

In 2017, the United States unveiled its South Asia Strategy, which encompasses a number of nations in the region, including Afghanistan as well as Pakistan, India, and the Central Asia nations. The current U.S. administration has stressed that the new strategy is a move away from the failed nation-building policies of past administrations. As of September 2018, Ambassador Zalmay Khalilzad's recent efforts as a special representative for the United States to Afghanistan have been focused on two primary objectives, getting the Taliban to engage with the Afghan government and implementing a long-term cease-fire in place to bolster peace negotiations (Kelemen, Hadid, and Romo 2018).

Without stronger progress toward peace, international organization-based nation-building programs will not succeed. The youth in Afghanistan agree with this assessment. Khadija,[4] a twenty-four-year-old political science student from Daikundi Province in central Afghanistan, reports being ready for political change in her country. To her, Afghanistan faces three primary political obstacles: "[The first is the] systemic political agenda of neighbor countries, keeping their interest intact which most of the time conflicts with other neighbors. [The second is the] absence of political will for a centralized, strong government within the national stakeholders due to their direct benefit from the conflict, namely financial and in terms of international influencers. [Finally,] ethnic decision-making blocks any kind of nationalization attempts." This political assessment from a young Afghan woman highlights a commonly expressed belief among the youth that outside experts and experienced tribal leaders are not the only ones who understand the political situation preventing lasting peace in Afghanistan. For the country's youth, whole entire lives have been lived in a context of conflict, and they have a firsthand understanding of potential solutions to bring about and sustain peace in their society. The fact that the majority of Afghanistan's population is very young makes this argument more compelling.

Following the passage of UNSCR 2250—and the earlier UNSCR 1325 on women, peace, and security—the U.N. formally recognized the critical role of youth and women in the global peace and security agendas. Hopes were high that more sustainable grassroots-level efforts would take hold in Afghanistan. In recent years, a number of international organizations have attempted to implement programs focused on prevention or one of UNSCR 2250's other four pillars for action—that is, participation, protection, partnerships, or reintegration (Amambia et al. 2018; U.N. Sri Lanka 2017). While all these organizations began with noble intentions and strove for effecting long-lasting, meaningful impact, many of them missed the mark. The programs they implement seem to remain at the national level; without local- and community-level engagement, the interventions they promote will not reach their intended targets. Furthermore, most of these projects fail to provide the king with the training and technology that would result in a long-term meaningful impact. As I elaborate in the next section, development programs in Afghanistan after 2001 intended to improve the lives of women and youth fell short of the mark due to the lack of funding, poor frameworks, and even failed institutions.

No Opportunities for Youth or Women in the Reconstruction of Afghanistan

Official policies by the Afghan government have sought to bring peace and sta- bility to Afghanistan through youth engagement. In 2013, Afghanistan's Ministry of Information and Culture drafted a National Youth Policy to incorporate youth and women into the peace and then later reconstruction processes. The draft discusses efforts to engage youth and women through government programs and increased engagement with international aid programs (Afghanistan Ministry of Information and Culture 2013). However, this policy never made it past the draft stage to any policy-supported level. In the context of stalled peace processes, the youth and women whom this policy was meant to benefit were never prioritized or even actually targeted.

It was not just public institutions that have failed youth. After 2001, Afghanistan was presented with a great opportunity for youth and women to be recognized and engaged as integral members of a modern and stable society. Afghanistan received billions in aid to reconstruct its civil society and revive its failing economy. After more than fifteen years of continuous aid, Afghanistan still ranks as the third most corrupt country and remains plagued by high levels of violence and poverty. While access to education and health care has increased, the quality of those ser- vices remains questionable (Samim 2016). The problem is not just the availability of funding, but rather the limited sustainability of most programs, the majority of which fail to engage with youth and women. Those two social groups constitute a demographic majority and have borne the brunt of the conflict and deprivation, yet they are often ignored in programs designed to bring peace and prosperity to their country.

In 2016, the World Bank published priorities for addressing Afghan economic instability, which were projected into 2030. The report assessed that protracted conflict, weak institutions, and a fragile economy were at the heart of Afghanistan's instability. The World Bank proposed, in the short term, public expenditures to bol- ster markets and increase investments and, in the long term, a broad-based growth model for sustained domestic revenue and foreign exchange (Nassif and Haque 2016). Glaringly, the possibility of the harnessing of Afghanistan's large and growing youth and women populations was not mentioned to provide a highly trained and resilient workforce for the country.

The U.S. Agency for International Development (USAID) is one of Afghan- istan's largest international partners in development. They have international assistance programs specific to women and youth, but while youth programs center on access to education and economic opportunities, women-specific programs are often limited to countering human trafficking or promoting better sexual health. Some programs seek to involve women in governance or the economy, but no effective programs are in place for involving youth and women in the peace process. USAID's Provincial Reconstruction Teams (PRT) in Afghanistan, now defunct, focused on engaging civil, military, societal, and religious leaders, almost exclusively men, while also reintegrating former insurgents and those affected by the conflict into society and the economic sectors (USAID 2019a, 2019b). Those kinds of nation-building programs have sometimes bolstered capacity building in general terms (McNerney 2006). On the other hand, PRTs did not directly address the effects of conflict on women or youth or engage them in efforts to secure enduring peace. Instead, PRTs seemed to hope for a "trickle-down" effect—an approach that ultimately failed to incorporated women's and youth's experiences and their potential contributions in securing lasting peace.

A few noteworthy exceptions do exist. For instance, the Youth Empowerment Program led by USAID from 2006 to 2008 worked to more directly involve youth in the processes of democratization and peace (USAID 2013c). From 2008 to 2011, the Afghanistan Skills Development Program assisted one thousand men and women develop specific skills in managerial, accounting, and information and communications technology (ICT) areas. The program also helped 6,750 men and women from poor, rural provinces learn targeted skills to better their lives (World Bank 2012). Other programs, such as USAID's Skills Training for Afghan Youth, offered to train youth from ages fifteen to twenty-four to be workforce ready in the modern world (USAID 2013c). For Afghan women, the Goldozi Project, cosponsored by USAID and FHI 360, seeks to provide women with marketable embroidery skills and access to training and facilities to pursue those newfound skills as sustainable jobs (USAID 2018). Similarly, the Women Enterprise Development focused on helping women enter the job market in larger numbers and enhancing their business opportunities and earning potential in today's career fields. This three-year project trained 301 women and 166 men in Afghanistan, creating seven joint ventures, technology transfers, and/or import-export transactions (USAID 2013b). Finally, USAID's Promote Project aims to mentor and train women for participation in civil society and in the promotion of sustainable peace and democracy (USAID 2019a). Unfortunately, although these programs saw initial traction, efforts were not sustained due to either insufficient funding or a lack of concrete results. With respect to ongoing programs, it remains unclear whether they are having the impact their parent organizations expected them to. I argue that, had young people been more engaged at local levels and given bigger roles in these interventions, these programs might still have enough momentum to continue driving them forward.

Afghan Youth and Women:
Participants but Not Beneficiaries of Current Initiatives

As the previous discussion has illustrated, even when taking steps in the right direction, most programs in Afghanistan have seldom achieved their stated goals. A report by the Special Inspector General for Afghanistan Reconstruction (SIGAR) concluded that the Promote Project referenced earlier, which intended to target seventy-five thousand women, only managed to assist roughly sixty despite its $280 million budget. The report further concluded that it was unclear what impact that project had on the lives of those sixty women and whether they benefited from their participation (Tolo News 2018). The report characterized the project as "poorly designed and oversold," ultimately failing to prepare women to get better jobs in any sector.

Similarly, an *Al Jazeera* article details that despite the billions of USAID poured into women's education projects, the programs were not effective. Nearly 66 percent of Afghanistan's girls do not attend schools. The ones that are lucky enough to be enrolled attend schools lacking basic facilities, teachers, and supplies, putting into question the quality of the education they are actually receiving. These girls also face discrimination and are negatively viewed by the more conservative factions in the country (Fung 2018). This goes back to a long history of the Taliban barring women and girls from education. The USAID and other international development programs—well funded but poorly designed—failed to consider the cultural and historical barriers to educating women and girls in Afghanistan.

Consequently, the projects discussed earlier did not result in widespread or sustainable outcomes for anyone in Afghanistan, let alone youth and women. Despite billions of U.S. dollars poured into the country since 2001, most of the reconstruction aid has been allocated primarily to rearming and policing Afghanistan, as revealed by U.S. government investigative reports and existing field-based scholarship (Lutz and Desai 2015). Another SIGAR report revealed over $15 billion in waste, fraud, and abuse of the U.S. Department of Defense–provided reconstruction funding from 2008 to 2018 (Ginsburg, Sweatt, and Massoudi 2018). A different SIGAR report further concluded that the World Bank did not properly audit their programs or publish the findings of their projects, calling into question their transparency and the actual results of their financial aid packages (SIGAR 2018a).

Compounding the poor security results, widespread fraud, waste, and dysfunction that have characterized many foreign interventions, those initiatives that have specifically sought to elevate the position of youth and women in the peace process, civil society, or Afghanistan's society at large tend to lack the funding and the political will to effect a widespread and lasting impact in the country. Even when well funded and conceptually aligned with nation-building initiatives, these programs lack a framework to successfully engage youth and women as the future maintainers of peace in Afghanistan. They focus on the agricultural sector to provide important infrastructure in a country where such systems do not exist. If they do attempt to involve women and youth in peace and leadership training, no additional resources or efforts are put into engaging community leaders or setting up avenues for youth and women to be involved in more formal political processes. If youth or women are not engaged at all levels of these projects and are not given the tools necessary to sustain these initiatives, these programs have little hope of making long-term impacts.

There have been no major programs designed in Afghanistan that truly engaged women and youth in the peace process. Youth and women tend to be targeted, if at all, as participants—not necessarily beneficiaries—in the economy, education, or health sectors. Initiatives tend to take the form of resources provided to them, with very little in terms of technology or training, rendering the process entirely unsustainable.

In an attempt to address these shortcomings, youth-run groups have sprung up, mainly in urban areas, over the past few years. Yet these groups are also marginalized from the peace process, especially at the national level, which limits the range of their potential impact. According to a 2018 Youth4Peace report, "With a continued sense that the current government is making little progress either in terms of economic development or securing a lasting peace agreement and a growing youth population, it is increasingly important to understand the views of youth on peace and security in Afghanistan" (Conciliation Resource 2018). As called for in UNSCR 2250, "Youth should be actively engaged in shaping lasting peace and contributing to justice and reconciliation," as they represent "a unique demographic dividend that can contribute to lasting peace and prosperity" if inclusive policies are put in place. Member states have been encouraged to engage local communities and nongovernmental actors "in developing strategies to counter the violent extremist narrative that can incite terrorist acts." They have also been encouraged to address conditions conducive to the spread of violent extremism by empowering youth; families; women; religious, cultural, and education leaders; and other concerned groups in civil society and by adopting "tailored approaches" to counterrecruitment to violent extremism. Within the category of prevention, member states have been urged to "facilitate an inclusive and enabling environment in which youth from different backgrounds are recognized and provided with adequate support to implement violence prevention activities and support social cohesion." The resolution further stressed the key role of inclusive policies, quality education, and other mechanisms to institute a culture of peace, tolerance, and dialogues that discourage youth participation in violence, terrorism, discrimination, and so on (UNSC 2015).

The youth of Afghanistan are ready to work for peace and contribute to transitioning their society away from its current conflict. During my interview with Jawid, a twenty-four-year-old student from Wardak Province, he noted, "I [want] to be an indirect part of resolving the war by rebuilding and strengthening the communities through giving [them] access for their basic needs, such as electricity, internet, clean water, and overall [a] better life. People who do not have much to lose in war do not care about war or peace. The gaps should be removed between rural and urban areas." As illustrated by Jawid's response, the youth in Afghanistan not only grasp the challenges that a postconflict Afghan society will face; they also have a clear understanding of what will be required to bring about lasting change in their country.

The three Ts framework that I outline in more detail in the next section constitutes a new, practical approach that can help guide specific programs and policies to involve youth and women in the building of a peace process that will have a sustained impact on Afghanistan. This framework emphasizes three traits that have been identified as commonly present in the most impactful programs to engage youth in both development and peacebuilding programs in postconflict states. Building on these best practices, the three Ts framework focused on community ties, technical training, and the effective use of technology.

Better UNSCR 2250 Implementation in Afghanistan with the Three Ts Framework

The proposed three Ts framework was developed to help Afghanistan transition from its current status of "underdeveloped" nation to one of "developed" country.

While the provision of basic services such as food, water, health programs and medicine, and institutional stability is clearly an important aspect of conflict prevention, the argument put forward here is that to be truly holistic and sustainable, international aid must go beyond the mere satisfaction of basic survival needs. It is particularly important for youth in countries like Afghanistan to be included in relevant policies and to provide them adequate tools to effectively operate in the modern world.

Community Ties

Local actors are better positioned to understand the lived realities of local communities, as they intersect with broader conditions at the country level. Youth, who constitute a large proportion of the Afghani population, are well aware of local challenges and opportunities. This is acknowledged in the *Amman Youth Declaration* that followed UNSCR 2250. This declaration underscores that all actors, including government, civil society, and faith-based organizations, should recognize and support young people by building upon their existing capacities and local ties (Youth4Peace 2015). The declaration also states that "national governments and local authorities must collaborate to create social and economic opportunities for young people, in both rural and urban locations." Furthermore, they must "invest in building young people's capabilities and equip them with skills to meet the labor demands through relevant education opportunities designed in a manner which promotes a culture of peace." UNSCR 2250 and the *Amman Declaration* both support local youth peace initiatives and indigenous processes for conflict resolution and promote the positive role of youth in the implementation of peace agreements (UNSC 2015). International development programs that are not designed with local realities in mind are likely to fail—and even make things worse—and have received highly critical evaluations in literature: "In *The Idealist*—a kind of 'where are they now?' for the ideas laid out in Jeffrey Sachs's *The End of Poverty*—Nina Munk discovers 'African villages were made squalid by the hopes and checkbooks of Western do-gooders.' Esther Duflo and Abhijit Banerjee's *Poor Economics* finds that dozens of 'common sense' development projects—food aid, crop insurance, microfinance—either don't help poor people or may even make them poorer" (Hobbes 2014). One noteworthy project in Afghanistan has been the National Solidarity Program (NSP). The NSP was established in 2002 to support local villages, support female participation, and make the postconflict environment safer for residents in addition to providing increased access to basic services (Center for Public Impact 2016). The program also established Community Development Councils (CDCs) tasked, at the local level, with identifying needs and planning, managing, and monitoring their development projects. As of 2016, nearly 35,000 communities had elected CDCs with over 150,000 female members. A total of 77,280 projects have been successfully financed through the project, and over $1.6 billion in block grants had been disbursed to the NSP's CDC subprojects. The success of this project is evidenced in the country's rural areas' increased support for democracy and youth and women empowerment; additionally, small water wells have been built where needed. The project's success has received positive national coverage. The follow-up to the NSP project, the Citizens' Charter, is currently trying to provide the CDC program a more solid structure and establish linkages with government entities (World Bank 2016). This will be an important step toward institutionalizing community-level engagement in the governance of the country; the local communities that are the beneficiaries of the projects will play a direct role in the whole process, which will greatly enhance its sustainability in the long-run.

It is vital to ensuring that target communities identify their own needs and shape assistance policies, especially through the contributions of young champions for the youth and women advocating for the female population; local women and youth possess a clearer understanding of the local on-the-ground realities, gender-based differences, and the suitability of development and peacebuilding interventions at the community level. Building on the structure of the CDCs and establishing a network of young champions would be an excellent starting point.

Technical Training

Afghanistan's formal education sector is outdated, with the current post–high school merit-based exam, known as Kankor, as one of the oldest methods for higher education enrollment (CSRS 2018). The Kankor exam has led to a significant number of youths getting into fields of study that they did not prefer. The available options for training in technical fields are rather limited. Furthermore, the location of the place of study is in most cases predetermined and inflexible, posing additional challenges for students and their families.

Poor-quality primary-level schooling does not prepare young people for study at the university level, and the lack of capacity, quality, and availability of higher education does not prepare youth for a competitive labor market. The high numbers of returnees from Pakistan and other countries who need to be absorbed into the current education system and workforce represent an additional difficulty. The time required for young people to be prepared to enter the labor market—provided that any employment opportunities exist for them—is currently exceedingly long. Given Afghanistan's present realities, alternative approaches to youth education and employment must be considered (Ariana News 2016).

In spite of the number of international aid programs devoted to improving education in Afghanistan, education remains an unreliable component of daily life for Afghani youth. Khair, a twenty-year-old student from Kabul, reported his conviction that the education he received failed to adequately prepare him to contribute to Afghanistan's postconflict peacebuilding and sustainability efforts. He believes that getting a higher education more focused on technical training would better allow him to positively impact his community and, by extension, his country. This standpoint is in line with UNSCR 2250 and focuses on the importance of creating policies for youth that would positively contribute to peacebuilding efforts. Both Khair and this resolution emphasize supporting projects designed to grow local economies, provide employment opportunities and vocational training for youth, foster their education, and promote youth entrepreneurship and constructive political engagement. In Afghanistan, one of the reasons identified as contributing to youth involvement in the conflict is the lack of any other meaningful life opportunities. As UNSCR 2250 rightly pinpointed, youth vocational and technical training could pave the way for employment, entrepreneurship, and political engagement and could potentially discourage participation in conflict and extremist violence.

Conflict also has a direct influence on youth's outlook, sense of self-worth, and social position in society—a very important consideration in a gerontocratic nation like Afghanistan. Youth in all Afghani provinces express having a deep appreciation for skill-based training that can improve their employability. The greatest area of interest for program content is in skills-based training such as carpentry, embroidery, and computer science and coding skills that directly translate into employment opportunities (ICMA 2011). However, technical training alone does not necessarily change youth's support for political violence—more has to be done in that regard, in addition to providing the desired vocational training. Some programs—for example, the RAMP UP project—included interventions intended to provide economic and social opportunities for women in culturally appropriate ways and initiatives to engage youth, such as sports, internships, and skills development. Two additional crosscutting objectives of these initiatives were anticorruption and conflict mitigation (Glinski, n.d.).

Basic vocational training for youth supported with the provision of stipends, business start-up cash, and other forms of assistance has proven to be an effective tool to increase opportunities in a shorter period of time. As a case in point, Shahnoz, an Afghan female returnee from Iran, trained for a full year to be a tailor through a funded program. She subsequently opened her own business, which now employs other women (Counterpart International 2017). Shahnoz's case illustrates the success of a basic form of training program that could relatively quickly improve the situation of those Afghan youth in need of the most urgent assistance. Additional examples include an agriculture-focused program supported by the Japanese government called ex-PEACE (Japan International Cooperation Agency 2017), a coding school for girls (Code to Inspire 2019), and a project targeting "peace champions" (O'Brien 2019). Training as civilian support to the U.S. military has also been promoted as a viable opportunity as well for Afghan youths (U.S. DOD 2018).

Information technology, software development, and other internet-related skills (Gallagher 2018) are in high demand globally. These technical skills can be designed for youth, resulting in a quick turnaround in terms of training and employment opportunities. A large-scale technical training program followed by employment or business opportunities carried out in Afghanistan would provide youth with viable alternatives to engagement in conflict and extremist violence.

Technology

Technology innovations take place at a lightning pace; technology has fundamentally altered the nature of modern conflict, the strategies employed by peacebuilders to mitigate violence, and the way businesses operate. Countries with fewer infrastructures, if provided with the right opportunities, can also take advantage of these technologies. For instance, Foldscope, an origami-based paper microscope created by Stanford University, only costs $1 and can be easily made available to children in poor and rural areas (Foldscope, n.d.); a mobile application is being used to connect artisans in rural Afghanistan to consumers worldwide (iFWorld-Design 2020); an inexpensive device enables households to cook a meal while heating water to temperatures high enough to eliminate bacteria; a hydropower plant uses local waterways alongside other energy innovations to provide energy to 1.4 billion people (Palma 2018); and energy-efficient "infant warmers" can address the risk of hypothermia that threatens thirteen million premature babies born each year (Huber 2013). The World Bank and other organizations have conducted risk surveys and community focus-group discussions involving CDC members and using technology such as social media and phone interviews. In the finance sector, the use of mobile money has been supported by multiple agencies and the government in many cases to pay teachers, the army, and other institutions (Borgen Project 2018); and Afghanistan has adopted an electronic national ID system and many other e-governance projects.

While the technology sector in Afghanistan has expanded considerably, there is much more that could be done to assist youth, especially young women, achieve better results. One of the biggest areas Afghanistan needs to leverage is the use of the internet to connect local businesses and talent to international markets. Except for the telecommunications sector, other ICT components are not developed institutionally in Afghanistan.

While acknowledging the pervasiveness of moral panics about the use of social media for the online radicalization of youth, I offer that technological skills are one of the potential advantages that young people can leverage—especially those raised in a more technologically advanced context than was the case for their elders. Successful examples from other countries support this argument, as discussed by Grace Atuhaire (chapter 2, this volume) and Willice Onyango (chapter 10, this volume). Providing Afghan youth with access to the information technology they need to connect with international markets and businesses in their region and beyond would allow them to acquire outside experience in various sectors. This experience can be then adapted and applied to the Afghani context in a more practical and sustainable sense.

A significant barrier to this strategy is the currently inadequate ICT infrastructure of Afghanistan, which cannot support modern information-transfer systems. The Afghan government thus needs to develop an in-country system development policy for all its ICT needs. This will enable the private sector in the country to flourish, allow youth to connect with the rest of the world through education and employment, and reduce the drivers pushing youth to participate in conflict and extremist violence.

Moving Forward

The fragile, conflict-prone conditions endured by the population of countries like Afghanistan should not serve as justification for only the most basic employment opportunities to be offered to the young population. Youth all over the world have the same amount of potential regardless of local circumstances; it could even be argued that the hardship endured by youth in countries such as Afghanistan adds further incentives and drive for them to succeed.

As the earlier discussion on the situation in the Shamshato refugee camp illustrated, the absence of a viable way to access education services and information severely limited youth's and women's opportunities for employment and life betterment, leading them to believe that their only livelihood options were with insurgent or radicalized groups. If more youth were provided access to information technologies and better community-based education programs and training that would prepare them to live and work in the modern world, the appeal or necessity to propagate radical philosophies or participate in violent conflict would diminish significantly. Social media could play a positive role in war-torn Afghanistan by providing a vehicle for citizens to become better informed and formulate and share their thoughts.

Notably—and not surprisingly—young people constitute the major drive behind this push for technological advancement. Many, like Maryam Ghulami, a twenty-year-old girl living in Herat, are convinced that their generation will bring about the change that their parents never could (Hindu Press 2019). Maryam is learning graphic design and computer science through an online academy. While she acknowledges that Afghanistan faces many problems, she has faith that her generation can effect positive change. Maryam remarks, "The new generation can change Afghanistan with knowledge, with technology."

After billions of dollars in aid has been invested in Afghanistan, we have witnessed one of the biggest failures of state-building efforts. The reconstruction and development efforts undertaken in Afghanistan have not been successful largely because the programs implemented were guided by flawed theories of change and did not target the root causes of fragility or effectively engage the right stakeholders. Conflict and the risk of radicalization need to be understood from local and historical perspectives; solutions for peace need to be context specific and customized. If the approach proposed in UNSCR 2250 can be translated from policy to action on the ground and young people are indeed brought in as part of the solution, the situation in Afghanistan would rise above its current bleakness. As previously noted, most of the Afghan population is under twenty-five, a fact that offers the promise of a human capital comparative advantage—or demographic dividend—as a foundation for Afghanistan's development. Nevertheless, Afghanistan's economy is still failing, and its political processes are stalled while the country remains torn by violence and conflict. Leveraging the country's large albeit undervalued youth population, a framework such as the three Ts model can pave the way for Afghanistan and countries in similar circumstances to better engage in global arenas. Empowering Afghani youth economically and facilitating their access to the community ties, training, and technology they need to succeed are, I argue, actionable strategies for society at large to follow the path toward modernization and bring an end to their forty-year conflict.

NOTES

1. This chapter draws primarily on Western sources and programmatic policy to analyze the effectiveness of current development strategies in Afghanistan, as those are the main available sources. In Afghanistan, policies on development are often centered on Western development models, and Afghanistan has produced limited native scholarship analyzing the effectiveness of international development programs.

2. All references in this section on the Shamshato refugee camp are based on a compilation of personal accounts experienced firsthand by the author or secondhand by his family and friends who also spent time in the same or a similar refugee camp.

3. All interviews were conducted by the author between August 28 and August 31, 2019, in Kabul, Afghanistan. An exploratory questionnaire with four open-ended questions was administered to five participants concerning their views on the conflict and peacebuilding in Afghanistan, any potential role they saw themselves having in it, and what role, if any, could education play in that process.

4. Names have been changed to maintain the anonymity of study participants.

REFERENCES

Afghanistan Ministry of Information and Culture. 2013. *Afghanistan National Youth Policy Draft*. Accessed February 28, 2019. www.youthpolicy.org/national/Afghanistan_2013_Draft _National_Youth_Policy.pdf.

Amambia, S. C., F. Bivens, M. Hamisi, I. Lancaster, O. Ogada, G. Okumu, N. Songora, and R. Zaid. 2018. *Participatory Action Research for Advancing Youth-Led Peacebuilding in Kenya*. Washington, D.C.: United States Institute of Peace.

Ariana News. 2016. "Mohe Announces Kankor Examination Results." Accessed June 10, 2019. https://ariananews.af/mohe-announces-kankor-examination-results.

Borgen Project. 2018. "New Developments: Afghanistan's Technology Is Growing." *Borgen Project Blog*, March 12, 2018. Accessed February 28, 2019. https://borgenproject.org/afghanistans-technology-growing-developing.

Center for Public Impact. 2016. "Building Trust in Government: Afghanistan's National Solidarity Programme." Accessed February 28, 2019. www.centreforpublicimpact.org/case-study/building-trust-in-government-afghanistans-national-solidarity-program.

Code to Inspire. 2019. "Building Afghanistan 2.0." Accessed June 10, 2019. www.codetoinspire.org.

Coleville, Rupert. 1997. "Afghanistan: The Unending Crisis." UNHCR. Accessed February 28, 2019. www.unhcr.org/publications/refugeemag/3b680fbfc/refugees-magazine-issue-108 -afghanistan-unending-crisis-biggest-caseload.html.

Collier, Paul, and Anke Hoeffler. 2004. "Greed and Grievance in Civil War." *Oxford Economic Papers* 56:563–595.

Conciliation Resources. 2018. *Youth Perspectives on Peace and Security: Afghanistan*. Youth4Peace, April 2018. Accessed February 28, 2019. www.youth4peace.info/system/files/2018 -04/1.%20FGD_Afghanistan_CR_0.pdf.

Counterpart International. 2017. "Young Afghan Aspirations: Peace and Stability." Accessed February 28, 2019. www.counterpart.org/stories/young-afghan-aspirations -peace-stability.

CSRS (Center for Strategic and Regional Studies Kabul). 2018. "Kankor and the Situation of Afghan Higher Education." Accessed April 30, 2020. https://csrskabul.com/en/?p= 3158.

DOD (U.S. Department of Defense). 2018. *Enhancing Security and Stability in Afghanistan*. Report to Congress. Accessed February 28, 2019. https://media.defense.gov/2018/Dec/20/ 2002075158/-1/-1/1/1225-REPORT-DECEMBER-2018.pdf. (URL inactive.)

Foldscope. n.d. "Our Story: Mission Statement." Accessed June 11, 2019. www.foldscope.com/ our-story.

Fung, Melissa. 2018. "Where's the Aid Money Gone? Afghan Girls' Struggle for Education." Al Jazeera. Accessed February 28, 2019. www.aljazeera.com/indepth/features/aid-money -afghan-girls-struggle-education-180606134316480.html.

Gallagher, Adam. 2018. "How 'Peace Tech' Is Changing Global Conflict." United States Institute of Peace. Accessed February 28, 2019. https://reliefweb.int/report/world/how-peace -tech-changing-global-conflict.

Ginsburg, Alexander B., Glenn Sweatt, and Kevin Massoudi. 2018. "New SIGAR Report Identifies 'Waste, Fraud, and Abuse' in Afghanistan." Pillsbury Law. Accessed February 28, 2019. www.pillsburylaw.com/en/news-and-insights/sigar-waste-fraud-afghanistan .html.

Glinski, Stephanie. n.d. "Training Young Entrepreneurs." Welt Hunger Hilife. Accessed February 28, 2019. www.welthungerhilfe.org/our-work/countries/afghanistan/vocational-training -in-afghanistan.

Goldstone, Jack A. 2010. "The New Population Bomb: The Four Megatrends That Will Change the World." *Foreign Affairs*. Accessed January 19, 2019. www.jstor.org/stable/20699781.

Hindu Press. 2019. "Afghan Youth Are Wary of Taliban's Return." February 1, 2019. Accessed February 28, 2019. www.thehindu.com/news/international/afghan-youth-are-wary-of-talibans-return/article26155023.ece.

Hobbes, Michael. 2014. "Stop Trying to Save the World." *New Republic,* November 17, 2014. Accessed February 2, 2019. https://newrepublic.com/article/120178/problem-international-development-and-plan-fix-it.

Huber, Rolf. 2013. "Meet 7 Startups That Are Innovating for the Developing World Online." Accessed July 11, 2017. https://venturebeat.com/2013/10/30/meet-7-startups-that-are-innovating-for-the-developing-world.

Human Rights Watch. 2016. "Afghanistan: Taliban Child Soldier Recruitment Surges." Accessed February 28, 2019. www.hrw.org/news/2016/02/17/afghanistan-taliban-child-soldier-recruitment-surges.

ICMA (International City/County Management Association). 2011. "Regional Afghan Municipalities Program for Urban Populations." ICMA, December 15, 2011. Accessed February 28, 2019. https://icma.org/programs-and-projects/regional-afghan-municipalities-program-urban-populations.

Jain, Rupuam. 2018. "Afghanistan's Poverty Rate Rises as Economy Suffers." Reuters, May 7, 2018. Accessed February 28, 2019. www.reuters.com/article/us-afghanistan-economy/afghanistans-poverty-rate-rises-as-economy-suffers-idUSKBN1I818X.

Japan International Cooperation Agency. 2017. "Enhancing Afghan Agriculture through Learning from the Expertise of the Agricultural Production in Japan." Accessed February 28, 2019. www.jica.go.jp/project/english/afghanistan/012/news/general/170331.html.

Kelemen, Helen, Dia Hadid, and Vanessa Romo. 2018. "Zalmay Khalilzad Appointed as U.S. Special Adviser to Afghanistan." NPR, September 5, 2018. Accessed February 28, 2019. www.npr.org/2018/09/05/641094135/zalmay-khalilzad-appointed-as-u-s-special-adviser-to-afghanistan.

Lutz, Catherine, and Sujaya Desai. 2015. "US Reconstruction Aid for Afghanistan: The Dollars and Sense." Costs of War, January 5, 2015. Accessed February 28, 2019. https://watson.brown.edu/costsofwar/files/cow/imce/papers/2015/US%20Reconstruction%20Aid%20for%20Afghanistan.pdf.

McNerney, Michael. 2006. "Stabilization and Reconstruction in Afghanistan: Are PRTs a Model or a Muddle?" *US Army War College Quarterly* 35. Accessed February 28, 2020. www.researchgate.net/publication/265539793_Stabilization_and_Reconstruction_in_Afghanistan_Are_PRTs_a_Model_or_a_Muddle.

Nassif, Claudia, and Tobias Haque. 2016. "Afghanistan to 2030: Priorities for Economic Development under Fragility." World Bank. Accessed February 28, 2019. http://documents.worldbank.org/curated/en/156881533220723730/pdf/129161-WP-P157288-Afghanistan-to-2030-PUBLIC.pdf.

O'Brien, Sarah. 2019. "Here Are the Most In-Demand Jobs for 2019." CNBC, January 24, 2019. Accessed February 28, 2019. www.cnbc.com/2019/01/24/here-are-the-most-in-demand-jobs-for-2019.html.

Palma, Julian. 2018. "Technology Can Help Afghanistan Better Manage Its Natural Disasters." *World Bank Blogs,* September 1, 2018. Accessed February 28, 2019. http://blogs.worldbank.org/endpovertyinsouthasia/technology-can-help-afghanistan-better-manage-its-natural-disasters.

Radio Free Radio Europe Radio Liberty. 2009. "Hope and Fears of Young Afghans as Taliban Talks Advance." Accessed February 28, 2019. www.rferl.org/a/afghanistan-society-politics/29746089.html.

Redden, Jack. 2002. "Pakistan Refugee Camp Once Famous for Arrivals Now One-Third Empty." UNHCR, November 11, 2002. Accessed February 28, 2019. www.unhcr.org/news/

latest/2002/11/3dcfa3144/pakistan-refugee-camp-once-famous-arrivals-one-third-empty .html.

Samim, Mohammad. 2016. "Afghanistan's Addiction to Foreign Aid." Diplomat, May 19, 2016. Accessed February 28, 2019. https://thediplomat.com/2016/05/afghanistans-addiction-to -foreign-aid.

SIGAR. 2018a. "Afghanistan Reconstruction Trust Fund." SIGAR. Accessed February 28, 2019. www.sigar.mil/pdf/audits/SIGAR-18-42-AR.pdf.

———. 2018b. "Stabilization: Lessons from the U.S. Experience in Afghanistan." SIGAR. Accessed February 28, 2019. www.sigar.mil/pdf/lessonslearned/SIGAR-18-48-LL.pdf.

Tolo News. 2015. "Unemployment Rates Spike in Afghanistan." Accessed February 28, 2019. www.tolonews.com/afghanistan/unemployment-rate-spikes-afghanistan.

———. 2018. "US Program for Afghan Women Falls Short: SIGAR." Accessed February 28, 2019. www.tolonews.com/afghanistan/us-program-afghan-women-falling-short-sigar.

UNFPA (United Nations Populations Fund). 2015. "Young People in Afghanistan." UNFPA. Accessed June 10, 2019. https://afghanistan.unfpa.org/en/node/15227.

United Nations Security Council. 2015. Resolution 2250, S/RES/2250. Accessed June 10, 2019. www.un.org/en/ga/search/view_doc.asp?symbol=S/RES/2250(2015)&referer=/english/ &Lang=E.

United Nations Sri Lanka. 2017. "Youth and Peacebuilding." Accessed February 28, 2019. http:// unvlk.org/youth_and_peacebuilding. (URL inactive.)

UNSC (United Nations Security Council). 2015. "Security Council Unanimously Adopts 2250 Resolution." United Nations, December 9, 2015. Accessed February 28, 2019. www.un.org/ press/en/2015/sc12149.doc.htm.

Urdal, Henrik. 2004. "The Devil in the Demographics: The Effect of Youth Bulges on Domestic Armed Conflict, 1950–2000." *Social Development Papers: Conflict Prevention and Reconstruction* 14:1–31.

———. 2006. "A Clash of Generations? Youth Bulges and Political Violence." *International Studies Quarterly* 50, no. 3 (September): 607–629.

Urdal, Henrik, and Kristian Hoelscher. 2012. "Explaining Urban Social Disorder and Violence: An Empirical Study of Event Data from Asian and Sub-Saharan African Cities." *International Interactions* 38, no. 4, 512–528.

USAID (U.S. Agency for International Development). 2013a. "Skills Training for Afghan Youth (STAY+)." USAID. Accessed February 28, 2019. www.usaid.gov/node/50576.

———. 2013b. "Women Enterprise Development." USAID. Accessed February 28, 2019. www .usaid.gov/node/52211.

———. 2013c. "Youth Empowerment Project." USAID. Accessed February 28, 2019. www .usaid.gov/node/51981.

———. 2018. "The Goldozi Project." USAID. Accessed February 28, 2019. www.usaid.gov/ news-information/fact-sheets/goldozi-project.

———. 2019a. "PROMOTE." USAID. Accessed February 28, 2019. www.usaid.gov/afghanistan/ promote.

———. 2019b. "Provincial Reconstruction Teams: Afghanistan." USAID. Accessed February 28, 2019. www.usaid.gov/provincial-reconstruction-teams. (URL inactive.)

World Bank. 2012. "Afghanistan Encouraging Skills Development and Musical Talent." Accessed February 28, 2019. http://documents.worldbank.org/curated/en/703321468182347774/ Afghanistan-Encouraging-skills-development-and-musical-talent.

———. 2016. "Project: Citizens' Charter Afghanistan." Accessed February 28, 2019. http:// projects.worldbank.org/P160567?lang=en.

Youth4Peace. 2015. "Global Forum on Youth, Peace, and Security." Accessed February 28, 2019. www.youth4peace.info/system/files/2016-10/AMMAN%20YOUTH%20DECLARATION %20%28English%29_0.pdf.

PART IV

Partnerships

CHAPTER 7

Climate Change, Environmental Action, and the Youth, Peace, and Security Agenda

GLOBAL POLICIES, LOCAL EFFORTS

Marisa O. Ensor

Conflicts triggered by competition over natural resources, the negative impact of climate change, and environmental degradation are among the greatest challenges in twenty-first-century geopolitics. Often compounding each other, these factors present serious threats to human security at global, national, and local levels. Young people, who constitute the largest demographic sector in many of the affected countries (Feseha 2018; OECD 2013), are frequently the most severely impacted. Climate action, on the other hand, can also serve as a vehicle for peacebuilding and environmental cooperation. Ensuring that these opportunities are both effective and inclusive would require the meaningful participation of youth together with other relevant partners. Yet young women's and men's increasingly active role in environmental action and the ways in which climate change uniquely impacts the security and development prospects of youth remain as of yet understudied.

Following the recommendations of *The Missing Peace: Independent Progress Study on Youth, Peace and Security,* this chapter seeks to spotlight efforts to facilitate youth's engagement in environmental issues and the extent to which this environmental action supports peacebuilding and enhances human security. Initiatives involving youth from South Sudan, a war-torn country whose very young population must confront the interrelated challenges of protracted conflict and climate change, serve as the primary case study. Based on longitudinal ethnographic fieldwork conducted among various youth-led organizations in South Sudan and in refugee camps in Uganda, I examine the challenges and opportunities facing conflict-affected South Sudanese youth in these two countries in their efforts to address the impacts of climate change, alleviate security challenges, and promote sustainable peace for all. The information on these networks' organizational structure and activities was collected through a combination of desk research and multisited ethnographic fieldwork undertaken in the fall of 2018 and spring/ summer of 2019. Field data-gathering methods included focus-group discussions and key informant interviews conducted with the networks' leaders and field staff as well as with female and male youth in both countries. Participatory resource mapping, risk calendars, and gender and conflict analysis tools were also implemented with young interlocutors.

Findings support the premise that mobilizing youth's capacities for peacebuilding and environmental action requires a targeted and long-term approach. This must include adequate consideration of conflict-related challenges (e.g., protracted displacement, loss of education, lack of employable skills, destruction of a stable family environment) as well as environmental circumstances also present during times of peace (e.g., rising temperatures; erratic rains and frequent droughts and floods, sometimes in the same season; increasingly violent competition over land, water, and grazing pastures) (Ensor 2018, 3). These findings may guide current peacebuilding initiatives in South Sudan and the South Sudanese diaspora. Lessons emerging from this research may also inform the global youth, peace, and security (YPS) agenda so that it better responds to on-the-ground realities, hence promoting more sustainable and inclusive approaches to long-lasting peace, development, and environmental action.

CLIMATE CHANGE AND SECURITY CHALLENGES

Climate change and current global security challenges are interrelated and mutually constitutive. The negative impacts of climate change increase vulnerability, exacerbate grievances, and deepen preexisting fragility, contributing to protracted crises. In effect, protracted crises are often driven by a combination of recurring causes, including human-induced factors and natural hazards that may result in breakdowns in food-provision systems and other threats to people's livelihoods. Unstable governance impairs economic performance and limits the capacity to implement adaptation and mitigation measures, which in turn increase the vulnerability to climate impacts. Climate change is thus commonly understood as a threat multiplier as it aggravates already fragile situations and contributes to social upheaval and violent conflict in regions where security challenges already exist. It is estimated that almost half a billion people live in over twenty countries affected by protracted human-environmental crises, mostly in Africa. Elevated hunger rates, another common risk in protracted crisis situations, are almost three times higher in Africa than in other developing contexts (FAO 2016, 4), threatening the survival and compromising the human security of this continent's young population.

The Intergovernmental Panel on Climate Change (IPCC) defines human security as a condition that exists when "the vital core of human lives is protected, and when people have the freedom and capacity to live with dignity" (IPCC 2014, 759). The concept of human security is also related to Johan Galtung's (1981) notion of "positive peace," as contrasted with "negative peace." Negative peace has historically denoted the absence of war and other forms of large-scale violent human conflict. Positive peace, on the other hand, also requires the amelioration of all structural and systemic obstacles to peace. In addressing the need for justice, equity, and democracy and an end to structural violence, positive peace promotes human security and broadens the focus beyond the end of war and physical violence toward recovery and sustainable development.

For many populations that already have limited capital assets and are resource dependent and socially marginalized, human security will be progressively undermined as the climate changes. It is further estimated that by 2030, climate impacts could push an additional 100 million people into poverty and, by 2050, as many as 143 million people could become climate migrants in just three regions— Sub-Saharan Africa, South Asia, and Latin America (IPCC 2014). Sub-Saharan Africa is particularly vulnerable to the impacts of climate change due to a number of factors, including poverty, recurrent droughts, inequitable land distribution, and overdependence on rain-fed agriculture. An analysis of the impact of climatic events on youth, peace, and security is critical for understanding the underlying mechanisms for how displacement, conflict, and security challenges apply specifically to young people (Payne, Warembourg, and Awan 2017, 6) in South Sudan and other war-torn countries. Additional scholarly and policy attention must thus focus on the ways in which climate change, conflict, and displacement uniquely impact the security and development prospects of the world's youth populations.

A Focus on African Youth

The positioning of youth in any society has a bearing on their leadership potential and their possible role in peacebuilding and postconflict recovery. The tension between young and old has been one of the key features of intergenerational shifts pertaining to the control over power, resources, and political space worldwide. This issue is particularly poignant in South Sudan, where young people make up over 70 percent of the population (UNESCO 2018).

Trapped in protracted refugee situations and struggling to transition into social adulthood, conflict-affected African youth often inhabit a liminal space that Mozambique-born anthropologist Alcinda Honwana termed "waithood" (2013). Africa's population as a whole is very young, with 60 percent of the entire continent below the age of twenty-five, making it the youngest continent in the world (Adegoke 2017). In 2010, 70 percent of the region's population was under the age of thirty, and slightly more than 20 percent was between the ages of fifteen to twenty-four. In 2015, youth in Africa constituted 19 percent of the global youth population, numbering 226 million (U.N. DESA 2015). African Union figures estimate that 40 percent of the continent's population was under the age of fifteen (AU 2017, 6). By 2030, it is predicted that the number of youth in Africa will have increased by 42 percent (U.N. DESA 2015). Given such demographic realities and the recent wave of social upheavals, deteriorating environmental conditions, and humanitarian crises in Africa—and in many other regions of the world—youth's agency and their potential for (positive or negative) change are the subjects of growing research and policy interest.

As discussed throughout this volume, young people's roles in peacebuilding have been gaining further momentum as a result of the United Nations Security Council Resolution (UNSCR) 2250, unanimously adopted in 2015. UNSCR 2250 urges member states to recognize the potential of young people to act as constructive change agents for peace (Lopes Cardozo and Scotto 2017, 6). This legally binding instrument—the first-ever thematic resolution on YPS—recognizes and legitimizes the efforts of youth in building peace.[1] By urging member states to increase the representation of youth in decision-making at all levels, UNSCR 2250 shifts the international focus from seeing youth as passive victims or a security threat to recognizing young people as a large sector of the population with the potential to contribute to constructive change.

A parallel development in Africa is the *African Union Agenda 2063: The Africa We Want* (AU 2013), which aims at removing all forms of systemic inequalities, exploitation, marginalization, and discrimination affecting young people to ensure that youth issues are mainstreamed in all development initiatives. Both U.N. and AU agendas acknowledge that youth are more likely to avoid violence and engage in peacebuilding if provided with meaningful opportunities to engage in political participation, forge connections with their community, prepare to join the workforce, and build constituencies for peace. U.N. and AU frameworks for youth participation are positive developments, but they offer limited detailed guidance on how YPS agendas are to be operationalized on the ground and are no substitute for locally driven efforts. There is still a distance to go to ensure the active and meaningful engagement of young people in national and local peace processes. Environmental activism can contribute to preparing conflict-affected youth to engage in—and potentially lead—peacebuilding and development initiatives. Examples from South Sudan are illustrative of these processes.

The Context of Conflict, Peace, and Environmental (In)security in South Sudan

South Sudan has a long history of conflict, displacement, and environmental crises. The Second Sudanese Civil War (1983–2005) between the government in Khartoum and the Sudan People's Liberation Army (SPLA)—largely a continuation of the First Sudanese Civil War (1955–1972)—triggered one of the worst humanitarian disasters of the twentieth century. It resulted in over two million casualties, most of them civilians, many of whom died of starvation and disease. Over five million people were forced to flee their homes (Johnson 2005). A peace agreement put an end to the conflict on January 9, 2005, and the Republic of South Sudan became an independent nation on July 9, 2011.

The South Sudanese Civil War, one of the most brutal and destructive conflicts of the twenty-first century, erupted on December 15, 2013, less than three years after their hard-won independence. A power struggle between President Salva Kiir, a member of the Dinka ethnic group, and his former vice president, Riek Machar, a Nuer, divided the national army along ethnic lines, prompting soldiers from each faction to turn against each other in Juba, the nation's capital. The fighting soon spread across the country, giving way to a deadly pattern of revenge and counter-revenge attacks along Dinka-Nuer ethnic lines. Exacerbated ethnic divisions have, however, been largely acknowledged as a consequence rather than a cause of the conflict, as ethnic identity has become an easily manipulated structure for exploiting intertribal differences and maintaining or gaining power.

Political instability and armed conflict have remained pervasive in South Sudan for most of its eight years of independence, resulting in massive waves of forced displacement, including distress migration (FAO 2016).[2] The U.N. High Commissioner for Refugees (UNHCR) estimates that over 4.3 million people have been forced to flee their homes, the majority of whom are women and children (2019). Conflict and large-scale displacements combined with drought and failing crops have brought 4.8 million people to the brink of famine, according to estimates by the U.N. Office for the Coordination of Humanitarian Affairs (U.N. OCHA 2017), and resulted in four hundred thousand excess deaths (Checchi et al. 2018, 2). The latest war in the world's newest country caused over 382,000 casualties (Checchi et al. 2018).

Numerous initiatives—that is, peace negotiations mediated by the Intergovernmental Authority on Development (IGAD), a regional political and economic development block for Eastern Africa; international sanctions; arms embargoes; and intraparty dialogues—culminated in several peace agreements, all of which were almost immediately violated. Renewed fighting erupted in mid-July 2016, resulting in reintensified violence and insecurity throughout the country (UNICEF 2017). A new peace agreement was reached on September 12, 2018—known as the Revitalized Agreement on the Resolution of Conflict in South Sudan (R-ARCSS)—which has largely held in most, but not all, areas. While politically motivated conflict has declined, intercommunal fighting has not abated.

Youth and Conflict in South Sudan

Within a context of rapidly switching allegiances, youth's propensity to resolve disagreements with violence has reportedly increased. The U.N. Mission in South Sudan (UNMISS) has focused on alleviating the population's massive humanitarian needs, including, above all, the protection of some two hundred thousand civilians who had sought refuge within U.N. bases—in areas known as Protection of Civilian (PoC) sites—since the conflict began (Arensen 2016). With a third of the population having been displaced—most of them youth—lacking opportunities, traumatized by war, and ethnically divided, the situation became a perfect storm for the protraction of the conflict.

The numbers of out-of-school children and adolescents/youth, particularly females and those affected by conflict and other emergencies, are very high despite the range of nongovernmental organizations (NGOs) providing educational frontline services (UNICEF 2016). Most young people, especially in the countryside, are uneducated, as near-term survival has been prioritized over the long-term benefits of education and skills training. In this volatile environment, the already fragile education system has deteriorated even further. Educational outcomes are very poor, as most primary school teachers are untrained. The capacity of the Ministry of General Education and Instruction to respond to students' needs remains limited; numerous teachers left their schools due to insufficient, delayed, and unpaid salaries as well as insecurity (UNICEF 2016). As a result, only 27 percent of the population over the age of fifteen is literate, and 94 percent of the youth engage in jobs without any vocational qualification (JAICA 2017).

South Sudanese youth—young males, in particular—are perceived by most other stakeholders to be active participants in conflict. Large and idle youth populations have proven easily manipulable, especially those harboring unaddressed grievances against certain groups (tribal, religious, political). Desperation in the

absence of any other viable alternatives has led many to join armed groups to provide for themselves and their families and to acquire a sense of purpose. Whether
instigating violence, engaging in cattle rustling and banditry, or defending their
homes and communities, youth's perceived propensity for violent behavior is also
believed to increase their likelihood to join armed militias. In many communities (e.g., Aweil, Bor, Rumbek, and Wau), inadequate educational and economic
opportunities have led to high youth unemployment rates, with youth under the
age of twenty-five reportedly more likely to resort to violent means of conflict resolution than any other demographic sector. Additionally, large numbers of street
children are engaged in criminal activities that, whether ethnically motivated or
opportunistic, thrive in an environment lacking functioning accountability mechanisms (SCG 2015). While positive steps have recently been taken—including the
ratification of the R-ARCSS—much remains to be done in all areas both to seek
the lasting political solutions required to address security, justice, and governance
needs and to transition to positive peace.

Youth and Environmental Factors in South Sudan

Even before the two warring parties began laying waste to the country, South
Sudan's young population lived in a context characterized by deteriorating environmental conditions, long-standing economic deprivation, underdevelopment,
and lack of service provision, compounded by weak governance, persistent political instability, marginalization, and acute insecurity easily exploited by militants
(Ensor 2016). Intercommunal conflicts had also intensified (SHBA 2012), often
centering on competition over land for pasture, cattle raiding, and the abduction
of women or children (Deng 2013).

The *Climate Change Vulnerability Index 2017* ranks South Sudan among the
five most vulnerable countries in the world, alongside the Democratic Republic
of Congo, Central African Republic, Haiti, and Liberia. The country is among
the most rapidly warming locations on the globe, with temperatures increasing as
much as 0.4 degrees per decade over the past thirty years—2.5 times faster than
the global average (Maplecroft 2017, 1). Environmental conditions are becoming
increasingly arid, with intensified and prolonged periods of drought punctuated
by erratic and brief but torrential rains. "The resulting flash floods often destroy
existing crops and pasture and wash away the topsoil, further compromising agricultural yields and food availability" (Ensor 2013b, 527). These trends constitute a
serious threat to the survival of a vast proportion of the population. Up to 95 percent of the people in South Sudan—more than eleven million—are dependent on
climate-sensitive activities for their livelihoods, including agriculture, animal hus-
bandry, forestry resources, the gathering of wild foods, and fishing. Only 4 percent
of the land is currently actively cultivated, even though more than 95 percent of
the country's total area is considered to be suitable for agriculture (Stalon 2017).
Pastoralist groups have traditionally perceived farming as undignified—a livelihood derogatorily referred to as "digging" among young people (Ensor 2013a, 37).

As climate change causes temperatures to rise and rains to become more erratic,
crop failures and livestock deaths become more common, as do conflict over
dwindling water sources and grazing areas among nomadic pastoralists—cattle
keepers who follow their herds in their seasonal migrations—and between farmers

and pastoralists. These conflicts involve primarily youth and often revolve around cattle, land, and water. Young nomadic cattle keepers who accompany their cows as they migrate to find pasture during the increasingly long and unpredictable dry season must also protect their animals from raiders. After years of on-and-off integration into military service, heavily armed young cattle raiders mount military-style attacks that may claim dozens or even hundreds of lives at a time. This type of communal violence preceded South Sudan's current ethnopolitical conflict, and unless its drivers are adequately addressed, it is likely to succeed it (Krause 2019).

Fighting and displacement coupled with the increasing global demand for ivory and extreme poverty have also placed tremendous pressure on the country's abundant wildlife and are driving poaching and bushmeat hunting. Logging and rapid deforestation are on the rise, and so are illegal exports of mahogany, teak, and charcoal. Trafficking operations exploit the current insecurity and governance vacuum in many areas of the country (Ensor 2018, 4; 2019).

Although violence and deprivation remain pervasive in South Sudan, many individuals, groups, and communities are mobilizing to pursue sustainable solutions. Many of those involved in grassroots peacebuilding efforts are young women and men whose potential contribution as drivers of peace is being encouraged and supported through initiatives such as capacity development for peacebuilding and environmental action.

South Sudanese Youth Networks as Environmental Peacebuilding

"Central to negotiating continuity and change in any context" (Ensor 2013a, 31), South Sudanese youth have emerged as key stakeholders in these profound transformations that characterize their war-torn country. The humanitarian community's emergency response has focused primarily on the provision of basic needs—food, water, shelter, and health care. However, at the time of this writing, many young South Sudanese have already been displaced for close to seven years and require more longer-term approaches. A recent study by Search for Common Ground concluded that "not only are South Sudanese, and youth in particular, at risk of becoming desensitized to persistent violence, but they also risk seeing violence as a justified and effective tool to rectify grievances" (Smith 2017, 14). On the other hand, youth were also found to be the age group most optimistic about future peace in South Sudan as well as the most likely group to identify as South Sudanese—a national identity that crosses tribal divisions (SCG 2017).

A number of initiatives have been recently implemented in the country seeking to capitalize on youth's energy to address climate and other environmental concerns while promoting inclusive positive peace in South Sudan. The United Nations Environment Programme (UNEP) released *South Sudan: First State of Environment and Outlook Report 2018* on June 5, 2018, to mark World Environment Day. This report examines the role of sustainable resource management as a vehicle for peace. Gender dynamics are underscored as an important factor. Key policy recommendations are an example of environmental peacebuilding—that is, they draw on the premise that building and sustaining inclusive peace in conflict-affected societies like South Sudan require the consideration of environmental factors and natural resource management. As posited by Dresse and her colleagues (2018), environmental peacebuilding rests on the premise that environmental factors can act as incentives for cooperation and peace rather than violence and competition. Environmental peacebuilding thus represents a paradigm shift from a standpoint of environmental scarcity to one of environmental peace (Dresse et al. 2018).

South Sudan Wildlife Service is already engaged in this type of approach. They have partnered with the NGO Fauna & Flora International and Bucknell University to train young men—and also a smaller number of young women—as community wildlife ambassadors. I visited their facilities in Yambio in Western Equatoria State, where hundreds of minors associated with the armed forces have been recently demobilized, to discuss how access to meaningful opportunities in conservation can facilitate reintegration and discourage youngsters from reenlisting (UNICEF 2019). Another case in point is the work of the Wildlife Conservation Society (WCS). Its conservation-security initiatives include joint community-wildlife-police patrolling to protect wildlife and local communities, including preventing cattle raiding and detecting armed-group movements. A related initiative, the U.S. Agency for International Development (USAID)–WCS Livelihoods Small Grants Program, targets young women and young men for projects linking livelihoods with environmental conservation and climate action (WCS 2019).

Partnerships and external support for peacebuilding and environmental action like those previously mentioned have an essential role to play. South Sudanese ownership of peace initiatives is, however, critical. As one of my young interlocutors remarked, "The youth in South Sudan are two-thirds of the present and all of the future." Yet even though only 3 percent of the population is over sixty-four, elders—older males, to be precise—are leading the war-torn country. Overcoming local perceptions of youth as violence prone, a growing number of young leaders in Juba, in other locations throughout the country, and in the diaspora have taken the initiative to establish networks dedicated to mobilizing their peers to become a positive force for change. Many of these initiatives have a peacebuilding and environmental focus. Seeking to overcome their typically limited skills and professional capacities, these youth-led initiatives often prioritize the acquisition of peacebuilding tools together with vocational education and training to ensure that young people do not become what some authors termed a "lost generation" (Cruise O'Brien 1996).

"We need to close the gap between local and international peacebuilders," exhorted Malual Bol Kiir, a South Sudanese peace activist and founder of the African Youth Action Network (AYAN). Guided by the premise that illiteracy is one of the major causes of conflict in South Sudan, AYAN is one of the many youth-led organization networks aiming at bringing together youth of various ethnic groups—both female and male—to discuss issues related to the conflict in South Sudan as well as issues specific to refugee communities. AYAN was founded in June 2015 in Uganda by young South Sudanese refugees and is currently registered in South Sudan and Uganda. With support from the U.N. High Commissioner for Refugees (UNHCR) through their Youth Initiative Fund, AYAN has been training young refugees and host community youth in peacebuilding and conflict resolution. Their stated objective is to promote young people's rights by building their leadership and strengthening youth-led training and other initiatives in the areas of peacebuilding, environmental stewardship, gender, sexuality, health, education, the arts, and good governance.

The specific activities implemented vary according to the program. Most of the initiatives involve training workshops and awareness-raising campaigns among youth in refugee camps as well as schools, colleges, churches, mosques, and barazas (public meetings) to promote national cohesion and respect for human and environmental diversity. Young participants are trained as mentors and peer educators to conduct peace awareness, open-forum workshops, panel discussions, and other methods of community advocacy focusing on the R-ARCSS and its implementation. Their ultimate objective is to equip young refugees to contribute to creating conditions conducive to return and recovery.

Another example is the Whitaker Peace and Development Initiative (WPDI). Founded by Forest Whitaker in 2012, WPDI's stated goal is to strengthen communities impacted by conflict, armed violence, insecurity, ethnic tensions, and limited opportunities for sociopolitical development. Youth-focused but not necessarily youth-led, WPDI operates in the United States, Mexico, South Sudan, and Uganda. With a strong presence in the Kiryandongo refugee settlement in Uganda,[3] where part of this study was conducted, WPDI peacebuilding initiatives seek to foster peace, reconciliation, and prosperity in disadvantaged and fragile communities in this African country. WPDI workshops provide training on peacebuilding, conflict resolution, and mediation tools as well as natural resource management and life, vocational, and information and communications technology skills. On-the-ground programs offer support to economic and cultural community projects, broadcast series, social events, and awareness-raising campaigns on various cultural and environmental topics.

A further component of WPDI is the Global Peacemaker Network, an open-source virtual space described on their website as "an online platform for students, teachers, conflict resolution and peacebuilding professionals, policy makers and global citizens." Their website provides access to online materials on issues including peacebuilding, community building, global security, conflict resolution, natural resources, and development. It is worth noting, however, that while many young "peacemakers"—as WPDI members call themselves—have cell phones and less often smartphones, most of them do not own a computer and have only sporadic access to the internet. Furthermore, connectivity in refugee camps and settlements is often unreliable, greatly reducing the extent to which peacemakers can avail themselves of these online resources.

The Golden Youth for Peace and Development also operates in the Kiryandongo settlement, and its motto is "to promote peace and prosperity for all." Unlike AYAN and the Global Peacemaker Network, the Golden Youth do not have a web page and rely on their Facebook page as a means to post photographs and announcements about their activities. As was the case with the two previous networks, this group emphasizes capacity development to mobilize and support youth to work collaboratively for peace, both in Ugandan refugee settlements and in South Sudan. Their activities include training seminars aimed at enhancing participants' skills in mediation and conflict-resolution techniques and in effective communication with direct relevance to contexts of violence and environmental fragility. Various volunteering schemes—planting trees, cleaning the streets and collecting garbage, and maintaining the boreholes on which settlement residents depend for water—and participation in community cultural activities provide young people with additional spaces to practice their newly acquired skills and voice their aspirations for their future and that of their kin and peers.

CHALLENGES AND LIMITATIONS

Youth-led networks in South Sudan and those formed by South Sudanese refugee youth in Uganda are operating in a sociopolitical and environmental context that is both challenging and unpredictable, as the relationship between the South Sudanese government, some internal stakeholders—most prominently the opposition—and some of its international partners remain considerably vexed. Initiatives focusing on training and capacity building can be effective instruments for mobilizing young people for peace, environmental management, and integrated development, helping overcome the barriers to youth participation in peace and governance processes. This mobilization needs to be strategic and sustained to effect a meaningful impact on the ground.

Membership in the youth networks discussed in this chapter is very fluid and reportedly in the upper hundreds in each of them. Actual numbers are impossible to determine with any accuracy—new youth networks are being established, and membership records are not frequently updated, if at all kept. Many youths belong to more than one network and engage in the various initiatives offered on the basis of scheduling—which tends to happen on a rather ad hoc basis—and interest in the topic. Female attendance is roughly equal or only slightly lower than male attendance, but their active participation is noticeably higher in female-only groups, underscoring the importance of attending to gender as well as generational dynamics. Much of the language used in "girl empowerment" activities is aspirational and inspirational; a superficial sense of optimism about the possibility of positive change pervades youth networks' activities and members' conversations. Upon deeper interrogation in key informant interviews and focus-group discussions, however, many girls and young women demonstrate a sobering recognition that "females in South Sudan carry the burden of a heavy workload, early marriages, and bride prices, while gender roles and negative stereotypes contribute to the unequal distribution of resources" (Ensor 2014, 18).

Exacerbated by wartime circumstances, these concerns involve structural as well as sociocultural conditions of inequality that are unlikely to be corrected through participation in youth-led environmental peacebuilding initiatives alone. As noted in the Committee on the Elimination of All Forms of Discrimination against Women's (CEDAW) *General Recommendation No. 37*, "Women, girls, men and boys are affected differently by climate change and environmental extremes, with many women and girls experiencing greater risks, burdens and impacts. Situations of crisis exacerbate pre-existing gender inequalities and also compound intersecting forms of discrimination" (2018, 3).[4] It is also worth noting that the development of self-confidence and assertiveness, some of the attributes encouraged in the peacebuilding training offered by most youth networks, may have different consequences for females than for males. As I concluded in an earlier study of gender issues among displaced South Sudanese youngsters, young females "display self-assurance and express progressive views on social issues—i.e., marriage, women's participation in public life—that may be categorized as trans-gressive and even perceived as a deliberate affront to South Sudanese tradition" (Ensor 2014, 16). Other studies of conflict-affected female youth have similarly noted that "resilience in the context of war often carries a high price" (Swaine and Feeny 2004, 83). In effect, "confronting deeply engrained cultural and social norms dictating a subordinate and mostly silent role for young females ... may place girls in a difficult and even dangerous position" (Ensor 2014, 16). The instrumentality of females of all ages in peacebuilding is broadly recognized, at least at the discourse level. It is, however, essential to ensure that young female peacebuilders are not co-opted and that their participation leads to their empowerment without placing them at heightened risk.

Young males, for their part, and especially those from cattle-keeping groups, often express concern about their inability to attain social adulthood through marriage. Bride prices, which must be paid in cattle to the family of the bride for the marriage to be effected, soared in South Sudan as donor money poured into the country after its 2011 independence from Sudan. Many young men felt that they would not be able to afford to get married unless they raided cattle from other com-munities. At the same time, guns flooded the country as both sides armed young herders and mobilized them to fight. Militarized cattle keepers started carrying automatic rifles instead of their traditional spears. Cattle raids, a generations-old phenomenon, have often escalated into massacres and endless cycles of revenge killings (Wild, Madut Jok, and Patel 2018). Clashes among pastoralists and between pastoralists and farmers have also become more violent and more frequent as a result of the environmental disruptions caused by climate change.

While generally enthusiastic about the environmental peacebuilding oppor-tunities made available to them, most study participants, female and male, noted that the lack of coordination among youth networks and the ad hoc nature of the workshops offered made planning difficult and often resulted in duplications and/ or gaps in desired training. Limited funding and other resources were a perennial concern. Most youngsters underscored the importance of responding not only to peacebuilding imperatives but also to deteriorating environmental conditions that affect livelihoods, evolving market demands, and projected reconstruction needs. Participants argued for flexible approaches that could be frequently reevaluated as circumstances changed. Accommodating the diverse challenges faced by multiple tribal communities, females, vulnerable youth, ex-combatants, and unemployed youth both in South Sudan and in refugee settlements abroad was also mentioned as a high priority.

Overall, participants agreed that the main contribution to peacebuilding and environmental action made by the youth-led efforts discussed in this study is that of capacity development through the training of youth peace leaders. Their initia-tives are believed to reinforce participants' culture of constructive dialogue and peaceful resolution of conflicts; they also strengthen participants' understanding of climate change and other issues affecting youth. Stress management, trauma relief and healing, resilience, self-knowledge, creativity and innovation, communication skills, leadership, teamwork, decision-making, interpersonal skills, and volunteer-ing spirit are additional benefits mentioned by youth network members.

While recognizing the importance of training in peacebuilding and environmental action and providing them with tools for collective engagement, most study participants cited entrepreneurship and employment opportunities as paramount among their concerns. Unless they are equipped with the skills to support their own livelihoods, young people will remain vulnerable to political manipulation. Economically oriented interventions whose primary purpose is to help young people enter the labor market are vital in societies recovering from violent conflict, where employment and affording a decent livelihood tend to be critical but daunting challenges for all demographic sectors (Date-Bah 2003). Short-term external interventions have a rather narrow view of these economic-development approaches. Vocational training alone does not provide a quick fix to building peace sustainably or mitigating and adapting to the long-term consequences of climate change. Rather, when these types of initiatives are not designed in a historically grounded, context-responsive, and inclusive manner, they risk doing more harm than good by replicating existing inequalities or creating unmet expectations (Lopes Cardozo 2017, 41; see also chapter 5, this volume). The management of expectations is thus crucial, as a lack of employment opportunities following vocational training initiatives or limited participation in decision-making processes following political awareness training may exacerbate youth's frustrations. Resulting grievances would then drive rather than mitigate conflict and alienation (Lopes Cardozo, Higgins, and Le Mat 2016; Mercy Corps 2015).

Moreover, missing from current approaches is the establishment of fora for meaningful discussions between young leaders and different local and national authorities and political actors. Training youth to become leaders for environmental peacebuilding and development means enabling them through guidance, not manipulating them for self-serving purposes. Yet most study participants expressed a concern with the limited extent to which youth have a real influence or decision-making capability in political parties, the army, and the government. Many acknowledged the risk of becoming merely implementers of top-down decisions made by others. While community perceptions toward youth have shifted in refugee camps—that is, instead of being seen only as actors in violent conflict, young people are beginning to be viewed as active agents of peace—this does not appear to be the case in their homeland, where intergenerational as well as gender dynamics remain problematic.

An additional challenge is the scarcity of well-documented information on project outcomes and thoughtful reflection on the challenges encountered. In general terms, "youth-led organizations are not equipped to document and write up their work in a way that is recognized and understood as legitimate by the wider, international community" (Amambia et al. 2018, 7). As a result, there is a limited repository of locally driven knowledge about the experiences of youth networks and the successes or failures of the initiatives implemented. When any data are collected, the focus is on outputs (e.g., number of youths trained, number of centers established) rather than outcomes (e.g., measurable resulting achievements). Furthermore, because no follow-up (e.g., monitoring and evaluation) is undertaken, it cannot be empirically established whether any observable impact is attributable to participation in any of the activities implemented by the youth networks. Training and guidance on the implementation of participatory action research (PAR) and other variants of participatory community-based research focused on the cogeneration of knowledge would go a long way in alleviating this shortcoming.

THE WAY FORWARD: ENVIRONMENTAL PATHWAYS TO HUMAN SECURITY AND POSITIVE PEACE

The United Nations World Population Prospects statistics estimate that there are 1.3 billion fifteen- to twenty-four-year-olds in the world. Nearly one billion of them live in developing, fragile, and conflict-prone countries (U.N. 2015), with six hundred million living in regions where conflict and forced displacement (UNDP 2014) threaten their human security.

There is a well-documented link between climate change and fragility, conflict, and violence. Climate change disrupts livelihoods, compromises food security, and leads to water stress, economic recessions, and forced and distress migration. Acting as a stress on global economic, political, and social systems, climate change can undermine the quality of institutions, especially in fragile situations where governments have limited coping capacities and means to help their populations adapt.

As the IPCC concludes, "The impact of climate change on human well-being, peace and security is going to worsen, especially for the poorest. Many of the people most affected live in fragile states. Such communities are suffering not only from persistent poverty, poor infrastructure, weak natural resource governance or unsustainable resource management, and lack of access to the world market, but also from other types of societal insecurity such as the fragility of state institutions, political instability, and the effects of recent armed conflict or the threat of approaching violence" (2014). Climate change is, of course, a global problem that affects us all, but its impacts are more severe on youth from conflict-affected countries. Moving from global policies to effective climate action at the local level "will require a comprehensive understanding of the interplay between climate change and youth empowerment" (Payne, Warembourg, and Awan 2017, 62).

As I have argued elsewhere, "Conflict and peacebuilding in Africa are complicated phenomena that cannot be fully understood without interrogating the historical, structural, and cultural factors within African countries and the global economic and political systems in which they are enmeshed" (Ensor 2012, 8). The current situation in South Sudan is one of multiple complex challenges, with the majority of youth having grown up surrounded and influenced by violence and deprivation. Ravaged by continued violence and persistent insecurity, South Sudan is also grappling with the devastating effects of climate change. The environmental circumstances and political milieu in which the population of South Sudanese youth are brought up will define who they will become in society and their ability to play a constructive role in it.

Rural youth, who constitute the majority of South Sudanese youngsters, are at a particular disadvantage—little has been done until recently to provide them with an education and to facilitate their meaningful participation in the modern economy. A multiplicity of unfavorable circumstances has led many to engage in violent activities such as cattle rustling and banditry; others join militias for political reasons, to settle personal disputes, or as one of the few livelihood strategies available to them. Access to meaningful livelihood opportunities is indeed a key issue for most young people. Unemployment is as much a serious concern for the many jobless youngsters found in Juba's town center as for their rural counterparts and for the displaced youth living in refugee settlements. Many of those who are contributing to support their families express a sense of urgency to acquire skills quickly and connect them to viable economic opportunities. They are otherwise liable to resort to settling for any opportunity offered to them, including high-risk, violent, and/or unlawful behavior in the absence of other viable options. The enormous number of idle youngsters languishing in PoC camps—a fertile ground for extremist narratives and "the radicalisation of South Sudan youth groups" (SSPC 2014, 24)—has potentially explosive political ramifications. Nevertheless, as the case study discussed in this chapter illustrates, these youngsters show tremendous potential for renewal through engagement in locally rooted environmental peacebuilding and development initiatives.

An additional hurdle is the misguided but widespread tendency to apply the category "youth" only to young males. Young women are often deeply involved in and affected by the dynamics of conflict, violence, and deprivation; their concerns must thus be addressed in environmental peacebuilding and development programs if these are to be inclusive and sustainable. For youth of any gender to feel empowered to inspire and lead change, they need opportunities for meaningful engagement beyond the refugee camps in which many of them currently live—for example, in their local communities back in South Sudan and, through social media, connecting with other relevant actors around the world. In order to reach their full potential, they must be able to access educational opportunities, including training in soft skills. Since multiyear, formal education is not an option for most refugee youth, alternative and more flexible educational models must be implemented. Bearing all of this in mind, gender considerations must be mainstreamed in the design and implementation of youth policy and the programming of any initiatives targeting youngsters.

Enhancing structures that promote the participation of youth in peacebuilding processes will actively contribute to young people's positive engagement with decisions and activities that affect their well-being. Capacity development aimed at preparing youth leaders for meaningful environmental peacebuilding must be based on critical analysis and case-by-case inquiry to ensure that youth participation lives up to its transformative potential rather than serving a tokenistic approach. Environmental peacebuilding efforts should be considered within a broader framework of climate action and sustainable livelihood support as well as equity so that the dividends of peace can be reaped by all, not only those in privileged positions.

The growing number of South Sudanese youth networks cater to their members' eagerness to learn, to live up to their full potential, to become the best version of themselves, and to contribute to the peace and development of their country. Current youth-led initiatives like the ones discussed in this chapter have certain limitations, however, and by themselves do not guarantee a successful outcome. Effective strategies to build peace require a supportive environment across all levels; they must connect high-level efforts with the realities of multilevel, intergenerational conflict, engaging the grassroots, middle-level leaders and elites. Furthermore, they must address both decades-old grievances and contemporary challenges (Milner 2018, 1). A failure to recognize young people as political actors would cause their potential contributions to postconflict recovery to be ignored, wasted, or at best underutilized. These young people must be consulted, encouraged, and supported to contribute to or even lead efforts to overcome the negative impacts of conflict, environmental degradation, and climate change.

In South Sudan, as in the rest of the globe, climate change is among the defining issues of our time. As Mary Robinson writes in her recent book on *Climate Justice*, "The threat to our planet may be dire, but the potential opportunity is also historic—the chance to stop an existential threat, to conquer poverty and inequality, and to empower those who have been left behind and neglected" (2018, 132). Youth have a greater stake in the impacts of climate change and will be instrumental in developing solutions in the future. Their voices and opinions must be considered in climate-change agreements and debates at international, national, and local levels, especially when those local circumstances are fraught with violence, deprivation, and fragility. In spite of seemingly insurmountable odds, many young South Sudanese women and men are organizing, seeking partnerships with local and international organizations, and mobilizing to contribute to finding local solutions to global threats of climate change and security challenges. May their courageous efforts lead to a more peaceful and prosperous future for their beleaguered country.

NOTES

1. There exists some disagreement among legal commentators whether U.N. Security Council resolutions are legally binding or not. Writing about UNSCR 1325, Tryggestad (2009) argues that the main factor in assessing bindingness is whether the resolution in question is adopted under chapter 6 (noncoercive measures) or under chapter 7 (coercive measures) of the U.N. Charter. The United Network of Young Peacebuilders notes that UNSCR 2250 pertains to the "'Maintenance of International Peace and Security' which is a reference to Chapter 7, Article 39 in the U.N. Charter. Security Council Resolutions under Chapter 7 are binding" (2016, 6). Joyner offers a different interpretation, arguing that "the legal obligation for U.N. Charter states parties to comply with the decisions of the Security Council, contained in Article 24 and 25 of the Charter, is not contingent upon the Council's acting in exercise of its Chapter VII powers. Any decision of the Security Council is legally binding upon all U.N. member states, whether or not the text of the resolution explicitly references Chapter VII" (2017, 1). It is, nevertheless, the case that no dedicated enforcement mechanism exists—a situation also common with international human rights law provisions.

2. The Food and Agricultural Organization of the United Nations defines *distress migration* as human mobility whose root causes include "food insecurity, rural poverty, limited income opportunities, inequality and environmental degradation" (Avis 2017, 2).

3. Located approximately 225 kilometers (140 miles) northwest of Kampala, Uganda, the Kiryandongo refugee settlement hosts almost sixty thousand refugees, the majority of whom are from South Sudan, with a small number from the Democratic Republic of Congo, Burundi, Rwanda, and Sudan (UNHCR 2018).

4. CEDAW is an international treaty adopted in 1979 by the United Nations General Assembly.

REFERENCES

Adegoke, Yinka. 2017. "The Youngest Continent Will Keep Being Run by Its Oldest Leaders." *Quartz Africa*, December 28, 2017. https://qz.com/africa/1162490/the-youngest-continent -keeps-on-being-run-by-the-oldest-leaders/.

Amambia, S. C., F. Bivens, M. Hamisi, I. Lancaster, O. Ogada, G. O. Okumu, N. Songora, R. Zaid. 2018. *Participatory Action Research for Advancing Youth-Led Peacebuilding in Kenya*. Peaceworks. Washington, D.C.: United States Institute of Peace. www.usip.org/sites/default/ files/2018-10/pw142-participatory-action-research-for-advancing-youth-led-peacebuilding -in-kenya.pdf.

Arensen, M. 2016. *If We Leave We Are Killed: Lessons Learned from South Sudan Protection of Civilian Sites 2013–2016*. Juba: International Organization for Migration. https:// publications.iom.int/system/files/pdf/if_we_leave_0.pdf.

AU (African Union). 2013. *African Union Agenda 2063: The Africa We Want*, April 2015. https://au.int/sites/default/files/documents/36204-doc-agenda2063_popular_version _en.pdf.

———. 2017. *State of Africa's Population 2017: Youth, Health and Development: Overcoming the Challenges towards Harnessing the Demographic Dividend*. Addis Ababa: African Union. https://au.int/sites/default/files/newsevents/workingdocuments/32187-wd -state_of_africas_population_-_sa19093_-e.pdf.

Avis, William Robert. 2017. *Scoping Study on Defining and Measuring Distress Migration*. Helpdesk Research Report. Rome: Food and Agricultural Organization of the United Nations. www.gsdrc.org/wp-content/uploads/2017/04/HDR1406.pdf.

CEDAW (Committee on the Elimination of Discrimination against Women). 2018. *General Recommendation No. 37 on Gender-Related Dimensions of Disaster Risk Reduction in the Context of Climate Change*. CEDAW/C/GC/37. https://tbinternet.ohchr.org/Treaties/ CEDAW/Shared%20Documents/1_Global/CEDAW_C_GC_37_8642_E.pdf.

Checchi, F., A. Testa, A. Warsame, L. Quach, and R. Burns. 2018. *Estimates of Crisis-Attributable Mortality in South Sudan, December 2013–April 2018*. London: London School of Hygiene and Tropical Medicine.

Cruise O'Brien, D. 1996. "Youth Identity and State Decay in West Africa." In *Postcolonial Identities in Africa*, edited by R. Werbner and T. Ranger, 55–74. London: Zed.

Date-Bah, Eugenia. 2003. *Jobs after War: A Critical Challenge in the Peace and Reconstruction Puzzle*. Geneva: International Labour Organization.

Deng, D. K. 2013. *Challenges of Accountability: An Assessment of Dispute Resolution Processes in Rural South Sudan*. Juba: South Sudan Law Society. www.pactworld.org/library/ challenges-accountability-assessment-dispute-resolution-processes-rural-south-sudan.

Dresse, Anaïs, Itay Fischhendler, Jonas Østergaard Nielsen, and Dimitrios Zikos. 2018. "Environmental Peacebuilding: Towards a Theoretical Framework." *Cooperation and Conflict* 54, no. 1, 99–119.

Ensor, Marisa O., ed. 2012. *African Childhoods: Education, Development, Peacebuilding and the Youngest Continent*. New York: Palgrave Macmillan.

———. 2013a. *Displaced Youth's Role in Sustainable Return: Lessons from South Sudan*. Migration Research Series, 47. Geneva: International Organization for Migration.

———. 2013b. "Youth, Climate Change, and Peace in South Sudan." *Peace Review's Special Issue on Climate Change and Peace* 25, no. 4, 526–533. Guest edited by Richard Matthew.

———. 2014. "Displaced Girlhood: Gendered Dimensions of Coping and Social Change among Conflict-Affected South Sudanese Youth." *Refuge* 30, no. 1, 15–24.

———. 2016. "Refugee Girls and Boys and the Dilemmas of (Un)sustainable Return in South Sudan." In *Children and Forced Migration: Durable Solutions in Transient Years*, edited by M. O. Ensor and E. M. Gozdziak, 105–127. New York: Palgrave Macmillan.

————. 2018. "Youth's Role in South Sudan's Perfect Storm: Climate Change, Conflict, and the Prospects for Peacebuilding in the World's Newest Nation." *Global Peace Services USA* 19, no. 3 (December): 1–10.

————. 2019. "Is Environmental Peacebuilding the Answer to South Sudan's Conflict?" *New Security Beat: The Blog of the Environmental Change and Security Program*, September 12, 2019. www.newsecuritybeat.org/2019/09/environmental-peacebuilding-answer-south -sudans-conflict/.

FAO (Food and Agriculture Organization of the United Nations). 2016. *Migration and Protracted Crisis: Addressing the Root Causes and Building Resilient Agricultural Livelihoods.* Rome: FAO.

Feseha, Minas. 2018. "The Nexus between 'Youth Bulge' and Armed Conflict." African Portal. Centre for International Governance Innovation. Accessed May 9, 2019. www.africaportal .org/features/nexus-between-youth-bulge-and-armed-conflict/.

Galtung, Johan. 1981. "Social Cosmology and the Concept of Peace." *Journal of Peace Research* 18, no. 2, 183–199.

Honwana, Alcinda. 2013. "Youth, Waithood, and Protest Movements in Africa." International African Institute, August 12, 2013. http://africanarguments.org/2013/08/12/youth -waithood-and-protest-movements-in-africa-by-alcinda-honwana/.

IPCC (Intergovernmental Panel on Climate Change). 2014. *Climate Change 2014: Impacts, Adaptation, and Vulnerability. Part A: Global and Sectoral Aspects.* Geneva: IPCC.

JAICA (Japan International Cooperation Agency). 2017. "Trainings for the South Sudan Vocational Training Instructors Were Conducted in Kiryandongo, Uganda and Juba, South Sudan." www.jica.go.jp/south_sudan/english/office/topics/171127.html.

Johnson, Douglas. 2005. *The Root Causes of Sudan's Civil Wars: Old Wars and New Wars.* Expanded 3rd ed. Woodbridge, Suffolk: Boydell & Brewer.

Joyner, Dan. 2017. "Legal Bindingness of Security Council Resolutions Generally, and Resolution 2334 on the Israeli Settlements in Particular." *EJIL: Talk! Blog of the European Journal of International Law*, January 9, 2017. www.ejiltalk.org/legal-bindingness-of-security-council -resolutions-generally-and-resolution-2334-on-the-israeli-settlements-in-particular/.

Krause, Jana. 2019. "Stabilization and Local Conflicts: Communal and Civil Wars in South Sudan." *Ethnopolitics* 18, no. 5, 478–493.

Lopes Cardozo, M. T. A., S. Higgins, and M. L. J. Le Mat. 2016. *Youth Agency and Peacebuilding: An Analysis of the Role of Formal and Non-formal Education. Synthesis Report on Findings from Myanmar, Pakistan, South Africa and Uganda.* Amsterdam: University of Amsterdam. https://educationanddevelopment.files.wordpress.com/2016/06/youth-agency-synthesis -report-final16.pdf.

Lopes Cardozo, M. T. A., and G. Scotto. 2017. "Youth, Peacebuilding and the Role of Education." INEE/YPS Thematic Paper. April 11, 2018. www.youth4peace.info/system/files/ 2018-04/11.%20TP_Education_Cardozo%20%26%20Scotto.pdf.

Maplecroft. 2017. *Climate Change Vulnerability Index 2017.* Verisk Maplecroft. https:// reliefweb.int/sites/reliefweb.int/files/resources/verisk%20index.pdf.

Mercy Corps. 2015. *Youth and Consequences: Unemployment, Injustice and Violence.* Portland, Ore.: Mercy Corps. www.mercycorps.org/sites/default/files/MercyCorps_Youth ConsequencesReport_2015.pdf. (URL inactive.)

Milner, C. 2018. *In It for the Long Haul? Lessons on Peacebuilding in South Sudan.* Juba, South Sudan: Christian Aid. www.christianaid.org.uk/sites/default/files/2018-07/In-it-for-the -long-haul-lessons-peacebuilding-south-sudan-jul2018.pdf.

OECD (Organisation for Economic Co-operation and Development). 2013. *Fragile States: Resource Flows and Trends.* Conflict and Fragility. Paris: OECD.

Payne, Julian, Antoine Warembourg, and Jalal Awan. 2017. *Impacts of Climate Change on Youth, Peace and Security.* Sustainable Development Solutions Network—Youth. Paris:

SDSN Youth. www.unsdsn.org/resources/publications/impacts-of-climate-change-on
-youth-peace-and-security/. (URL inactive.)

Robinson, Mary. 2018. *Climate Justice: Hope, Resilience, and the Fight for a Sustainable Future.*
New York: Bloomsbury.

SCG (Search for Common Ground). 2015. *Baseline Assessment Communicating for Peace in
South Sudan: A Social and Behavior Change Communication Initiative.* Search for Common
Ground Interview with Jonglei State Women's Association. www.sfcg.org/wp-content/
uploads/2016/02/SFCG_UNICEF-Conflict-Baseline_Format-2.pdf.

———. 2017. *Combined Final Evaluation for "'I Love My Country': Strategic Communications
for Peacebuilding in South Sudan" and Baseline Evaluation for "'I Love My Country': Promoting Localized Understanding and Peaceful Coexistence in South Sudan."* www.sfcg.org/
wp-content/uploads/2017/09/SFCG-ILMC-Evaluation-Final-ILT-approved.pdf.

SHBA (Sudan Human Security Baseline Assessment). 2012. "Women and Armed Violence in
South Sudan." Small Arms Survey. Accessed April 30, 2019. www.smallarmssurveysudan
.org/fileadmin/docs/facts-figures/south-sudan/womens-security/HSBA-women-and
-armed-conflict.pdf.

Smith, K. 2017. "Building a Constituency for Peace in South Sudan." Search for Common
Ground. Accessed April 30, 2019. www.sfcg.org/wp-content/uploads/2017/08/Building-a
-Constituency-for-Peace-in-South-Sudan. (URL inactive.)

SSPC (South Sudan Protection Cluster). 2014. *Protection Trends Analysis May 2014.* Accessed
April 30, 2019. https://reliefweb.int/sites/reliefweb.int/files/resources/20140519-South
-Sudan-Protection-Cluster-Trends-Analysis.pdf.

Stalon, Jean-Luc. 2017. "Confronting Climate Change in South Sudan." United Nations Africa
Renewal. Accessed June 15, 2019. www.un.org/africarenewal/news/confronting-climate
-change-south-sudan.

Swaine, A., and T. Feeny. 2004. "A Neglected Perspective: Adolescent Girls' Experiences of the
Kosovo Conflict of 1999." In *Children and Youth on the Frontline,* edited by Jo Boyden and
Joanna de Berry, 63–84. New York: Berghahn.

Tryggestad, Torunn L. 2009. "Trick or Treat? The UN and Implementation of Security Council Resolution 1325 on Women, Peace and Security." *Global Governance* 15, no. 4, 539–557.

U.N. DESA (United Nations Department of Economic and Social Affairs). 2015. *Population
Facts: Youth Population Trends and Sustainable Development.* United Nations Department
of Economic and Social Affairs, Population Division, 2015. www.un.org/esa/socdev/
documents/youth/fact-sheets/YouthPOP.pdf.

UNDP (United Nations Development Programme). 2014. "UNDP Youth Strategy 2014–2017:
Empowered Youth, Sustainable Future." Accessed July 4, 2019. www.undp.org/content/
dam/undp/library/Democratic%20Governance/Youth/UNDP_Youth-Strategy-2014-17
_Web.pdf.

UNEP (United Nations Environmental Programme). 2018. *South Sudan: First State of Environment and Outlook Report 2018.* Nairobi: UNEP.

UNESCO (United Nations Educational, Scientific, and Cultural Organization). 2018. "First-
Ever National Youth Conference Held in South Sudan." Accessed July 5, 2019. www.unesco
.org/new/en/media-services/single-view/news/first_ever_national_youth_conference
_held_in_south_sudan_wit/.

UNHCR (United Nations High Commissioner for Refugees). 2018. *Uganda Refugee Response
Monitoring.* Settlement Fact Sheet: Kiryandongo. January 2018. https://reliefweb.int/sites/
reliefweb.int/files/resources/UGA_Factsheet_Kiryandongo_Gap%20Analysis_January
_2018.pdf.

———. 2019. "South Sudan Emergency." August 31, 2019. www.unhcr.org/en-us/south-sudan
-emergency.html.

UNICEF (United Nations Children's Fund). 2016. "South Sudan—Education; the Challenge: Situation Overview." www.unicef.org/southsudan/education.html.

———. 2017. "2018 Humanitarian Needs Overview: South Sudan." November 2017. https://reliefweb.int/sites/reliefweb.int/files/resources/South_Sudan_2018_Humanitarian_Needs_Overview.pdf.

———. 2019. "More Than 3,000 Children Released from Armed Groups in South Sudan since Conflict Began, but Thousands More Continue to Be Used." UNICEF Press Release, February 19, 2019. www.unicef.org/press-releases/more-3000-children-released-armed-groups-south-sudan-conflict-began-thousands-more.

United Nations. 2015. "Security Council, Unanimously Adopting Resolution 2250 (2015), Urges Member States to Increase Representation of Youth in Decision-Making at All Levels." December 9, 2015. www.un.org/press/en/2015/sc12149.doc.htm.

U.N. OCHA (United Nations Office for the Coordination of Humanitarian Affairs). 2017. "South Sudan: A Humanitarian Crisis of Catastrophic Proportions." September 20, 2017. www.unocha.org/story/south-sudan-humanitarian-crisis-catastrophic-proportions.

UNOY (United Network of Young Peacebuilders). 2016. *A Guide to Security Council Resolution 2250.* http://unoy.org/wp-content/uploads/Guide-to-SCR-2250.pdf.

WCS (Wildlife Conservation Society). 2019. "Key Wildlife Populations Remaining in South Sudan despite Five and a Half Years of Armed Conflict." WCS Newsroom, June 21, 2019. https://newsroom.wcs.org/News-Releases/articleType/ArticleView/articleId/12506/Key-Wildlife-Populations-Remaining-in-South-Sudan-Despite-Five-and-a-Half-Years-of-Armed-Conflict.aspx.

Wild, Hannah, Jok Madut Jok, and Ronak Patel. 2018. "The Militarization of Cattle Raiding in South Sudan: How a Traditional Practice Became a Tool for Political Violence." *Journal of International Humanitarian Action* 3, no. 2, 1–11.

CHAPTER 8

Putting Youth on the Agenda

INTERSECTIONS WITH THE WOMEN, PEACE, AND SECURITY FRAMEWORK

Jeni Klugman and Matthew Moore[1]

The future of humanity and of our planet lies in our hands. It lies also in the hands of today's younger generation who will pass the torch to future generations.
—2030 Agenda

It is time for women. It is time for young people.
It is time for us to decide our future and implement our vision.
—Pashtana Arabzai, twenty-seven years old, Afghan parliamentary candidate, 2018 (Mohamed 2018)

The global community's commitments to sustainable, comprehensive, and inclusive peace have greatly expanded over the last two decades. Key milestones include the women, peace, and security (WPS) agenda set forth in United Nations Security Council Resolution (UNSCR) 1325 (2000) and seven subsequent WPS resolutions;[2] the youth, peace, and security (YPS) agenda set forth in UNSCR 2250 (2015); and the evolving concept of sustaining peace—which also have important implications for the Sustainable Development Agenda, to which 193 governments committed in 2015.

The UNSCR 2250—on YPS—has clear echoes of the WPS agenda. However, as documented in the 2015 global study on WPS and will be outlined later, progress on the WPS agenda remains uneven and challenging (U.N. Women 2015a). Underlying both agendas is the motivation to reverse historical exclusion and to promote the inclusion—political, social, and economic—of both women and youth in security and peacebuilding. Women make up roughly half of the world's population, and young women and young men between the ages of fifteen to twenty-nine currently count for approximately one in four people—yet both women and young people have been traditionally excluded from the realm of peace and security (U.N. Women 2018).

Today's generation of youth (ages fifteen to twenty-nine years[3]) is close to 1.8 billion—of whom about 90 percent live in developing countries and about

140 million live in the thirty-six countries classified by the multilateral development banks as fragile and conflict-affected states.[4] More than a third of the Sustainable Development Goals (SDGs) reference young people, with a focus on empowerment, participation, and/or well-being (Andersson 2016). Young people's engagement is also key to the participation, inclusion, accountability, and global engagement embedded in goals 16 (peaceful, just, and inclusive societies) and 17 (partnerships and implementation).

The economic dimensions of youth exclusion are often manifested in high rates of unemployment, whereas large numbers of women are excluded from the labor market or, when they are in paid work, earn low returns. Political exclusion is reflected in limited political representation of both women and youth in formal institutions and their underrepresentation in political leadership.

The position of young women is a clear intersection between the WPS and YPS agendas, often manifested in their overlapping disadvantages. Yet the larger constraints facing young women tend not to be explicitly highlighted in either agenda. This neglect is associated with another shortcoming that characterizes both agendas—the lack of gender- and age-disaggregated data. Oftentimes, gender-disaggregated data are not age-disaggregated. The absence of data that are both gender and age disaggregated impedes understanding the experience of salient groups—such as young women—and the crafting and monitoring of evidence-based policies and programs.

The main objective of this chapter is to identify and explore the links and synergies between these two major global agendas and reflect upon the extent to which the youth agenda has addressed evident shortcomings of the WPS agenda in light of the fifteen years of WPS implementation experience and missed opportunities. There are clearly commonalities between the two agendas—both seek to promote inclusion in all phases of peacebuilding, political transitions, and other processes related to peace and security. Yet there are also important differences in focus and approach.

We seek to deepen the understanding of the linkages between these interdependent fields of practice and scholarship to advance a better informed and more gender-sensitive global YPS agenda. It is, as far as we are aware, the first attempt to undertake comparative analysis and outline the policy implications. The YPS and WPS agendas are natural allies linked by a common framework based on the Security Council's mandate to maintain international peace and security.[5] Scholars and practitioners need to avoid "WPS-only" or "YPS-only" silos, which neglect the many opportunities for collaboration between the two agendas.

The chapter is structured as follows: The next section sets the scene empirically, and the following section presents a more systematic comparative analysis of the founding and subsequent resolutions, highlighting differences as well as similarities and reflecting on such crosscutting issues as accountability and monitoring. Case studies on Afghanistan, Colombia, and the United Kingdom illustrate how the YPS and WPS approaches have unfolded across a range of countries. The final section highlights implications for policy and possible ways forward.

SETTING THE SCENE

It is useful to set the stage in terms of the situation of women and youth, who are often relatively disadvantaged in terms of inclusion, justice, and security. This is referenced in the statements of U.N. bodies and other international institutions—sometimes both are mentioned together as "vulnerable groups" warranting special attention,[6] although this characterization tends to fail to recognize and promote the role young women can play in building sustainable peace.

Here we take advantage of a recent innovation on the empirical front to illustrate ways to think about the peace and security agendas. The WPS Index is designed to measure and track progress on women's inclusion, justice, and security through a single number and ranking (Georgetown Institute for Women, Peace and Security and Peace Research Institute Oslo 2017).

Three broad dimensions of women's well-being are aggregated:

- *Inclusion* has multiple aspects—economic, social, and political—with indicators ranging from employment and financial inclusion to cell-phone access and parliamentary representation.
- *Justice* is captured in both formal laws, drawing on the World Bank's Women, Business and the Law database and informal discrimination, as reflected by lack of acceptance of women working and son bias (World Bank Group 2018).
- *Security* is measured at the family, community, and society levels.

The 2019/2020 edition of the WPS Index was estimated for 167 countries, covering over 98 percent of the world's population, using transparent and reliable data that are publicly available. As illustrated by figure 8.1, which shows the top and bottom dozen countries, Norway led the world rankings, and Yemen was in last place.

All of the current bottom dozen, except Pakistan, are classified as fragile or conflict-afflicted states, and six are in Sub-Saharan Africa. Looking behind these aggregate results reveals extensive unevenness in performance—only about thirty countries score in the top third for all three dimensions. This underlines the universality of the gender and security agenda.

While there are clear regional patterns in performance, there are also major differences within each region, which suggests that reaching the standards of neighbors should be feasible. There are countries in all regions that outperform the global average, including Nepal in South Asia; Tanzania, Ghana, Zimbabwe, South Africa, Rwanda, Namibia, and Mauritius in Sub-Saharan Africa; and many in Latin America and the Caribbean, including Argentina, Bolivia, Chile, Costa Rica, and Jamaica.

Echoing what the United Nations Development Programme's (UNDP) *Human Development Report* has underlined for many years, money matters, but it is not the whole story (2016). Many countries do far better on the WPS Index—or far worse—than their per-capita income rank. Six countries rank at least 50 places higher than their per-capita income rank, including Rwanda, Jamaica, and Moldova. But Saudi Arabia plummets 108 places on the WPS Index relative to its income ranking, Kuwait 88 places, and Iran drops 61 places, as shown in figure 8.2.

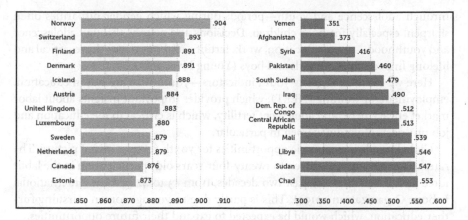

Figure 8.1. The top and bottom dozen countries on the WPS Index, 2017/2018

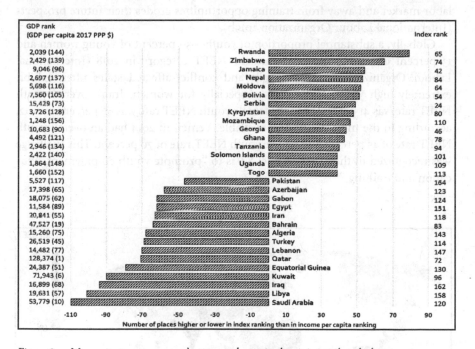

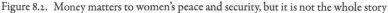

Figure 8.2. Money matters to women's peace and security, but it is not the whole story

How does this picture relate to the situation of youth? Do countries that do well on the WPS Index tend to do relatively well for youth? And is the reverse true?

Age-disaggregated data are even scarcer than gender-disaggregated data. For example, while information about education enrollments is widely available, as is child vaccination coverage and mortality rates, much less about youth is tracked, especially in the eighteen to twenty-nine age range indicated by UNSCR 2250. The relative availability of data appears to mirror the global policy focus. Since around 2000, growing attention to children has led to impressive achievements in infant and child mortality and primary education. But attention seems to taper off through adolescence and youth—periods during which gender disparities often sharpen, especially for poor children. Decisions and actions through adolescence and youthhood—about education, work, fertility, and marriage—have critical and lifelong impacts for both girls and boys (Young Lives 2015).

Here we focus on two key youth indicators—youth who are not in education, employment, or training (NEET), which provides important insights about labor market engagement, and adolescent fertility, which is critical to the education and job prospects of young women in particular.

Global trends in economic opportunities for youth reveal a mixed picture. The rates of female youth's (fifteen to twenty-four years old) participation in the labor force have fallen over the past two decades, from 53 to 42 percent (International Labour Organization 2019a). This is partly due to young women pursuing further education, which would be expected to expand their future opportunities.

However, increasing numbers of young women and men are not receiving an education and are out of the labor force.[7] Especially for youth, time out of the labor market and away from training opportunities erodes their future prospects (International Labour Organization 2019b).

Globally, a substantial proportion of youth—30 percent of young women and 13 percent of young men—fell into the NEET category in 2018 (International Labour Organization 2019c). Fragile and conflict-affected states often exhibit extremely high youth NEET rates—especially for women. Iraq's overall youth NEET rate was 41 percent, and the female youth NEET rate was 66 percent in 2012, according to the most recent data available. Yemen in 2014 had an overall youth NEET rate of 45 percent and female youth NEET rate of 70 percent. This challenge was recognized in the SDGs—target 8.6 is to "promote youth employment, education and training."[8]

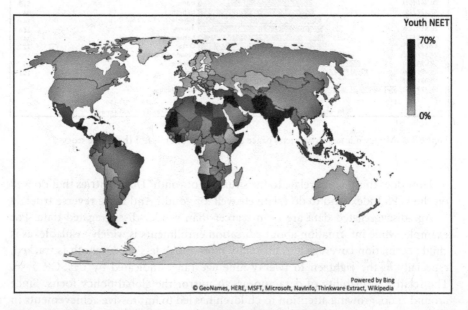

Figure 8.3. Youth not in education, employment, or training (NEET)

It is striking that in most countries, more females are NEET compared to males. The key stylized facts are as follows:

- In 191 countries, about one in three young women are counted as NEET, ranging from an average of 13 percent in developed regions to a massive 49 percent in South Asia, compared with 14 percent for young men.
- In South Asia, the youth gender gap for NEET is huge: 49 percent for women and 14 percent for men.
- In the Middle East and North Africa, Algeria and Egypt had 2019 NEET rates for young women 25 percentage points higher than for young men.

This stands in contrast to the typical focus on disenfranchised young men and underlines the importance of a gender lens.

Figure 8.4 shows the association between the WPS Index and overall NEET rates across 128 countries. The correlation is marked around 0.55. Among the countries that do well on both fronts are Iceland and Norway, whereas Afghanistan, Yemen, Iraq, Mali, and Pakistan do badly on both fronts. There are some countries that do very poorly on engaging youth, but not as poorly on the WPS Index—notably Laos, Zimbabwe, and Trinidad and Tobago.

Adolescent fertility is an important measure of the status and opportunities of female youth. Having children this early in life exposes adolescent women to unnecessary risks, and early childbearing greatly reduces the likelihood of a girl completing her education and limits her opportunities for training and employment (Wodon et al. 2017).

Globally, over recent decades, adolescent fertility has been declining, albeit unevenly. In developing countries, adolescent fertility averages 13 births per 1,000 young females in 2017 compared to 28 in 1990. The highest regional rate is in

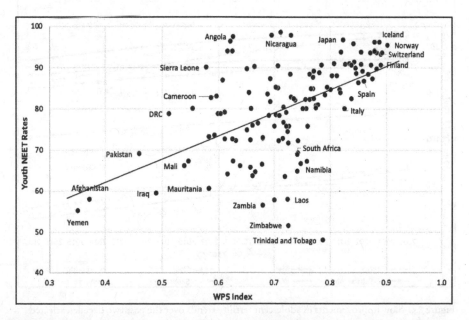

Figure 8.4. The association between the WPS Index and NEET rates

Sub-Saharan Africa at 103. The average rate is lower in Latin America and the Caribbean, but in countries in this region with the highest rates, there has been little change (World Bank Group 2017). Figure 8.5 shows how average rates have declined in some countries but remained persistently high in others, including Niger, Mali, and Chad.

How is the WPS Index associated with adolescent fertility? We might expect significant correlations, since the status of women as captured by the WPS Index is predictive of major health outcomes, including maternal and infant mortality (Klugman et al. 2018). High adolescent fertility raises major issues around women's sexual and reproductive health and early marriage.[9] Girls living in poverty are more likely to marry young. And the poor are likely to suffer more from the negative impacts of child marriage due to the various constraints they face, such as barriers to health and education services (Wodon et al. 2018).

Figure 8.6 shows the patterns across countries, with an overall correlation coefficient of 0.6. Among the countries that do well on both fronts are Iceland and Norway, whereas certain countries, including Mali and Niger, do poorly on both. For example, countries in the top twenty-fifth percentile of the WPS Index uniformly do well with regard to adolescent fertility, as illustrated by the absence of countries in the upper-left quadrant. While there are outliers, such as Lebanon and Pakistan, which do relatively well on adolescent fertility but less so on the WPS Index, the overall pattern is clear.

In sum, countries that do well on the WPS Index tend to do well on measures of youth status, with better outcomes for women associated with better opportunities and outcomes for youth. Additionally, for example, the youth literacy rate and gender parity in youth literacy are both strongly associated with the WPS Index.[10]

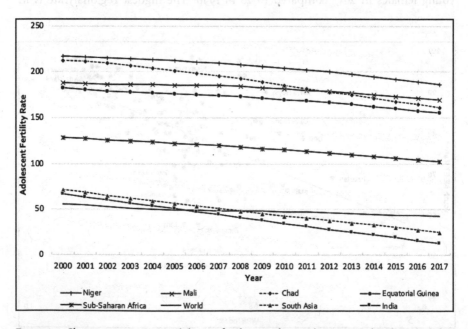

Figure 8.5. Slow improvements in adolescent fertility trends over the past two decades, selected regional and country examples

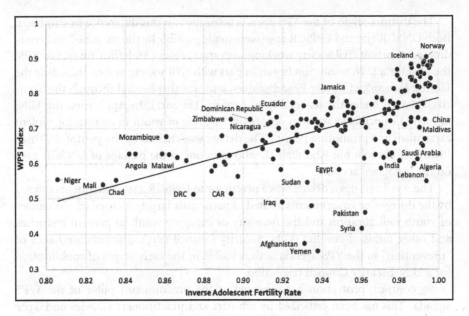

Figure 8.6. The association between the WPS Index and adolescent fertility

This association supports the argument, already intuited by advocates working in both fields, that there is much overlap and space for collaboration between the WPS and YPS agendas. We now turn to the shared agenda.

Youth and Women: Shared Agendas?

In light of common challenges, how do the global WPS and YPS agendas compare in practice?

We focus on the explicit pillars for action, to which we add two major issues for both agendas—namely, accountability and the international legal framework. The following analysis further considers the issue of stakeholders and champions.

There are significant synergies between the YPS and WPS agendas. The symmetry is most obvious for three of the pillars: participation, protection, and prevention. However, it is also interesting that activities postconflict have different labels and a somewhat different focus. The YPS agenda has tended to emphasize the inclusion of youth in disarmament and related activities. The relief and recovery pillar of the WPS agenda is generally regarded as having been relatively neglected and weakly developed in practice (O'Reilly 2019).

Despite the apparent symmetry of the agendas, each has evolved distinct areas of emphasis. Since the adoption of UNSCR 1325, the protection pillar has been most prominent in scholarship and practice on WPS, and the majority of subsequent WPS resolutions have focused on this pillar (Shepherd 2019). The YPS agenda has had less time to evolve areas of emphasis, but *The Missing Peace: Independent Progress Study on Youth, Peace and Security* has described prevention as the YPS agenda's "central pillar" (Simpson 2018).

The distinct origin of the YPS agenda helps explain this difference in emphasis. Both UNSCR 1325 and UNSCR 2250 were made possible by the sustained and coordinated efforts of civil society working with state actors (Anderlini 2019). For YPS, the idea for a U.N. resolution began in part with civil society actors, including the United Network of Young Peacebuilders, and was shepherded through the Security Council under the leadership of Jordan (Lie 2017). In April 2015, the U.N. Security Council held an open debate on "the role of youth in countering violent extremism and promoting peace." The debate was chaired by the youthful Crown Prince Al Hussein bin Abdullah II, who announced the passage of UNSCR 2250 on his Instagram account.

The April 2015 open debate was a precursor to UNSCR 2250. Statements offered by the thirty-nine governments invited to participate largely focused on the danger of youth radicalization and the necessity of engaging youth to prevent terrorism and other forms of conflict (U.N. Security Council 2015). The predominance of "prevention" in the YPS agenda is thus visible in the early stages of mobilization for a U.N. Security Council resolution.

By contrast, protection has emerged as the predominant pillar of the WPS agenda. This has been criticized by scholars and practitioners (Davies and True 2019). Since the adoption of UNSCR 1325, four of seven subsequent WPS resolutions focused on protection-related themes. UNSCR 1820 (2008) focused on conflict-related sexual violence and "set the nascent WPS agenda on [its] trajectory" (Shepherd 2019).

While prevention has been the least emphasized WPS pillar, the most recent WPS resolution, UNSCR 2242 (2015), is framed in terms of the prevention of extremism and terrorism as evidence grew about the various roles that women play in both fueling and preventing violent extremism (Gowrinathan 2014) and links to the YPS agenda's concern with countering violent extremism. We also know that where women are included in peacemaking processes and where their rights are respected, peace and stability are more likely to prevail (Hudson et al. 2009; O'Reilly, Ó Súilleabháin, and Paffenholz 2015). The superficial differences between the WPS and YPS agendas diminish once the interdependence of the pillars is recognized.

First, the language of the youth resolutions is less mandatory in tone, couched in terms of "considering" and "taking into account." By way of contrast, the WPS agenda declared that various changes would be ensured. This suggests a lesser degree of commitment of the international community to the youth agenda.

Second, UNSCR 2250 makes no reference to young women and men or gender but rather connotes youth in gender-neutral—or gender-blind—terms. This is a concern, especially given the differences in needs, opportunities, and constraints for young women and young men. More encouragingly, the *Missing Peace* report underscores the importance of supporting and promoting positive, gender-equitable identities and roles.

Because the gender-related dimensions are not explicit in the YPS agenda, there is a risk that this disadvantage will not be addressed and that gender and age biases will continue to exclude young women from formal political and peace processes. As noted by U.N. Women, stereotypes and assumptions about the capabilities and credibility of young people—and young women in particular—as unqualified and too inexperienced result in their exclusion (U.N. Women 2018). In Uganda, for example, young women reported persistent negative stereotypes from some members of the community, limiting their participation in a leadership and anti-corruption campaign (Walker et al. 2014).

Third, UNSCR 2250 defines what types of activities are included in each pillar. The protection pillar includes the directive to "end impunity" and prosecute per-petrators of crimes. This specificity may be intended to advance progress through greater specificity, in contrast to UNSCR 1325.

Fourth, the partnerships dimension was not explicit in the formulation of the WPS agenda, while the YPS agenda highlights the resource needs of relevant U.N. agencies as well as actors at different levels.[11] This may be a response to the evident underresourcing of the WPS agenda (U.N. Secretary-General 2018). In 2015, when the YPS agenda was defined in UNSCR 2250, "the failure to allocate sufficient resources and funds has been perhaps the most serious and persistent obstacle to the implementation of the women, peace and security agenda" (U.N. Women 2015a).

The accountability mechanisms established as part of the YPS agenda appear to be weaker than those put in place to monitor WPS. A major global review undertaken in 2015 on UNSCR 1325 amounted to a "call to action," with rec-ommendations endorsed by the secretary-general (U.N. Women 2015b). Official reporting takes place annually and is considered each October in an open debate of the Security Council. This is an occasion to spotlight achievements as well as con-tinued challenges and gaps in the WPS agenda. Additionally, in 2016, UNSCR 2240 formalized an Independent Experts Group on WPS at the Security Council, which meets regularly to monitor implementation. Another piece of the accountability architecture is the set of twenty-six indicators laid out by the U.N. secretary-general in 2010 (U.N. Security Council 2010b), although in practice, the indicators have not been systematically collected and the associated data remain sparse. While far from perfect, these various mechanisms have helped sustain the focus of the WPS agenda and facilitated civil society scrutiny and engagement.

By contrast, the YPS resolutions establish far fewer formal mechanisms for monitoring progress. The founding resolution, UNSCR 2250, requested a report, *The Missing Peace: Independent Progress Study on Youth, Peace and Security*, which was completed in 2018. The Security Council has also requested that the secretary-general provide a report on the implementation of the YPS agenda by May 2020. However, no annual or regularized reporting mechanism, similar to the WPS open debate and report, currently exists.

One possible way forward would be to link to discussions related to the develop-ment agenda. In 2018, participants at the 2018 U.N. Economic and Social Council (ECOSOC) Youth Forum called for engaging youth in monitoring and implement-ing the SDGs, including through countries' voluntary national reviews, using more accessible language and fostering skills relevant to the future of work, among other priorities (Lebada 2018).

Finally and relatedly, addressing data constraints is critical. This is especially urgent for the youth agenda and remains crucial for WPS. Lack of sufficient data, reporting, and monitoring means that the picture of the needs and strengths of young people is incomplete. It also means that youth organizations and young leaders are unable to track impacts and attract resources to scale their efforts.

The YPS and WPS agendas are linked both in the formal content of the resolutions and in their shared opportunities and constraints. An obvious point of intersection is the role of young women in building and sustaining peace in fragile and conflict situations. We turn now to the cases of Colombia, Afghanistan, and the United Kingdom to highlight how these issues have played out in three very different contexts.

Colombia: Model of Participation?

In 2016, the signing of a peace agreement ended the Colombian government's decades-long conflict with the Revolutionary Armed Forces of Colombia (FARC) guerilla group. The conflict disproportionately impacted women and youth as civilians and activists, mediators, and sometimes combatants (Bouvier 2016).[12] Rates of intimate partner violence are high, affecting almost one in five (18 percent) of Colombian women annually,[13] while more than one in five youth were out of education and work. Both youth and women will play a critical role in determining prospects for Colombia's peace and security.

The Colombian peace accords have been held up as a model for the inclusivity of women. As the agreement was negotiated in Havana, women's groups and civil society groups regularly met with FARC and government representatives to ensure their concerns were on the agenda (Dayal 2018). Women representatives were eventually included on both sides, and a gender subcommission (GSC) was established (Carvajal and Álvarez-Vanegas, 2019). This resulted in the inclusion of 130 gender stipulations in the final agreement, including land reform for rural women, measures to address gender-based violence, and women's political representation. It is noted that while the agreement is considered a model in terms of gender inclusion, as of 2018, only about half of the gender-related commitments had not been initiated and only 4 percent had been fully implemented (Kroc Institute 2018), while the women human rights defenders who played critical roles in the peace process have faced increased violence (U.N. News 2020).

The Colombian case illustrates the mutually reinforcing interaction of the participation and the protection pillars of the WPS agenda. The participation of women negotiators and civil society activists obtained measures to further protection, such as the ban on impunity for crimes of sexual violence.

While the inclusion of women was an explicit goal of the negotiating parties, youth were not. This may reflect that the parties and international actors involved had internalized the WPS agenda to a greater degree than the more recent YPS agenda. It may also be traced to UNSCR 2250's softer language on the participation of youth. While UNSCR 1325 calls on states to "ensure" the increased representation of women in peace negotiations, UNSCR 2250 asks them to "consider" ways to incorporate the views of youth in peace negotiations "as appropriate."[14]

Yet despite their absence from formal negotiations, Colombian youth have played positive roles in peacebuilding and civic engagement before, during, and after the FARC peace process. Examples include a network for young peacebuilders in the state of Antioquia as well as a UNDP initiative to facilitate conversations between one hundred thousand young people and the government office in charge of negotiations, showing the willingness of youth to work for peace (Andersson 2016). In 2018, the U.N. Mission in Colombia noted that youth groups have assumed "expanded roles" in reintegration and reconciliation activities (U.N. Security Council 2018b).

Young women have played a major role in advocating for human rights and building peace in Colombia. However, women are underrepresented in senior leadership among youth peacebuilding groups. A 2018 study on *Jovenes por Jovenes* (Spanish for "youth for youth") found that seven out of ten youth leaders are male, and only one in six youth peacebuilding organizations carries out activities related to gender, for example (Ochoa 2018). Greater support for young women's leadership in these groups would advance both the YPS and WPS agendas in Colombia.

Afghanistan: Limited Progress, Significant Potential

Afghanistan is one of the world's youngest countries, with about 63 percent of the population below twenty-five years of age (U.N. Population Fund 2018b; see also chapter 7, this volume). At the same time, the disadvantage of women is well known. The country ranked second last in the 2019/2020 WPS Index. While progress has been limited in the implementation of both the WPS and YPS agendas, there is significant potential for gains in the role of young women in advancing peace.

It was not until 2015 that Afghanistan adopted a national action plan (NAP) for WPS (Afghanistan Ministry of Foreign Affairs 2015), and protection and participation have lagged behind. In 2009, Afghanistan adopted the Elimination of Violence against Women (EVAW) law, which criminalizes various forms of violence against women and establishes duties for the government to investigate and prosecute certain cases, but implementation has fallen short, resulting in "de facto impunity" in many cases, and insecurity for women and other groups remains widespread (U.N. Assistance Mission in Afghanistan and U.N. Office of the High Commissioner for Human Rights 2018).

Implementation of the participation pillar has also been inadequate in Afghanistan, with some bright spots. There has been a "notable absence" of women from negotiations in peace talks and summits overall (U.N. Secretary-General 2018), dating back to 2002 (Duncanson and Farr 2019). The February 2020 peace deal between the Taliban and the United States was negotiated without Afghan government representatives and civil society and lacks guarantees to protect women's rights and their inclusion in the upcoming intra-Afghan talks (Verveer and Koppell 2020).

Women's increasing domestic political engagement, however, has been notable. In 2018, 418 women candidates—the highest number in Afghanistan's history—ran for the national parliament (Mohamed 2018). Afghanistan's constitution reserves 27 percent of seats in the lower house for women.[15] On the YPS front, government, civil society, and grassroots initiatives have sought to engage youth in peacebuilding. For example, in 2018, the Afghan Youth Parliament, an initiative supported by the national government and the United Nations Population Fund, brought together youth representatives elected from youth councils and civil society from around the country (about one-third women) to discuss education, employment, and political participation (U.N. Population Fund 2018b).

Young women have gained a larger role in domestic politics and building peace in Afghanistan, certainly relative to the low baseline in 2000. The 2018 parliamentary election saw a number of young women candidates, such as Sabri Andar, a disabled (she uses a wheelchair) twenty-six-year-old who ran for a seat representing Kabul (Mohamed 2018). Gita Bashardoost, a Kunduz-based activist, has used civic activism to push for the inclusion of young people in peace initiatives (U.N. Assistance Mission in Afghanistan 2018). Sharbat, a pseudonym used by a respondent to a 2017 survey on youth, founded a group to teach computer and design skills to youth, using entrepreneurship to offer them employment and, indirectly, to further peace (United Network of Young Peacebuilders 2018). It is clear that young women in Afghanistan are engaged on several fronts relevant to the WPS and YPS agendas, which provide important foundations for future progress.

The United Kingdom:
Support for Implementing the Agendas

The United Kingdom has been engaged in the WPS and YPS initiatives from the outset. The government has made a strong public commitment to pursuing WPS objectives through its foreign policy, including in its third four-year national action plan (NAP) for 2018–2022 (United Kingdom Foreign and Commonwealth Office 2018), which is externally focused.[16] Importantly, the NAP recognizes that the challenges women and girls encounter differ by age and observes that adolescent girls are "a particularly important group to support to bring about change in the long term" (United Kingdom Foreign and Commonwealth Office 2018).

The United Kingdom has also committed to supporting the YPS agenda (Pierce 2018) and pursued a number of relevant initiatives under the WPS mandate, as noted in the U.K. NAP report to Parliament (United Kingdom Foreign and Commonwealth Office 2018), including funding for a program to change norms around gender-based violence that focuses on youth and women's groups in South Sudan, supporting a women's leadership network in improving literacy and political empowerment for women from the Shan minority in Myanmar, and developing a program to protect vulnerable young women living on the streets in Kinshasa.

The United Kingdom's efforts on WPS and YPS predominantly focus on fragile and conflict states. This "outbound" emphasis has been criticized domestically by academics and civil society. However, donor states like the United Kingdom do play an important role in financing the implementation of both agendas. In recent years, the largest donors, including the United Kingdom and a handful of other wealthy states (and the EU), contributed more than 80 percent of bilateral aid dedicated to gender equality in fragile and conflict states (U.N. Secretary-General 2018).

The WPS and YPS agendas, of course, apply to the United Kingdom domestically, but the United Kingdom's explicit "inbound" initiatives on both have been more limited. Efforts to support the political participation of youth are illustrated by the British Youth Council, an elected body of six hundred young people that sits in the House of Commons annually and debates a subject determined by youth ballot (Pierce 2018). Relevant to the prevention pillar, the United Kingdom's domestic counterterrorism policy specifically targets outreach to women and youth to counter violent extremism in their communities (Bigio and Vogelstein 2016).

Looking Ahead

Over the first two decades of the twenty-first century, the international community has promoted a more inclusive and sustainable approach to global peace and security. Initiated in 2000, the WPS agenda called on states to recognize and promote the role of women in preventing and sustaining peace. The YPS agenda, established fifteen years later, similarly emphasizes the importance of youth. The agendas parallel each other in significant ways—addressing the underlying exclusion issues and the formal structure and areas of emphasis of the founding UNSC resolutions. In 2020, some leading civil society networks were calling to integrate both agendas into the Beijing +25 Generation Equality Forum.[17]

On the empirical front, various measures of youth well-being were found to broadly correlate with the WPS Index, which assesses women's well-being on the dimensions of inclusion, justice, and security. Countries that do well on the WPS Index, for example, tended to do well on measures for adolescent fertility and for youth not in employment, education, or training. Although our analysis does not imply causality, it suggests that often where women do well, youth also do well across these indicators and indicates potential synergies in efforts to overcome exclusion.

Formally, the WPS and YPS agendas share three core pillars—participation, protection, and prevention. In practice, the agendas have evolved differing emphases. Protection is widely seen as the most prominent WPS pillar, although recent scholarship has called for increased attention to other pillars, such as participation and also recovery (O'Reilly 2019). Less time has elapsed to allow the YPS agenda to evolve a distinct emphasis, although prevention is emerging as a key pillar (Simpson 2018). At the same time, the pillars are clearly interdependent: where women's and youth's *participation* in peace negotiations is advanced, for example, they are able to further *protection* by ensuring the inclusion of relevant provisions in a resulting agreement.

The larger disadvantages faced by young women are clearly at the intersection of both agendas. We underlined the extensive exclusion of young women from both education and work and the need for efforts to engage young people in productive work to include women as well as men. Expanding access to economic opportunities is important for young women and men, which involves efforts of the private sector as well as government and development partners. Access to safe and legal contraception and abortion services are important elements of policies and programs to be addressed, alongside efforts to address early marriage, which is closely associated with adverse norms and poor prospects for young women.

There are major policy agendas associated with advancing the prospects for women and youth that are beyond the scope of this chapter. A whole range of evidence is accumulating about what works for girls' education, for example, and empowerment more broadly. For education, making schools affordable—reducing direct costs by eliminating school fees and reducing indirect costs through scholarships and stipends—is important, while a greater focus on connecting education to jobs improves perceived rates of return and thus families' investment in girls' education (Sperling and Winthrop 2016). Increasing the supply of quality education is also important. Recent studies also find that reducing the average distance from home to school in Afghanistan, reducing the class size in Uganda, and offering school meals and school uniforms in Kenya improved girls' test scores (Masino and Niño-Zarazua 2016).

Evaluations of programs to empower adolescent girls suggest that the most effective programs have several characteristics (Cassaday, Chakravarty, Fox, and Haddock 2015), including locally appropriate and deliberate recruitment strategies to reach marginalized girls; appropriate support and structures, including training, transportation, and child care; incentives for providers so they have a vested interest in the success of participants; and links to the local labor market and economic opportunities—for example, support for business development in Liberia, where wage jobs are scarce. Overall, evidence suggests that the most promising programs for female youth take place in girl-friendly settings and provide a combination of information about sexual and reproductive health and complementary training and assets, although it is hard to know exactly which components contributed the most to successful outcomes and for whom (Baird and Özler 2016).

Looking ahead, as the agendas address common challenges, there is scope for greater learning and synergies both among the pillars of each agenda and between the women and youth agendas for peace and security. For both, addressing data constraints and shortcomings in monitoring is critical, alongside the development of more robust accountability mechanisms. The recognition of the importance of participation and improvements in monitoring and accountability processes, including the establishment of the Independent Experts Group, suggest that the WPS agenda has adapted to challenges and gaps, even if progress has been uneven—which is a useful lesson going forward for the YPS agenda.

In adopting the WPS and YPS resolutions, the Security Council sought to recognize and advance the role of women and youth, respectively, in the global peace and security agenda. By working to address the many areas of common concern between the agendas—as well as mutual challenges—scholars, policy makers, and practitioners can ensure that both agendas can realize their potential to advance sustainable peace in the coming decades.

NOTES

1. Thanks to Agathe Christien, Anne Della Guardia, Haiwen (Bryan) Zou, and Chen Zheng for research assistance and Amie Gaye for statistical inputs.

2. U.N. Security Council Resolution 1820 (June 19, 2009), U.N. Security Council Resolution 1888 (September 30, 2008), U.N. Security Council Resolution 1889 (October 9, 2009), U.N. Security Council Resolution 1960 (December 16, 2010), U.N. Security Council Resolution 2106 (June 24, 2013), U.N. Security Council Resolution 2122 (October 18, 2013), U.N. Security Council Resolution 2242 (October 13, 2015).

3. The definition of *youth* varies by organization and region. The U.N., for example, has defined *youth* as persons from the ages of fifteen to twenty-four "for statistical purposes" (United Nations Youth 2013). UNSCR 2250 defines *youth* as persons from the ages of fifteen to twenty-nine for purposes of the YPS agenda, and it is this definition we use here.

4. Countries are classified as such based on weak policies and institutions and/or the presence of a U.N. and/or regional peacekeeping or peacebuilding mission during the past three years (World Bank Group 2019).

5. UNSCR 1325 (October 31, 2000); UNSCR 2250 (December 9, 2015).

6. A characteristic example is UNSCR 1208 (November 19, 1998), on refugee protection, which emphasizes the "security needs of women, children and the elderly, who are the most vulnerable groups in refugee camps and settlements."

7. This means that unemployment is often not a good measure of labor force status in developing countries; the reported rates are typically low in poor countries, but that does not mean that people—and youth, in particular—are gainfully employed.

8. The official definition is the proportion of youth (ages fifteen to twenty-four years) not in education, employment, or training.

9. Contraceptive prevalence is the percentage of women who are currently using, or whose sexual partner is currently using, at least one method of contraception. Sub-Saharan Africa, which has the highest regional adolescent fertility rate (103 births per 1,000), also has the lowest regional contraceptive prevalence rate at 28 percent (U.N. Department of Economics and Social Affairs 2019).

10. The correlation between youth literacy rate and gender parity in youth literacy is 0.65 and 0.61, respectively.

11. UNSCR 2250.

12. According to U.N. Women, more than half of FARC fighters were recruited at a young age. Women and youth served as combatants on all sides of the Colombian conflict.

13. WPS Index, "Colombia Country Profile," https://giwps.georgetown.edu/country/colombia.

14. UNSCR 2250.

15. At the time of this writing, only one-third of the results have been certified due to allegations of election fraud.

16. The nine priority countries identified in the U.K. NAP are Afghanistan, Burma, Democratic Republic of Congo, Iraq, Libya, Nigeria, Somalia, South Sudan, and Syria.

17. See https://gnwp.org/open-letter-beijing25-an-uphill-battle-for-the-women-and-peace-and-security-and-youth-and-peace-and-security-agendas.

REFERENCES

Afghanistan Ministry of Foreign Affairs. 2015. *Afghanistan's National Action Plan on UNSCR 1325—Women, Peace and Security.* PeaceWomen. www.peacewomen.org/sites/default/files/NAP%20Afghanistan.pdf.

Anderlini, S. N. 2019. "Civil Society's Leadership in Adopting 1325 Resolution." In *The Oxford Handbook of Women, Peace and Security,* edited by S. E. Davies and J. True. New York: Oxford University Press. https://doi.org/10.1093/oxfordhb/9780190638276.013.65.

Andersson, K. 2016. "Young People Building Peace in Colombia." U.N. Development Programme. www.undp.org/content/undp/en/home/blog/2016/2/2/Los-j-venes-consolidan-la-paz-en-Colombia.html.

Baird, S., and B. Özler. 2016. "Sustained Effects on Economic Empowerment of Interventions for Adolescent Girls: Existing Evidence and Knowledge Gaps." Center for Global Development. www.cgdev.org/sites/default/files/sustained-effects-economic-empowerment.pdf?callout=2-2.

Bigio, J., and R. Vogelstein. 2016. *How Women's Participation in Conflict Prevention and Resolution Advances U.S. Interests.* Council on Foreign Relations. www.cfr.org/report/how-womens-participation-conflict-prevention-and-resolution-advances-us-interests.

Bouvier, V. M. 2016. *Gender and the Role of Women in the Colombian Peace Process.* U.N. Women. www.unwomen.org/en/digital-library/publications/2017/2/gender-and-the-role-of-women-in-colombias-peace-process.

Carvajal, I. M., and E. Álvarez-Vanegas. 2019. "Securing Participation and Protection in Peace Agreements: The Case of Colombia." In *The Oxford Handbook of Women, Peace and Security*, edited by S. E. Davies and J. True. New York: Oxford University Press. https://doi.org/10.1093/oxfordhb/9780190638276.013.36.

Cassaday, K. A., S. Chakravarty, L. Fox, and S. E. Haddock. 2015. *The Spirit of Boldness: Lessons from the World Bank's Adolescent Girls Initiative*. World Bank Group. http://documents.worldbank.org/curated/en/725871467996978832/The-spirit-of-boldness-lessons-from-the-World-Bank-s-adolescent-girls-initiative.

Davies, S. E., and J. True. 2019. "Women, Peace, and Security: A Transformative Agenda?" In *The Oxford Handbook of Women, Peace and Security*, edited by S. E. Davies and J. True. New York: Oxford University Press. https://doi.org/10.1093/oxfordhb/9780190638276.013.1.

Dayal, A. 2018. *Connecting Informal and Formal Peace Talks: From Movements to Mediators*. Georgetown Institute for Women, Peace and Security. https://giwps.georgetown.edu/resource/connecting-informal-and-formal-peace-talks.

Duncanson, C., and V. Farr. 2019. "Testing the WPS Agenda: The Case of Afghanistan." In *The Oxford Handbook of Women, Peace and Security*, edited by S. E. Davies and J. True. New York: Oxford University Press. https://doi.org/10.1093/oxfordhb/9780190638276.013.42.

Georgetown Institute for Women, Peace and Security and Peace Research Institute Oslo. 2017. *Women, Peace and Security Index 2017–18*. Washington, D.C.: GIWPS and PRIO.

Gowrinathan, N. 2014. "The Women of ISIS: Understanding and Combating Female Extremism." Foreign Affairs. www.foreignaffairs.com/articles/middle-east/2014-08-21/women-isis.

Hudson, V., M. Caprioli, B. Ballif-Spanvill, R. McDermott, and C. Emmett. 2008. "The Heart of the Matter: The Security of Women and the Security of States." *International Security* 33, no. 3, 7–45.

ILO (International Labour Organization). 2019a. "Labour Force Participation Rate by Sex and Age—ILO Modelled Estimates, July 2019 (%)—Annual." ILO. https://ilostat.ilo.org/data.

———. 2019b. "World Employment Social Outlook: Trends 2019." ILO. www.ilo.org/global/research/global-reports/weso/2019/lang--en/index.htm.

———. 2019c. "Share of Youth Not in Employment, Education or Training (NEET) by Sex and Rural / Urban Areas—ILO Modelled Estimates, Nov. 2019 (%)." ILO. https://ilostat.ilo.org/data.

Klugman, Jeni, Li Li, Kathryn M. Barker, Jennifer Parsons, and Kelly Dale. 2019. "How Are the Domains of Women's Inclusion, Justice, and Security Associated with Maternal and Infant Mortality across Countries? Insights from the Women, Peace, and Security Index." *Social Science and Medicine—Population Health* 9 (December 2019).

Kroc Institute. 2018. *Special Report of the Kroc Institute and the International Accompaniment Component, UN Women, Women's International Democratic Federation, and Sweden, on the Monitoring of the Gender Perspective in the Implementation of the Colombian Final Peace Accord*. https://kroc.nd.edu/assets/297624/181113_gender_report_final.pdf.

Lebada, A. M. 2018. "Youth Express Needs, Recommendations for SDG Implementation." SDG Knowledge Hub. https://sdg.iisd.org/commentary/generation-2030/youth-express-needs-recommendations-for-sdg-implementation.

Lie, K. K. 2017. *On the Front Lines: Youth, Peace and Security*. Norwegian Children and Youth Council. www.lnu.no/wp-content/uploads/2017/04/2250-lnu-rapport-14-e.pdf.

Masino, S., and M. Niño-Zarazua. 2016. "What Works to Improve the Quality of Student Learning in Developing Countries?" *International Journal of Educational Development* 48:53–65. www.sciencedirect.com/science/article/pii/S0738059315300146.

Mohamed, H. 2018. "'It Is Time': Afghanistan's Female Candidates Promise Change." *Al Jazeera*. www.aljazeera.com/news/2018/10/time-women-candidates-afghanistan-promise-change-181019091831158.html.

Ochoa, L. 2018. *Peacebuilding in Colombia: A Youth Perspective, Program of Alliances for Reconciliation*. Search for Common Ground. www.sfcg.org/wp-content/uploads/2018/02/Peacebuilding_in_Colombia-A_YOUTH_PERSPECTIVE_highlights.pdf.

O'Reilly, M. 2019. "Where the WPS Pillars Intersect." In *The Oxford Handbook of Women, Peace and Security*, edited by S. E. Davies and J. True. New York: Oxford University Press. https://doi.org/10.1093/oxfordhb/9780190638276.013.17.

O'Reilly, M., A. Ó Súilleabháin, and T. Paffenholz. 2015. *Reimagining Peacemaking: Women's Roles in Peace Processes*. International Peace Institute. www.ipinst.org/wp-content/uploads/2015/06/IPI-E-pub-Reimagining-Peacemaking.pdf.

Pierce, K. 2018. "Statement by Ambassador Karen Pierce, UK Permanent Representative to the UN, at the Security Council Debate." www.gov.uk/government/speeches/youth-peace-and-security.

Shepherd, L. 2019. "WPS and Adopted Security Council Resolution." In *The Oxford Handbook of Women, Peace and Security*, edited by S. E. Davies and J. True. New York: Oxford University Press. https://doi.org/10.1093/oxfordhb/9780190638276.013.7.

Simpson, G. 2018. *The Missing Peace: Independent Progress Study on Youth, Peace and Security*. UNFPA. www.unfpa.org/resources/missing-peace-independent-progress-study-youth-and-peace-and-security.

Sperling, G., and R. Winthrop. 2016. *What Works in Girls' Education: Evidence for the World's Best Investment*. Brookings Institution Press. www.brookings.edu/wp-content/uploads/2016/07/What-Works-in-Girls-Educationlowres.pdf.

UNDP (United Nations Development Programme). 2016. *Human Development Report 2016*. http://hdr.undp.org/en/2016-report.

———. 2017. "Fast Facts: Youth as Partners for the Implementation of the SDGs." www.undp.org/content/undp/en/home/librarypage/results/fast_facts/fast-facts--youth-as-partners-for-the-implementation-of-the-sdgs.html.

UNFP (United Nations Population Fund). 2018b. "Young People Make Their Voices Heard through the Afghan Youth Parliament." https://afghanistan.unfpa.org/en/news/young-people-make-their-voices-heard-through-afghan-youth-parliament.

United Kingdom Foreign and Commonwealth Office, Department for International Development and Ministry of Defence. 2018. *National Action Plan on Women, Peace and Security 2018–2022: Annual Report to Parliament 2018*. www.gov.uk/government/publications/uk-national-action-plan-nap-on-women-peace-and-security-wps-2018-to-2022-report-to-parliament-december-2018.

United Nations Assistance Mission in Afghanistan. 2018. "Young Afghans Essential for Peacebuilding in Country's Northeast." https://unama.unmissions.org/young-afghans-essential-peace-building-country%E2%80%99s-northeast.

United Nations Assistance Mission in Afghanistan and United Nations Office of the High Commissioner for Human Rights. 2018. *Injustice and Impunity: Mediation of Criminal Offences of Violence against Women*. www.ohchr.org/Documents/Countries/AF/UNAMA_OHCHR_EVAW_Report2018_InjusticeImpunity29May2018.pdf.

United Nations Department of Economic and Social Affairs. 2019. "Contraceptive Use by Method 2019." www.un.org/en/development/desa/population/publications/pdf/family/ContraceptiveUseByMethodDataBooklet2019.pdf.

United Nations Secretary-General. 2018. *Report of the Secretary-General on Women and Peace and Security*. S/2018/900. https://undocs.org/S/2018/900.

United Nations Security Council. 2010a. "Statement by the President of the Security Council." S/PRST/2010/22. www.securitycouncilreport.org/un-documents/document/WPS-S-PRST-2010-22.php.

————. 2010b. *Women and Peace and Security: Report of the Secretary-General.* S/2010/173. https://undocs.org/S/2010/173.

————. 2015. 7432nd meeting. "Maintenance of International Peace and Security." S/PV.7432. www.securitycouncilreport.org/atf/cf/%7B65BFCF9B-6D27-4E9C-8CD3-CF6E4FF96FF9 %7D/spv_7432.pdf.

————. 2018a. *United Nations Verification Mission in Colombia: Report of the Secretary-General.* S/2018/723. https://colombia.unmissions.org/sites/default/files/n1845592.pdf.

————. 2018b. *Women, Peace and Security.* S/PV.8382. October 25, 2018. https://undocs.org/en/S/PV.8382.

United Nations Women. 2015a. "Financing of the Women, Peace and Security Agenda." In *A Global Study on the Implementation of United Nations Security Council Resolution 1325.* http://wps.unwomen.org/financing.

————. 2015b. *Preventing Conflict, Transforming Justice, Securing the Peace: A Global Study on the Implementation of United Nations Security Council Resolution 1325.* www.peacewomen .org/sites/default/files/UNW-GLOBAL-STUDY-1325-2015%20(1).pdf.

————. 2018. *Young Women in Peace and Security: At the Intersection of the YPS and WPS Agendas.* Progress Study on Youth, Peace and Security. New York: U.N. Women, April 2018. www.unwomen.org/en/digital-library/publications/2018/4/young-women-in -peace-and-security.

United Nations Youth. 2013. "Definition of Youth." www.un.org/esa/socdev/documents/ youth/fact-sheets/youth-definition.pdf.

United Network of Young Peacebuilders. 2018. *Peacebuilders, beyond Dividing Lines: The Reality of Youth-Led Peacebuilding in Afghanistan, Colombia, Libya and Sierra Leone.* http:// unoy.org/wp-content/uploads/Final-Version-Research-Report_Beyond-Dividing-Lines _UNOY.pdf.

U.N. News (United Nations News). 2020. "Colombia: 'Staggering Number' of Human Rights Defenders Killed in 2019." https://news.un.org/en/story/2020/01/1055272.

Verveer, M., and C. Koppell. 2020. "Afghan Women: Essential for Peace." The Hill. https:// thehill.com/opinion/international/486302-afghan-women-essential-for-peace.

Walker, D., and P. Pereznieto, with G. Bergh and K. Smith. 2014. "Partners for Change: Young People and Governance in a Post-2015 World." Relentless Development. http:// restlessdevelopment.org/file/partners-for-change-young-people-and-governance-in-a -post-2015-world-pdf. (URL inactive.)

Wodon, Q., C. Male, C. Montenegro, H. Nguyen, and A. Onagoruwa. 2018. "Educating Girls and Ending Child Marriage: A Priority for Africa." World Bank Group. http:// documents.worldbank.org/curated/en/268251542653259451/Educating-Girls-and-Ending -Child-marriage-A-Priority-for-Africa.

Wodon, Q., et al. 2017. *Economic Impacts of Child Marriage: Global Synthesis Report.* World Bank Group. http://documents.worldbank.org/curated/en/530891498511398503/Economic -impacts-of-child-marriage-global-synthesis-report.

World Bank Group. 2017. "Adolescent Fertility Rate (Births per 1,000 Women Ages 15–19)." https://data.worldbank.org/indicator/sp.ado.tfrt.

————. 2018. *Women, Business and the Law 2018.* http://documents.worldbank.org/curated/ en/926401524803880673/Women-Business-and-the-Law-2018.

————. 2019. "Harmonized List of Fragile Situations FY19." www.worldbank.org/en/topic/ fragilityconflictviolence/brief/harmonized-list-of-fragile-situations.

Young Lives. 2015. *How Gender Shapes Adolescence: Diverging Paths and Opportunities* (Policy Brief No. 22). www.younglives.org.uk/content/how-gender-shapes-adolescence-diverging -paths-and-opportunities.

PART V

Disengagement and Reintegration

CHAPTER 9

Securitized Youth, Transitional Justice, and the Politics of Disengagement in Rwanda

Victoria R. Bishop

The adoption and implementation of transitional justice (TJ) mechanisms and the (re)establishment of the rule of law in postconflict societies have been widely debated. Postconflict justice is currently at the forefront of international development and security discourse (Siitonen 2011; Ni Aolain 2016; Ladisch 2018). Recognized as having "particular relevance to YPS [Youth, Peace and Security]" (Simpson 2018, 103), TJ requires establishing effective accountability mechanisms for human rights abuses—failure to do so would result in impunity and has the potential to exacerbate or prolong the suffering of victims and survivors. When human rights abuses are ignored, the consequences impede the ability of affected community members and youth alike to move toward reconciliation (Ketelaars 2014). Justice is essential for societies to transition from conflict to sustainable peace and establishes an indispensable foundation for conflict-affected youth to navigate the fragile circumstances that follow repression and gross human rights abuses.

Recently, the peacebuilding community has reflected on opportunities to meaningfully engage youth in peacebuilding processes and has recognized youth's capabilities as agents of change and sustainability (McEvoy-Levy 2011; Atran 2015; Berents and McEvoy-Levy 2015; McGill and O'Kane 2015; U.N. and World Bank 2017). The 2015 United Nations Security Council Resolution (UNSCR) 2250 on the global YPS agenda and the 2010 U.N. Report's guiding principles to transitional justice advocate for youth's involvement in peacebuilding. In practice, however, youth are often pushed aside by the political and institutional elite during political transitions (Ladisch 2018, 4). A significant deficit in trust among youth in their governments, multilateral bodies, and civil society organizations is a common consequence of this exclusion. Gendered stereotypes of young people as either perpetrators of violence (males) or passive victims (females) often pervade the mutual lack of trust (Simpson 2018). These perceptions limit youth's ability to contribute to the peacebuilding discussions, let alone advocate for their rights as youth.

The case of postgenocide Rwanda is illustrative of the progressive securitization of youth—that is, the increasing tendency to consider youth primarily or even exclusively in terms of their relation to security matters, a phenomenon that was crystallized in the adoption of UNSCR 2250 and subsequent related frameworks but that greatly predates the global impact of these documents. As my 2016 field visit to Kigali, Butare, and Kibeho corroborates, recent discussions of youth's role in current Rwandan society (e.g., Ensor 2019; Sommers 2012; Waldorf 2009) highlight their ambivalent position vis-à-vis their older counterparts in a context of shifting regional and global priorities. Rwandan youth remain "stuck" (Sommers 2012) between expectations of increased social agency and challenges that impede their transition to social adulthood. Young people are thus uncomfortably situated in a postconflict space where gender-sensitive international standards must be reconciled with local cultural values that do not always give due weight to the views of young people (Ensor 2013). Rwandan youth's engagement in the global YPS agenda, as framed by the turbulent postgenocide context that has dominated social life in their country for over twenty-five years, is the guiding driver of this chapter.

The disengagement and reintegration pillar of UNSCR 2250, which engages youth primarily from a securitized perspective during peacebuilding processes, is an additional lens through which these dynamics are examined. The chapter further assesses the accomplishments and limitations of the various mechanisms implemented in Rwanda since the 1994 genocide, with an emphasis on the link between increasingly securitized constructions of youth and youth-related justice processes that do not always promote meaningful disengagement and reintegration. I combine insights derived from an examination of recent literature, applicable theoretical and policy frameworks, and discussions with a range of stakeholders (scholars, aid workers, legal experts, educators, and young people themselves) in both Rwanda and the United States. I argue that the following elements should be considered in regard to the securitization of youth in the Rwandan case: (1) youth's unique role in the design and implementation of TJ mechanisms and disarmament, demobilization, and reintegration (DDR) approaches for sustaining peace as both objects and subjects and (2) the crucial role of culture in these processes.

Contextual Frameworks
Who Are Considered Youth?

While youth in Rwanda constitute a demographic majority, the ironic reality is that young people are often viewed and treated as social minorities (Sommers 2015). In international development and security discourse and practice, youth in Africa are often overshadowed by preconceptions of the youth-bulge theory, which refers to a country's development when a country has a large population of children and young adults due to lower infant mortality rates and higher fertility rates in women (Lin 2012). The so-called youth bulge has a quantitative, demographic focus that paradoxically results in the exclusion of youth (State of the Union Africa 2010, 27). Quantitative data devoid of social context, however, offer limited explanatory value. Approaches inspired by youth-bulge theoretical concerns fail to incorporate the views and perspectives of youth and instead isolate young people, who are perceived as problems to be mitigated or contained.

Youth often fall through the cracks due to inconsistent conceptualizations among stakeholders and policy makers of what age groups or social events define youth. Most African governments, including Rwanda, define youth to be between fifteen and thirty-five years of age (UNSCR 2015; Simpson 2018). The United Nations' approach classifies youngsters as children (zero to fourteen years of age), adolescents (ten to nineteen years of age), teens (thirteen to nineteen years of age), and young adults (twenty to twenty-four years of age; United Nations Economic and Social Council 2011). While the U.N. has made attempts at standardizing the international conception of age groups, the operational definition of youth varies in different societies and is contingent on societies' cultures and not always defined in fixed, chronological parameters (Watkins 2012). Rather than a definitive age number, these cultures "primarily define 'youth' as the life phase between childhood and adulthood" (Sommers 2015, 12). Cultural constructions of age and life cycles are important elements in the discourse of the securitization of youth and are not always adequately addressed.

Gendered Youth

Examining increasingly securitized constructions of youth requires addressing the gendered circumstances of young people in both conflict and postconflict contexts. Gendered stereotyping is common, with female youth often viewed as "troubled" and male youth identified as "troublesome" (Stainton-Rogers and Stainton-Rogers 1992). War and/or post-violent-conflict conditions have the tendency to exacerbate the alienation of both young females and young males, but they do so in different ways, as seen in the case of postgenocide Rwandan youth (De Berry 2001; Martin 2004; Ensor 2014). The combination of gendered bias and the securitization of youth is problematic, as these attitudes often privilege the perspectives and agendas of male youth. For example, many societies fail to view females as political, economic, or educated actors (Mazurana et al. 2002). Similarly, "girls continue to be marginalized in programs for child soldiers at both national and community levels" (Mazurana et al. 2002, 119) despite females' participation in armed conflicts, such as the case of female youth's involvement in the Rwandan genocide (Ensor 2014).

Gendered bias harms both female and male youth and detracts from local and global efforts to promote peace and security. A growing number of scholars (Hendrixson 2004; Grabska 2010; Ensor 2013; Sommers 2015) have recognized the double standards often associated with gendered constructions of youth in conflict-affected contexts. In discussions of gender differences, the term *gender* is assumed to be coterminous with women—adult women, to be precise. On the flip side, when speaking of youth, the subtext commonly references male youth, which leaves female youth largely ignored (Hendrixson 2004). Gender inequalities compound all other forms of discrimination. Efforts to adequately engage female as well as male youth in peacebuilding will fall short if policy makers fail to acknowledge the intersectionality of youth—especially if efforts lack a proper cultural framework. Furthermore, as I elaborate later in the chapter, the problematic reintegration of many youths following the Rwandan genocide and the challenges involved in fulfilling societal expectations of female and male roles created significant difficulties that have hampered the transition of young people in this country into social adulthood.

The Rwandan Genocide and Its Youth

April 7, 2018, marked a quarter of a century since this infamous genocide, which only lasted three months but took nearly a million lives, three hundred thousand of which were children under the age of eighteen (UNICEF 2004). The ethnic cleansing initiated by radical Hutu leaders claimed the lives of more than three-quarters of all ethnic Tutsi citizens (Kuperman 2001, 122). Since the end of the genocide, Rwanda has become the crown jewel to donors and the international development community (Storey 2001, 365). This country has the world's highest urbanization rates and has experienced economic growth and sociopolitical progress in the past twenty-five years (World Bank 2019). As the world remembers the horrors of the genocide and examines the lessons learned, the international community must build on these lessons as Rwanda seeks to deliver justice for those affected by gross human rights abuses. Notable progress has been achieved by this country in the past two decades, but the chasm of sociopolitical difficulties for marginalized groups remains open, particularly for Rwanda's youth.

World Vision East Africa was among the organizations that recognized the opportunity and necessity to involve youth in peacebuilding early on in the process. In 2005, a decade before the 2015 adoption of UNSCR 2250, World Vision East Africa's Promotion of Reconciliation Among Youth (PRAY) project incorporated youth involvement in advancing peacebuilding initiatives (Kamatsiko 2005). Groups of twelve to fifteen male and female youth gathered to discuss with local leaders their visions for lasting peace in Rwanda. Their feedback was incorporated in World Vision East Africa's Area Development Programmes (Kamatsiko 2005, 42).

Rwanda's postgenocide TJ mechanisms and their effect on Rwandan youth have only recently been systematically brought to the table as practitioners, scholars, and the international development and security communities reflect on Rwanda's progress in the last twenty-five years. Youth have, however, been discussed in securitized terms by the international community for some time now. Building on the 2004 *UN Secretary-General Comment on Transitional Justice*, the 2010 *Guidance Notes on Transitional Justice* (U.N. Secretary-General 2010) established the need to carefully consider the age dimensions of postconflict justice with an aim to support child-sensitive approaches. The UNSCR 2250 global policy framework, published five years after the U.N.'s guiding principles on TJ, further solidifies the global YPS paradigm. UNSCR 2250 explores how conflict impacts young people's lives and what actions must take place to mitigate the effects of war and mass atrocities in instances such as the Rwandan genocide.

More importantly, UNSCR 2250 exhorts the international community to find ways youth can be meaningfully included in creating and sustaining peace. This resolution shifts the parochial portrayal of youth exposed to the atrocities of extreme violence and war as mere victims the world needs to help or as perpetrators the world needs to criminalize to a new narrative where youth are agents of positive social change. Rwandan youth provide an example of young people's resiliency and highlight the possible contributions youth can bring to designing and sustaining peace initiatives.

Rwanda's Response to Postconflict Reconstruction

The corpus of research and literature on the complexities and motivations of the events leading up to the 1994 genocide is beyond the scope of this chapter. However, a brief outline of the most salient events provides the context in which transitional justice initiatives were implemented by the international community and the Rwandan government in the wake of the genocide. On April 6, 1994, a plane carrying former president Habyarimana of Rwanda and former president Ntaryamira of Uganda was shot down en route to Kigali, Rwanda, after the two attended peace talks in Arusha, Tanzania. The assassination of the two presidents is commonly recognized as the event that triggered the beginning of the massacre. Hutu extremists took control over the Rwandan government and launched the extermination campaign against Tutsi and moderate Hutus (Waldorf 2009; Ensor 2019). Tutsi members of the Rwandan armed forces (FAR) and Hutu militia groups, Interahamwe (Those who attack together) and Impuzamugambi (Those who have the same goal), began slaughtering Tutsis and moderate Hutus immediately after the collapse of the Rwandan government. Children were not spared as either victims or perpetrators, and Hutu youngsters were recruited to participate in the slaughter alongside their adult counterparts.

For the following three months, the Rwandan Patriotic Front (RPF) fought the Hutu extremists in one of the bloodiest civil wars in recent history. By July 1994, the RPF gained control over Kigali, the capital of Rwanda, and hundreds of Hutus fled to neighboring countries in fear of being retaliated against and charged with murder (Ensor 2019). Many Hutus who did not participate in the killings also fled in fear of being wrongly accused. In the aftermath of the genocide, the RPF established a coalition government. Pasteur Bizimungu became the president, and Paul Kagame, leader of the RPF forces during the genocide, became the vice president and defense minister. A new constitution adopted in 2003 eliminated all references to ethnicity in Rwanda (Rwanda Ministry of Justice 2008). The country's first legislative elections also took place that year, and Kagame was elected to serve a ten-year term as Rwanda's president (Meierhenrich 2006). Kagame, as of writing this chapter, remains president.

Securitized Youth: Survivors or Perpetrators

After the genocide ended in July 1994, reparations and the reintegration of the survivors as well as the perpetrators proved to be challenging but necessary tasks. Among the many crimes for which perpetrators were being tried in courts were those committed against youngsters (van Den Herik 2005). The United Nations Commission on Human Rights stated that between April 6, 1994, and July 15, 1994, the perpetrators of the Rwandan genocide violated Protocol II of Article 3 in the 1994 Geneva Conventions Article 4(3) of the 1977 Additional Protocol II that prohibits the recruitment of children under the age of fifteen (van Den Herik 2005, 205).

In December 1995, 2 percent of the prison population who were arrested for being active perpetrators in the genocide were minors under eighteen years of age (U.N. Commission on Human Rights 1996). It was also documented that many adult perpetrators of the genocide brought their children along with them while they committed acts of violence throughout the genocide (U.N. Commission on Human Rights 1996). The U.N. Commission on Human Rights (1996, 2000) reported that children were recruited on both sides of the conflict. Youth were encouraged by their parents or members of the militias to carry out the same acts of violence as their adult counterparts (Article I(iii) (27)). A United Nations International Children's Fund (UNICEF) report in 1995 found that 35 percent of the children interviewed in the study saw children killing or injuring other children (Human Rights Watch 2003). Youngsters as young as seven years of age were detained.

UNICEF concluded that nearly 96 percent of children in Rwanda witnessed massacres, 80 percent of Rwanda's children lost at least one family member, and an estimated ninety-five thousand children were left orphaned (UNICEF 2004). Many of those children who did not perish still endured physical and mental trauma both during and after the genocide (Pells, Pontalti, and Williams 2014, 299).

Furthermore, the raping of young girls was weaponized by genocidaires (U.N. Commission on Human Rights 2000). Young girls were often subjected to sexual violence, sometimes along with their older sisters and mothers, after having just been forced to watch their brothers and fathers being massacred (Ensor 2019). Young female survivors of both rape and genocidal violence were confronted with the additional plight of being deemed ineligible for marriage in the postgenocide period (U.N. Commission on Human Rights 2000). Girls who became pregnant as a result of rape were even more ostracized owing to the stigmatization suffered by unmarried mothers in Rwanda's heavily patriarchal culture.

International and domestic funding and programming have sought to promote reconciliation and healing primarily for female survivors, while the admittedly smaller number of young boys who also were also survivors of sexual violence received far less attention. Additionally, women have reported that "they consider that the United Nations bodies and NGOs have devoted most of their services to unaccompanied children and have tried to deal with women's psychological needs using methods developed elsewhere that do not take the specific aspects of Rwandan society into consideration" (U.N. Commission on Human Rights 2000, I (24)). The voices of youth who were survivors of these crimes and their experiences after the war must be also acknowledged postgenocide and in the country's period of reconstruction.

Other organizations, such as Never Again Rwanda (NAR), have created avenues for youth—both female and male—to engage in peacebuilding and social justice. NAR was established in 2002 in response to the Rwandan genocide and has since then promoted a path toward sustainable peace through local community dialogues, workshops, and programs (Never Again Rwanda 2019). The approach promoted by NAR not only invites Rwandan youth participation in its programs but also seeks to empower and engage youth in the processes of addressing the root causes of conflict. Further detail on youth in the courts and reintegration will be discussed later in this chapter.

TRANSITIONAL JUSTICE

Transitional justice paradigms—retributive, restorative, traditional (indigenous), and so on—are increasingly common mechanisms through which societies emerging from conflict deal with unresolved legacies of past violence.[1] TJ consists of judicial and nonjudicial processes and mechanisms in conformity with international legal standards and obligations—prosecution initiatives, facilitating initiatives of the right to truth, delivering reparations, institutional reforms, and national consultations (U.N. Secretary-General 2010, 1). Essentially, TJ refers to the range of measures associated with a country's attempt to come to terms with large-scale human rights abuses and aim to ensure accountability, serve justice, and achieve reconciliation (U.N. Secretary-General 2004, 4). Youth are critical stakeholders of TJ whose meaningful participation requires attention to the delicate balance between trauma and resiliency. These measures must be creatively designed and implemented while considering the coexistence of both agency and vulnerability among conflict-afflicted youths, replacing the older focus on assumed fragility and victimhood (Betancourt and Ettien 2010).

A wide range of retributive and restorative TJ initiatives were implemented in Rwanda in the years following the genocide (Ensor 2019). In November 1994, the United Nations Security Council established the International Criminal Tribunal for Rwanda (ICTR) in Arusha, Tanzania. Reflecting a retributive construction of justice, ICTR tribunals began indicting and trying perpetrators in 1995 (United Nations Security Council 1994; Sterio and Scharf 2019). Ninety-three individuals considered responsible for serious violations of international humanitarian law were indicted under the ICTR tribunal. The ICTR also became the first tribunal to define rape in international law and recognize rape as an act of genocide (U.N. International Residual Mechanism for Criminal Tribunals 2015).

The United Nations conducted more than seventy tribunal cases, while Rwandan courts tried up to twenty thousand individuals. However, trying individuals through the ICTR and domestic court systems proved to be an arduous and impractical process, as the locations of numerous perpetrators were unknown. Additionally, Rwanda's prisons became extremely overcrowded and could no longer structurally support the 120,000 incarcerated persons arrested and detained postgenocide (Reimers 2014, 121; Meyerstein 2017, 468).

Of the 120,000 people detained for involvement in the genocide, approximately 4,500 were reportedly minors, defined by the Rwandan Penal Code as persons between fourteen and eighteen years old at the time of the genocide (U.N. Commission on Human Rights 2000; Ensor 2019; Penal Code Article 77 1987). Rwanda became the first country to try minors for committing acts of genocide. The age of criminal responsibility postgenocide is fourteen years (Ensor 2019, 6; U.N. International Residual Mechanism for Criminal Tribunals 2015).

Article 74 of the Rwandan Law on Crimes against Humanity and Genocide stated that children under the age of fourteen at the time of the crime could not be held legally responsible for their actions or detained and that children over fourteen but under eighteen should receive reduced penalties (U.N. International Residual Mechanism for Criminal Tribunals 2015). Yet youth under fourteen years old were still arrested, detained, and not released from prison until 2001 (U.N. International Residual Mechanism for Criminal Tribunals 2015).

Nearly five thousand youth who were considered a security threat were arrested and detained in overcrowded prisons. The conditions of the prisons barely met international standards (Human Rights Watch Interview 1998). Imprisoned youth (aged fourteen to eighteen) often lacked the financial means, family support, or political clout to acquire basic supplies such as blankets, plates, or clothes (Human Rights Watch Interview 1998). A Human Rights Watch Report (2003) shared the testimony offered by Silas K., who was fifteen during the genocide:

> I don't get visits. I have no parents. My mother died a long time ago, and my father died during the war. I have a little brother who is now ten. He is at home alone in our house. I don't know how he is doing. He has nothing to eat himself, so how can he find food for me and bring it here? I have no blanket and no clothes. I don't have a plate or basin and eat my food in a palm-oil can that I share with someone else. One of the prisoners gave me these shorts I'm wearing out of kindness.

The Rwanda Ministry of Justice released 1,100 detainees who had been children in 1994 (2008). In January 2003, Rwanda's president, Paul Kagame, ordered the release of all "genocide minors," but only youth who had spent the maximum possible sentence in pretrial detention were eligible for release (Ensor 2019). In July 2005, 1,900 minors at the time of the genocide were released, but most were now approaching adulthood and had little resources for reintegrating back into society.

The released minors, along with the other released prisoners, were sent to two months of reeducation at solidarity camps throughout the country (Mgbako 2005; Penal Reform International 2010). These camps were known as ingando and served as stepping-stones to their provisional community release until their local court hearing, commonly known as the *gacaca* court system (Penal Reform International 2010). According to the Rwanda National Unity and Reconciliation Commission (NURC), ingando camps were "a civic education activity that has facilitated the smooth reintegration" of returnees to Rwanda, former Rwandan armed forces members, and provisionally released prisoners (Child Soldiers International 2008; Purdeková 2011).

BACKGROUND ON THE *GACACA* SYSTEM

By 1998, the total prison population reached its highest point at 130,000 persons, but only 1,292 people had been tried through the ICTR (Reimers 2014, 121; Meyerstein 2007, 468). To deal with the thousands of accused individuals and to foster reconciliation, a hybrid transitional justice approach and traditional community court system known as the *gacaca* was established. A pilot phase of an adapted *gacaca* court system was issued in June 2002 (Meyerstein 2007, 474). President Kagame officially administered the revised system in 2005. This transitional justice mechanism consisted of community-based judicial forums to address the concerns of the country coming to terms with justice and reconciliation and to process its massive population of incarcerated persons who were accused of being perpetrators in the 1994 genocide (Ingelaere 2008, 38).

Gacaca gatherings have been an aspect of Rwandan culture dating back to precolonial British rule. *Gacaca* in the local Kinyarwanda language refers to the lawn where community members gather to settle minor disputes among community members (Meyerstein 2007, 468). However, a *gacaca* court system was not immediately implemented by the government due to Rwanda's fragile state

(Longman 2009). There were arguments against using the *gacaca* to try crimes of genocide on grounds that the *gacaca* would minimize the seriousness of the crimes. Critics were also concerned about the ability of ordinary people who were not trained in judicial procedures to make decisions on the serious offenses under consideration (UNCHR 1996). These concerns were assuaged by President Kagame and proponents of using the *gacaca* courts. Supporters argued that trying genocide crimes in *gacaca* courts would not trivialize the process; rather, it would invite people to deal with such crimes on the level where they took place, which, they claimed, was essential in rebuilding Rwandan society. Furthermore, advocates of the *gacaca* courts were confident that ordinary people could be educated and trained to carry out judicial procedures (Office of the President of the Republic 1999).

Youth and the Gacaca

But what did the *gacaca* court systems mean for the nearly estimated 4,500 youth detained in prisons? Once the *gacaca* were officially implemented in 2002, the processing of alleged perpetrators at the time of the genocide who were minors—that is, age fourteen to eighteen—was especially challenging because by the time of the *gacaca* hearings, these minors were now adults (Rieder and Elbert 2013). Those who were minors in 1994 but adults in 2002 were still entitled to a reduction of penalties if convicted (Human Rights Watch 2003).

In 2007, an amendment to the *gacaca* law reduced the maximum penalty for minors convicted of crimes from a twelve-year sentence to a five-year sentence (Human Rights Watch 2003). Community leaders who oversaw the *gacaca* proceedings were required to adhere to the organic law that made special provisions for those who were minors at the time of the genocide. However, detainees were often treated as adults and charged with adult sentences, which could be up to twenty years (Human Rights Watch 2003; Hola and Brehm 2016). Courts sentenced numerous minors to full penalties instead of the reduced prison terms as mandated by Rwandan law.

In spite of its obvious shortcomings, the involvement of youth in the *gacaca* processes seemed promising, and for many youths, the *gacaca* provided a new beginning and release from imprisonment. However, the abuse of the term *minor* and the difficulty to verify the ages of detainees exacerbated the alienation of youth. Birth certificates were often unavailable, as births are not always recorded, and communal records had been destroyed during the genocide. Prosecutors claimed that prisoners had lied about their age in the hopes of receiving reduced penalties. Prosecutors were eventually pressured by the Rwandan government to give the benefit of the doubt to self-declared minors—but only after time-consuming investigations and litigation. There is also credible evidence that prison authorities beat detainees who attempted to attend training sessions on children's rights and the justice system (Human Rights Watch 2003).

THE CONTEXT OF DISENGAGEMENT

The fifth pillar of action of UNSCR 2250 addresses the key issue of disengagement and reintegration for sustainable peace. In prevalent peacebuilding discourse, disengagement and reintegration commonly refer to the various steps taken in peacekeeping operations—that is, DDR. Resolution 2250 requires those who implement DDR programs to consider the impact that DDR has on young people in recognition of the large proportion of former combatants that are youth (United Nations Security Council 2015).

Reintegration is generally understood as the economic and social processes through which former combatants attain civilian status and sustainable employment and income. While acknowledging the importance of economic opportunities and reintegration, my analysis of the situation in Rwanda is primarily concerned with the social reintegration of youth within the context of the global YPS agenda. Social reintegration refers to the processes through which ex-combatants and victims of war become part of and reaccepted by their communities (Kingma 2001a).

The reintegration of former combatants in African countries often reflects the widespread tendency for African governments and international organizations to direct resources and development investments toward rural areas and to help former combatants return to their former lives (Sommers 2006, 4). Former U.N. secretary-general Kofi Anan listed "the reintegration of ex-combatants and others into productive society" as part of the priorities of postconflict peacebuilding in the *Causes of Conflict and the Promotion of Durable Peace and Sustainable Development in Africa* (United Nations 1998, 14). The World Bank (2002) also underscores the necessity of implementing meaningful DDR practices for restoring security and sustaining peace.

In the context of postgenocide Rwanda, youth's participation in *gacaca* processes represented a form of disengagement, as it released young defendants from their involvement in violent acts and facilitated their reintegration into society. However, lingering stigmatization of youth perceived as violent security threats created considerable obstacles in their path toward successful reintegration and overall sustainable peace.

Rwanda's Securitization of Youth in Solidarity Camps and Exclusion of Child Soldiers

Since 1995, Rwanda has demobilized and reintegrated approximately fifty-four thousand combatants (Waldorf 2009). The Rwandan Demobilization and Reintegration Commission (RDRC) implemented a DDR program, the Rwandan Demobilization and Reintegration Program (RDRP), in two major phases, one from 1997 to 2001 and the other from 2002 to 2007 (Waldorf 2009, 8; World Bank 2018).

The disarmament and demobilization of child soldiers happened in three distinct phases. First came the child soldiers in the RPF from 1994 to 1998. When RPF forces gained control over Rwanda and ended the genocide, many Hutus fled to neighboring countries where youth were voluntarily recruited or forced to join armed rebel groups. The next two phases focused on DDR programs for those youth who were considered security threats. The second phase of disarmament and reintegration targeted the child soldiers who were involved in the Army for the Liberation of Rwanda (the Hutu rebels' last attack in Rwanda) incursion into Rwanda in 2001 (Waldorf 2009, 11; Human Rights Watch 2001). The final phase sought to disarm, disengage, and reintegrate Rwandan child soldiers associated with armed combatants in Congo (Waldorf 2009, 11).

Once youth were disarmed and demobilized, the subsequent step was to reintegrate them back into Rwandan society. The Rwandan government created the NURC to "rebuild the social fabric of the nation" (Rwanda 2013a). Similar to the youth who were released in 2001 by the presidential decree, youth who were transitioning from involvement with armed forces were also placed in *Ingando* solidarity camps.

Fewer than three thousand child soldiers were associated with the RPF—a third of those were officially registered by the RPF and given military numbers (Kingma 2001b). Child soldiers, or *kadogo*, were placed in *Ingando* as part of their demobilization after the genocide (Waldorf 2009; Child Soldiers International 2008). The *Ingando* provided reeducation courses in Rwandan history, civic education, national unity and reconciliation, *gacaca* procedures, and microfinancing (Waldorf 2009, 11; Mgbako 2005, 5). All ex-combatants received a basic needs kit of US$100 and basic household supplies when they completed *Ingando* training (Waldorf 2009, 11). Some also received reintegration support along with the basic needs kit. This allowance was between US$150 and US$2,000, depending on their rank (Waldorf 2009, 11). It is not clear whether minors received these allowances as well.

Successful DDR programs are often necessary bases for peace, and reintegration is often the precursor of sustaining peace (De Berry 2001; Shepler 2014). International agencies and the Rwandan government focused heavily on demobilizing these soldiers in the groups previously mentioned. The disengagement and reintegration of youth, and of child soldiers in particular, were, however, not systematically monitored (Waldorf 2009; Clark 2014).

Violence, Failed Adulthood, and the Current Context of Rwandan Youth

In a U.S. Institute of Peace Special Report titled *Youth in Rwanda and Burundi* (2011), Marc Sommers and Peter Uvin noted the struggle that female and male youth face as they transition into adulthood in Rwandan society. Unemployed, undereducated male youth were the dominant demographic among the foot soldiers during the Rwandan genocide (Sommers 2006, 5). The Interahamwe are believed to have included thousands of young men who were forced or recruited into the groups.

These young men embodied what some advocates of the youth-bulge theory predicted regarding male youth as security threats (Waldorf 2009). It was the common belief that Interahamwe were violent, fearsome young men who slaughtered thousands of their fellow Rwandan citizens. However, the reality is that youth, even youth who participated in these horrific acts, were indeed victims as well (Hendrixson 2004). A combination of coercion and promises of a better life caused those male youth who were in desperate situations to become easy targets for recruitment to violent groups. These male youths, nevertheless, constituted a small fraction of the youth as a whole. Their actions, horrific as they were, do not support the claim that *all* male youth are potential violent threats (Peters, Richards, and Vlassenroot 2003; Hendrixson 2004; Waldorf 2009).

The process of implementation of DDR programs must also acknowledge the existing tension between Rwandan societal expectations for youth and the challenges that impeded their transition into social adulthood. Rwandan male youth who were soldiers during the 1994 genocide remained on the margins of society and have received little attention or support as they transitioned into adulthood. Additional scholars (Hendrixson 2004; Urdal 2004) reject the outdated idea that concentrated numbers of African male youth are dangerous and found that even in the most desperate, humiliating circumstances, most youth remain more or less peaceful. Sommers and Uvin's (2011) investigation of the experiences of Rwandan male youth within the context of African urbanization and its rapidly growing population adds a further dimension to our understanding of this complex situation. Young women and young men who were minors at the time of the genocide have become too old to be considered youth, yet they are not fully considered women and men until certain societal benchmarks are achieved. This begs the question: How do youth become adults, and what happens when youth are unable to transition into society's standard of adulthood? In contexts where youth have experienced "failed adulthood," it is often owing to unfavorable institutional and power structures that inhibit youth voices.

As the *Missing Peace* report notes, "Young women and men both struggle to transition into adulthood, but in different ways" (2018, 11). In Rwanda, to become a man, a male youth must build a house before marriage and children. Masculinity is fragile and dependent on elements to which young males have limited access—receiving a good education, owning a house, getting married, having kids, and keeping a job are social indicators of masculinity in Rwandan culture (Sommers 2012). If a male does not manage to achieve one of these elements, then his masculinity is jeopardized and questioned. This, in turn, impacts female youth's ability to transition into social womanhood, which is dependent on marriage.

Illustrative of this situation, a young female student (aged fourteen at the time) in a rural part of Kibeho, Rwanda, where I worked in 2016 commented on and admired an older woman's long hair (she herself had a shaven head). My young interlocutor commented that she was waiting to start growing her hair out until she was married; she further offered that one of her motivations for striving to be top of her class was to attract a suitable husband. This young woman was one of the few youths in her village to attend primary school.

The minimum legal marrying age in Rwanda is twenty-one for both females and males. But if males cannot manage to obtain suitable housing due to land shortages and strict government regulations in Rwanda, young women are left with no other option than to keep waiting in social limbo (Sommers 2012). Rwanda's combination of cultural tradition and the demands of the government leave youth with few or no alternatives to traditional expectations but without the means to meet these expectations (Sommers and Uvin 2011).

A thirty-five-year-old male from Kigali who was assisting our onsite project instructing primary school English students in Kibeho in 2016 underscored this reality. He often noted that, on one hand, the opportunity to learn English in the Rwandan school system had obvious benefits to Rwandan youth; on the other hand, obtaining an education and learning English as a status symbol in Rwandan culture, he argued, "produces uncultivated scientists, and research results that will never answer the vital questions of the society concerned" because privileging English neglects Rwanda's own language, culture, and values. His comment illustrates the tension between traditional cultural values and evolving notions of youth's role in Rwandan modern society.

CONCLUSION

As the previous discussion illustrates, young people in Rwanda have been constructed in securitized terms at least since the genocide that so dramatically altered the current sociopolitical relations in this small African country. The participation of Rwandan youth in the global YPS agenda is currently framed by multiple factors. These include recognizing youth's capabilities as agents of change, promoting young people's disengagement from violent structures through the implementation of DDR measures, integrating cultural considerations in the design and implementation of transitional justice mechanisms, and creating avenues for youth participation in peacebuilding processes.

Without negating Rwandan youth's past engagement in violent conflict and genocidal behavior or minimizing their current struggles to overcome exclusion and achieve social adulthood, Rwandan youth provide an encouraging example of young people's resiliency in the face of seemingly insurmountable odds. Their experiences underscore the positive contributions that, provided with the right opportunities, youth can make to building and sustaining peace. Rwandan youth represent the future of their country, which continues to deal with the residual effects of the genocide. Female and male youth represent strategically important stakeholders in transitional justice and DDR processes; their experiences can inform efforts to implement institutional reforms, rebuild civic trust, and ensure that crimes will not be repeated (Simpson 2018). Transitional justice processes provide youth with a vehicle for active participation and opportunities to contribute to rebuilding war-torn societies. It is thus vital for the international development and security communities to acknowledge young women and men's capacities as active, creative protagonists in peace and security efforts.

TJ mechanisms and DDR practices for youth will not be successful unless practitioners and policy makers design them with due consideration of the cultural context in which these measures are to be implemented. Efforts must be taken to create conditions for justice, equality, inclusivity, and the meaningful engagement of youth in achieving positive peace. Negative peace, which denotes the absence of overt violence, is simply not enough (Schnabel 2005, 27). This will require the full participation of all members of society, including youth, as well and the political will and commitment of local and international partners (UNICEF 2008, 17).

The success and failures of the *gacaca* court system and the challenges facing Rwandan youth as they strive to overcome the legacy of the genocide, bring positive peace to their country, and achieve social adulthood remain the objects of much discussion. This chapter has argued for the culturally meaningful engagement of youth in the design and implementation of transitional justice procedures and DDR approaches in the context of the global YPS agenda. Rwanda's youth involvement in their country's transitional justice and DDR initiatives is not without contradictions and inconsistencies. These efforts do, nevertheless, reflect Rwanda's unique approach to procedural fairness from the standpoint of their own cultural norms and societal ideals. In line with UNSCR 2250, facilitating Rwandan youth's engagement in their country's approach to justice and sociopolitical life is an essential step toward advancing Rwanda's postgenocide peace and security.

NOTE

1. Retributive justice emphasizes a punitive approach in which perpetrators are most likely prosecuted (Huyse and Salter 2008, 5). Justice through the lens of restorative mechanisms identifies needs and responsibilities where the accountability lies with understanding the impact of the transgressions and repairing harm (Meyerstein 2007, 465; Ingelaere 2008; Huyse and Salter 2008, 53). Restorative justice seeks to restore the sense of normalcy prior to violent conflict. The traditional justice paradigm makes an argument for the use of a country's traditional practices to be adopted and/or adapted to develop more appropriate responses tailored to specific cultures (Ingelaere 2008).

REFERENCES

Atran, Scott. 2015. "The Role of Youth in Countering Violent Extremism and Promoting Peace." Address to United Nations Security Council, April 23, 2015. www.unisa.edu.au/Global/EASS/MnM/Publications/Address_UN_Security_Council_Scott_Atran.pdf.

Berents, Helen, and Siobhan McEvoy-Levy. 2015. "Theorising Youth and Everyday Peace(building)." *Peacebuilding* 3, no. 2, 115–125. https://doi.org/10.1080/21647259.2015.1052627.

Betancourt, T. S., and A. Ettien. 2010. "Transitional Justice and Youth Formerly Associated with Armed Forces and Armed Groups: Acceptance, Marginalization and Psychosocial Adjustment." UNICEF. Innocenti Working Paper, IWP 2010–2017.

Child Soldiers International. 2008. "Child Soldiers Global Report 2008—Rwanda." RefWorld. www.refworld.org/docid/486cb129c.html.

Clark, Phil. 2014. "Bringing Them All Back Home: The Challenges of DDR and Transitional Justice in Contexts of Displacement in Rwanda and Uganda." *Journal of Refugee Studies* 27, no. 2, 234–259. https://doi.org/10.1093/jcs/fet051. (URL inactive.)

De Berry, J. 2001. "Child Soldiers and the Convention on the Rights of the Child." *Annals of the American Academy of Political and Social Science* 575, no. 1, 92–105. https://doi.org/10.1177/000271620157500106.

Statutory order establishing the penal code, Official Gazette of the Republic of Rwanda, 17th year, number 13. July 1, 1987, First Book ("Penal Code") Art. 77.

Ensor, Marisa O. 2013. "Drinking the Bitter Roots: Gendered Youth, Transitional Justice and Reconciliation across the South Sudan-Uganda Border." In "Peace Education, Memory and Reconciliation in Africa: Contemporary Perspectives on Conflict Transformation," edited by Marisa O. Ensor. Special issue, *African Conflict & Peacebuilding Review* 2, no. 3, 171–194.

———. 2014. "Displaced Girlhood: Gendered Dimensions of Coping and Social Change among Conflict-Affected South Sudanese Youth." *Refuge* 30, no. 1, 15–24.

———. 2019. "Child Rights and Transitional Justice: Retributive and Restorative Approaches in the Aftermath of the Rwandan Genocide." In *Transitional Justice and Forced Migration: Critical Perspectives from the Global South*, edited by Nergis Canefe, 83–107. Cambridge: Cambridge University Press.

Grabska, Katarzyna. 2010. "Lost Boys, Invisible Girls: Stories of Sudanese Marriages across Borders." *Gender Place and Culture* 17, no. 4, 479–497. https://doi.org/10.1080/0966369X.2010.485839.

Hendrixson, Anne. 2004. "Angry Young Men, Veiled Young Women: Constructing a New Population Threat." *Corner House Briefing* 34 (December): 1–16. www.thecornerhouse.org.uk/sites/thecornerhouse.org.uk/files/34veiled.pdf.

Hola, Barbora, and Hollie N. Brehm. 2016. "Punishing Genocide: A Comparative Empirical Analysis of Sentencing Laws and Practices at the International Criminal Tribunal for Rwanda (ICTR), Rwandan Domestic Courts, and Gacaca Courts." *Genocide Studies and Prevention: An International Journal* 10, no. 3, 58–80.

Human Rights Watch. 2001. "Rwanda: Observing the Rules of War?" *Human Rights Watch Report* 13, no. 8(A), 4–5.

———. 2003. "Rwanda Lasting Wounds: Consequences of Genocide and War for Rwanda's Children." *Human Rights Watch Report* 15, no. 5(A), 1–80. www.hrw.org/reports/2003/rwanda0403.

Huyse, Luc, and Mark Salter, eds. 2008. *Traditional Justice and Reconciliation after Violent Conflict: Learning from African Experiences*. Stockholm: IDEA.

Ingelaere, Bert. 2008. "The Gacaca Courts in Rwanda." In *Traditional Justice and Reconciliation after Violent Conflict: Learning from African Experiences*, edited by L. Huyse and M. Salter, 25–58. Stockholm: IDEA.

Kamatsiko, Valarie V. 2005. "Small Feet, Deep Prints: Young People Building Peace with World Vision East Africa." World Vision Africa. www.wvi.org/sites/default/files/Small_Feet_Deep_Prints.pdf.

Ketelaars, Elise. 2014. "Transitional Justice, Culture and Society: Beyond Outreach." *International Journal for Court Administration* 6, no. 2, 106–109.

Kingma, Kees. 2001a. *Demobilisation and Reintegration of Ex-combatants in Post-war and Transition Countries*. Eschborn, Germany: Deutsche Gesellschaft für Technische Zusammenarbeit.

———. 2001b. *The Rwanda Demobilisation and Reintegration Program: Evaluation Report Prepared for the United Nations Development Programme*. Kigali: United Nations Development Programme (UNDP).

Kuperman, Alan. 2001. *The Limits of Humanitarian Intervention: Genocide in Rwanda*. Washington, D.C.: Brookings Institution Press. www.jstor.org/stable/10.7864/j.ctt127xzj.

Ladisch, Virginie. 2018. "A Catalyst for Change: Engaging Youth in Transitional Justice." International Center for Transitional Justice. www.ictj.org/publication/catalyst-change-engaging-youth-transitional-justice.

Lin, Justin Y. 2012. "Youth Bulge: A Demographic Dividend or a Demographic Bomb in Developing Countries?" *World Bank Blogs*. Accessed March 2020. https://blogs.worldbank.org/developmenttalk/youth-bulge-a-demographic-dividend-or-a-demographic-bomb-in-developing-countries.

Longman, Timothy. 2009. "An Assessment of Rwanda's Gacaca Courts." *Peace Review* 32, no. 2, 304–312.

Martin, S. F. 2004. *Refugee Women*. Lanham, Md.: Lexington.

Mazurana, Dyan E., Susan A. McKay, Khristopher C. Carlson, and Janel C. Kasper. 2002. "Girls in Fighting Forces and Groups: Their Recruitment, Participation, Demobilization, and Reintegration." *Peace and Conflict: Journal of Peace Psychology* 8, no. 2, 119.

McEvoy-Levy, Siobhan. 2011. "Children, Youth, and Peacebuilding." In *Critical Issues in Peace and Conflict Studies: Theory, Practice, and Pedagogy*, edited by Thomas Matyok, Jessica Senehi, and Sean Byrne, 159–177. Lanham, Md.: Lexington.

McGill, Michael, and Claire O'Kane. 2015. "Evaluation of Child and Youth Participation in Peacebuilding." Global Partnership for Children and Youth in Peacebuilding. http://unoy.org/wp-content/uploads/3MEvaluation-Global-report-Child-and-YouthParticipation-in-Peace-builing.pdf. (URL inactive.)

Meierhenrich, Jens. 2006. "Presidential and Parliamentary Elections in Rwanda, 2003." *Electoral Studies* 25, no. 3, 627–634. https://doi.org/10.1016/j.electstud.2005.10.003.

Meyerstein, Ariel. 2007. "Between Law and Culture: Rwanda's Gacaca and Postcolonial Legality." *Law & Social Inquiry: Journal of the American Bar Foundation* 32:467–1095.

Mgbako, Chi. 2005. "'Ingando' Solidarity Camps: Reconciliation and Political Indoctrination in Post-genocide Rwanda." *Harvard Human Rights Journal* 18:201–224.

Ministry of Justice. 2003. "Imbonerahamwe Igaragaza Ibisabwa n'intangazo Ryaturutse Muri Perezidansi ya Republika/Chart Showing What Was Required by the Communiqué of the President of the Republic." Accessed March 2020. www.refworld.org/docid/486cb129c.html.

Never Again Rwanda. 2019. *Annual Report 2018*. http://neveragainrwanda.org/wp-content/uploads/2017/08/ANNUAL-REPORT-2018-Official_compressed.pdf.

Ni Aolain, Fionnuala. 2016. "The 'War on Terror' and Extremism: Assessing the Relevance of the Women, Peace and Security Agenda." *International Affairs* 92, no. 2, 275–291. https://doi.org/10.1111/1468-2346.12552.

Nordstrom, Carolyn. 1999. "Visible Wars and Invisible Girls, Shadow Industries, and the Politics of Not-Knowing." *International Feminist Journal of Politics* 1, no. 1, 14–33.

Office of the President of the Republic. 1999. *Government of Rwanda, Report on the Reflection Meetings Held in the Office of the President of the Republic from May 1998 to March 1999.* Kigali: Office of the President of the Republic, 1999.

Pells, Kirrily, Kirsten Pontalti, and Timothy P. Williams. 2014. "Promising Developments? Children, Youth and Post-genocide Reconstruction under the Rwandan Patriotic Front (RPF)." *Journal of Eastern African Studies* 8, no. 2, 1–17. https://doi.org/10.1080/17531055.2014.892672.

Penal Reform International. 2010. "'Eight Years On . . .': A Record of *Gacaca* Monitoring in Rwanda." *Penal Reform International.* Accessed March 2020. https://cdn.penalreform.org/wp-content/uploads/2013/05/WEB-english-gacaca-rwanda-5.pdf.

Peters, Kirin, Paul Richards, and Koen Vlassenroot. 2003. *What Happens to Youth during and after Wars? A Preliminary Review of Literature on Africa and Assessment on the Debate.* The Hague: RAWOO. www.raoo.nl/pdf/youthreport.pdf. (URL inactive.)

Purdeková, Andrea. 2011. "Rwanda's Ingando Camps—Liminality and the Reproduction of Power." Working Paper Series No. 80. Refugee Studies Centre, University of Oxford. www.refworld.org/pdfid/55c9fb404.pdf.

Reimers. B. C. 2014. "The 'Intra-Tutsi Schism' and Its Effect on Truth, Justice, and Reconciliation in the Rwandan Gacaca Courts." In *Indigenous Conflict Management Strategies: Global Perspectives*, edited by A. Adebayo, J. Benjamin, and B. Lundy, 121–133. Lanham, Md.: Lexington.

Rieder, Heide, and Thomas Elbert. 2013. "Rwanda—Lasting Imprints of a Genocide: Trauma, Mental Health and Psychosocial Conditions in Survivors, Former Prisoners and Their Children." *Confl Health* 7, no. 6, 1–13. https://doi.org/10.1186/1752-1505-7-6.

Rwanda Ministry of Justice. 2008. *Constitution of the Republic of Rwanda 04 June 2003.* Kigali.

Schnabel, Albrecht. 2005. "Preventing and Managing Violent Conflict: The Role of the Researcher." In *Researching Conflict in Africa: Insights and Experiences*, edited by Elizabeth Porter, Gillian Robinson, Marie Smyth, Albrecht Schnabel, and Eghosa Osaghae, 24–43. Tokyo: United Nations University Press.

Shepler, Susan. 2014. *Childhood Deployed: Remaking Child Soldiers in Sierra Leone.* New York: New York University Press. https://doi.org/10.1080/10402659.2015.1037668.

Siitonen, Lauri. 2011. "Human Security and State Rebuilding in Post-conflict Nepal: Peace at the Cost of Justice? (ASIA)." *Regions and Cohesion* 1, no. 1, 54–77. https://doi.org/10.3167/reco.2011.010105.

Simpson, Graeme. 2018. *The Missing Peace: Independent Progress Study on Youth, Peace and Security.* UNFPA. www.unfpa.org/sites/default/files/youth/youth-web-english.pdf.

Sommers, Marc. 2006. "Fearing Africa's Young Men: The Case of Rwanda." *Social Development Papers: Conflict Prevention and Reconstruction* 32:1–18. http://documents.worldbank.org/curated/en/303071468105531710/pdf/351490RW0Youngomen0WP3201PUBLIC1.pdf.

———. 2012. *Stuck: Rwandan Youth and the Struggle for Adulthood.* Athens: University of Georgia Press.

———. 2015. *The Outcast Majority: War, Development, and Youth in Africa.* Athens: University of Georgia Press.

Sommers, Marc, and Peter Uvin. 2011. "Youth in Rwanda and Burundi: Contrasting Visions." *United States Institute of Peace Special Report* 293. www.usip.org/sites/default/files/resources/sr293.pdf.

Stainton-Rogers, R., and W. Stainton-Rogers. 1992. *Stories of Childhood: Shifting Agendas of Child Concerns.* Hemel Hempstead, UK: Harvester Wheatsheaf.

State of the Union Africa. 2010. "State of the Union Continental Report Africa—2010." Accessed August 25, 2011. http://allafrica.com/download/resource/main/main/idatcs/00020200:265d13f9960ba253a8e4b1d32adc899c.pdf.

Sterio, Milena, and Michael Scharf. 2019. *The Legacy of Ad Hoc Tribunals in International Criminal Law: Assessing the ICTY's and the ICTR's Most Significant Legal Accomplishments.* Cambridge: Cambridge University Press.

Storey, Andy. 2001. "Structural Adjustment, State Power and Genocide: The World Bank and Rwanda." Review of African Political Economy 28, no. 89, 365–385. www.jstor.org/stable/4006616.

UNCHR (United Nations Commission on Human Rights). 1996. *Question of the Violation of Human Rights and Fundamental Freedoms in Any Part of the World, with Particular Reference to Colonial and Other Dependent Countries and Territories.* Report on the Situation of Human Rights in Rwanda. http://hrlibrary.umn.edu/commission/country52/68-rwa.htm.

———. 2000. *Report on the Situation of Human Rights in Rwanda.* www.unhcr.org/en-us/3ebf9bb60.pdf.

UNICEF (United Nations Children's Fund). 2004. "Rwanda: Ten Years after the Genocide." UNICEF. www.unicef.org/infobycountry/rwanda_genocide.html.

———. 2008. "The State of African Children 2008: Child Survival." UNICEF. Accessed September 15, 2011. www.unicef.org.

United Nations. 1998. *The Causes of Conflict and the Promotion of Durable Peace and Sustainable Development in Africa.* Report of the U.N. Secretary-General. A/52/871-S/1998/3/318. New York: United Nations.

United Nations and World Bank. 2017. *Pathways for Peace: Inclusive Approaches to Preventing Violent Conflict—Main Messages and Emerging Policy Directions.* Washington, D.C.: World Bank. https://reliefwcb.int/sites/reliefweb.int/files/resources/211162mm.pdf.

United Nations Economic and Social Council. 2011. "Youth: Frequently Asked Questions." United Nations Department of Economic and Social Affairs, Social Policy and Development Division. http://undesadspd.org/Youth/FAQs.aspx.

United Nations International Residual Mechanism for Criminal Tribunals. 2015. "The ICTR in Brief." United Nations International Residual Mechanism for Criminal Tribunals. Accessed June 2020. https://unictr.irmct.org/en/tribunal.

United Nations Secretary-General. 2004. *The Rule of Law and Transitional Justice in Conflict and Post-conflict Societies.* Report of the Secretary-General, U.N. Document S/2004/616 2004.

———. 2010. "Guidance Note of the Secretary-General: United Nations Approach to Transitional Justice." www.un.org/ruleoflaw/files/TJ_Guidance_Note_March_2010FINAL.pdf.

United Nations Security Council. 2015. Resolution 2250, S/RES/2250. December 9, 2015. www.un.org/en/ga/search/view_doc.asp?symbol=S/RES/2250(2015)&referer=/english/&Lang=E.

Urdal, Henrik. 2004. "The Devil in the Demographics: The Effect of Youth Bulges on Domestic Armed Conflict, 1950–2000." *Social Development Papers: Conflict Prevention and Reconstruction* 14:16.

van Den Herik, L. J. 2005. *Contribution of the Rwanda Tribunal to the Development of International Law.* Leiden: Brill.

Waldorf, Lars. 2009. *Transitional Justice and DDR: The Case of Rwanda*. New York: International Center for Transitional Justice. www.ictj.org/sites/default/files/ICTJ-DDR-Rwanda-CaseStudy-2009-English.pdf.

Watkins, Tammy. 2012. "Turnkana Children's Contributions to Subsistence and Household Ecology in Kenya." In *African Childhoods: Education, Development, Peacebuilding, and the Youngest Continent*, edited by M. Ensor, 61–77. New York: Palgrave Macmillan. https://doi.org/10.1057/9781137024701.

World Bank. 2002. *Greater Great Lakes Regional Strategy for Demobilization and Reintegration*. Washington, D.C. Accessed February 2020. https://reliefweb.int/report/angola/greater-great-lakes-regional-strategy-demobilization-and-reintegration.

———. 2018. *Implementation Completion and Results Report on a Grant in the Amount of SDR 5.2 Million and Trust Fund Grants in the Amount of US$9.1 Million Additional Trust Fund Grants in the Amount of US$3.1 Million and an Additional Credit in the Amount of SDR 5.8 Million to the Republic of Rwanda for the Second Emergency Demobilization and Reintegration Project*. Report no. ICR00004278. Accessed January 2020. http://documents1.worldbank.org/curated/en/842721529346104263/pdf/P112712-Implementation-Completion-and-Results-Report-ICR-Document-06132018.pdf.

———. 2019. "Future Drivers of Growth in Rwanda: Innovation, Integration, Agglomeration, and Competition." World Bank Result Briefs. www.worldbank.org/en/results/2019/05/10/future-drivers-of-growth-in-rwanda.

CHAPTER 10

Digital Media as the Next Frontier for Fighting Violent Extremism among Youth?

Willice Onyango

Over the past ten years, the dynamics of digital social networks have been investigated by researchers in a range of disciplines including technology, education, political science, psychology, and sociology, with the focus on the digital universe of games, videos, blogs, and forums (UNESCO 2017). Some of this research has specifically examined the link between social media and the growing role of personal, political, ethnic, religious, and violent radicalization of youth in sectarian or political groups (UNESCO 2017; Thompson 2011). Indeed, it is often claimed that the internet is increasingly an active vector for violent radicalization that facilitates the proliferation of extremist ideologies in low-cost, fast, decentralized, and globally connected networks (Awan, Hoskins, and O'Loughlin 2011; Archetti 2013). This claim is understandable given that terrorism is a resource-intensive operation, with new recruits continually being sought in order to replace individuals lost to fighting, suicide bombings, and arrests (Bloom 2011), together with the need to expand their operations.

Digital media presents vast opportunities for violent extremist groups seeking to radicalize young audiences online, disseminating propaganda messages in order to attract recruits and sympathizers (Conway 2005). With their highly effective packaging, the internet is an ideal recruitment tool for groups such as the Islamic State (ISIS) and al-Qaeda (Venhaus 2010). Terrorist group presence is spread throughout the internet, with cyberspace offering a myriad of opportunities for online recruitment and the broadcasting of violent content (UNESCO 2017). Young people are being exposed to hate and violent extremist content online both purposefully and accidentally (Grizzle and Tornero 2016). The extent of this exposure is significant, especially considering that almost one-third of the world's total population uses mobile phones (Statista, n.d.), leading some to conclude that violent extremism is a form of communication (Ferguson 2010). This is particularly worrying, since the heaviest users are young people (Lee 2005).

This chapter examines these trends in the context of a recent case study—the Kenyan Youth Manifesto—which was a project aimed at using the digital sphere to foster a more peaceful and just society. This online initiative was created by young people for young people. Its purpose was to harness the wisdom of young people through social media to determine how they want to be situated in their country's socioeconomic and political life. This initiative was based on the premise that in order to counter violent extremism among youth, the conditions and factors that underlie the rise of violent extremism among youth need to be understood and addressed. The Kenya Youth Manifesto tested whether an effective pathway to counter extremism could be developed by enabling young people to work in partnership with other youth across the country to surface and resolve the key challenges they were facing socially, economically, and politically.

This case study of youth engagement supports the findings of the 2017 U.N. Progress Study, which states that in the absence of meaningful opportunities to engage socially, politically, and economically, "marginalized young people are strikingly creative in forging alternative places of belonging and meaning through which to express themselves" (6). Additionally, this work aligned with the United Nations Security Council Resolution (UNSCR) 2250's conclusion that "young people play an important and positive role in the maintenance and promotion of international peace and security" (UNSCR 2250 2015). It sought to engage with the U.N.'s fifth pillars for action—"disengagement and reintegration"—which exhorts all relevant parties to "invest in youth affected by armed conflict through employment opportunities, inclusive labor policies and education promoting a culture of peace" (Simpson 2018, 2).

The objectives were twofold: first, to overview the growing body of literature on social media as a vector of violent extremism and, second, to explore whether a process such as the Kenyan Youth Manifesto, a youth-led social media intervention, partnering with youth to envision a more positive future for young people, could act as a counterforce to social media being used to foster youth extremist violence.

THE CONTEXT OF THE KENYA YOUTH MANIFESTO

There have been numerous efforts to narrow or shut down dissenting online voices, particularly by authoritarian governments. These have, however, frequently resulted in human rights violations (Simpson 2018). Other more benign efforts have tried to counter the perceived threat of violent radicalization online by, for example, developing social media initiatives that encourage youth to participate in creating more peaceful and secure societies. Examples include the PeaceTech Lab (Simpson 2018), which works to reduce violent conflict using technology, media, and data to accelerate and scale peacebuilding efforts, and the Stanford Peace Innovation Lab (Simpson 2018), which uses behavior modeling, innovation, and persuasive and social technologies to increase positive peace. The Youth Café, a Pan-African youth organization headquartered in Kenya, is such a group.[1] As part of its mission, it seeks to promote the utility of public diplomacy programs on social media and internet platforms as a way of reducing the number of young people who are susceptible to online radicalization.

As an integral part of this effort, the Kenya Youth Manifesto (Youth Café 2018), developed by and with youth, served as a demonstration of how the manifesto's pillar of "Peace, Security and Social Cohesion" could be fostered through a partnership with young people. This process enabled youth to work in a loose relationship to highlight issues of importance to them, including how their lives could be improved to mitigate their potentially dire circumstances. The aim was to enable young people to suggest the sort of society that would hold a more positive future for them rather than simply reacting with either anger or disaffection to the circumstances that were out of their control. It hoped to explore whether young people could cocreate an online initiative that would deter susceptible youth from seeking the dangerous alternative of violent extremism. Thus it focused on whether an engagement process run by and for Kenyan youth to develop their preferred future would provide insights about what it might take to deter youth from violent extremism. It could furthermore determine whether young people themselves prioritized peace and the need to deter youth from violent extremism. Moreover, it would provide a pathway forward in this discovery effort.

RESEARCH OVERVIEW

The literature review component of the study aimed first at providing an understanding of the current thinking on social media's role in youth violent extremism. Though statements abounded regarding the internet serving as an active vector for violent radicalization and its ideologies, there was no definitive evidence of a direct link between the internet and the violent radicalization of youth (UNESCO 2017). There was evidence that ill-intended people are indeed heavily spread throughout the internet, and there is growing knowledge regarding how terrorists use cyberspace. However, evidence about the actual role the internet plays in violent radicalization remains inadequate. Limited information regarding gender is available, although there is a more recent focus on women as violent actors, their pathways to radicalization, and their roles within violent extremist groups, as well as their roles in countering violent extremism (UNESCO 2017). Methods for deradicalization using social media were absent, as was evidence-based policy for preventing and countering violent radicalization. Finally, neither policy nor research seemed to take into account the importance of context—that is, that policies and actions to prevent online recruitment in some places were unlikely to work in other settings.

The second issue the literature review aimed to understand was that although youth were centrally featured in the literature, they seemed to be peripheral in efforts to resolve it. This was despite the connection, made for over fifty years of research, between a youth bulge (a high proportion of young people relative to the total population) and the risk of wars, increased violence, and political instability (UNESCO 2017). It has also been proposed that a youth demographic dividend could be realized instead; it would be led by the economic growth potential resulting from shifts in a population's age structure, particularly when the share of the working-age population was larger than the non-working-age population (UNFPA 2016). Though not explicitly evidenced in the literature, the clash between these two alternative phenomena could partially explain the paucity of meaningful partnerships between decision-makers and youth. What is clear is that this absence of effective relationships has limited society's understanding of how digital media has served violent extremism and could serve to counter extremism among young audiences. Mutual, trust-based partnerships between youth and governments have not featured in the literature. It is a weakness that needs rectifying and is explored in this chapter.

The final issue investigated in the literature review was whether the prevalent focus on youth's engagement in radical extremist violence was warranted. Scholars have questioned the assumptions underlying the proposition of a direct link between the internet and youth radicalization (Aliaga and O'Farrell 2017; Apua 2016). Representations of youth have often been stereotypic, focusing on the distorted partnering and policy priorities of youth influenced by violent extremist groups. Policy makers have assumed that it is predominantly young people joining these groups. This concern is supported by some evidence: "The majority of Boko Haram fighters are teenagers, the typical ISIS recruit is around 26 years old, and most Jemaah Islamiyah members are young and male" (Search for Common Ground 2017, 3). In addition, the majority of gang members—whether in Central America, the Caribbean, South Africa, Côte d'Ivoire, or Chicago—fall into the youth age category. However, such data distort the fact that youth who join violent or extremist groups constitute only a minute fraction of the youth population. Youth have argued that despite legitimate social, political, and economic grievances, the vast majority of young people are peaceful and resist urges to become involved in violent extremism. Moreover, it is stigmatizing to young women and men if an implicit assumption is made that they are all at risk of joining violent extremist groups (Aliaga and O'Farrell 2017, 22).

PERCEPTIONS AND VERACITY OF VIOLENT YOUTH EXTREMISM IN THE DIGITAL SPHERE

Given the ubiquitous nature of the digital world for young people today, it is understandable why there has been a preoccupation with youth and violent radicalization online. This is also clearly understood by the perpetrators of radicalization. For example, Klausen (2015) notes that ISIS members and their supporters use a variety of social media apps and file-sharing platforms, from Facebook and Ask.fm (a global social networking site where users create profiles and can send each other questions) to kik (a cross-platform mobile application used for instant messaging) and YouTube, providing, for example, rap videos and online magazines with messages aimed directly at disaffected youth. In 2015, ISIS operated seventy thousand Twitter accounts and tweeted two hundred thousand times per day, Mexico's Sinaloa cartel's Twitter account had more than thirty-four thousand followers, and a Latin American gang called the Mara Salvatrucha, or MS-13, had over forty thousand likes on Facebook, communicating online with its members across the Americas (SecDev Group 2018, 1–2). Understandably, governments have been preoccupied with the fear of online platforms being vehicles for the promotion, mobilization, and recruitment of youth into violent extremism and organized crime. This fear has been exacerbated by the likelihood that renowned violent extremist groups are better equipped than governments to use digital technologies to engage excluded and marginalized young people (UNESCO 2017).

Recent research has highlighted the sophistication of violent groups' social media. These organizations have tailored their marketing and branding strategies toward young people in specific country and regional contexts (Rogers 2017). Such groups seek to offer "a ready-made community, identity, and the opportunity to be part of a cause that can be particularly attractive to young people" (Littman 2015, 2). One study of al-Qaeda recruits noted that the organization successfully targeted confused young people seeking an individual identity that would fulfill them—for example, some seeking revenge and needing an outlet for their frustration, some seeking status, some seeking group acceptance, and some seeking adventure (Venhaus 2010). Media content, videos on YouTube, interaction with others, and propaganda photos are all aimed at meeting such needs (Payne 2009, 32).

It is difficult to understand the radicalization phenomena by exploring the different acts of terrorism in the world, let alone the actual role of the internet and social media platforms in the radicalization of such terrorists. Trying to find a window into this phenomenon, researchers have examined the browsing patterns on communication devices popular among at-risk/potential extremists under the age of thirty-five and assessed the outcomes of microtargeted strategic communications propagating violent extremist ideologies. Investigators have also explored how sites such as Facebook, Twitter, YouTube, and Instagram function as radicalizing milieus (Bloom 2013) within which young people are introduced to extremist messages, are networked to others with similar perspectives, and in some cases, are actively recruited to join violent terrorist groups (Stevens and Neumann 2009; Venhaus 2010). However, the collective intelligence gained by such research has been insufficient to understand enough about causal sequencing to build more effective responses to online violent radicalization.

Little is known about the role young women play in cyberspace and violent radicalization (Bloom 2011; 2013). Existing gender, social media, and radicalization research is highly exploratory and descriptive. The gender issue in social media studies is virtually nonexistent. Females' role in online radicalization remains underresearched and underestimated. Overall, gender issues are largely under-studied due to complex and varied factors including cultural, social, and societal power dynamics. However, there is much to be gained by undertaking a more inclusive study of gender dynamics in the context of violent extremism, especially since the risks of not doing so could manifest in an increase in violent extremism among females. Research has focused predominantly on ISIS, and there is little interdisciplinary/intercultural research on extreme right-wing, left-wing, or radical feminist women's involvement on the internet and social media, which is a prob-lematic trend that detracts from efforts to address extremism in a holistic manner (Stevens and Neumann 2009; Venhaus 2010).

GOVERNMENT RESPONSES TO ONLINE VIOLENT RADICALIZATION OF YOUTH

There have been few constructive government responses to online violent radical-ization. On the contrary, they have often exacerbated the problem. The use of social media by violent groups, terrorist organizations, and organized crime has triggered what has been called a "moral panic" (Sukarieh and Tannock 2017; Shafer 2002). This has motivated many governments to monitor online activities, limit freedom of expression, target legitimate political activities, and silence dissenting youth voices. Repressive governments have used national wholesale blocking of social media and even internet shutdowns to control online activity. Nonauthoritarian regimes also have been ambivalent about the internet's power of social mobilization. While admiring democracy activists organizing online, outrage is expressed when ISIS recruits remotely (Human Rights Watch 2017, 42). It would appear that attempts to counter violent extremism assume the internet and globalization are threats and hence need to be inhibited. However, cutting off their key means of accessing other young people's perspectives and experiences and connecting with others can lead to even greater disaffection and alienation. Furthermore, the anticipation or suspicion of terrorism and violent extremism has triggered some governments not only to narrow or shut down the availability of civic spaces for dissenting youth voices but also to disregard human rights and arrest, jail, and even target and attack youth (CIVICUS 2017).

Particularly in countries that have been facing insurgencies led by violent extremist groups—such as Libya, Mali, Nigeria, Somalia, and Tunisia (Cilliers 2015, 236; Boukhars 2017)—it has been suggested that communities are more fearful of their government's continual violations of human rights than they are of extremist groups. Indeed, this has been cited as a highly significant motivation in young people's decisions to participate in violent extremist groups in Africa (United Nations Development Programme 2017). In fact, researchers have proposed that "police tactics are also the best recruiting tools for terrorist groups" (18) and that repressive reactions of governments have been used by violent groups as a tactic to persuade or recruit new members and to gain legitimacy among nonviolent resistance and social movements (Neumann 2017, 25; Novelli 2017).

Young people across the globe, not just in developing countries, often feel deeply fearful of the police and the violence they face at the hands of law enforcement personnel. Young people do not necessarily experience justice; precisely because of their status as youth, they often encounter issues with the police and other elders (Neumann 2017, 25; Novelli 2017). Though the consequences and extent of government abuses of power vary, the common experience among youth of feeling victimized is nonetheless striking. To that end, it seems obvious that if governments want to establish more constructive relationships with youth, then shutting down spaces for young people, dissenting or not, is not a helpful strategy. This is especially true because the virtual world also offers many positive opportunities for young people to participate in creating more peaceful societies.

To date, there have been few attempts by governments to partner with young women and men in action research to learn how to counter radicalization using digital and new media. Not learning from and with young people has been a lost opportunity, particularly given youths' high and continually growing use of social media. Young people are at the forefront of the rapid take-up of social media platforms transforming communication and influence. Yet rather than partnering with youth, government action tends to be driven more by preemptive security-based approaches (Nordås and Davenport 2013), which are not based on evidence or a commitment to preventive interventions (SecDev Group 2018). Although some approaches to the prevention of violent extremism do acknowledge the importance of youth empowerment, participation, and inclusion, such as the United Nations secretary-general's Plan of Action to Prevent Violent Extremism (United Nations Secretary-General 2016), the prevailing policy orientation continues to taint the youth population as a whole, exacerbating rather than addressing their underlying experiences of marginalization (Attree 2017).

ALTERNATIVE APPROACHES

Rather than focusing on the problems of youth disengagement, there is a growing body of evidence showing how young people are actively engaged within their communities, from community service and civic engagement to advocating for the needs of their communities or participating in formal institutions. The positive roles young people can and do play in society are an important counterweight to the prevalence of research findings regarding online violent extremism and youth. The U.N. initially adopted this approach in 2015, UNSCR 2250, with the first Security Council Resolution recognizing the important role that young women and men play in the maintenance and promotion of international peace and security. It was largely civil society organizations, including youth-serving organizations, that drove this outcome. These organizations had identified the need for a global framework to support young people's peacebuilding efforts that could engage member states and United Nations entities. Then in 2018, the United Nations Population Fund progress report entitled *The Missing Peace: Independent Progress Study on Youth, Peace and Security* focused on youth's positive contribution to peace processes and conflict resolution and urged member states to "increase, as appropriate, their political, financial, technical and logistical support, that take account of the needs and participation of youth in peace efforts, in conflict and post-conflict situations" (Simpson 2018, 72).

Globalization has led today's youth to have higher expectations for self-direction, freedom, and opportunity. The information age has taught them their human rights and given them a broader vision of what their lives could be (UNFPA 2014, 79). Young people are mobile not only physically through migration but also virtually. Two-thirds of the world's internet users are the age of thirty-five, and half are under the age of twenty-five (UNFPA 2014). Young people's horizons are being reshaped by their growing access to information and varied worldviews via social media and the internet. They are increasingly aware of their rights and deprivation relative to other people in their communities and around the world as well as opportunities that may exist in other places (Simpson 2018). Globalization brings the power of expanding horizons and visibility, the space for connectivity, and platforms for expanding direct social, political, and economic participation. However, globalization also has negative consequences including terrorism, currency fluctuation, displacement of workers, abandonment of culture (Shopina, Oliinyk, and Finaheiev 2017), and of course, the recent devastating coronavirus disease (COVID-19) global pandemic.

The World Youth Report highlighted that cyber technologies offer unique organizational tools for peace and positive forms of digital organization as well as platforms for civic participation among youth (United Nations Department of Economic and Social Affairs 2016). Since the internet can both "enable and inhibit the spread of violent conflict" (United Nations and World Bank 2017, 10; Simpson 2018), approaches that conscript young people into using technologies to work together to build more positive and peaceful communities need to be a key focus.

Young people already use innovations in social media, communication plat-forms, and cyber technologies in their engagement for peace. Social media and information and communication technologies (ICTs) serve as tools to build global networks and connect youth in multiple locations in a broad array of constructive interests. ICTs offer innovative mechanisms for young people in conflict-affected and divided societies to communicate and network in search of desired outcomes (UNESCO 2017)—for example, WhatsApp, which is being used for multiple pur-poses and peacebuilding courses (Klausen 2015). ICTs represent much more than cyber toolboxes. They represent innovative spaces claimed by youth for dialogue and participation. Notably, ICTs have enabled young people to monitor, docu-ment, and publish human rights violations in situations of violent conflict and to inform and protect vulnerable communities. Young videographers have captured and uploaded videos documenting atrocities in embattled conflict zones. In Syria, SalamaTech, an online platform for Syrians in war zones, oft used by young people, helps sustain dialogue and communication, providing updates on the situation and assisting in the coordination of humanitarian responses for those in need. In Egypt, HarassMap is an online app that enables young women to report their experiences of sexual violence or harassment (Skalli 2013).

Other online initiatives have been developed by youth, or youth are the key users and audience. They include online video-gaming technologies adapted to peacebuilding, such as PeaceMaker (Israel–Palestine), which developed an award-winning game revolving around finding peaceful solutions to the conflict in the region (Simpson 2018). Other "peace tech" platforms include Bytes (Lupaianez-Villanueva et al. 2018), which focuses on trust building through ICT (games, apps, websites, social media) to engage young people, particularly in North Ireland. Another platform, A Scuola di OPENCOESIONE (Lupaianez-Villanueva et al. 2018), uses open data for civic engagement through an educational online pathway designed for students in Italian secondary schools.

Unfortunately, there is limited information on the roles and active contribu-tions of young women to peace in their communities. Once again, this is likely the result of social norms and historical circumstances that marginalize women. Despite significant obstacles, young women find creative ways to organize and form networks, foster safe spaces for engagement, and promote social cohesion. This peacebuilding work, not only undertaken but often initiated and led by young women, demands greater attention and visibility (as a case in point, see chapter 2, this volume, discussing a young Kenyan woman's successful use of social media as a conflict mediation tool). The prevalence of female-led peacebuilding endeavors is especially noteworthy given the restraining influence of pervasive traditional gender norms of girls and young women—a remnant of the "gerontophallic post-colonial Africa" (chapter 7), which almost two decades of WPS implementation has not succeeded in mitigating (chapter 8). One effort to ameliorate such disadvantage has been in the Kurdistan region of Iraq, which provides training (Simpson 2018). It is a significant and deleterious anomaly that while women's peacebuilding efforts have gone unrecognized, there is a mounting body of evidence of the role that young women have played as both direct perpetrators and indirect instigators of violence (Attree 2017; Cilliers 2015).

THE KENYA YOUTH MANIFESTO PROCESS

This case study focused on establishing partnering relationships to enable youth to use the digital sphere to develop a Youth Manifesto to improve young people's lives in Kenya. The research was made possible by the support and participation of key stakeholders—including representatives of civil society and business; United Nations organizations including U.N.-Habitat, UNICEF, U.N. Women, and U.N. Democracy Fund; and international development agencies, academia, relevant government agencies, and the media—working together with Kenyan youth (Onyango 2018). Without any formal commitments, there was an intersectoral collaboration aimed at working with youth in the interests of the future of young people in Kenya.

The Kenya Youth Manifesto process focused on digital communication to understand the world of young people and to learn how they wanted to go about improving it. It exemplified UNSCR 2250's imperative of inclusivity in matters of peace and security, highlighting the crucial contributions of young actors and opening avenues for those traditionally excluded from participation in policy development and decision-making—in particular, young people.

This was achieved through the following process: first, partnering with diverse youth groups to coordinate an online initiative, eliciting young people's participation from across the nation, and ascertaining youth's key concerns and suggestions for addressing their main challenges; then, after collaboratively creating a draft Youth Manifesto from their combined inputs, confirming with them that this accurately reflected their views; and finally, continuing to update them on any progress regarding decision-makers' serious consideration and response to the manifesto. The online process involved the use of a series of topical social media and TweetChats under the hashtag #YouthManifestoKE, reaching over two million social media impressions as well as eliciting over eleven thousand youth responses.[2] The tweets ranged from how to transform ethnic and divisive politics, to corruption as a driver of extremism, to the role of digital platforms in amplifying youth voices.

The online forum provided a platform for sharing experiences, ideas, and knowledge on constructive strategies for countering violent extremism. Discussions shed light on the different types of radical ideologies (political, identity-based, and religious) and provided insights into extremist group ideologies through the narrative of disengaged youths' real-life experiences (Onyango 2018; Youth Café 2018). The numerous youth-centered consultations took seriously the need to reflect the diversity of Kenyan youth. The manifesto process clarified young people's preferred vision for youth in Kenyan life, including opportunities critical to their future. Additionally, it surfaced and improved understanding of the drivers of youth radicalization—in particular, the marginalization of youth in Kenyan society, which is exacerbated by human rights violations and the unequal treatment of young women. The pressures of young people's lives described in the online platform unsurprisingly mirrored issues documented by U.N. reports on preventing violent extremism, including the following.

Human Rights Violations

The U.N. highlighted reactive, short-sighted responses with "a single-minded focus only on security measures and an utter disregard for human rights, have often made things worse" (U.N. Secretary-General 2016, para. 9; Organization for Security and Co-operation in Europe 2014). An example given was that after receiving a beating from the police, a Mombasa youth felt "even more vulnerable, angry and disempowered than before" (Simpson 2018). Similar concerns were expressed by Youth Manifesto participants. The following comments were made by a diverse mix of young men and women drawn from all over Kenya in response to the question, Why is it important to engage young people in Kenya's political process leading to the general elections?

> Youth remain the centerpiece of a nation's political, economic and social fabric. Our voices emancipate our participation towards our peace building and countering extremism in Kenya. But let us use soft approaches in addressing underlying factors that lead to radicalization as opposed to countering them with force as the government is doing things.

> I think it's a social issue. How are we cultured to counter extremism? Laws are as good or bad as the people making them, hence the gaps in our laws. Is our legislative and criminal justice system working?

> As youths we must talk about corruption that is largely leading us into extremism. The need to have what we want instantly. We cannot talk about peace without talking about corruption in Kenya. Corruption is heavily linked to violent extremism.

These comments reflect an interest by young people to have their voices heard and evidence a clear grasp of basic issues that affect their communities. We can thus conclude that providing safe spaces for young people to be engaged is vital if we are to address their grievances before they escalate into violent tendencies.

Gender Differences

The U.N. noted that both young women and young men struggle to transition into social adulthood, but they do so in different ways. The shifting roles and societal responsibilities that signal the transition from youth to adulthood can be markedly different for young women and young men and for young members of sexual and gender minorities (SGMs). Positive gender-equitable identities and roles need to be at the forefront of global policies, including cultivating nonviolent masculinities. Not doing so will exacerbate young men's vulnerability to extremism and leave the door open for young girls to be further enticed into extremist groups. Manifesto participants also pointed to gender-based concerns. The following are several comments from young women and men who responded to the manifesto's request for public input in the months leading up to the 2017 Kenyan elections:

> When young women in Nairobi's informal settlements bear children, their status as mothers generally trumps their age as the key characteristic defining their social status. Women and young people have been active participants in

propagation of violence and have been recruited in terrorist groups as young people who have been lured by financial incentives; and thus, the role of women in violence and terrorism should be addressed.

These remarks speak to the clear imperative to take gender dynamics into account, particularly the role of young women, in any engagement processes with youth—local, national, or international. They also attest that young women are ready and able to contribute effectively in proposing solutions to extremism and that their voices and ideas should not be muted by gender norms that deny them the necessary spaces for expression.

THE STEP-BY-STEP PROCESS TAKEN BY THE KENYA YOUTH MANIFESTO

Rather than a stand-alone initiative, the Kenya Youth Manifesto process built on years of policy work spearheaded by the Youth Café. Specifically, in 2017, the Youth Café planned consultations on how to counter extremism, offline as well as online, through a series of TweetChats. The forum provided a platform for sharing experiences, ideas, and knowledge on constructive strategies for preventing violent extremism. Discussions shed light on the different types of radical ideologies (political, identity based, and religious) and provided insights into the deep-rooted beliefs and ideologies of extremist groups through the narratives of disengaged individual's real-life experiences.

The Kenya Youth Manifesto began with a different frame—that of discerning the socioeconomic, political life Kenyan youth wanted to live. Though this inevitably brought to the fore issues of violent radicalization, the focus was more on envisaging and codesigning the future young people wanted in Kenya. The manifesto participatory consultations emerged out of a coordinated process of building a broad youth constituency and developing individual and group capacities. Through a series of consultations with youth groups across the country, tweet chats, and short mobile messages, the Coalition for Kenya Youth Manifesto was created as the umbrella body to coordinate the development of the Youth Manifesto. The initial core manifesto team widened its scope and participation to accept youth-led organizations that were interested in the project and had a history of working on similar issues. Diverse organizations and individuals formed the membership of the coalition, with each taking a lead role in the diverse aspects of the manifesto's engagement process. The coalition had over sixty-one youth-serving organizations as members, altogether reaching three hundred skilled youth advocates and champions with varied talents. The various roles they took on included online and offline outreach, fundraising, preparing drafts of the manifesto, and the public launch event. The coalition had a total of thirty-six males and twenty-five female members.

A diverse technical team of seven young researchers—four females and three males—and youth workers visited numerous regionally representative tertiary institutions and high schools between January and March of 2017 to provide the opportunity for many students and young artists to contribute to the consultations. The engagement with political parties—and in some cases, their youth wings—ensured that politically active youth were not left out of the process.

It was understood from the outset that to be taken seriously, the Youth Manifesto would need to be informed, carefully considered, and not simply repetitive of other policy statements. To assist in this process, thirteen young research volunteers combed through all existing youth policies and interventions and their impacts across the country, making useful contributions regarding the place of young people in peace and security. These contributions ensured that the manifesto did not duplicate policies but rather filled evident gaps that were in related youth blueprints, such as the Kenyan constitution, the National Youth Policy, the East African Community Youth Policy, the African Youth Charter, and the United Nations World Program on Youth.

Creativity was actively encouraged. Many young people and some older adults with internet access contributed through social media platforms in very imaginative ways, such as using memes and short vlogs (social media accounts for regular short video posts). Altogether, these activities yielded 5,473 inputs such as opinions, voices, and perspectives, mainly in written form, either as individual responses based on templates developed by the project team or as activity reports outlining youth positions and recommendations.[3] As a result, the project team was able to develop a database of all inputs received. Based on these inputs, the drafting team prepared thematic summaries, clustering the inputs under twelve thematic issues, with "Peace, Security, and Social Cohesion" being a key theme.[4] This enabled the drafting team to develop a final draft of the report, with the support of the steering committee members. This draft report was subjected to a thorough review by young people through various platforms, including online consultations.

Participant Suggestions regarding Social Cohesion

Experiences of exclusion were often raised. These included lack of voice, inadequate opportunity, and limited access to education and broader development opportunities. Meaningful political inclusion was a central demand underlying all other forms of exclusion. Some concerns were as follows:

We are living in a century where creativity and technology have changed a lot of assumptions. The best way could be having a good engagement discussion with youth on what works well and what their mission in life and later form a joint action point to support them in economic inclusion.

Our generation has the potential to transform ethnic politics. That's not hyperbole, it's the truth. Young people who participate politically in their community early from early on are more likely to become better citizens.

Since time immemorial we've been told that youths are the leaders of tomorrow. It's never reaching. It has to be today!! Nothing has been fair in politics or political processes.

Comments like these highlight the crucial need for the effective and efficient political inclusion of young people if manifestations of youth exclusion are to be addressed. It is also evident that concerted and continuous intergenerational dialogues are important to bridging gaps between the young and old generations.

However, youth participation and partnership were not unconditional. Inclusion in corrupt, undemocratic, or oppressive systems was understood to be neither legitimate nor acceptable. Many challenged the whole concept of inclusion, with suggestions for creating their own alternative spaces for political engagement:

> Participation in informal political process enables young people to build a vote of confidence from the community and trust that they are willing to carry out transformative leadership.

There was also a loss of confidence in economic systems that exclude youth as key stakeholders and reflect growing levels of inequality. For many, economic inclusion primarily involved fair access to meaningful and reliable employment. There were suggestions about how this could be achieved. For example, one participant proposed the following:

> To reduce poverty and unemployment, the government should reduce the cost of starting businesses. Currently, all the profit goes to tax and rent. Living with the internal struggle of being skillful but not being able to obtain desired jobs is difficult. Also, passing of critical information to the youths is key. Lack of information on employment and access to sustainable economic opportunities has made young people engage in acts of violence and enhanced ideological extremism.

Comments such as these underscore the importance of economic inclusion in any efforts aimed at political inclusion. With ever-rising youth unemployment in Kenya, many young people who spoke were actively looking for ways of creating self-employment and wanted conducive environments for their future ventures to thrive. Without resolving youth unemployment, more young people will remain vulnerable to recruitment in violent extremist groups.

Participants also discussed limited access to education and access to the broader development process. From those in remote areas to those involved in transnational networks, education was seen as indispensable to building peace, preventing violence, and addressing the systemic exclusion of youth. There was an almost universal understanding that education was a core peace and security concern that provided a place of social cohesion and belonging. For example,

> Education is one of the most important means of empowering young people in any society. Tied to that is the need to curb corruption and internal conflicts through equitable distribution of wealth across generations, participatory democracy, and inclusive economic development.
>
> It is especially important to consider the cultural point of view and historical narratives on how youth have been supportive of conflict prevention and being in leadership roles. This will not only inspire the current generation but also will help in having well-documented analyses on the cultural practices and youth leadership position in the community.
>
> Beyond countering violent extremism, I think there's an important role for youth spaces such as Kenya Youth Manifesto in facilitating conversations, encouraging awareness, and dispelling misinformation to tackle associated prejudices.

These statements underscore the almost universal agreement among youth that education and, more specifically, educated young people are key to achieving peace, cohesion, and security. Targeted investments in supporting young people to acquire the education and digital skills necessary in the twenty-first century are required.

The analysis of participants' comments undertaken to develop the themes highlighted how participants brought to the fore not only the challenges they faced with respect to violent extremism as both victims and active participants but also how they are using or could use digital media to address violent extremism.

ANALYSIS OF PROCESS AND OUTCOMES OF THE KENYA YOUTH MANIFESTO

Overall, the manifesto process was comprehensive. It elicited, themed, and recommended priority ideas and viewpoints of Kenya's youth and endeavored to implement priority actions. It used a variety of online opportunities and face-to-face workshops to broaden inclusion and deepen understanding of diverse youth concerns and suggestions. The consideration and development of themes and priority actions involved the broad stakeholder groups, and extensive feedback was invited to make amendments and additions. The final manifesto was widely disseminated.

Understanding the obstacles to implementation, recommended actions were directed to a broad range of stakeholders including the government, civil society, the private sector, the U.N., donors, and the international community, as well as young people themselves. Given the paucity of resources and the need to avoid fragmentation and duplication, the aim was to make the implementation of these recommendations a collaborative response to the call to action.

Writing an actionable manifesto in any democratic country is beset with difficulties including the following: the issues of those it aims to be representing; creating an agenda that is forward thinking but more practical than idealistic; developing specific targets that are difficult but at least potentially achievable; advancing an agenda that is broad enough to encompass the range of issues and diversity of participants, including those who are rarely heard, while not being so broad as to be platitudinal; and in terms of implementation, spreading the load more broadly than just on the shoulders of government. Given the snags of navigating such difficult currents, the Kenya Youth Manifesto managed relatively well. It was probably never feasible for substantial numbers of recommendations to be implemented without significant changes to local and national budgetary priorities. Since there was little regional or national government buy-in to this initiative, this was not going to happen. Concomitantly, there was little likelihood that the young people participating would feel highly satisfied that their voices had resulted in significant change. Despite understanding the lack of resources and political will to make the sort of changes likely to be recommended, the Kenya Youth Manifesto project team persisted, doing what they could to increase the likelihood of being heard and the possibility of enacting change. Even more to their credit, there were some successes in terms of implementation.[5]

The Kenya Youth Manifesto case study examined whether an effective way to understand and address extremism could be created by enabling young people to work in partnership with youth across the country to surface and resolve the key challenges they were facing socially, economically, and politically. This proposition was supported, with Kenyan youth from different socioeconomic groups and regional areas making it clear that if their basic needs for education, economic security, health and well-being, and meaningful civic participation were met, young people would be deterred from being lured into violent extremism. Overall, the Kenya Youth Manifesto initiative was successful in achieving its stated aims, at least to the extent feasible given the enormous challenges it faced. Achieving as much as it did, the manifesto was an impressive effort, achieving international acclaim.[6]

CONCLUSION

Rather than focusing on how digital media can ignite violent radicalization among marginalized and disengaged youth in Kenya, this chapter chose an alternative pathway—focusing on the potential for youth to use social media to reenvision and cocreate a more peaceful, secure, and just future. It described the case study of the Kenyan Youth Manifesto. Rather than youth assuming the role of passive actors in their socioeconomic political lives, this online initiative was created by young people, with young people, to improve the lives of young people. Youth wanted to explore how, via digital media, they could potentially counter violent extremism among Kenyan young people by giving them the opportunity to describe and resolve the key challenges they faced—socially, economically, and politically. The Kenya Youth Manifesto was not simply a one-off event but rather one element of a longer-term process to involve youth in creating a more equitable, secure, peaceful life in Kenya.

The manifesto-writing process demonstrated the ability of young people to design and implement a large-scale, complex engagement procedure. Its results clearly showed that the young people involved believed that if their concerns could be addressed—including their basic needs for education, economic security, health and well-being, and meaningful civic participation—Kenyan youth would be unlikely to be lured into violent extremism.

In terms of its biggest challenge—securing and maintaining the Kenyan government's involvement, thereby enabling a significant shift from policy to delivery on youth concerns—it was not so successful. However, in terms of goals over which it had more control—a process run by and for youth that was inclusive, collaborative, and empowered and that produced tangible, potentially implementable results—it was highly successful. Moreover, in terms of research, it provided a replicable model for youth organizations and youth leaders seeking to contribute to peace and security. Indeed, it set the groundwork for achieving a transformative shift toward decision-makers working in partnership with youth to counter violent youth extremism. It provided a framework for action that could be adopted by young people, governments, multilateral organizations, civil society, and other actors to work together to support youth innovation in countering violent youth radicalization and building sustainable peace.

NOTES

1. See the website at www.theyouthcafe.com/.

2. A TweetChat is a public conversation around a unique hashtag that allows one to follow and participate in a discussion.

3. The online templates included the following information-gathering questions: (1) What can political leaders do to show more support to the concerns of Kenyan youth? (2) What are some of the reasons you think that youth are used to propagate violence during particularly in electoral contexts? and (3) How important to you is youth participation in democracy and peacebuilding? The activity reports were drawn from recent partner documents such as the National Youth Convention report, whose outcomes enriched the manifesto in a special way.

4. The twelve thematic issues covered the following: (1) poverty eradication; (2) education and training; (3) employment; (4) youth in the diaspora; (5) entrepreneurship; (6) health, girls and boys; (7) youth living with disabilities; (8) juvenile delinquency, peace and conflict prevention; (9) participation in decision-making; (10) media and ICT; (11) environment; and (12) arts, sports, and recreational activities.

5. The Kenyan government increased the Youth Enterprise Development Fund from Ksh. 500,000 to Ksh. 2 million, which was one of the recommendations of the manifesto. In addition, the proposal to have free secondary education was adopted by leading presidential aspirants, though not yet implemented, and the government introduced health coverage for the youth in the form of the National Health Insurance Fund, as recommended by the manifesto.

6. The Youth Café's executive director presented the manifesto at the 2018 International Conference for Participatory Democracy, organized by the International Observatory for Participatory Democracy. Also, the Youth Café participated in a workshop organized by the Kettering Foundation Deliberative Democracy Institute by virtue of the contents of the manifesto. Africa, Ethiopia, Ghana, and Botswana have used the manifesto as a template to develop one of their own. In addition, the manifesto was reviewed by Prof. Peter Levine of Tuffs University.

REFERENCES

Aliaga, L., and K. Tricot O'Farrell. 2017. *Counter-terror in Tunisia: A Road Paved with Good Intentions?* London: Saferworld. https://saferworld-indepth.squarespace.com/counter-terror-in-tunisia-a-road-paved-with-good-intentions.

Apua, R. 2016. Youth and Violent Extremism Online: Countering Exploitation and Use of the Internet. New York: Routledge.

Archetti, C. 2013. *Understanding Terrorism in the Age of Global Media: A Communication Approach.* Basingstoke, U.K.: Palgrave Macmillan.

Attree, L. 2017. *Shouldn't YOU Be Countering Violent Extremism?* London: Saferworld. https://saferworld-indepth.squarespace.com/shouldnt-you-be-countering-violent-extremism.

Awan, A. N., A. Hoskins, and B. O'Loughlin. 2011. *Radicalization and Media: Connectivity and Terrorism in the New Media Ecology.* New York: Routledge.

Bloom, M. 2011. *Bombshell: Women and Terrorism.* Philadelphia: University of Pennsylvania Press.

———. 2013. "In Defense of Honor: Women and Terrorist Recruitment on the Internet." *Journal of Postcolonial Studies* 4, no. 1, 150–195.

Boukhars, A. 2017. *The Geographic Trajectory of Conflict and Militancy in Tunisia.* Washington, D.C.: Carnegie Endowment for International Peace. https://carnegieendowment.org/files/CP313_Boukhars_Tunisia_Final.pdf.

Cilliers, J. 2015. "Violent Islamist Extremism and Terror in Africa." *Institute for Security Studies Paper* 5, no. 3, 22–110.

CIVICUS. 2017. *State of Civil Society Report 2016*. CIVICUS. www.civicus.org/documents/reports-and-publications/SOCS/2016/summaries/SoCS-full-review.pdf.

Conway, M. 2005. "Determining the Role of the Internet in Violent Extremism and Terrorism: Six Suggestions for Progressing Research." *Studies in Conflict and Terrorism* 40, no. 1, 77–98.

Ferguson, K. 2010. *Countering Violent Extremism through Media and Communication Strategies: A Review of Evidence*. New York: Routledge.

Grizzle, A., and J. M. Perez Tornero. 2016. "Media and Information Literacy against Online Hate, Radical, and Extremist Content: Some Preliminary Research Findings in Relation to Youth and a Research Design." In *Media and Information Literacy: Reinforcing Human Rights, Countering Radicalization and Extremism*, edited by J. Morgan and C. Piere, 45–199. New York: Routledge. www.gcedclearinghouse.org/sites/default/files/resources/180167eng.pdf.

Human Rights Watch. 2017. *World Report 2017*. www.hrw.org/sites/default/files/world_report_download/wr2017-web.pdf.

Klausen, J. 2015. "Tweeting the *Jihad*: Social Media Networks of Western Foreign Fighters in Syria and Iraq." *Studies in Conflict & Terrorism* 38, no. 1, 1–22.

Lee, L. 2005. "Young People and the Internet: From Theory to Practice." Accessed May 14, 2020. http://journals.sagehub.com. (URL inactive.)

Littman, S. 2015. "A Personal Reflection on Good and Evil on the Internet." In *The Routledge International Handbook on Hate Crime*, edited by N. Hall, A. Corb, P. Giannasi, and J. G. D. Grieve, 289–292. New York: Routledge.

Lupaianez-Villanueva, F., A. Theben, F. Porcu, and I. Pena-Lobez. 2018. *Study on the Impact of the Internet and Social Media on Youth Participation and Youth Work*. New York: Routledge.

Neumann, P. R. 2017. *Countering Violent Extremism and Radicalization That Lead to Terrorism: Ideas, Recommendations, and Good Practices from the OSCE Region*. www.ocse.org/chairmanship/346841.

Nordås, R., and C. Davenport. 2013. "Fight the Youth: Youth Bulges and State Repression." *American Journal of Political Science* 57:926–940. https://doi.org/10.1111/ajps.12025.

Novelli, M. 2017. "Education and Countering Violent Extremism: Western Logics from South to North?" *Compare: A Journal of Comparative and International Education*, 47, no. 6, 835–851.

Onyango, W. 2018. *Kenya Youth Manifesto*. Nairobi: Longman.

Organization for Security and Co-operation in Europe. 2014. *Preventing Terrorism and Countering Violent Extremism and Radicalization That Lead to Terrorism: A Community-Policing Approach*. London: Oxford University Press.

Payne, K. 2009. "Winning the Battle of Ideas: Propaganda, Ideology, and Terror." *Studies in Conflict & Terrorism* 37, no. 3, 33–220.

Rogers, A. E. 2017. *Children and Extreme Violence: Viewing Non-state Armed Groups through a Brand Marketing Lens: A Case Study of Islamic State*. New York: Routledge.

Search for Common Ground. 2017. *Transforming Violent Extremism: A Peacebuilder's Guide*. Washington, D.C.: Search for Common Ground. www.sfcg.org/wp-content/uploads/2017/04/SFCG-Peacebuilders-Guide-to-Transforming-VE-final.pdf.

SecDev Group. 2018. *Digitally Enabled Peace and Security: Reflections for the Youth, Peace and Security Agenda*. New York: Routledge.

Shafer, J. A. 2002. *Spinning the Web of Hate: Web-Based Propagation of Extremist Organizations*.

Shopina, I., O. Oliinyk, and V. Finaheiev. 2017. "Globalization and Its Negative Impact on the Global Economy." *Baltic Journal of Economic Studies* 40, no. 3, 22–45.

Simpson, Graeme. 2018. *The Missing Peace: Independent Progress Study on Youth, Peace and Security*. UNFPA. www.unfpa.org/sites/default/files/youth/youth-web-english.pdf.

Skalli, L. 2013. "Young Women and Social Media against Harassment in North Africa." *Journal of North African Studies* 30, no, 2, 199–206.

Statista. n.d. "Social Media Statistics and Facts." Accessed December 10, 2020. www.statista
.com/topics/1164/social-networks.

Stevens, T., and P. R. Neumann. 2009. *Countering Online Radicalization: A Strategy for Action*.
London: Oxford University Press.

Thompson, L. 2011. "Radicalization and the Use of Social Media." *Journal of Strategic Security* 4, no. 2, 22–89.

UNESCO (United Nations Educational, Scientific, and Cultural Organization). 2017. "Youth
and Violent Extremism on Social Media: Mapping the Research." Paris: UNESCO.

United Nations. 2015. "Security Council, Unanimously Adopting Resolution 2250 (2015), Urges
Member States to Increase Representation of Youth in Decision-Making at All Levels." U.N.
Meetings Coverage, December 9, 2015. www.un.org/press/en/2015/sc12149.doc.htm.

United Nations and World Bank. 2017. *Pathways for Peace: Inclusive Approaches to Preventing
Violent Conflict—Main Messages and Emerging Policy Directions*. Washington, D.C.: World
Bank. https://reliefweb.int/sites/reliefweb.int/files/resources/211162mm.pdf.

United Nations Department of Economic and Social Affairs. 2016. *World Youth Report 2015:
Youth Civic Engagement*. Geneva: U.N.

United Nations Development Programme. 2017. *Journey to Extremism in Africa: Drivers,
Incentives and the Tipping Point for Recruitment*. Geneva: U.N.

United Nations Population Fund. 2014. *The Power of 1.8 Billion Adolescents, Youth and the
Transformation of the Future*. Geneva: U.N.

———. 2016. *Demographic Dividend*. Geneva: U.N.

(UNFPA) United Nations Population Fund. 2016. "The State of the World Population
Report 2016." New York, NY: United Nations Population Fund. Available at: https://www
.unfpa.org/sites/default/files/sowp/downloads/The_State_of_World_Population_2016
_-_English.pdf [accessed February 12, 2021]

United Nations Secretary-General. 2016. U.N. Secretary-General's Remarks at General Assembly. Geneva: U.N.

UN Security Council, Security Council resolution 2250. 2015. [on youth, peace and security],
18 March 2016, S/RES/2250 (2015). Available at: https://www.refworld.org/docid/56ebfd654
.html [accessed February 10, 2021]

Venhaus, J. M. 2010. *Why Youth Join al-Qaeda*. United States Institute of Peace Special
Report 236. www.usip.org/sites/default/files/SR236Venhaus.pdf.

Youth Café. 2018. *Kenya Youth Manifesto*. Accessed December 5, 2020. www.theyouthcafe.com/
kenya-youth-manifesto.

Conclusions

SECURITIZING YOUTH—LESSONS LEARNED

Marisa O. Ensor

With a global population of 1.8 billion, the twenty-first-century generation of youth is the largest in history (Ozerdem 2016). Nearly 1 billion of them live in developing and fragile countries, which also tend to be more conflict prone. In effect, the median age in war-torn countries is less than twenty-five years (Ozerdem 2016). Young women and men are critical stakeholders in contexts of conflict and fragility and are also at the front lines of the efforts to build peaceful and inclusive societies, yet their contributions remain underrecognized, understudied, and underfinanced.

As the United Nations Development Program's Bureau for Crisis Prevention and Recovery lamented almost fifteen years ago, "There is an automatic tendency to problematize youth as a factor in violent conflict while overlooking their many positive contributions to a society, including their potential role in sustaining the social fabric and peace, as well as their survival in impossible environments" (UNDP 2006, 9). Still prevalent today, this outdated standpoint has tended to overemphasize the involvement of young people in perpetuating violent conflicts without adequately considering the ways in which youth can also act as positive instruments in peacebuilding and postconflict recovery processes. In effect, uncritical categorizations of youth as "spoilers" have until recently dominated humanitarian policy and practice. The majority of national and international policy pronouncements or security-related programs in postconflict and fragile contexts continue to reflect a polarized discourse. Attitudes—and consequently, policy and practice—toward the young have often oscillated between the two extremes of "infantilizing" and "demonizing." On the one hand, youths are viewed as vulnerable, powerless, and in need of protection. On the other, they are feared as dangerous, violent, apathetic, and threats to security. Either way, youths as a conceptual category have been frequently "othered" in the discourse on conflict.

As the chapters that compose this volume have illustrated, the international community is progressively, if unevenly, moving away from a victim-perpetrator binary. More nuanced understandings of youth agency are directing attention to young people's positioning in relationship to the broader cultural, social, and political context in processes of both conflict and peace (Lopes Cardozo et al. 2015; Lopes Cardozo, Higgins, and Le Mat 2016). As discussed in the introduction to this volume, the recent ascendance of youth in global narratives of peace and security has not been universally celebrated. Detractors highlight the disconnection between discourse and practice and the challenges—or even desirability—of applying global frameworks to particular local realities. Others, including some volume contributors, have voiced a concern with the overly optimistic but empirically unproven expectation that youth engagement would automatically result in positive gains. Closer attention to intergenerational and gendered power relations and the way in which youth agency is conceptualized at the policy level and how this framing translates into programmatic responses are called for.

Responding to these global constraints and opportunities, the global normative frameworks for sustainable, comprehensive, and inclusive peace have greatly expanded over the last twenty years. As Klugman and Moore discuss in detail in chapter 8, this framework encompasses the women, peace, and security (WPS) agenda set forth in U.N. Security Council Resolution (UNSCR) 1325 (2000) and seven subsequent WPS resolutions together with the youth, peace, and security (YPS) agenda set forth in UNSCR 2250 (2015). The parallel YPS and WPS frameworks "seek to address a significant gap in the international community's efforts to address the increasingly complex challenge of preventing conflict and sustaining peaceful and inclusive societies through more comprehensive approaches" (U.N. Women 2018, 7). Together with the concept of "sustaining peace," outlined in parallel resolutions of the Security Council Resolution 2282 (2016) and General Assembly 70/262 (2016), the WPS and YPS agendas call for inclusive planning, program design, policy development, and decision-making processes for conflict prevention, resolution, and recovery.

Also increasingly promoted is targeted environmental and socioeconomic policy-making that takes into consideration the potential risks posed by global processes such as climate change, environmental degradation, and related mass forced displacement while also recognizing the ways in which youth can uniquely shape positive outcomes (Payne, Warembourg, and Awan 2017, 57; see also chapter 7, this volume). Subsequent related initiatives include the 2017 adoption of a global Gender Action Plan (GAP) by the U.N. Framework Convention on Climate Change. This GAP seeks to achieve gender-responsive climate policy and action (UNFCCC 2017).

Inviting reflection on the many achievements, challenges, and opportunities heralded by these recent developments in global policy, scholarship, and practice, *Securitizing Youth* bears testimony to the enormous diversity of young people's realities, evidencing youth's agency, resourcefulness, and ability to cope with challenging circumstances. This approach must not be limited to rhetorical discussion but should also aim at informing the implementation of practical measures. Increasing young people's participation in policy, programming, and decision-making processes has catalytic potential for efforts to prevent, mitigate, and recover from conflict. Contributing authors identify gaps and barriers to the full engagement, recognition, and contribution of young women and men in building sustainable peace. We spotlight areas where more targeted research and analysis is needed to better inform policy development and continue to expand the evidence base supporting the important contribution that young women and men make as agents of change in fostering positive peace. In line with trends identified in the global YPS agenda, we offer policy recommendations structured according to UNSCR 2250's five pillars for action,[1] suggesting effective responses at the local, national, and international levels.

Youth and the Changing Global Peace and Security Landscape

As the world welcomes the second decade of the second millennium, conflict and violence impact more young people than at any point over the last two decades. Successfully navigating postconflict environments—understood as the period following armed conflict when kinetic violence has largely halted but grievances, mistrust, and social upheaval often persist—requires that youth be able to respond to often unfavorable gerontocratic power dynamics prevalent in the societies where most of them live. It is also increasingly recognized that peacebuilding is itself a highly politicized process, as "the dichotomies of right and wrong that war produces do not disappear with the end of the conflict" (Pingel 2010, 112). Fluid sociocultural, political, economic, and environmental circumstances affect young people's ability to contribute to peacebuilding efforts, their changing identities, and their ability to transition to social adulthood.

Conflict, Violence, and Fragility

The current generation of young women and men has inherited a world plagued by a series of interrelated threats to peace and security. These include more violent armed conflicts than at any time in the past thirty years driving 80 percent of all humanitarian needs and the largest forced displacement crisis since World War II. The weakening of core state functions and concomitant collapse in basic services delivery that characterize most conflict-affected countries represent both a humanitarian and a development challenge. These dynamics have a clear impact on poverty, with extreme poverty rates rising almost exclusively in fragile countries (Cuaresma et al. 2018), and disproportionately affect youth.

Relatedly, interpersonal and gang violence annually cause the deaths of many more people than violent conflicts. Recent estimates indicate that for each person who dies at war, between five and thirteen are victims of interpersonal violence (Pettersson and Wallensteen 2015). Today's most violent situations are linked to gang warfare, organized or drug-related crime, state brutality, murders by nonstate actors, and heightened levels of interpersonal violence. These situations are at the core of fragility and are very often protracted. They impact the development of entire regions—for example, Central America—and contribute to massive flows of migrants. Young women and men are particularly affected. Over 35 percent of women and girls—and, to a lesser extent, also boys and younger men—globally report physical or sexual violence; conflict, postconflict, and displacement situations exacerbate violence against women and girls and lead to sexual and gender-based forms of violence, including rape, forced marriage, trafficking, and sexual exploitation (WHO 2017).

The global fragility landscape has worsened significantly in recent years. The nature of violent conflicts is evolving, affecting both low- and medium-income countries. While the number of interstate conflicts has declined, regional and domestic instability has risen largely due to the increase of intrastate conflicts in medium-income countries. In other cases—for example, Afghanistan (see chapter 6, this volume) or South Sudan (see chapter 7, this volume)—decades-long conflicts have fluctuated in intensity but have never been fully resolved, becoming an intrinsic aspect of sociopolitical life. In 2016, 75 percent of people in fragile settings lived in medium-income countries, which also counted more than twice as many conflicts as low-income countries, a trend that has continued in more recent years (World Bank Group 2020, 3).

Regardless of country income levels, a particularly insidious phenomenon affecting youth in fragile states is the legacy of past violence: "Protracted armed conflict can lead to a vicious cycle in which violence becomes the norm. Young ex-combatants often face particularly big challenges in returning to civilian life and at high risk of further involvement in violence" (Hilker and Fraser 2009, 4). Nevertheless, the majority of young people—even those living in conflict-affected and fragile states—do not get involved in violence. As the various chapters that compose *Securitizing Youth* have illustrated, most of them are striving to make a positive contribution to peacebuilding and development.

Gender Matters in Youth, Peace, and Security

While attention to gender dynamics has by now become somewhat of a research orthodoxy, particularly in social science, the consistent and effective implementation of gender-inclusive approaches in peace and security endeavors remains elusive. The experiences of young women and young men in both conflict and peace are "strongly determined by gender, or more precisely, by how the rights, roles, responsibilities and capabilities of females and males are defined within a particular social context" (U.N. 2005, 151). Yet there is a lack of empirical evidence and analysis specifically on young women's experiences in peace and security contexts and processes. There is still relatively limited age-disaggregated data and research on WPS as a whole and even more limited research on youth, peace, and security that incorporates a gender lens. As several chapters in this volume have illustrated (chapters 3, 7, and 8), there is a critical need to engage in comprehensive intersectional analysis to improve policies and increase young women's participation, which is essential to building inclusive and sustainable societies.

While the necessity to integrate a gender dimension is acknowledged, at least in theory (UNDP 2006, 17), most studies on youth and violence implicitly or explicitly refer to young men, reflecting a pronounced gender imbalance. Indeed, the term *youth* in the peace and security discourse has been customarily used to refer only to young men (United Nations Inter-agency Network on Youth Development's Working Group on Youth and Peacebuilding 2016), a pattern also common in the "youth and development" and "youth and conflict" literatures (Sommers 2015). However, expectations of masculinity—that is, "the various ways of being and acting, values and expectations associated with being and becoming a man in a given society, location and temporal space" (OECD 2019, 9)—tend to remain invisible and unquestioned, as they are often seen as the norm (Naujoks and Thandar Ko 2018). Conflict undermines the possibilities of many men to live up to societal expectations to be economic providers, protectors, or decision-makers (Wright

2014; Dolan 2002; 2009), precluding boys from achieving social adulthood and manhood (Sommers 2012). It is not uncommon for women to assume the role of primary economic provider while male partners are at war. Expanding social and economic opportunities for women and girls may lead to fears of loss and a backlash from men and boys. When conflict ends and men return, the subsequent colliding of gender roles can lead to increased rates of violence within the home (Rustad, Ostby, and Nordas 2016).

Analyses of females' actions have similarly been closely shaped by gendered stereotypes (Smeulers 2015) that neglect or misrepresent female agency. As Nordstrom argues, "The lack of political, economic and educational development for girls is a symptom of many societies' failure . . . to see women as political, economic or educated actors" (1999, 44–45). This pattern is particularly pervasive in conflict-affected contexts and distorts interpretations of young women's engagement in armed struggles (Boutron 2016) and peacebuilding efforts (Sievers 2017). Inaccurate presumptions about the motivations, needs, and contributions of women and girls, as well as social and cultural perceptions and norms, have served to limit engagement with female actors in peacebuilding efforts. It is therefore critical to underscore the importance of applying both gender and age lenses in conflict analysis and to ensure the participation of young women—not only young men—in the design and implementation of programs and policies.

Youth and the Violence of Exclusion

The legitimacy of the state in the eyes of the population as a whole, and especially the young, should be a key consideration in peacebuilding interventions. Youth-bulge demographics affect intergenerational dynamics and can be especially challenging in gerontocratic societies characterized by vast age differences between the country's leadership and its population. Excluding young people from political processes and failing to facilitate their participation can lead to grievances that are played out through violence that contributes to instability and undermines peace (Cummins and Ortiz 2012; Affa'a Mindzie 2015).

In fragile situations where the state has limited capacity, an important consideration centers on how services are delivered to maximize inclusion and (re)build trust. The provision of increased economic and education opportunities, as Nasrat Khalid proposes in chapter 6 in the context of Afghanistan, can facilitate this process. Beyond building capacity, strengthening state and local institutions is a first-order priority to confer legitimacy, renew the social contract between young citizens and the state, and foster social cohesion. Special attention to legitimacy is required to promote civic engagement and transparency, support local institutions, and address security and justice issues. International interpretations of justice must be reconciled with local cultural values, giving due weight to youngsters' views, as Victoria R. Bishop cautions us in chapter 9. In turn, stronger and more legitimate institutions can more effectively manage power sharing, redistribution, and non-violent dispute resolution (World Bank 2017).

Recent evidence suggests that young people perceive peace as controlled solely by authorities and governments that they have little trust in or one that is dominated by the elite. This is amplified when the only meaningful way to participate in peace and security efforts is limited to the political sphere, one that is inaccessible and not trusted by many youngsters who grow up seeing its inefficacies and corruption. As some young commentators have underscored, "What is frequently pointed to by adults as political apathy is more often an active withdrawal from political systems in which young people have lost faith and trust" (United Nations 2018).

The lack of political representation only exacerbates this issue. A 2016 Interparliamentary Union (IPU) Report ascribed this lack of representation to three main reasons: (1) restrictive minimum age requirements; (2) disillusionment among youth, which is correlated with lower voting rates; and (3) party bias in favor of older candidates with more extensive political backgrounds. Additional barriers facing youth in their efforts to increase their access to political spaces and elected offices include lack of experience—and few opportunities to acquire it—limited name recognition, and fewer connections and financial resources than their older counterparts. Young people often report a constant need to "prove themselves as real politicians." The murder of Abass Abdullahi Sheikh Siraji, Somalia's youngest cabinet minister, is often referenced to support the argument for additional attention to the significant risks of personal violence against politically involved youth (Mohamed and Ibrahim 2017). The intersection of gender with youth identity results in even greater obstacles for young females (IPU 2015, 9).

The consequence of these high barriers to entry into politics is that youth voices are marginalized in the most critical governmental and organizational decisions around peace and security. Policy then poorly represents their most pressing needs. As youth interviewed by the U.N.'s Progress Study underscored, discussions around youth, peace, and security are often too shallow, focusing on only a subset of issues such as "unemployment, HIV-AIDS, crime and deviant behavior" (United Nations 2018). Stigma and negative stereotypes of youth, especially of youth from ethnic minorities, as Diana Budur discusses in chapter 3 with respect to Roma youngsters, lead to less political involvement and poorer representation. If unaddressed, these may in turn provoke disillusionment, further disengagement from peace and security-related decision-making processes, and even potential radicalization.

Preventing and Countering Violent Extremism (PVE/CVE)

The *Arab Human Development Report 2016* argues that "violent radicalization has become a particular concern—indeed, a defining feature—across the Arab region, particularly among youth" (UNDP 2016, 36). Similarly, the *Youth Action Agenda to Prevent Violent Extremism* notes that "the appeal of violent extremism is growing around the world" as "a sense of disengagement and marginalization, despite the inter-connected world we live in, leaves young people vulnerable to recruitment wherever they are" (Global Youth Summit 2015, 1).

An overriding concern in the global YPS agenda is indeed that youth, and particularly surplus populations of youth excluded from economic opportunity, are at risk of becoming radicalized and pulled into violent forms of extremism. Resolution 2250 (UNSCR 2015, 2) warns that "the rise of radicalization to violence and violent extremism, especially among youth, threatens stability and development." This pervasive focus has resulted in the increasing securitization of youth—that is, the propensity for young people to be seen through a lens of threat and insecurity. In chapter 5, Ali Altiok reports that even youth-led peacebuilding organizations are not impervious to this tendency.

The rise in the proliferation of arms and political extremism in the last fifteen years is often attributed to the disillusionment of young men and sometimes young women. The tone in such discussions tends to be rather accusatory. The extent to which youth are themselves disproportionately the victims of violence, political extremism, and terrorism is, on the other hand, often understated or unacknowledged. Causal pathways to violence are neither linear nor generally traceable except in hindsight, negating effective predictive models. PVE/CVE programming is made more complex because there is no typical youth demographic, while motivations for joining extremist groups vary across regions. The three key drivers generally identified as pushing youth to engage in violent activities—that is, injustice, discrimination, and violence—are highly nuanced from individual to individual, community to community, and region to region. It is also important to note that many young women and men affiliated with violent extremist groups have not necessarily been radicalized; a real or perceived lack of viable alternatives to satisfy material needs, a stable income, the promise of marriage or personal and/or familial safety may motivate them to join violent groups (Ensor 2017).

The comparatively small but persistent number of youth who are involved in violence and targeted to join extremist groups demonstrates that current approaches to peacebuilding, conflict mitigation, and PVE/CVE must be reevaluated. Rather than focusing on maximizing short-term security efforts, evidence shows that long-term community-based development initiatives that address the complex push-and-pull factors causing a small minority of youth to engage in violence can actually increase youth voices, contribute to PVE, and strengthen youth participation in peacebuilding (DEVEX 2015; see also Altiok, chapter 4, and Onyango, chapter 10, this volume).

Resolution 2250 encourages governments, international organizations, and civil society to actively engage youth populations as partners in shaping peace and security processes and implementing promising practices related to comprehensive, community-based solutions so that they may have greater peace dividends. This resolution is predicated on the premise that youth engagement in positive alternatives to violence should be maximized in order for peace writ large to take hold. As Carole MacNeil offers in chapter 1 of this volume, comprehensive positive youth development (PYD) approaches may offer valid alternatives to meet young people's need for meaning, belonging, and recognition. The Youth Café, discussed by Willice Onyango in chapter 10, provides further insights into young people's use of digital media platforms to identify constructive strategies to prevent radicalization and extremist violence.

Education and Employment as Peace and Security Concerns

Issues of youth, peace, and security are cross-cutting priorities at the heart of the 2030 Agenda for Sustainable Development (UNGA 2015), as they apply across the full spectrum of the Sustainable Development Goals (SDGs). The focus on YPS in development also serves to highlight the unique contributions that youth can make to conflict prevention. As reported in the *Missing Peace* study (Simpson 2018) discussed at more length in the introduction to this volume, most young women and men see education as indispensable to building peace, promoting development, and preventing violent conflict.

As Diana Budur discusses in the context of marginalized Roma youth (chapter 3, this volume) and Nasrat Khalid offers in the case of conflict-affected young Afghanis (chapter 6, this volume), education can serve as both protective and preventive factors in peace and security programming. Actors involved in disengagement and reintegration efforts are also encouraged to invest in youth affected by armed conflict through employment opportunities, inclusive labor policies, and education promoting a culture of peace. It is, however, imperative to eschew unfounded assumptions of a natural progression for unemployed or uneducated youth to engage in armed or extremist violence. Short-term economic integration approaches to countering violent extremism have proven ineffective and counterproductive (Novelli 2017).

It is furthermore worth noting that youngsters across the globe report having lost their confidence in economic systems that exclude them as key stakeholders: "For many young people who participated in the [Missing Peace] study, economic inclusion manifested primarily as fair access to meaningful and reliable employment" (Simpson 2018, xii). Valeria Izzi (chapter 4, this volume) offers a sobering analysis of what she terms the "youth employment for peacebuilding mantra" and the potentially problematic role that labor-focused approaches play in relation to the securitization of youth.

Dichotomous youth-bulge / youth-dividend constructions are also troublesome in this context. Youth-bulge theories have historically treated youth either as passive actors at best or, more commonly, as sources of political and economic instability, violence, and risk (see Ensor, introduction, this volume). In recent years, more positive policy and programmatic approaches have been developed seeking to leverage the skills, capacities, and creative energy of youth: "Countries with the greatest demographic advantages for development are those entering a period in which the working-age population will have a low proportion of young dependents, and the benefits of good health, quality education and decent employment. . . . When this happens, the national economic payoff can be substantial, leading to a demographic dividend" (UNFPA 2016). Thus understood, the demographic dividend constitutes a source of resilience that acknowledges young people's potential contributions to peace and security. On the other hand, valuing youth's potential contributions primarily in terms of their purported demographic dividend—that is, their expected economic or development benefits to society at large—risks depriving young women and men of their full agency (Simpson 2018, 22). These considerations spotlight the importance of moving the conversation beyond access to education and employment to a more nuanced understanding of young people's stake in the wider community and broader development processes.

Youth and Social Media

Youth across the globe constitute the largest demographic group online. This is particularly the case in Africa, Asia, and the Middle East, where young people are connecting in record numbers (WBG 2016). As with any other tool, the benefits and risks associated with social media and digital technologies depend on the way they are used. On the positive side, cyber-enabled communication can be a powerful tool in the global YPS agenda. Social media can be used to help draw attention to political violence, spread messages of peace, and promote tolerance and mutual understanding (Madzima-Bosha 2013; USIP 2012). It offers a window for young people to express their opinions, access information, and communicate with people outside of their physical social circles. These platforms allow young women and men to engage in collective action and bring issues that matter to them to the attention of a broader audience—in the face of barriers to their entry into civic and public spaces (Darmapuri 2017; Loiseau and Nowacka 2015).

On the negative side, it is worth remembering that not all youth are benefiting equally. As the 2016 World Development Report indicated, "There also are persistent digital divides across gender, geography, age, and income" (World Bank Group 2016, 5). Furthermore, social media is also being used to spread violent extremist ideologies and racist and misogynist narratives, incite violence, and threaten peace, social cohesion, and gender equality. Online violence is an insidious and growing phenomenon in cyberspace—social media can and is being used to stir up hatred and harassment, instigate bullying, promote offline violence, and destroy people's lives. As Phumzile Mlambo-Ngcuka, executive director of U.N. Women, remarked at the launch of the report *Combatting Online Violence against Women & Girls: A Worldwide Wake-Up Call* (September 24, 2025), "Online violence has subverted the original positive promise of the internet's freedoms and in too many circumstances has made it a chilling space that permits anonymous cruelty and facilitates harmful acts towards women and girls."

Given these concerning realities, young women's and men's engagement in building peace through alternative means, such as social media and the internet, begs further exploration. While technology offers opportunities to increase young people's participation in the public sphere, it is important to also understand the risks they face both online and in public spaces. Willice Onyango's research on youth-led public diplomacy programs on social media and internet platforms, presented in chapter 10, is a case in point. As he concludes, countering commonly held views on the use of the internet as a recruitment tool, online platforms can facilitate young people's sharing of experiences and ideas on constructive strategies to prevent radicalization and extremist violence. Social media's role in youth activism is also discussed in chapter 2. Drawing on her fieldwork in Nairobi's Kibera slum, Grace Atuhaire discusses how young local activists successfully used social media to de-escalate a conflict triggered by the forced eviction of a large number of families. Additionally, information and communications technology (ICT) is one of the components of the Three Ts framework proposed by Nasrat Khalid in chapter 6.

Environmental Governance and Climate Change

Recent World Bank data estimate that 65 percent of current conflicts have a significant land dimension, while conflicts around fresh water are increasing, particularly at the subnational level, as that resource becomes scarcer (World Bank Group 2020, 9). In parts of Africa, tensions between pastoralists and agriculturists over access to land and water have escalated to violence that often involves youth (Ensor 2018; 2019). Approaches to preventing conflicts linked to the management of natural resource assets and extractive industries need to be strengthened and expanded. While natural resources can play an important role in supporting economic growth, extractive resources and their revenues represent a major risk of violent conflict if not managed (World Bank Group 2020, 9).

There is a well-documented link between climate change and matters of peace and security. One of the greatest threats facing humanity, climate change has far-reaching and devastating impacts on people, the environment, and the economy. As a "threat multiplier," climate change is aggravating already fragile situations and contributing to more social upheaval and even violent conflict. Climate risks—for example, extreme weather events and disasters, volatile food prices, and sea-level rise and coastal degradation—increase vulnerability, exacerbate grievances, and deepen preexisting fragility. In fact, by 2030, climate impacts could push an additional 100 million people into poverty, and by 2050, as many as 143 million people could become climate migrants in sub-Saharan Africa, South Asia, and Latin America (World Bank Group 2020, 3).

Climate impacts affect all regions of the world and cut across all sectors of society. They also put an unfair burden on future generations. Solutions to these climate-related inequities must address underlying power structures, with particular attention to gender and generational dynamics. Typically, efforts to mitigate and adapt to climate change have mainly focused on institutional measures and overlooked the capacity of young people to promote viable mitigation and adaptation measures. This is a concern, for as Corner et al. (2015, 530) note, "Young people do not necessarily see what they can do in response to climate change, and when perceived self-efficacy is limited, personal engagement with climate change is likely to be lower." Young women and men nonetheless represent a unique opportunity for positive change given both their potential to contribute to development processes and the time-sensitive nature of the current climate crisis (Payne, Warembourg, and Awan 2017). As the Global Commission for Adaptation recently noted, "As inheritors of the effects of climate change, youth are also integral to generating political momentum, addressing inequalities, and advancing solutions" (GCA 2019, 12).

There has been a long-standing contention that participation in politics and engagement with environmental issues such as climate change are the preserve of well-resourced and educated youth (Ingelhart 1997; Ødegård and Berglund 2008). My fieldwork among South Sudanese activist youth living at home and in refugee settlements in Uganda counters this assertion. As I discuss in chapter 7, effective youth-inclusive approaches to peacebuilding and conflict prevention need to be informed by the threats and opportunities posed by changes in climate and other critical environmental conditions. Efforts to improve global peace and security cannot be successful through siloed approaches. Youth-led organizations should position their comparative advantages to contribute to broader international efforts in support of peace, stability, and environmental action. Partnerships of young people working on climate change, as well as partnerships between existing youth-focused organizations, should be encouraged if human and planetary well-being are to be safeguarded.

The Multifaceted Nature of Current Youth Mobility

A surge in violent conflict since 2010 has led to historically high numbers of people forcibly displaced or migrating under distress than ever before (Avis 2017). Globally, there are about 70.8 million refugees, internally displaced persons, and asylum seekers who have fled their homes to escape violence, conflict, and persecution

(UNHCR 2018a). Afghan refugees represent one of the world's largest protracted refugee populations (see chapter 6, this volume, for a discussion of the situation in Afghanistan), as do those from South Sudan (see chapter 7, this volume). For other young people—for example, survivors of genocide in Rwanda (see chapter 9, this volume) and Romani youngsters (see chapter 3, this volume)—uprootedness is as much cultural and structural as it is geographic. According to data from the United Nations Department of Economic and Social Affairs (U.N. DESA), the number of people aged nineteen or under living in a country other than the one where they were born rose from 28.7 million in 1990 to 37.9 million in 2019 (U.N. DESA 2019). More than one-third of the world's refugees are estimated to be young people. The U.N. Refugee Agency's current Policy on Age, Gender and Diversity Accountability does not, however, recognize youth as a distinct population group or make explicit reference to youth in its Core Actions (UNHCR 2018b).

Poor governance and political instability, which often underlie or lead to the outbreak of conflict and violence, have been increasingly compounded by accelerated environmental degradation and the negative impacts of climate change worldwide. Combined, these multiple and interrelated factors pressure people to migrate in order to protect their livelihoods and limit their exposure to persecution and other security risks. My analysis of the situation in South Sudan (chapter 7, this volume) illustrates these increasingly common dynamics. The growing attention to environmentally induced displacement evident in scholarly and policy circles (Ayazi 2019; Milan, Oakes, and Campbell 2016; UNHCR 2015) is critical for understanding the underlying mechanisms for how forced migration, conflict, and security challenges apply specifically to young people.

Environmental and natural resource factors including drought, land dispossession, water scarcity, and climate change exacerbate conflict risks such as poverty and economic shocks and the associated pressures to move. The combination of these factors can lead to what the Food and Agriculture Organization of the United Nations (FAO) refers to as "distress migration." This can happen directly or indirectly through extreme livelihood deterioration over a prolonged period of time. In particular, protracted crises reduce household livelihood security by (1) restricting access to economic opportunities, land, and natural resources, either temporarily or permanently; (2) reducing investment choices; and (3) depleting household assets. As the crisis becomes protracted, the economy shrinks, and ways of earning a living continue to dwindle. Migration thus becomes a necessary means for survival, as traditional livelihoods and safety nets are disrupted (FAO 2016, 7). Between 2008 and 2014, a total of 184 million people worldwide were displaced by environmental disasters alone (FAO 2016, 7).

The vulnerability of those engaged in this type of "distress migration" is compounded by the fact that there is no protection framework for environment / climate change–displaced persons; existing legislation, policies, and institutional arrangements are largely inadequate to address this specific type of human mobility. As noted by the Global Migration Group, "Environmental change, both sudden and gradual, directly and indirectly influences the propensity to migrate; these factors and resulting displacement are expected to increase in the coming years and will particularly impact youth" (Cortina, Taran, and Raphael 2014, 8). A better understanding of the experiences and decisions made by displaced youth is needed to inform policymakers and humanitarian actors' responses and ensure that actions taken to enhance young people's well-being reflect those circumstances.

YOUTH ACTION MOVING FORWARD

Resolution 2250 (2015) on youth, peace, and security was the first ever U.N. Security Council Resolution to recognize the positive role young people play in the maintenance and promotion of peace and security. Subsequently, UNSCR 2419 (2018) reiterated the importance of youth participation by urging for the inclusive representation of young people. These instruments have shaped the modern global YPS agenda but are not the first international efforts aimed at giving a voice to the world's youth. Founded in 1989, the United Network of Young Peacebuilders (UNOY Peacebuilders) is a global network of young people and youth organizations active in the field of peacebuilding and conflict transformation, especially in conflict-affected and postwar regions. Aimed at translating YPS policy into practice, UNOY's "Guide to Kick-Starting UNSCR 2250 Locally and Nationally" was released shortly after the adoption of this resolution (UNOY 2016).

Another institution that has been instrumental in these efforts over the years is the United Nations Major Group for Children and Youth (UNMGCY)—the U.N. General Assembly–mandated, official, formal, self-organized space for children and youth under thirty. Since its inception in 1992, UNMGCY has consulted with more than one billion youth in over 175 countries. In their own words, UNMGCY acts "as a bridge between children and youth to the U.N. system in order to ensure that their right to meaningful participation is realized" (UNMGCY 2018).

One of the primary ways UNMGCY supports Resolution 2250 is through its Humanitarian Affairs Working Group, including its facilitation of the Youth Working Group at the World Humanitarian Summit. At the 2016 World Humanitarian Summit, the Compact for Young People in Humanitarian Action was launched in recognition of the pressing need to protect youth rights and engage them in conflict response efforts (UNMGCY 2018). UNMGCY connected youth to the World Humanitarian Summit and played a large role in the compact itself, being the active leading entity and the convenor for the youth engagement taskforce (UNMGCY 2018). This compact drew on the Doha Youth Declaration on Reshaping the Humanitarian Agenda; the Global Refugee Youth Consultations; the SCR 2250 on Youth, Peace and Security; and all prior youth consultations. In 2018, the following imperatives were announced (UNMGCY 2018):

Action 1: Promote and increase age- and gender-responsive and inclusive programmes that contribute to the protection, health and development of young women, young men, girls and boys within humanitarian settings.

Action 2: Support systematic inclusion of engagement and partnership with youth, in all phases of humanitarian action through sharing of information and involvement in decision-making processes at all levels, including budget allocations.

Action 3: Recognize and strengthen young people's capacities and capabilities to be effective humanitarian actors in prevention, preparedness,

response and recovery, and empower and support local youth-led initiatives and organizations in humanitarian response, such as those targeting affected youth, including young refugees and internally displaced
persons living in informal urban settlements and slums.

Action 4: Increase resources intended to address the needs and priorities
of adolescents and youth affected by humanitarian crises, including
disasters, conflict and displacement, and identify ways to more accurately
track and report on the resources allocated to young people in humanitarian contexts.

Action 5: Ensure the generation and use of age- and sex-disaggregated data
pertaining to adolescents and youth in humanitarian settings. (UNFPA
and IFRC 2018, 6–7)

In a world of division, young people are standing up for collective action. Building fruitful bridges between research-based evidence and action on behalf of
youth—and by youth—is indeed one of the most pressing challenges facing those
working to improve the lives of young women and men worldwide. There is a recognized need for continued dialogue about the best means of connecting research,
policy, and practice. A more integrated research agenda that would encourage
cross-disciplinary and cross-thematic dialogue involving youth would have a
more positive impact on research outcomes in both academic and policy terms.
Ultimately, although there are still significant challenges in accomplishing the main
objectives of the YPS agenda, the extensive global efforts currently underway hold
immense potential. Acknowledging the intersection of cultural, socioeconomic,
political, and environmental factors in international peace and security, institutions
such as UNMGCY and others can support young women and men to become not
just the leaders of tomorrow but critical stakeholders of today.

Concluding Thoughts

By 2050, the world's population is projected to reach 9.6 billion, up from 7.5 billion currently. Nearly all population growth will occur in less-developed, fragile, and
conflict-affected countries that are expected to continue to have very large youth
cohorts (U.N. DESA 2019). The roles of youth in peace and security, conflict and
peacebuilding are complex phenomena that cannot be fully understood without
interrogating the historical, structural, and cultural factors within particular countries
and the global political, economic, and environmental systems in which they are
enmeshed. As the previous discussion has illustrated, current efforts to promote a
more inclusive approach to global peace and security agendas require the meaningful
engagement of young women and men as indispensable partners. Drawing on empirical research findings and robust policy analyses of cases of young people's engagement with the peace and security field, the contributors to this volume have advanced
our central argument—that is, that the particular challenges and opportunities that
young women and men face must be investigated and factored into relevant policy
and practice, promoting more sustainable and durable solutions in the process.

The chapters contained in *Securitizing Youth* vividly illustrate that the largest
generation of young people in history displays enormous creativity in the various

roles they play and demonstrate remarkable determination in their efforts to overcome a turbulent climate of social instability, violent conflict, and environmental uncertainty. Refusing to be passive subjects of history, young women and men on all continents are actively participating in key social, political, economic, and climate action developments and, in the process, constructing their own identities and the present and future character of their nations. Looking toward the future, we urge scholars and practitioners alike to acknowledge young women and men as active, politically and socially aware individuals, not objectified, passive victims or a problem to be solved. Research design, policymaking, and project programming should start with their input. Much has already been accomplished and yet, given the complexity of the challenges at hand, much more remains to be done.

NOTE

1. As discussed in the introduction of this volume, UNSCR 2250's five pillars for action are the following:

1. Participation. Taking youth's participation and views into account in decision-making processes, from negotiation and prevention of violence to peace agreements
2. Protection. Ensuring the protection of young civilians' lives and human rights and investigating and prosecuting those responsible for crimes perpetrated against them
3. Prevention. Supporting young people in preventing violence and promoting a culture of tolerance and intercultural dialogue
4. Partnerships. Engaging young people during and after conflict when developing peacebuilding strategies, along with community actors and United Nations bodies
5. Disengagement and reintegration. Investing in youth affected by armed conflict through employment opportunities, inclusive labor policies, and education promoting a culture of peace

REFERENCES

Affa'a Mindzie, M. 2015. "Building Peace and Development in the Sahel: Enhancing the Political Participation of Women and Youth." New York: International Peace Institute. www.ipinst.org/wp-content/uploads/2015/02/IPI-Rpt-Building-Peace.pdf.

Avis, William Robert. 2017. *Scoping Study on Defining and Measuring Distress Migration.* GSDRC Helpdesk Research Report no. 1406. Rome: Food and Agricultural Organization of the United Nations. www.gsdrc.org/wp-content/uploads/2017/04/HDR1406.pdf.

Ayazi, Hossein. 2019. *Climate Refugees: The Climate Crisis and Rights Denied.* Othering & Belonging Institute. Berkeley, Calif.: UC Berkeley. https://belonging.berkeley.edu/climaterefugees.

Boutron, Camille. 2016. "From Peru to Colombia: The Silenced Voices of Women Fighters." The Conversation, September 30, 2016. http://theconversation.com/from-peru-to-colombia-the-silenced-voicesof-women-fighters-65817.

Corner, A., O. Roberts, S. Chiari, S. Völler, E. S. Mayrhuber, S. Mandl, and K. Monson. 2015. "How Do Young People Engage with Climate Change? The Role of Knowledge, Values, Message Framing, and Trusted Communicators." *WIREs Climate Change* 6, no. 5, 523–534. https://doi.org/10.1002/wcc.353.

Cortina, Jeronimo, Patrick Taran, and Alison Raphael. 2014. "Migration and Youth: Challenges and Opportunities—Key Messages and Policy." Global Migration Group, UNICEF. https://globalmigrationgroup.org/system/files/23._Key_Messages_and_Policy_Recommendations.pdf.

Cuaresma, Jesús Crespo, Wolfgang Fengler, Homi Kharas, Karim Bekhtiar, Michael Brottrager, and Martin Hofer. 2018. "Will the Sustainable Development Goals Be Fulfilled? Assessing Present and Future Global Poverty." *Palgrave Communications* 4, no. 29, 1–8.

Cummins, M., and I. Ortiz. 2012. "When the Global Crisis and Youth Bulge Collide: Double the Jobs Trouble for Youth." Social and Economic Policy Working Paper. February 2012. New York: U.N. Children's Fund (UNICEF).

Darmapuri, Sahana. 2017. "Empowering Women in Fragile States through Social Media." Our Secure Future, April 2017. http://oursecurefuture.org/blog/empowering-women-fragile-states-through-social-media.

DEVEX. 2015. "Youth Will." Devex. https://pages.devex.com/youth-will.html.

Dolan, Chris. 2002. "Collapsing Masculinities and Weak States—a Case Study of Northern Uganda." In *Masculinities Matter! Men, Gender and Development*, edited by F. Cleaver, 57–84. London: Zed.

———. 2009. *Social Torture: The Case of Northern Uganda 1986–2006*. Oxford: Berghahn.

Ensor, Marisa O. 2017. "Refuge and Radicalization in Chad: Dilemmas of Refugee Protection in Central Africa." In *Maintaining Refuge Anthropological Reflections in Uncertain Times*, edited by David Haines, Jayne Howell, and Fethi Keles, 19–26. Committee for Refugees and Immigrants. American Anthropological Association. Arlington, VA.

———. 2018. "Youth's Role in South Sudan's Perfect Storm: Climate Change, Conflict, and the Prospects for Peacebuilding in the World's Newest Nation." *Global Peace Services USA* 19, no. 3, 1–10.

———. 2019. "Is Environmental Peacebuilding the Answer to South Sudan's Conflict?" *New Security Beat: The Blog of the Environmental Change and Security Program*, September 12, 2019. www.newsecuritybeat.org/2019/09/environmental-peacebuilding-answer-south-sudans-conflict/.

FAO (Food and Agriculture Organization of the United Nations). 2016. *Migration and Protracted Crisis: Addressing the Root Causes and Building Resilient Agricultural Livelihoods*. Rome: FAO.

GCA (Global Commission on Adaptation). 2019. *Adapt Now: A Global Call for Leadership on Climate Resilience*. Last updated September 13, 2019. https://cdn.gca.org/assets/2019-09/GlobalCommission_Report_FINAL.pdf.

Global Youth Summit. 2015. *Youth Action Agenda to Prevent Violent Extremism and Promote Peace*. UNOY, September 28, 2015. https://unoy.org/wp-content/uploads/Youth-Action-Agenda-to-Prevent-Violent-Extremism-and-Promote-Peace.pdf.

Hilker, Lyndsay McLean, and Erika Fraser. 2009. *Youth Exclusion, Violence, Conflict and Fragile States*. Report prepared for DFID's Equity and Rights Team, April 30, 2009. www.dmeforpeace.org/peacexchange/wp-content/uploads/2015/12/youth-exclusion-violence-conflict-and-fragile-states.pdf.

Ingelhart, Ronald. 1997. *Modernization and Postmodernization: Cultural, Economic, and Political Change in 43 Societies*. Princeton, N.J.: Princeton University Press.

IPU (Inter-parliamentary Union). 2015. *Youth Participation in Parliaments and Peace and Security*. www.ipu.org/sites/default/files/documents/tp_youth_participation_in_parliaments_and_peace_and_security_ipu.pdf.

Loiseau, E., and K. Nowacka. 2015. "Can Social Media Effectively Include Women's Voices in Decisionmaking Processes?" OECD Development Centre, March 2015. www.oecd.org/dev/development-gender/DEV_socialmedia-issuespaper-March2015.pdf.

Lopes Cardozo, M. T. A., S. Higgins, and M. L. J. Le Mat. 2016. *Youth Agency and Peacebuilding: An Analysis of the Role of Formal and Non-formal Education Synthesis Report on Findings from Myanmar, Pakistan, South Africa and Uganda*. Amsterdam: University of Amsterdam. https://educationanddevelopment.files.wordpress.com/2016/06/youth-agency-synthesis-report-final16.pdf.

Lopes Cardozo, Mieke, Sean Higgins, Elizabeth Maber, Cyril O. Brandt, Nebil Kusmallah, and Marielle Le Mat. 2015. *Literature Review: Youth Agency, Peacebuilding, and Education*. Amsterdam: University of Amsterdam. http://dare.uva.nl/record/1/490433.

Madzima-Bosha, Tadzie. 2013. "Harnessing the Power of Social Media for Conflict Prevention." Peace Insight. Accessed September 15, 2019. www.insightonconflict.org/blog/2013/07/socialmedia-conflict-prevention/. (URL inactive.)

Milan, Andrea, Robert Oakes, and Jillian Campbell. 2016. *Tuvalu: Climate Change and Migration—Relationships between Household Vulnerability, Human Mobility and Climate Change*. Bonn: United Nations University Institute for Environment and Human Security. http://collections.unu.edu/eserv/UNU:5856/Online_No_18_Tuvalu_Report_161207_.pdf.

Mohamed, Hussein, and Mohamed Ibrahim. 2017. "Somali Public Works Minister Seen as 'Rising Star' Is Shot to Death." *New York Times*, May 4, 2017. www.nytimes.com/2017/05/04/world/africa/abbas-abdullahi-sheikh-siraji-shot-somalia.html?_r=0.

Naujoks, Jana, and Myat Thandar Ko. 2018. "Behind the Masks: Masculinities, Gender, Peace and Security in Myanmar." International Alert. Accessed September 18, 2019. www.international-alert.org/sites/default/files/Myanmar_MasculinitiesGenderPeaceSecurity_EN_2018.pdf.

Nordstrom, Carolyn. 1999. "Girls and War Zones: Troubling Questions." In *Engendering Forced Migration: Theory and Practice*, edited by Doreen Indra, 44–45. New York: Berghahn.

Novelli, Mario. 2017. "Education and Countering Violent Extremism: Western Logics from South to North?" *Compare: A Journal of Comparative and International Education* 47, no. 6 (July), 835–851.

Ødegård, Guro, and Frode Berglund. 2008. "Political Participation in Late Modernity among Norwegian Youth: An Individual Choice or a Statement of Social Class?" *Journal of Youth Studies* 11, no. 6, 593–610.

OECD (Organisation for Economic Co-operation and Development). 2019. "Engaging with Men and Masculinities in Fragile and Conflict-Affected Settings." OECD Development Policy Papers, no. 17. March 2019.

Ozerdem, Alpaslan. 2016. "The Role of Youth in Peacebuilding: Challenges and Opportunities." Oxford Research Group, October 26, 2016. www.oxfordresearchgroup.org.uk/blog/the-role-of-youth-in-peacebuilding-challenges-and-opportunities.

Payne, Julian, Antoine Warembourg, and Jalal Awan. 2017. *Impacts of Climate Change on Youth, Peace and Security*. Paris: Sustainable Development Solutions Network Youth. www.unsdsn.org/resources/publications/impacts-of-climate-change-on-youth-peace-and-security/. (URL inactive.)

Pettersson, T., and P. Wallensteen. 2015. "Armed Conflicts, 1946–2014." *Journal of Peace Research* 52, no. 4, 536–550.

Pingel, Falk. 2010. "The Power of the Curriculum." In *Even in Chaos: Education in Times of Emergency*, edited by Kevin M. Cahill, 109–135. New York: Fordham University Press and the Center for International Humanitarian Cooperation.

Rustad, S. A., G. Ostby, and R. Nordas. 2016. "Artisanal Mining, Conflict, and Sexual Violence in Eastern DRC." *Extractive Industries and Society* 3, no. 2, 475–484. https://doi.org/10.1016/j.exis.2016.01.010.

Sievers, Lara. 2017. "Young and Female: The Future Mediators in Conflicts." Dag Hammarskjöld Foundation. Accessed September 10, 2019. www.daghammarskjold.se/young-female-future-mediators-conflicts/.

Simpson, Graeme. 2018. *The Missing Peace: Independent Progress Study on Youth, Peace and Security*. UNFPA. www.unfpa.org/sites/default/files/youth/youth-web-english.pdf.

Smeulers, Alette. 2015. "Female Perpetrators—Ordinary and Extra-ordinary Women." *International Criminal Law Review* 15:207–253.

Sommers, Marc. 2012. *Stuck: Rwandan Youth and the Struggle for Adulthood*. Athens: University of Georgia Press.

———. 2015. *The Outcast Majority: War, Development, and Youth in Africa*. Athens: University of Georgia Press.

U.N. DESA (United Nations Department of Economic and Social Affairs). 2019. "International Migrant Stock by Age and Sex." Population Division, International Migration. Accessed September 12, 2019. www.un.org/en/development/desa/population/migration/data/estimates2/estimates19.asp.

UNDP (United Nations Development Programme). 2006. *Youth and Violent Conflict: Society and Development in Crisis?* New York: UNDP.

———. 2016. *Arab Human Development Report 2016*. New York: UNDP.

UNFCCC (United Nations Framework Convention on Climate Change). 2017. "The Gender Action Plan." UNFCCC. Accessed September 15, 2019. https://unfccc.int/topics/gender/workstreams/the-gender-action-plan.

UNFPA (United Nations Population Fund). 2016. "Demographic Dividend: Overview." UNFPA, May 5, 2016. www.unfpa.org/demographic-dividend.

UNFPA and IFRC (United Nations Population Fund and International Federation of Red Cross and Red Crescent Societies). 2018. *Igniting Hope: Compact for Young People in Humanitarian Action*. Accessed December 21, 2020. www.unfpa.org/publications/compact-young-people-humanitarian-action.

UNGA (United Nations General Assembly). 2015. *Transforming Our World: The 2030 Agenda for Sustainable Development*. A/RES/70/1, October 21, 2015. www.refworld.org/docid/57b6e3e44.html.

UNHCR (United Nations High Commissioner for Refugees). 2015. *Guidance on Protecting People from Disasters and Environmental Change through Planned Relocation*. Geneva: UNHCR. www.unhcr.org/protection/environment/562f798d9/planned-relocation-guidance-october-2015.html.

———. 2018a. "Global Trends: Forced Displacement in 2018." Accessed August 10, 2019. www.unhcr.org/globaltrends2018/.

———. 2018b. "UNHCR, Policy on Age, Gender and Diversity Accountability 2018." Accessed August 10, 2019. www.unhcr.org/protection/women/5aa13c0c7/policy-agegender-diversity-accountability-2018.html.

United Nations. 2005. *World Youth Report*. Accessed August 1, 2019. www.un.org/esa/socdev/unyin/documents/wyr05book.pdf.

———. 2018. "Adopting Resolution 2419 (2018), Security Council Calls for Increasing Role of Youth in Negotiating, Implementing Peace Agreements." Accessed August 1, 2019. www.un.org/press/en/2018/sc13368.doc.htm.

United Nations Inter-agency Network on Youth Development's Working Group on Youth and Peacebuilding. 2016. "Young People's Participation in Peacebuilding: A Practice Note, with Support from PeaceNexus Foundation." Accessed August 2, 2019. www.un.org/en/peacebuilding/pbso/pdf/Practice%20Note%20Youth%20&%20Peacebuilding%20-%20January%202016.pdf. (URL inactive.)

United Nations Women. 2018. *Young Women in Peace and Security: At the Intersection of the YPS and WPS Agendas*. Progress Study on Youth, Peace and Security. New York: U.N. Women. www.unwomen.org/-/media/headquarters/attachments/sections/library/publications/2018/research-paper-young-women-in-peace-and-security-en.pdf?la=en&vs=2849.

United Network of Young Peacebuilders and Search for Common Grounds for the United
    Nations Inter-agency Working Group on Youth and Peacebuilding. 2016. "Translating
    Youth, Peace & Security Policy into Practice; Guide to Kick-Starting UNSCR 2250 Locally
    and Nationally." Accessed August 1, 2019. http://unoy.org/wp-content.
UNMGCY (United Nations Major Group for Children and Youth). 2018. "Five Actions."
    Accessed August 1, 2019. www.youthcompact.org/five-key-actions.
UNSC (United Nations Security Council). 2015. *Security Council Resolution 2250 (2015)
    [on Youth, Peace and Security]*, S/RES/2250. March 18, 2016. www.refworld.org/docid/
    56ebfd654.html.
USIP (United States Institute of Peace). 2012. *Social Media and Conflict Prevention*. Washington,
    D.C.: USIP. www.usip.org/publications/2012/12/social-media-and-conflict-prevention.
WBG (World Bank Group). 2016. *World Development Report Digital Dividends*. Washing-
    ton, D.C.: WBG. http://documents.worldbank.org/curated/en/896971468194972881/pdf/
    102725-PUBReplacement-PUBLIC.pdf.
———. 2020. *World Bank Group Strategy for Fragility, Conflict, and Violence 2020–2025*. Wash-
    ington, D.C.: WBG. http://documents.worldbank.org/curated/en/844591582815510521/
    pdf/World-Bank-Group-Strategy-for-Fragility-Conflict-and-Violence-2020-2025.pdf.
WHO (World Health Organization). 2017. "Violence against Women." Accessed August 3,
    2019. www.who.int/news-room/fact-sheets/detail/violence-against-women.
World Bank. 2017. *World Development Report: Governance and the Law*. Washington, D.C.:
    World Bank. https://openknowledge.worldbank.org/handle/10986/25880.
Wright, Hannah. 2014. "Masculinities, Conflict and Peacebuilding: Perspectives on Men through
    a Gender Lens." Saferworld, October 2014. www.saferworld.org.uk/resources/publications/
    862-masculinities-conflict-and-peacebuilding-perspectives-on-men-through-a-gender-lens.

Notes on Contributors

ALI ALTIOK is an independent researcher and advocate for youth and peacebuilding. He coauthored the global policy paper *We Are Here: An Integrated Approach to Youth Inclusive Peace Processes* for the U.N. Office of the Secretary-General's Envoy on Youth. He worked as a researcher at the United Nations Peacebuilding Support Office and United Nations Population Fund Secretariat, supporting research, data analysis, and narrative development of *The Missing Peace: Independent Progress Study on Youth, Peace and Security*, mandated by the United Nations Security Council under Resolution 2250. Ali is a former member of the United Networks of Young Peacebuilders and coordinator of its youth, peace, and security research network. He holds an MA in political, legal, and economic philosophy from the University of Bern (Switzerland) and an MA in peace and security studies from the University of Hamburg (Germany) and is originally from Turkey.

GRACE ATUHAIRE holds an MA in global studies, a joint program of Addis Ababa University and Leipzig University. She is an accredited member of FemWise-Africa, Moremi Initiative Leadership Empowerment and Development (MILEAD), Rotary International, and Uganda Women Writers Association. With a background in communication and advocacy, she has worked as an editorial officer at the Institute for Peace and Security Studies, Addis Ababa University. Previously, she held different positions with ActionAid International. Grace is currently enrolled in a PhD in political science at the University of Tubingen. Her doctoral project investigates "Anti-terrorism and State Securitization of Border Communities in Africa" using a comparative study of Kasese, Uganda; Garrisa, Kenya; and Bamako, Bayangs community in Mamfe, Cameroon.

VICTORIA R. BISHOP, MPA, is an applied researcher and scholar with a background in applied statistics and sociology. She currently works at the U.S. Institute of Peace, where her work has helped facilitate the institute's Inaugural Women Building Peace Award Ceremony. She continues to provide programmatic support to high-level projects of strategic institutional priority. Victoria previously worked for the Center for Global Impact (CGI) at the International Republican Institute (IRI), a nonpartisan international organization based in Washington, D.C., with active programs and projects in over eighty-five countries. She assisted CGI's fragility and resiliency programs for preventing violent extremism worldwide. Prior to joining IRI, Victoria gained experience in operations management, policy design, and policy implementation in Washington, D.C., government. She has also spent time in Kibeho, Rwanda, where she worked with local youth. Her research interests focus on the role of culture in the design and implementation of transitional justice mechanisms in sub-Saharan Africa as well as international prison systems.

DIANA BUDUR, PhD, completed a doctorate in anthropology at Princeton University and a bachelor of arts in human biology at Stanford University. Her dissertation, "Gypsy Myths and Romani Cosmologies in the New World: The Roma and Calons in Brazil," was published in 2017. It was based on long-term ethnographic fieldwork on the Romani diaspora subgroups in Rio de Janeiro and São Paulo. It elaborated on the ethnic members' use of language, food, gender, sexuality, spirituality, and taboos in relation to the majoritarian society. It also analyzed Romani psychic readers' discourses of illness and health, along with discourses of assimilation and resistance, power, mental health, and gender inequalities. Sexuality and gender roles are also the focus of her latest publication, a self-reflexive contribution to the volume *Sex: Encounters* (2018) edited by Richard Martin and Dieter Haller. Diana is an applied anthropology consultant, researching meditation and mindful-movement curriculums in the education sector.

MARISA O. ENSOR, PhD, LLM, the editor of this volume, is a gender and youth specialist with a background in the human dimensions of disasters, environmental change, conflict, displacement, and security. Trained in political ecology (environmental anthropology) and human rights law, Dr. Ensor has fifteen-plus years of scholarship and practice in conflict-affected and environmentally fragile countries in Africa, Europe, the MENA region, and Latin America. Much of her work examines women's and girls' positive roles in conflict prevention, peacebuilding, human mobility, disaster risk management, and environmental governance, including climate action, focusing on the identification of context-specific solutions. She is currently based at Georgetown University—Justice and Peace Studies Program and Institute for the Study of International Migration, School of Foreign Service. Prior to joining Georgetown, she taught at several other universities in the United States and abroad, including the American University in Cairo's Center for Migration and Refugee Studies. Marisa has published five books and over forty journal articles, book chapters, and policy briefs and has presented her work in a wide range of global venues.

VALERIA IZZI, MSc, PhD, is an independent researcher and consultant and an honorary fellow at the Centre for African Studies at the University of Edinburgh. Her research interests focus on the interplay between development policy and interventions and local-level social, political, and cultural structures and dynamics, with a particular interest in the theory and practice of youth-specific interventions in peacebuilding. Valeria is a coauthor of the study "Jobs Aid Peace—a Review of the Theory and Practice of the Impact of Employment Programmes on Peace in Fragile and Conflict-Affected Countries" (Berlin, International Security and

Development Center), commissioned by the U.N. Peacebuilding Support Office, the International Labour Organization, UNDP, and the World Bank. The study served to inform the joint statement "Employment Programmes and Peace—a Joint Statement on an Analytical Framework, Emerging Principles for Action and Next Steps," published by the four agencies in 2016. Valeria holds an MSc from the School of Oriental and African Studies, University of London, and a PhD from the Scuola Superiore Sant'Anna, Pisa, Italy.

NASRAT KHALID is the founder and chief strategist of AWAL, an international development firm focusing on transformational development and the force behind ASEEL, an e-commerce solution that provides a global market to handmade products from war-torn and underdeveloped countries. He has previously served in various capacities with the World Bank Group, USAID, and other major development agencies. Designing innovative strategies and putting technology at the core of the solution, Nasrat has been able to initiate causes, organizations, and teams that have transformed and accelerated the establishment of different sectors in developing countries. Nasrat has presented in global forums and conferences and is a TEDx speaker. He has established four organizations that have been recognized by the G20, World Bank, ICANN, UNIGF, and the government of Afghanistan.

JENI KLUGMAN, PhD, is the managing director at the Georgetown Institute for Women, Peace and Security and a fellow at the Kennedy School of Government's Women in Public Policy Program at Harvard University. She recently became VicHealth's second leading thinker, together with Iris Bohnet, under an initiative that aims to make behavioral insights practical and accessible for Victorian government, industry, and not-for-profit organizations. She has served as the director of Gender and Development at the World Bank and as the director and lead author of three global Human Development Reports published by the UNDP. Jeni sits on several boards and panels, including for the World Economic Forum and the *Journal of Human Development and Capabilities*. She holds a PhD in economics from the Australian National University and postgraduate degrees in both law and development economics from the University of Oxford, where she was a Rhodes Scholar.

CAROLE MACNEIL, PhD, is the founder and principal of MacNeil and Associates Consulting, which focuses on promoting learning, fostering leadership, and inspiring and advancing social change, with young people at the center. Carole is a specialist in youth and community development, youth civic engagement, youth-led peacebuilding, intergenerational partnerships, youth program development, and community-based/participatory research with over twenty-five years of experience in working with youth, communities, schools, youth-serving organizations, and international development organizations. She has worked with youth and communities all over the world, with a particular focus on fragile and conflict-affected contexts in Africa and the Middle East, and has partnered with multiple international agencies and organizations, including USAID, U.N.-Habitat, the World Bank, Women Deliver, IREX, Chemonics, and RET. In previous roles, Carole has served as a Fulbright Scholar to Kenya and visiting professor at the University of Nairobi, national director of the 4-H Youth in Governance Initiative, statewide director of the California 4-H Youth Development Program, and executive director / cofounder of the nonprofit organization Project YES (Youth Envisioning Social change). Currently, she also serves as a research affiliate with the University of Colorado's Community Engagement, Design, and Research Center (CEDaR). Carole earned her EdM from Harvard University's Graduate School of Education, her PhD from the University of Colorado, and a certificate in nonprofit organizations from the University of Colorado's School of Public Administration. She has presented worldwide and authored dozens of publications on youth-led development, youth leadership, and youth-adult partnerships.

MATTHEW MOORE is the 2018–2019 Hillary Rodham Clinton Law Fellow with the Georgetown Institute for Women, Peace and Security. Matt received his JD from Georgetown University Law Center and a MA from Columbia University's School of International and Public Affairs. At Georgetown Law, Matt published an article on the legal consequences of Brexit and was the articles editor for the *Georgetown Journal of International Law*. He served as a summer associate at the Public International Law and Policy Group, where he researched human rights issues in Iraq and Yemen, and as a judicial intern with the U.S. District Court for the District of Columbia. During graduate school, Matt completed field research in Medellín, Colombia, on peacebuilding and the demobilization of combatants. He served as a graduate student research consultant for Human Rights Watch and the Carnegie Council for Ethics in International Affairs and as an intern at the *New Yorker*. Previously, Matt worked in New York at the quarterly political journal *Dissent*.

WILLICE ONYANGO is the founder and executive director of the Youth Café, a premier Pan-African youth organization based in Kenya. He previously served as a global youth representative to the U.N. High Level Panel of Eminent Persons on Post 2015 that was cochaired by the British prime minister and the Liberian and Indonesian presidents. He also served in the African Union Working Group on Food Security and Demographic Dividend and as the chairperson for the International Youth Council, Kenya. Willice has been invited to speak at numerous international forums spanning twenty-eight countries; including the sixty-eighth U.N. General Assembly, World Bank Youth Forum, AU Heads of State Summit, and European Investment Bank's Africa Day, among other conferences on youth, development, and democracy. He is also an alumnus of the One Young World, International Young Leaders Assembly, and completed civic leadership at the Staley School of Leadership, Kansas State University. He is the author of *The Kenya Youth Manifesto*, which unified the aspirations of the ordinary Kenyan youth into a common philosophy, leading to the publication and launch of the first ever nonpartisan blueprint for Kenyan youth. He is a regular columnist for the *Star*, the *Standard*, Huffington Post, Open Democracy, and World Economic Forum, among other publications.

Index